Gender Equality in Post-War Kurdistan

Cameron Compton

Abstract

This book analyses the effects of gender inclusive policies or the lack of such on development at a time of conflict transformation.

It has nowadays been established that the presence of women and the existence of gendered policies at a time of peace building are vital for the development of any country or region presently in this situation. Despite this knowledge, inclusion of women and gender has remained scarce and effects of their integration have thus proven difficult to measure.

It is the aim of this thesis to support research in this area, by demonstrating the implications of incorporating or failing to implement different types of gender inclusive policies on the example of the actions taken in the Kurdistan Region of Iraq.

The Kurdistan Region is currently in a unique position of its development. After withstanding decades of armed conflict, the region today is greatly autonomous and economically prosperous. For the previous decade it has been the government's aim to decrease the potential of new conflict, to become internationally competitive and to increase positive development for its people. One of their stated foci was thereby the promotion of gender and women's inclusion in public policies.

By comparing the policies deployed in the Kurdistan Region with experiences and knowledge from around the world, and by using the citizens of the region themselves as validators, this thesis will examine if the existing policies have had the desired effect, and if not, what should be changed.

This will be done in the political, economic and social sphere (focusing on education), with the outcome that policies introduced by Kurdistan's decision makers are partly positive, but lack in consistency, inclusiveness and gender sensitivity. This leads to a loss of human resources for the region, as well as to unequal effects within society, and thus to a lack of sustainable peace.

Table of Contents

A. Title Page 1

B. Abstract 2

C. Table of Contents 3

D. Acknowledgments 6

E. Abbreviations 7

I. Introduction 9

A. Aims, Objectives and Contributions of the Thesis 10

B. Hypothesis and Leading Questions 17

C. Structure of the Thesis 17

II. Methodology - Methods and Procedure 19

A. Library- and Internet based Research 20

B. Field Research 21

    1. Methods of Data Collection 22

C. Influences on the Conduct of the Research 27

III. Setting the Scene 29

A. Reflections on War, Peace and Gender 30

B. Kurdistan's History – The Long Path to Autonomy 42

C. Women During the Time of Conflict 57

    1. Women as Victims during Armed Conflict and Beyond 58

    2. Women as Actors 69

D. Women and Gender Equality in the Kurdistan Region – Then and Now 75

IV. Gender, Women and Politics 102

    1. A Theoretical Overview 104

A. Gender and Women in Peace Negotiations 108

    1. Women's Involvement in Negotiations 111

    2. Gendering the Contents of Agreements 121

B. Gender, Women and Parliament 125

   1. Supporting Women's Inclusion 127

   2. Searching for Gender Equality 136

C. Other Political Activism 145

   1. The Kurdistan's Women's Movement – A Historical Abstract 149

   2. Grassroots Political Activism Today 154

V. Gender, Women and the Economy 175

   1. A Theoretical Overview 179

   2. Legal Foundation 185

A. Influencing the Economy from a National Level– Macroeconomic Policies 190

   1. The KRG & Economic Measures for Conflict Transformation 194

   2. Budgeting for Gender Equality 197

   3. National Strategies – Putting Theory into Practice? 201

B. Women, Gender and the Labour Market 205

   1. Including Women into the Workforce – Raising the Numbers 208

   2. From Work to Gender Equality? 212

   3. The Effects of Women's Employment Situation on Individual and Social Transformation 220

C. Running Businesses to Achieve Equality 225

   1. Raising Economic Productivity – The Microfinance Sector 230

VI. Gender, Women and Society – The Power of Education 236

   1. A Theoretical Overview 241

   2. Legal Foundation 252

A. Children's Schooling 254

   1. Access to Schooling 257

   2. Quality of Schooling 263

B. Higher Education and Social Research 274

    1. Supporting Equality in Higher Education 278

    2. Quality of Higher Education – Searching for Critical Thinking and the Inclusion of Gender 286

C. Women's Education – Education by Women 293

    1. Literacy as a Way forward 293

    2. Women as Educators for a New Generation 301

VII. Conclusion 308

  A. Politics 310

  B. Economy 314

  C. Education 319

VIII. Bibliography 326

IX. Appendix 359

  A. Field Research - Information on Interviews & Interviewees 359

  B. Map of Iraq and the Kurdistan Region 359

  C. The Kurdistan Region in Pictures 360

  D. Women's Situation in Numbers 371

  E. United Nations Security Council Resolution 1325 (2000) 376

  F. Convention on the Elimination of All Forms of Discrimination Against Women 1979 379

  G. Constitution of Iraq 2005 389

  H. Draft Constitution of the Iraqi Kurdistan Region 2009 419

CEDAW – Convention on the Elimination of All Forms of Discrimination Against Women 1979

CEO – Chief Executive Officer

FGM – Female Genital Mutilation

GCPE – Global Campaign for Peace Education

GDP – Gross Domestic Product

GFIW – General Federation of Iraqi Women

HCDP – Human Capacity Development Program in Higher Education

HDC – Center for Humanitarian Dialogue

IAU – Inter-Agency Information and Analysis Unit

ICCPR – International Covenant on Civil and Political Rights 1966

ICESCR – International Covenant on Economic, Social and Cultural Rights 1966

ICG – Iraqi Central Government

IDPs – Internally Displaced People

ILO – International Labour Organisation

IOM – International Organisation for Migration

IOW – Independent Women's Organisation

IRI – International Republican Institute

KDP – Kurdistan Democratic Party

KHRW – Kurdish Human Rights Watch

KIU – Kurdish Islamic Union

KRG – Kurdistan Regional Government

KWRW – Kurdish Women's Rights Watch

MFI – Microfinance Institution

MP – Member of Parliament

NGO – Non Governmental Organisation

NIWC – Northern Ireland Women's Coalition

OHCHR – Office of the High Commissioner for Human Rights

PDA – People's Development Association

PKK – Kurdistan Workers' Party

PUK – Patriotic Union of Kurdistan

Resolution 1325, or Res 1325 – UN Security Council Resolution 1325 (2000)

SC – Security Council

TAL – Transnational Administrative Law

UKH – University of Kurdistan Hawler

UN – United Nations

UN WOMEN – UN Entity for Gender Equality and the Empowerment of Women

UNAMI – United Nations Assistance Mission for Iraq

UNDEF – United Nations Democracy Fund

UNDP – United Nations Development Programme

UNESCO – United Nations Educational, Scientific and Cultural Organisation

UNICEF – United Nations Children's Fund

UNIFEM – United Nations Development Fund for Women

WEO – Women Empowerment Organisation

I.   Introduction

Interviews in the Kurdistan Region, 2012:

Question: *"How do you think it is possible to prevent further war?"*

Answer: *"We need equality through respect, and a stop to discrimination."* [1]

Question: *"And how do you think equality is achievable?"*

Answer: *"We just need equality in all areas: political, economic and social."* [2]

The time of conflict transformation is probably one of the most demanding circumstances any leaders of any state or region will ever have to face. The challenges seem endless and criticism is never far away.

One region, which is currently in this position, is the Kurdistan Region of Iraq. Since the fall of Saddam Hussein, the region has seen vast changes, but the ideal situation is said yet to be achieved. This is especially so when it comes to the enhancement of gender equality in society, the inclusion of women and gender[3] in the region's dealings as a whole, and the providing of sustainable peace for all citizens.

How exactly the leading figures of the region have dealt with these issues, by including women and gender into their policies, and how successful these efforts have been, or if indeed some constructive criticism is required, will the subject of this thesis.

It will be the focus of the following and first subchapter to elaborate, precisely which aims and objectives the thesis is led by when exploring this subject matter and what its unique contributions are to the area of study concerned:

---

[1] Interview AR, Sulaimaniya on 21/05/2012
[2] Interview BF, Erbil on 29/06/2012
[3] 'Gender' thereby being understood as the sexual attribute in correlation with other types of personal identities, such as ethnicity, religion, age, or class.

A.   Aims, Objectives and Contributions of the Thesis

"Women's involvement is essential to achieving sustainable peace".[4]

Already over two decades ago, the UN and the international community in general, started to recognize and to highlight women's distinct suffering during war, as well as their unused capabilities when it comes to the work for peace.[5] This has been preceded by an increase of academic interest on the matter, which has led to the establishment of the recognised correlation of gender equality and positive conflict transformation.[6] As the UN Security Council stated on 8 March 2000, the first Women's Day of the new Millennium, *"Peace is inextricably linked with equality between women and men"*,[7] or as promoted by NGOs such as the Working Group on Women, Peace and Security, sustainable peace can only be achieved with the full and equal participation of women in all levels of decision-making.[8]

Despite this knowledge, women today are still marginalized when it comes to the inclusion in peace building and the importance of gender quality throughout the process is, while often theoretically recognized, not implemented in practice.[9] This was also acknowledged by the UN Secretary General in 2010.[10] A study of academic writings and official reports over the decades reveals that little has changed. Reports[11] which were written about 15 years ago on the necessity of gender consideration and women's inclusion in the peacebuilding process have the same or similar critique, as those written today. This is despite several attempts during this period, for example through Resolution 1325, to change the existing

---

[4] Deniz Kaniyoti, "Reconstruction & Women's Rights in Afghanistan," *ISIM Review* 20 (2007): 20.

[5] United Nations Economic and Social Commission for Asia and the Pacific, *Women and Armed Conflict, A Regional Analysis on Asian and the Pacific* (Bangkok: December 2009), 4.

[6] Donna Pankhurst, "The 'Sex War' and Other Wars: Towards a Feminist Approach to Peace Building" *Development in Practice* 13(2/3) (2003): 154.

[7] United Nations. Press Release SC/6816. "Peace inextricably linked with equality between women and men says Security Council in International Women's Day statement" (8. March 2000) http://www.un.org/News/Press/docs/2000/20000308.sc6816.doc.html. (Accessed on 10.10.2011)

[8] Sarah Taylor and Kristina Mader, *Mapping Women, Peace and Security in the UN Security Council, Report of the NGOWG Monthly Action Points, 2009-2010* (NGO Working Group on Women, Peace and Security, October 2010), 4.

[9] Donna Pankhurst, "The 'Sex War' and Other Wars: Towards a Feminist Approach to Peace Building" *Development in Practice* 13(2/3) (2003): 154.

[10] Security Council, *Women and Peace and Security* (Report of the Secretary-General 173, 2010).

[11] Such as the report by Brigitte Sorensen, *Women and Post-Conflict Reconstruction, The War-torn Societies Project* (Occasional Paper No. 3, 1998).

prejudices and to convince countries to enhance the inclusion of women and gender in their official dealings.

It follows that still more work needs to be done to make the public, as well as the policy makers, aware of the importance of the issue. One way of doing so is by demonstrating how successful implementation or the lack of inclusion of gender policies influences the development of a country or region and its society. It is the aim of this thesis to do so on the example of the Kurdistan Region of Iraq.

This will be done by firstly establishing potential effects of gender inclusive policies on the development of countries and regions and their people at a time of conflict transformation, by drawing on the experience of academics working in the field around the world, as well as on the established know-how of the international community. It is thereby the aim to use a vast variety of expertise, from different ends of the spectrum, in order to find common ground between them, as to be able to come to a conclusion on the most likely effects of gender inclusive policies in the respective areas of interest, and on how they have to be deployed and implemented in order to have a positive effect on wider development within a region, as well as on the individual lives of the citizens.

It is further the aim of this thesis to test how the policies deployed and the actions taken by the Kurdistan Regional Government (KRG) compare to the established theory, as to conclude which effects the respective policies, or the lack of such, have on the development of the region and its people at the time of conflict transformation.

The results of the extensive interviews conducted during field research in the area will thereby be used as a 'checking system'. The concrete and implied answers, as well as the behaviour of the interviewees will show the practical effects of the KRG's policies.

It is thus the aim of the thesis to evaluate the effects of the existence or non-existence of different types of gender inclusive policies on national and individual development in a region at a time of conflict transformation, by using both, academic and practitioners' expertise, and local knowledge of the people affected.

The analysis of the policies deployed is thereby not restricted to a single sphere of interest. Three areas have been chosen, namely politics, the economy and education; in all of which the existing gender policies and their effects will be evaluated. While these three spheres are far from inclusive when it comes to the fields to be considered at a time of conflict transformation, they are amongst the main areas to be dealt with when aiming for enhanced development and sustainable peace for all. By choosing to widen the focus and to not merely concentrate on one are of interest, the objectives of the thesis are threefold: It is firstly the aim to demonstrate the difficulties faced at the time of peace building, when it is also impossible to merely concentrate on one concern and to thus paint a slightly more realistic picture of the issue at stake. This was of special importance to the author, since he sole focus on gender inclusive policies, in comparison to policies considering children, the elderly, the disabled, different ethnic groups, religious groups etc., is already a very restricted one, when bearing in mind the amount of necessary issues to be considered at the time of conflict transformation. Secondly, it is the intention of the thesis to demonstrate the interconnectedness of the different spheres considered, and to thereby underline once more that there is never a single solution when it comes to enhance certain development. Finally, by analysing the deployment and their respective effects of gender inclusive policies in a variety of areas, it is the goal of the thesis to derive to a more inclusive conclusion on the KRG's actions for the enhancement of gender equality within the region as a whole and its overall effects.

By showing up the different effects gender inclusive policies or the lack of such have on development within the region and its citizens, it is the aim of the thesis to function as a tool to demonstrate to other academics, the public and also to policy makers how their considerations on gender inclusion effect wider development on a variety of levels. While the thesis can thus also be used as a guideline for other regions in similar situations, it has to be seen as a contemporary and context specific document, with its specificities being aimed at the Kurdistan Region in the year of 2012.

In order to arrive at all of the goals outlined above, the thesis is based around several assumptions. It is the first assumption that positive peace has not yet been achieved anywhere in the world and that it is the aim of development in the country to move towards this positive peace.

It is a further postulation that if peace wants to be achieved for the whole population, including women, gender equality is needed at all levels.

In addition, it is the notion of the thesis is that 'peace' is more than merely the non-existence of armed conflict. Peace is necessary to be embedded in the minds and peace has to exist on a national, as well as on a personal level, to be able to truly talk about the existence of 'peace'. Additionally peace and development are composed of many aspects, including the necessity of equality between religious groups, social groups, ethnicity or gender. As a consequence to this notion, it is a further aim of this thesis to show up the existence of this intersectionality. It thereby has to be noted that while all forms of intersectionality are of great importance, this thesis will focus specifically on the intersectionality between gender and class – rather than religion or ethnicity – as this has proved to be the most significant factor when it comes to considering the effects of gender inclusive policies in the Kurdistan Region.

By achieving its different aims, this thesis will provide a series of contributions to different disciplines. Taking a feminist approach when analysing the time of conflict transformation on the example of the Kurdistan Region, the thesis will contribute to the areas of peace studies, gender studies, and will particularly form a unique contribution to the discipline of Kurdish studies.

According to Eifler and Seifert the issue of gender in internal and international conflicts as well as throughout transformation processes is in general still an under-researched terrain.[12] It can be observed that research in this area has been focused only on specific parts of the world, with various studies of women's participation in conflict situations existing about Africa, South America, Eastern Europe and infrequently Southern Asia, but independent research on the subject

---

[12] Christine Eifler and Ruth Seifert, *Gender Dynamics and Post-Conflict Reconstruction* (Frankfurt am Main: Peter Lang GmbH, 2009), 21.

being especially limited in the Middle East. While several international organisations such as the Heinrich Böll Stiftung,[13] the Center for Humanitarian Dialogue[14] and different UN organisations[15] have published findings on women's involvement in conflict transformation around the world, research is still limited when it comes to the Kurdistan Region.

In general, academic research on the Iraqi Kurdistan Region is still very restricted as a consequence of the decades of preclusion from international dealings, during which it was difficult to access material on the region, as well as to access the region itself. Reasonable stability has only recently given the Kurdistan Region the chance to be accessed by academics from outside and to establish their own academia, after years of physical and cultural destruction.

It is the aim of this thesis, by having conducted field research in the region with a focus on the civil society's views on the process of conflict transformation, to try to fill a gap of existing research in the field of feminist, conflict as well as Kurdish Studies:

While feminist academia was already occupied with the general issues of gender and conflict throughout the 1990s, with pioneers like Cynthia Cockburn[16], Cynthia

---

[13] Layla Al-Zubaidi, *Amdements to the Personal Status Law in Iraqi Kurdistan strengthen Women's Rights* (Heinrich Böll Stiftung, Interview, 2009).; Layla Al-Zubaidi, *Der Streit um Frauenrechte und das Personenstandsrecht: Testfall für die Demokratie im Irak* (Beirut: Heinrich Böll Stiftung, 2009).

[14] Christine Bell and Catherine O'Rourke, *Opinion, UN Security Council 1325 and Peace Negotiations and Agreements* (Geneva: Center for Humanitarian Dialogue, March 2011); Cate Buchanan (ed.), *Women at the Indonesian peace table: Enhancing the contributions of women to conflict resolution* (Geneva: Center for Humanitarian Dialogue, November 2010); Center for Humanitarian Dialogue, *Meeting report, Oslo forum 2011, Annual Mediators' Retreat* (Oslo, Norway: 21-23 June 2011); Center for Humanitarian Dialogue, *Peacemaking in Asia and the Pacific: Women's participation, perspectives and priorities* (Geneva: March 2011); Center for Humanitarian Dialogue, *Promoting gender issues in peace negotiations* (Annual Report 2010, Geneva: 2010).

[15] Secretary-General, Report, *Improvement of the status of women in the United Nations system* (UN General Assembly, 65th session, Item 28(a), Advancement of women, 9.9.2010); UN ESCAP, *Women and Armed Conflict*; United Nations and World Bank, *Joint Iraq Needs Assessment* (October 2003); UNPO, *Presidential and Parliamentary Elections, Kurdistan Region of Iraq, 25 July 2009* (Election Observation Report, 2009).

[16] Cynthia Cockburn, "'Democracy without Women Is No Democracy': Soviet Women Hold Their First Autonomous National Conference," *Feminist Review* 39 (1991): 141-148; Cynthia Cockburn, "Gender Relations as Causal in Militarization and War" *International Feminist Journal of Politics* 12(2) (2010): 139-157; Cynthia Cockburn, "On 'The Machinery of Dominance: Women, Men and Technical Know-How'" *Women's Studies Quarterly* 37(1/2) (2009): 269-273.

Enloe[17], Deniz Kandiyoti,[18] Simona Sharoni[19], Christine Eifler, Ruth Seifert[20] and Donna Pankhurst[21] opening the doors for a whole new branch of academia, academic work on gender relations and women in the Kurdistan Region of Iraq has only really started after 2003 with academics like Nadje Al-Ali, Nicola Pratt[22], Andrea Fischer-Tahir[23], Karin Mlodoch[24], Shahrzad Mojab[25] and Fatma Incesu[26] taking the lead. Research on the Kurdistan Region in general and on gender issues in particular, is still scattered when considering the topics researched and it is still often conducted exclusively or at least partly from outside the region.

When considering research on conflict and peace, a similar pattern can be observed. While different academics work on the different concepts of peace

---

[17] Cynthia Enloe, "'Gender' Is Not Enough: The Need for a Feminist Consciousness" *International Affairs* 80(1) (2004): 95-97; Cynthia Enloe, "The Women behind the Warriors" *The Women's Review of Books* 10(5) (1993): 23-24; Cynthia Enloe, *Globalization and Militarism, Feminists make the Link* (Plymouth: Rowman & Littlefield Publishers, 2007); Cynthia Enloe, *Nimo's War, Emma's War, Making Feminist Sense of the Iraq War* (Berkley: University of California Press, 2010).

[18] Deniz Kandiyoti (ed.), *Gendering the Middle East, Emerging Perspectives* (London: L.B. Tauris Publishers, 1996); Deniz Kandiyoti (ed.), *Women, Islam and the State* (Basingstoke: Palgrave Macmillan, 1992)

[19] Simona Sharoni, "Middle East Politics Through Feminist Lenses: Toward Theorizing International Relations from Women's Struggles" *Alternatives: Global, Local, Political* 18(1) (1993): 5-28; Simona Sharoni, "The Myth of Gender Equality and the Limits of Women's Political Dissent in Israel" *Middle East Report* 207 (1998): 24-28; Simona Sharoni, "Women and Gender in Middle East Studies: Trends, Prospects and Challenges" *Middle East Report* 205 (1997): 27-29; Simona Sharoni, "Women and the Gulf" *Off Our Backs* 21(2) (1991): 22.

[20] Eifler and Seifert, *Gender Dynamics and Post-Conflict Reconstruction*; Christine Eifler und Ruth Seifert (Hrsg), *Soziale Konstruktionen – Militär und Geschlächterverhältnis* (Münster: Westfälisches Dampfboot, 1999).

[21] Donna Pankhurst (ed.), *Gendered Peace, Women's Struggles for Post-War Justice and Reconciliation* (New York: Routledge, 2008); Pankhurst, "The 'Sex War' and Other Wars,"154-177.

[22] Nadje Al-Ali and Nicola Pratt, "Women in Iraq: Beyond the Rhetoric" *Middle East Report* 239 (2006): 18-23; Nadje Al-Ali and Nicola Pratt, "Women's organizing and the conflict in Iraq since 2003" *Feminist Review* 88 (2008): 74-85; Nadje Al-Ali and Nicole Pratt, "Between Nationalism and Women's Rights: The Kurdish Women's Movement in Iraq" *Middle East Journal of Culture and Communication* 4 (2011): 337-353; Nadje Al-Ali and Nicola Pratt (ed.), *Women and War in the Middle East, Transnational Perspectives* (London: Zed Books, 2009).

[23] Andrea Fischer-Tahir, "Competition, cooperation and resistance: women in the political field in Iraq" *International Affairs* 86(6) (2010): 1381-1394.

[24] Karin Mlodoch, "'We Want to be Remembered as Strong Women, Not as Shepherds': Women Anfal Survivors in Kurdistan-Iraq Struggling for Agency and Acknowledgement" *Journal of Middle East Women's Studies* 8(1) (2012): 63-91.

[25] Shahrzad Mojab, "Kurdish Women in the Zone of Genocide and Gendercide" *Al-Raida* XXI(103) (2003); Shahrzad Mojab and Rachel Gorman, "Dispersed Nationalism: War, Diaspora and Kurdish Women's Organizing" *Journal of Middle East Women's Studies* 3(1) (2007): 58-85; Shahrzad Mojab, "Theorizing the Politics of 'Islamic Feminism'" *Feminist Review* 69 (2001): 124-146.

[26] Fatma Incesu, *Die Stellung der Frauen in der kurdischen Gesellschaft* (Frankfurt am Main: Peter Lang, 2004).

building, as Johan Galtung[27], Jonathan Goodhand[28], Oliver Richmond[29], as well as on conflict and gender relations in and around the Middle Eastern region, as Lila Abu-Lughod[30], Valentine Moghadam[31] or Simona Sharoni[32] and finally there also exists general academic work on the Kurdistan Region, as conducted by Ferdinand Hennerbichler[33], Faleh Jabar[34] or Kerim Yildiz[35], which all have an important role to play in the analysis of gender relations and conflict transformation in the Kurdistan Region and thus also form the basis of this thesis, academic research on the implications of national policies on gender relation's development and conflict transformation in the Kurdistan Region, as done by this paper, has not yet been conducted.

By concentrating on the issue of gender equality from a political side, as well as civil society's view, and by widening the focus through introducing the effects of gender politics in political, economic and educational developments in the region, the thesis will provide the English speaking population with a current testimony of the situation in the Kurdistan Region, which is otherwise not available in this way, and will at the same time add to the current research on gender and peace studies from a still academically difficult to access region.

---

[27] Johan Galtung, *Peace by Peaceful Means, Peace and Conflict, Development and Civilization* (Oslo: PRIO, International Peace Research Institute, 1996).

[28] Jonathan Goodhand, *Aiding Peace? The Roles of NGOs in Armed Conflict* (London: Lynne Rienner Publishers, 2006); Jonathan Goodhand and David Hulme, "From Wars to Complex Political Emergencies: Understanding Conflict and Peace-Building in the New World Disorder" *Third World Quarterly* 20(1) (1999): 13-26.

[29] Oliver Richmond (Review), "Peace and Development: Strange Bedfellows? Postconflict Development: Meeting New Challenges by Gerd Junne; Willemijn Verkoren" *International Studies Review* 7(3) (2005): 437-440; Oliver Richmond, "A Genealogy of Peacemaking: The Creation and Re-Creation of Order" *Alternatives: Global, Local, Political* 26(3) (2001): 317-348; Oliver Richmond, "Emancipatory Forms of Human Security and Liberal Peacebuilding" *International Journal* 62(3) (2007): 458-477.

[30] Lila Abu-Lughod, "Dialects of Women's Empowerment: The International Circuitry of the *Arab Human Development Report 2005*" *Int. J. Middle East Stud.* 41 (2009): 83-103; Lila Abu-Lughod, "Saving Muslim Women or Standing with Them?: On Images, Ethics, and War in our Times" *Insayat* 1(1) (2003): 1-12.

[31] Valentine Moghadam and Fatima Sadiqi, "Women's Activism and the Public Sphere: An Introduction and Overview" *Journal of Middle East Women's Studies* 2(2) (2006): 1-7; Valentine Moghadam, "Peacebuilding and Reconstruction with Women: Reflections on Afghanistan, Iraq and Palestine" *Development* 48(3) (2005): 63-72.

[32] Sharoni, "The Myth of Gender Equality," 24-28; Sharoni, "Women and Gender in Middle East Studies," 27-29; Sharoni, "Women and the Gulf," 22.

[33] Ferdinand Hennerbichler, *Die Kurden* (Mosonmagyaróvár: Edition fhe, 2004).

[34] Faleh Jabar and Hosham Dawod (ed), *The Kurds, Nationalism and Politics* (London: SAQI, 2006).

[35] Kerim Yildiz, *The Kurds in Iraq, The past, present and future* (London: Pluto Press in association with Kurdish Human Rights Project, 2004).

B.   Hypothesis and Leading Questions

It is the underlying hypothesis of this thesis that gender inclusive policies, if deployed and implemented correctly, will have a positive effect on gender equality within society, and will thus promote the establishment of sustainable peace and development for every person individually, the decrease of conflict potential, and the increase of positive national development.

Following from the above, the hypothesis continues, when applied on the example of the Kurdistan Region, that while development is clearly visible, the fact that gender equality and positive peace is not yet a reality for all in the region, conflict potential is still clearly present, and national development is not as enhanced as it arguably could be, is partly due to gender policies not being deployed and implemented inclusively.

This hypothesis leads to a series of questions including the following:

- Does enhanced gender equality truly promote sustainable peace?
- Which policies have been deployed by the KRG?
- What are their effects on society and on the national level?
- What steps have to be taken to support the development of gender equality and sustainable peace?

These questions and many more will be discussed in the thesis and arguments will be presented to support the hypothesis.

C.   Structure of the Thesis

The thesis is divided in seven chapters, with chapters I and II introducing the topic as well as the methodology of the thesis, chapter III providing the necessary background information, and chapters IV, V and VI forming the heart of the thesis, by analysing the research findings, before leading to a conclusion in chapter VII.

After giving an outline of the themes and objectives of the thesis, as well as the main hypotheses and values of it in chapter I, chapter II provides a description of the methods used and the challenges encountered as part of the research, especially going into depth on the field research conducted in the Kurdistan

Region. The researcher has thereby chosen not to include an extra 'theory chapter' as part of the introduction of the thesis, but rather to provide a section on the background of the theoretical and academic discussion at the beginning of each chapter it correlates to, for reasons of better legibility and wholeness.

Chapter III is the last of the background chapters and has as its aim to enable the reader to better understand the prevailing circumstances in the region of research, with the aim of ensuring enhanced understanding of the methods deployed by the politicians, as well as the reactions of civil society, which will be discussed in the subsequent chapters. As part of this aim, the third chapter therefore provides a short essay on the author's reflections on war, peace and gender, historical background information on the Kurdistan Region, an analysis of the roles of women during the time of conflict in general and more specifically during the previous conflicts, which took place in the region, and finally paints a picture of the development of women's status within society and the existence of gender equality throughout time within the region.

Chapter IV is the first of the three main chapters of the thesis, discussing the influence of different political actions and forces on gender quality in the country and consequently on the positive transformation of peace. Within the framework of the three subchapters it will be elaborated how women and gender have been included in Kurdistan Region's politics, what the current possibilities for the inclusion are, i.e. national and international legislation, as well actions by the officials, how this is influencing society, through analysing interviews conducted in Kurdistan, and the development of conflict transformation, by inter alia taking into consideration already existing research on the topic, and which further steps should be taken.

Chapter V will discuss how economy in general and women's and gender inclusion in it, when it comes to macroeconomic policies, employment, and business, have the ability to influence the development of gender equality, and conflict transformation. It will be discussed how the inclusion of women and gender in the region's economy or the lack thereof influences women's personal development and peace within the families and society and how it influences economic development in the region as a whole and consequently the rebuilding of an economically functioning region, which is considered to be a driving force in conflict transformation.

The last of the three main chapters, chapter VI, will have at its centre the role of education in shaping social development, gender equality and conflict transformation. It will be discussed how education influences society in general, and women and girls in particular, when it comes to the questions of equality, as well as war and peace; and how women themselves have the ability to change society through education, on the examples of children's schooling, higher education, adult education and women as educators in the Kurdistan Region.

Finally, chapter VII will, after a short summary of the outcomes of the chapters above, draw a general conclusion on the issue at stake, namely that the enhancement of gender equality does indeed support the development of positive peace - although differently on the national and the personal level - and that while theoretical achievements have been vast in the Kurdistan Region, their practical implementation remains slow, and issues, such as the gap between different groups of society, are challenges which will have to be tackled by the government, in order to ensure true enhancement of equality, as well as the prevention of further conflict.

II.   Methodology - Methods and Procedure

In order to access the material needed for this thesis, the researchers used two methods: library- and internet based research and field research. As a starting point, the researcher came into the field with certain hypotheses in mind, which were adapted and changed depending on the outcome of the research encountered. The researcher thereby tried to keep a very open mind and not to become static with the ideas previously developed, but to work with the different analyses and outcomes encountered as part of the research and to advance the thesis according to the new data established.

The following chapter will provide an overview of the techniques used to derive the data used in this thesis. It will elaborate challenges encountered and it will analyse the personal influences of the researcher on the data.

A. Library- and Internet based Research

Primary and secondary material for the study was derived through library based and internet based research.

Inevitably nearly all the accessible material was either written by people in the West or by people from around the world whose work has been published in Europe or America.

Special use was made of libraries from the different institutes of the University of Vienna, the library for development policy in Vienna, "C3: Bibliothek for Entwicklungspolitik", the Kurdish library Casme Calil in Eichgraben, Lower Austria, and the library of the University of Exeter.

Other material originated from extensive research online, comprising material from different UN institutions, such as the secretariat or UN Women, an extensive number of scholarly articles and various materials from different NGOs, as well as regional organisations.

Primary sources include resolutions, constitutions, national regulations, as well as government reports and newspaper articles. Additionally secondary sources were used, such as books and articles comparing and evaluating the measures taken and the research conducted in the area.

All the material was mainly in English or in German, with a few sources in Kurdish or Arabic. The limitation of language proved to be one of the challenges encountered as part of the research. As Kurdish is not the researcher's mother tongue, it was impossible to access all material in the Kurdish language, which resulted in a loss of certain material.

But even without the language barrier, it proved challenging to access authentic material when it came to research on the current situation inside the Kurdistan

Region. Material on the region is not yet freely available, and even when it is, it cannot always be trusted.

Similar challenges could be encountered when it came to the field research:

B.   Field Research

As explained in the introduction, it was the researcher's aim to get a comprehensive picture of the effects of the policies deployed by the government, by using the expertise of the people directly affected. In order to meet this goal, the researcher got together with people of all ages, as well as different social and religious backgrounds, in order to get a feeling from the whole population on what changes have been happening inside the region, and what the role of women and gender is playing in them. This is based on the understanding that it is necessary to look at the "ordinary" people to understand the whole picture, as explained by Cynthia Enloe.[36]

Since it was the interest of the author to look at the world views of members of a specific certain group and the author sees it as necessary to be sensitive to the participant's interpretation of their social world, the research was led in the tradition of the qualitative research strategy. Exactly how the research strategy was conducted and by which stimuli it was influenced, will be subject of this chapter.

Field research for the study was conducted exclusively in the Kurdistan Region of Iraq, as opposed to regions of Kurdish residence in other countries, or the whole of Iraq, for the reason of Kurdistan Iraq's unique position in the conflict transformation process, and consequently the people's unique experience from other parts of the region.

Research was conducted in the Kurdistan Region on an on and off basis throughout the year of 2012, with the researcher being based in Erbil as well as Sulaimaniya, and taking trips to other parts of the region, such as Dohuk or

---

[36] Cynthia Enloe, Connecticut College, Lectures, YouTube "Cynthia Enloe speaks on Women in Iraq" http://www.youtube.com/watch?v=BUVPmOvJINA (Accessed on 7.12.2011)

Halabja, with the research being based mainly on interviews, as well as personal observation.

While the movement between the different parts of the region and also between different groups of people meant for the researcher that she was able to gain a broader knowledge of the issues at stake, it meant at the same time that it was difficult to establish tight connections with too many people, which had an influence on the interviews, as will be seen below.

1.   Methods of Data Collection

Data was collected in two ways: personal observations and interviews. Even though the use of interviews was the main focus of the researcher, since it was the aim to draw conclusions from the points of views of the people involved in the situation, personal observation was of great Important to fill the gaps left by the interviews.

a)   *Interviews*

The researcher interviewed 63 men and women from different parts of the regions, the majority being from Erbil, then Sulaimaniya, the surrounding areas, as well as few from Kirkuk and Mosul.

With the explicit aim of reaching people from different social backgrounds, in comparison to for example only interviewing high level politicians, or NGO workers, several challenges crossed the path of the researcher.

As an "outsider" it is never easy to get into a community. In the particular case a lack of sufficient knowledge of the local languages, and the region as a whole, as well as the fact that it is seen as unacceptable in the region for a young woman to live alone by herself, made the situation more difficult.

In order for the researcher to get access to the local community in the Kurdistan Region, she first established contact with Kurdish people based in her own local community, in Austria, Vienna.

By becoming part of the Kurdish school of Vienna, by getting in contact with different politically engaged Kurds in Austria, by attending festivals and by getting involved with the first scientific Kurdish society of Austria, the basis was formed, which opened the researcher the way into the Kurdish society in their own home country.

The researcher got nearly all of her contacts of the interviewees through her already existing contacts in Kurdistan, which were different family members of Austrian Kurds, as well as university contacts.

As giving an interview was for many participants seen as a sign of trust and of doing a favour, it was necessary for the researcher to have a "reference" or be accompanied by a local, so that the other party could be sure that the researcher can be trusted.

This automatically narrowed down the groups of people who could be approached.

At the interviews conducted the gender balance of the interviewees proved reasonably equal, with 57 per cent of female interviewees and 43 per cent men, but the age balance was not.

There was a much higher percentage of younger women being interviewed as opposed to older women (with 60% of women interviewed being under the age of 29) and in contradiction there was a higher percentage of older men being interviewed as opposed to younger men (with 62% of men interviewed being between the age of 29 and 50), the reason being that those groups were far easier to access. As experienced by the researcher, the young women were reasonably outspoken, while the older women rather held back, and with the men it was exactly the other way round.

It was especially difficult to access people ready to be interviewed, who were over the age of 60, as they either did not want to be interviewed, or the people supporting the researcher were not ready to assist her in talking to the older people, either for reasons of respect for the elderly, or possibly uncertainty because of the type of interview questions, or because the elderly people were not regarding of still playing a role in today's politics.

The research was directed at women and men in their normal day-to-day life. Through not only targeting political elites, international institutions and current peace activists, the author aimed to promote the increased participation of women at all levels of society and in all situations. In order to obtain a wide variety of participants, the researcher targeted different groups: politicians, NGO workers, people living in urban areas, as well as people from the country side and people who are well educated, as well as people who are not. Through this *purposive sampling*[37] the researcher aimed at getting an insight into the views of the population as a whole, and not only of a specific group. Within diverse groups of people, the recruitment of participants was a *probability sampling*[38], which depended on accessibility. Interestingly, it could be observed that no real pattern emerged of a clear male or female line or of questions being answered according to social status or even education.

The interviews were held with students from different universities, teachers, doctors, workers, housewives, officials, people with very different religious believes (from very religious to atheists; Muslims, as well as Christians), different political opinions (PUK, KDP, Gorran, Islamic, or not political at all) and very different social backgrounds (from the very rich elite to families who could barely feed their children). Additionally, the researcher talked to people who have lived in Kurdistan their whole lives, as well as people who returned from exile and people who have decided to stay outside the country but who are regularly going for visits.

It was particularly difficult for the researcher to get in close contact with people actually living in the country side, although interviews were conducted with people who are originally from the country side, as the people supporting the researcher were either not willing or able to support her with contacts in the country side and several attempts to talking to people in the country side failed, partly as a consequence of cultural misunderstandings.

But language and cultural predicaments were only some of the obstacles faced by the researcher. A further challenge was provided by the issue discussed itself.

---

[37] Alan Bryman, *Social Research Methods* (Third edition, Oxford: Oxford University Press, 2008) 458.
[38] Ibid.

The interviews were from their layout semi-structured with open-ended questions and interviewees were encouraged to answer in whichever way they wanted, even if it did not correspond with the question in order to get an insight into what the interviewee sees as relevant and important.

In the interviews the interviewees were asked about their opinions on the situation of women in their country, their opinion on further inclusion of women, how this could be achieved, their satisfaction with the development of their country in general and their opinions on working methods of conflict transformation.

Thereby the different questions which had a connection to conflict transformation were mixed, so that the interviewee, when coming back to a specific topic, was able to see it from a different point of view.

The interviews were conducted one by one but also in small groups, in order to establish where and how people reacted differently in their answers.

Initially it was the researcher's intent to only conduct semi-structured interviews, but during the field research this proved impossible. While in some situations it was not possible to have any type of real interview, but rather merely a "loose conversation", such as for example with a few students at a university, who were scared that the usage of pen and paper while they were talking could get them into trouble, because interviews were not officially allowed on university premises, but it was not possible to go out for them as well, other people were ready to provide information, but only if they were allowed to fill out the interview themselves in private and on a piece of paper, as they did not want to discuss any type of political questions in public. There were also several people who refused to talk about the subject or to answer certain questions, as they were scared of getting problems for certain opinions. It is also for this reason that the researcher decided to not use any names or other characteristics, which could identify the interviewees, in her thesis.

As a result of the partial lack of free speech from several of the interviewees, the researcher could sometimes not be sure if the interviewees truly spoke what they were thinking or if they rather replied to questions in a way that they presumed the researcher wanted them to answer. As explained by a 23 year old student *"In our society there is the mentality that people give the "right" ("correct") answer to everything they are asked. There is no freedom in giving answers".*[39] These types of answers will be highlighted throughout the thesis.

While these were some of the more challenging moments of the research, it has to be said that the researcher also had long and very open conversations with people who were extremely happy to talk about the issue at stake.

In addition to the interviews, the researcher also relied on personal notes and observations:

b) *Personal Notes and Observations*

During the time of field research the researcher took notes on the general setting and circumstances, but also on the behaviour of participants during and around the time of interviews.

This way of collecting data helped to further learn about and appreciate the culture of the social group and to get a feeling of why the interviewees are thinking in the way they are. At the same time it helped to divide words from actions, as it could be observed that many participants' theoretical points of view were contradictory to their actions.

The researcher specifically spent time travelling the region, being part of social gatherings and attending political meetings, as an observer with the research questions in mind. This more distanced way of research and the consequent active reflection on the observations made through the writing of notes, provided the research with an understanding, which would not have been present otherwise.

While the researcher tried to be as objective as possible when conducting the research, this was impeded by more underlying influences:

---

[39] Interview BW, Sulaimaniya on 08/08/2012

C.　　Influences on the Conduct of the Research

"Different accounts and interpretations of events are linked to particular world-views and frames of mind."[40]

Personal experiences and values of the researcher have a great impact on the research conducted. It can have an impact on the choice of area, the formulation of the research question, as well as the analysis of data or the conclusions drawn from the data.[41]

Because of who we are (who speaks, who writes, where, what time, with whom, for whom…) there is always subjectivity. Even though researchers try to keep an objective distance, it is not possible to be truly objective. One's own experiences and personality are central to the research process and make it subjective.[42]

Concerning this difficult subject of personal influence on research, which is by many seen as having to be "objective", the author supports the point of view, as held by Turnbull, who stated at the beginning of his book:

> *"the reader is entitled to know something of the aims, expectations, hopes and attitudes that the writer brought to the field with him, for these will surely influence not only how he sees things but even what he sees."* [43]

It follows for the researcher that it is better to know about the author's personal influences than to read the thesis with false expectations.

The author of the thesis is a white, young, middle class, European female who grew up in an international environment, and who is married to an Iraqi citizen.

The author comes from a critically thinking background with feminist influence. She went into the research with a very positive view on the society researched and on the subject of women and it was her aim and hope to on the one hand point out the current reality of the researched subject, but to also work for social change.

---

[40] Nadje Al-Ali, *Iraqi Women, Untold Stories from 1948 to the Present* (London Zed Books, 2007) 2.

[41] Bryman, *Social Research Methods,* 24.

[42] James Clifford and George Marcus (ed.), *Writing Culture, The Poetics and Politics of Ethnography* (Berkeley: University of California Press, 1986) 13.

[43] Colin Turnbull, *The Mountain People* (London: Picador, Pan Books, 1974) 13.

While the situation of the researcher, as a young woman from the West and married to an Iraqi was very positive in certain situations, it could mean obstacles in others, when it came to research for the thesis.

Being a European and a woman meant that many people were rather prepared to talk to the researcher about issues, which they might not have discussed with somebody from inside the community or with a man. It was easier to get access to certain households and the researcher was not considered a threat.

Additionally the fact that a European was so interested in the region to even conduct research there was regarded highly by many who all wanted to offer help.

At the same time being a European meant that there existed several language as well as cultural misunderstandings, which are reflected in the choice of documents for the theoretical part of the research, as well as in the interviews. It was not possible to for the author to access official Kurdish documents and reports, in the same way as it would have been for a native speaker. At the same time, the researcher was not able to conduct or to fully understand the interviews in the interviewee's mother tongue, which resulted in a great loss of material and different cultural understandings lead to the interviewer misunderstanding certain actions, and while some of them were clarified, there are certainly still several which were not.

Being a European in the Kurdistan Region also meant that it was possible for the researcher to be allowed into the circle of high level politicians, as well as other wealthier families, but it also meant that it was more difficult to access other parts of society.

Finally the fact that the researcher is married to an Iraqi meant on the one hand that many people responded more friendly, for reasons of religious belief or other, and that the researcher already had some insight into the culture before arriving for her field research. On the other hand it also meant that certain restrictions applied, which would not have applied if the researcher had gone there as a single European woman, because the welfare of the wider family had to be taken into consideration.

All of the obstacles described and experienced by the researcher were proof to her that the field of Kurdistan, especially when it comes to gender studies and conflict transformation, is still an under-researched terrain and is consequently a work in progress. The researcher therefore hopes that her study will be able to play a part in opening the pathway to further research in the area. At the same time the researcher kindly asks the reader to keep in mind the challenges encountered when reading the thesis and to keep an open mind for different ways of interpretation.

Before starting off with the main analysis of the thesis, the following chapter will provide a variety of necessary background material:

III.   Setting the Scene

This thesis comprises a variety of challenging topics, and more experienced academics have already dedicated books to question every one of these issues individually. As can be derived from the title, it is the thesis' aim to discuss the interrelationship between gender and post-armed-conflict development, on the example of the situation in the Kurdistan Region. As to be able to fully and critically discuss the issue at stake, it is firstly necessary to derive a profound understanding of the different theories of "post-conflict development", in order to appreciate if and how gender policies can affect development at the time of peacebuilding; to increase insight into the situation of women and gender relations during the times of armed conflict, as to comprehend the different challenges faced at the time of conflict transformation; to gain knowledge of the past and present situation of the Kurdistan Region, in order to apprehend the precise circumstances the thesis is embedded in; and to develop familiarity with the situation of women and gender relations in the Kurdistan Region, as to appreciate the effects gender policies are likely to have on development of the region, and the people themselves.

It is the aim of the following chapter to provide this background knowledge, in the best way possible, by firstly reflecting on the issues of war, peace and gender, followed by an account of Kurdistan's history, and a discussion on women's roles during the time of conflict, to finally elaborate the issue of women and gender equality in the Kurdistan Region.

Tackling the most controversial question first, i.e. the existent relationship between gender equality and conflict transformation, is the first subchapter:

A.   Reflections on War, Peace and Gender

"Women are crucial partners in creating the conditions for sustainable peace: economic recovery, social cohesion and political legitimacy."[44]

War and peace are ever present concerns in today's world. Hardly a day goes by without people being confronted with violent conflicts either as individuals or through the media. At the same time there has emerged a global movement for peace. Millions are going rallying for peace on the streets, and ever more books and articles being written about wars as well as peace processes;[45] the principal aim of the UN is the achievement and maintenance of global peace[46], the international community increasingly supports peace-keeping activities and countries are sending their soldiers abroad in the name of peace. Nevertheless the number of conflicts around the world is not decreasing,[47] their methods are, through advances in technology, arguably even more gruesome than before, and the aim for a global and sustainable peace is very far from achieved.

The different violent conflicts occur for a variety of reasons and they all have their individual characteristics. Some wars are fought for economic reasons, such as challenging or defending established property rights[48], others aim to achieve regional hegemony or a level of global control, for instance the so-called "wars

---

[44] Kvinna till Kvinna Foundation, *Building Security – a contribution to the debate on security policy* (Stockholm 2011) 32.

[45] Roger Mac Ginty, *No war, no peace: the rejuvenation of stalled peace processes and peace accords* (Baskingstoke: Palgrave Macmillan, 2006) 12.

[46] See Article 1(1) of the UN Charter: *"The Purposes of the United Nations are: To maintain international peace and security, and to that end: to take effective collective measures for the prevention and removal of threats to the peace, and for the suppression of acts of aggression or other breaches of the peace, and to bring about by peaceful means, and in conformity with the principles of justice and international law, adjustment or settlement of international disputes or situations which might lead to a breach of the peace;"*

[47] UCDP, "Conflict Encyclopedia" Uppsala Universitet http://www.ucdp.uu.se/gpdatabase/search.php (Accessed on 12.09.2011)

[48] Tony Addison and Tilman Brück, *Making Peace Work, The Challenges of Social and Economic Reconstruction* (Basingstoke: Palgrave Macmillan, 2009) 2.

against terrorism".[49] Still others are caused by ethno-nationalist issues, by class issues, or by the oppression of one element of society by another.[50] But whatever their origins, all wars lead to destruction.

The logical question is how to re-establish or create a situation of peace out of the chaos and destruction of war.

As explained by Lederach:

> *"Conflicts do not just happen to people, people are active participants in creating situations and interactions they experience as conflict".*[51]

It follows that conflicts are created, which leads to the assumption that peace may also be created. But in order to overcome conflict, and be able to create peace and constructive development for all, it is firstly necessary to understand the underlying situation which led to the conflict.

All conflicts are multidimensional[52] and every conflict is unique.[53] The outbreak of war is thereby determined by pre-existing conditions, as is the behaviour of people during the conflict.[54] War does not occur as an isolated event, which can be eliminated through a single action never to return again. Rather it is a complex phenomenon which derives from socially and historically defined relations between the different parties to the conflict.[55] As Quincy Wright puts it:

> *"A war, in reality, results from a total situation involving ultimately almost everything that has happened to the human race up to the time the war begins".*[56]

---

[49] Vivienne Jabri, "Revisiting change and conflict: On Underlying Assumptions and the De-Politicisation of Conflict Resolution" *Berghof Research Center for Constructive Conflict Management* 5 (2006): 4.

[50] Cockburn, "Gender Relations as Causal in Militarization and War," 149.

[51] John Paul Lederach, *Preparing for Peace, Conflict Transformation Across Cultures* (New York: Syracuse University Press, 1996) 9.

[52] Richmond, "A Genealogy of Peacemaking," 326.

[53] Goodhand and Hulme, "From Wars to Complex Political Emergencies," 17.

[54] Chris Cuomo, "War is not just an event: Reflections on the significance of everyday violence" *Hypatia* 11(4) (1996): 33.

[55] Susanne Buckley-Zistel, *Conflict Transformation and Social Change in Uganda. Remembering after violence* (New York: Palgrave Macmillan, 2008) 21/22.

[56] William Nester, *Globalization, War, and Peace in the Twenty-first Century* (New York: Palgrave MacMillan, 2010) 28.

This includes the legacy of previous political leaders, the availability of economic opportunities and also the relationship between the genders.

While every circumstance surrounding the creation or de-escalation of armed conflict is important, the main focus of this thesis is with gender equality and with viewing the genesis of war and peace from a gender perspective.

In many ways, the conducting of armed conflicts, as well as the construction of peace, are gendered activities in a variety of ways. Men and women are generally prescribed different roles from one another, with the specifics depending on age, class and cultural background.

From a gendered perspective, wars deepen the divisions, which existed before, supporting men's roles as perpetrators of violence and women as victims. Once again war makes it clear that women are oppressed and exploited through their bodies, legitimizing sexual violence against women, such as mass rape.[57]

Furthermore, gender issues can be considered as root cause of war. As explained by Cynthia Cockburn *"they foster militarism and militarization. They make war thinkable. They make peace difficult to sustain"*[58]

Transition from a state of war to a state of peace can only occur through a number of stages. Actions by the military and civilian leaders are needed to halt imminent large scale violence. Measures have to be taken to provide the general population with their basic needs and to initiate reconciliation within society. Finally long term provisions are required to eliminate as much as possible the potential of future conflict, which includes the elimination of potential root causes. Clearly these three stages can or even should overlap and the measures necessary to achieve them will vary from region to region and also from decade to decade. However all of them are necessary to achieve a state of peace.

The concepts shortly outlined in the paragraph above are not new and are recognized by academics and practitioners today. However there is still arguably too much emphasis on the first of the three stages (i.e. action by the military and

---

[57] Cockburn, "Gender Relations as Causal in Militarization and War," 144.
[58] Ibid.p.149

civilian leaders) once a country or a region emerges from violent conflict. Even today it is still often assumed that it is only through the existence of armies and the threat or actual use of military force that peace can be achieved or maintained between nations.[59]

This assumption could also be verified on the example of Kurdistan. The Kurdistan Region is highly disputed territory. According to the peace-brief of the United States Institute of Peace in March 2011 several measures are necessary to prevent the outbreak of further conflict in or at the borders of the Kurdistan Region. These include the operation of integrated security forces, the declaration of a demilitarised zone across the disputed territories, having a negotiating committee to resolve the conflict over the disputed territory, to appoint a UN Special rapporteur on the issue as well as to develop a team of local authorities, who can respond first to tensions arising on the ground.[60]

While all these measures are necessary to prevent immediate conflict from arising, their militaristic and narrow character will not allow for sustainable peace to flourish. While it may be possible to achieve a short term peaceful solution by force, the goal of sustainable peace needs to be approached from a different angle. The main challenge with analyzing conflict and the subsequent building of peace is the number of different layers which have to be considered. It is not possible to come up with one formula that sorts everything. Various dimensions including human rights, gender, health, religion, language, education, psychology and business practice need to be considered.[61] It follows that the consideration of gender policies and their positive implementation are one of many steps to prevent further conflict by eliminating root causes and to work towards achieving sustainable, or even positive, peace within society.

---

[59]Bruce Bonta, "Conflict Resolution among Peaceful Societies: The Culture of Peacefulness" *Journal of Peace Research* 33(4) (1996): 409.

[60] Emma Sky, *Preventing Arab-Kurd Conflict in Iraq after the Withdrawal of US Forces*, (Washington: United Institution if Peace, Peacebrief 86, March 2011) 4/5.

[61] Charles Webel and Johan Galtung, *Handbook of Peace and Conflict Studies* (New York: Routledge, 2007) 299.

As defined by Galtung, peace thereby is a never-ending process,[62] which has to be maintained on a national, as well as a personal level.

Only at the very basic level is peace understood as the opposite of conflict or war. Many would define peace as a time in which soldiers are not sent to the front and organized killing exists at a minimal level. But while one group might have a feeling of peace once they are back home from the battle field, another group might only experience peace once they are able to leave their houses again without fear.

As Galtung explains there exist three types of violence: physical, structural and cultural.[63] Today's peace is defined through the elimination of only the first type of violence, the physical one and mainstream opinion is that the absence of large-scale physical violence is enough for countries and people to live at peace, a "negative peace". With negative peace there is no longer organized violence, but neither is there truly positive interaction and people are merely "coexisting peacefully". Galtung introduced two other forms of peace: "positive peace" and "unqualified peace". While there is some cooperation at a time of positive peace, but there are still occasional outbreaks of violence. "Unqualified peace" implies the total absence of violence in combination with a pattern of cooperation.[64]

While unqualified peace is arguably unachievable in the near future, it nevertheless insufficient to aim merely for negative peace. For many women, as well as men, peace does not necessarily mean the cessation of armed conflict. As long as all people's security needs are not met they will not feel in a state of peace. The meeting of these needs for women, if indeed they are ever achieved, will often take much longer than for men. Women will consequently experience a state of peace at a different time from men. Cynthia Enloe defines peace as "women's achievement of control over their lives". This would entail much more than violence outside their homes, or even violence at home, which many women experience

---

[62] Galtung, *Peace by Peaceful Means*, 265.

[63] Ibid.p.3

[64] Johan Galtung, *Peace: Research, Education, Action, Essays in Peace Research* (Volume 1, Copenhagen: Christian Ejlers, 1975) 29/30.

after a conflict. It involves the absence of poverty and the helplessness or dependency it creates.[65]

"Peace" is thereby something personal to every individual. The perception of "peace" is as much dependent on a person's beliefs and expectations as on his or her experience during war. Since everyone is different there are nearly as many ideas of peace as there are people.

When people in the Kurdistan Region were asked what they associated with "peace", the most common answer was "development".[66] Peace, for the people, goes together with development of the region, intellectually, but also economically[67]. It is peace that ensures the possibility of development of all aspects of society[68]. In the people's experience development does not exist without peace and at the same time, peace does not exist without development.[69]

Another very important aspect was that peace is what every human being needs for "life". Peace is the foundation of life and it is not possible to truly live without peace.[70]

Others commented that peace for them means to live in unity and harmony[71] and that peace needs to comprise all levels of society, in the sense that all the different ethnic and social groups can live together in harmony[72]. In general people rather thought of peace in a wider sense. They said that peace is to live together everywhere (in the whole world) without hate and envy and that peace means acceptance and a willingness not to enforce anything on anybody else.[73] For one person especially, peace meant that everybody in society can have the religion and

---

[65] Cynthia Enloe in Nadje Al-Ali, "Reconstructing Gender: Iraqi women between dictatorship, war, sanctions and occupation" *Third World Quarterly* 26(4-5) (2005): 742.

[66] See e.g. Interview AG, Erbil on 13/04/2012; Interview AH, Erbil on 15/04/2012; Interview AS, Sulaimaniya on 23/05/2012; Interview AW, Sulaimaniya on 01/06/2012; Interview BE, Erbil on 26/06/2012; Interview AX, Sulaimaniya on 03/06/2012, Interview BG, Erbil on 02/07/2012; Interview BN, Erbil on 17/07/2012

[67] Interview AG, Erbil on 13/04/2012

[68] Interview AN, Erbil on 03/05/2012

[69] Interview BG, Erbil on 02/07/2012

[70] Interview BT, Erbil on 24/07/2012

[71] Interview AV, Sulaimaniya on 28/05/2012

[72] Interview BW, Sulaimaniya on 08/08/2012

[73] Interview CE, Vienna on 21/10/2012

belief they want, that the private sphere is accepted and that everybody can have access to education.[74]

Still others considered peace as being "freedom", something that gives spirit and happiness to life[75]. Such "freedom" provides the basis to live in wealth and with stability[76]. In view of all these elements of 'peace' from a gender perspective, it can be concluded that "true" peace will only exist when it is possible for every man and woman to live in freedom, without oppression, either from the state or from the people around them; to live without discrimination; and to be empowered to develop themselves. In the words of one elderly woman: *"Peace means that there are no differences between men and women"*.[77]

The correlation between gender equality and the existence of peace is still a highly disputed theory among academics, as well as civil society. Many are of the opinion that while gender and other elements of equality amongst the population are significant, they do not rank in importance for peace building with other issues, such as disarmament, political actions and the reconstruction of the economy. At the same time people held the opinion that a correlation does necessarily exist. As explained by a 20 year old student,

> *"equality in a region leads to enhanced possibilities because of the different experience people have, and consequently makes the establishment of peace easier."*[78]

Additionally it was explained by a housewife and a middle-aged doctor that it is not possible to create a homogenous state without equality between the sexes and that equality and unity are the basis for peace, as people will always resume fighting and conflict, if they do not feel equal.[79]

From a feminist point of view peace is more than the mere absence of great-scale physical violence.[80] Peace encompasses humanitarian as well as social, economic,

---

[74] Interview CK, Vienna on 20/10/2012

[75] Interview AQ, Sulaimaniya on 19/05/2012

[76] Interview AK, Erbil on 20/04/2012

[77] Interview CD, Vienna on 21/10/2012

[78] Interview AE, Erbil on 09/04/2012

[79] Interview AY, Sulaimaniya on 04/06/2012; Interview AO, Sulaimaniya on 13/05/2012

[80] Goodhand and Hulme, "From Wars to Complex Political Emergencies," 15.

political and cultural issues. In order to achieve this "positive peace", as discussed above, structural as well as cultural violence need to be eliminated in all their forms. Structural violence, in the form of social exploitation and repression, together with cultural violence, namely symbolic violence in religion, ideology, language, art, science, law, media, education etc., create the justification for physical violence. It follows that only through their elimination will it be possible to have real peace. [81] And there is a need for social transformation when wanting to achieve true peace.[82]

Structural and cultural violence can arise from a variety of issues including economic classes, ethnic and religious groupings as well as sexual orientation and gender. To the extent that mainstream research on peace and armed conflict takes a gender neutral approach for granted, it may be argued that it implicitly assumes a male-centric approach. This has to change, since, according to Cynthia Cockburn, it is gender relations which *"push the wheel around"*.[83] Although gender relations have changed dramatically around the world in the previous 200 years, equality is far from achieved, either at a national, or at a personal level. Women are still underrepresented in decision making positions, little has changed in the sexual division of labour, and women are still disproportionately affected by violence, especially domestic violence.[84]

Women are exploited through not having the same opportunities as men for their personal development. This structural violence against women is maintained through *"socialization, gender stereotyping, and a constant threat of violence"* which identify women as inferior. Even if they manage to get outside the house, they do not have the same opportunities as men. Women often get inferior jobs receive less pay and thus enjoy fewer opportunities for public participation. Structural violence is created and sustained by cultural norms. It is therefore cultural violence which legitimises structural violence and gender issues are integral to both. Gender inequality exists in every state, and although women's

---

[81] Galtung, *Peace by Peaceful Means,* 3.

[82] Ibid.p.16

[83] Cockburn, "Gender Relations as Causal in Militarization and War," 149.

[84] Heinrich Böll Stiftung, *Gender Politics Makes A Difference, Experiences of the Heinrich Böll Foundation Across the World* (Berlin: Heinrich Böll Stiftung, 2009) 5.

power varies across regions and states, full equality is yet still to be achieved in any state.[85]

It follows that from a gender point of view positive peace does not exist in today's world. More and more scholars are agreeing with the concept of a continuum effect, when it comes to war. Wars are no longer seen as single events, but rather as being timeless conflicts, at different stages of development. For feminists it is especially so, since women report that they are experiencing similar coercion by men during the so-called peace time as during war.[86]

Women's equality is as much a prerequisite for sustainable peace, as sustainable peace is for women's equality. War determines and deepens gender differences and positive peace will only be achievable if all forms of inequality are extinguished. It follows that movements for peace and movements for gender, as well as for religious, ethnic and class equality, need to go hand in hand.

Women, as approximately fifty per cent or more of the population, play an important role in the transformation of the country and the development of society. But rather than receiving support after the end of armed conflicts, women often suffer a backlash in their relations not only with men but also against any new-found freedoms and they are forced back into their "traditional roles".[87]

In order to achieve peace in a country it is necessary to have a plan for an effective, multi-layered structure, comprising political reconstruction of a legitimate and capable state, economic reconstruction, social reconstruction, including the build-up of a democratic society, and to provide general security.[88] All of the different components interact with one other and if any of them are missing, it is not possible to achieve a successful reconstruction of a state.

Elements of the international community have recognized and long worked on a "new vision of peace". Already in 1992, UNESCO adopted its Culture of Peace

---

[85] Mary Caprioli, "Primed for Violence: The Role of Gender Inequality in Predicting Internal Conflict" *International Studies Quarterly* 49(2) (2005): 164.

[86] Cockburn, "Gender Relations as Causal in Militarization and War," 146/148.

[87] Pankhurst, "The 'Sex War' and Other Wars," 161.

[88] Larry Diamond, "What went wrong in Iraq" *Foreign Affairs* 83(5) (2004): 37.

Action Programme, and called at the international peace conference in Yamoussoukro, Cote d'Ivoire in 1989 for

> *"a new vision of peace culture based on the universal values of respect for life, liberty, justice, solidarity, tolerance, human rights and equality between women and men"*[89]

In 2000 the UN initiated the *Year of a Culture of Peace*, which was widened to the *Decade for a Culture of Peace and Non-Violence for the Children of the World* (2001-2010)[90].[91]

The *Culture of Peace*, in comparison with related research, focuses specifically on the content and conditions of peace. As described by David Adams:

> *"A culture of peace consists of values, attitudes, behaviours and ways of life based on non-violence, respect for human rights, intercultural understanding, tolerance and solidarity, sharing and free flow of information and the full participation of women"*[92]

The *Culture of Peace*, has to start on all levels: political, legal, educational and social. It defines peace as *"the well-being of all"*, including social justice.[93]

As one of the key priorities of a *Culture of Peace*, peace researchers, like Werner Wintersteiner, see the necessity of social inclusion and of gender democracy.[94] The *Culture of Peace*, from its beginnings included the necessity of equality between the sexes and full participation of women in the community[95].

But while the need for a new outlook on peace has become more and more acceptable, especially in the academic sphere, practice still largely seems very different.

---

[89] first book by Father Felipe MacGregor in Viktorija Ratkovic and Werner Wintersteiner (Eds.), *Yearbook Peace Culture 2010, Culture of Peace, A Concept and A Campaign Revisited* (Klagenfurt: Drava Verlag 2010) 10/11.

[90] See resolution A/53/25 from November 10, 1998

[91] Ratkovic and Wintersteiner (Eds.), *Yearbook Peace Culture 2010*, 10.

[92] Ibid.pp.10/11

[93] Ibid.p.12

[94] Ibid.p.11

[95] see Manifesto 2000 for a Culture of Peace and Non-Violence, and The Declaration and Programme of Action on a Culture of Peace by the UN, Article 1 in Ratkovic and Wintersteiner (Eds.), *Yearbook Peace Culture 2010*, 18.

Peace is not a passive concept. It has to be worked for, by individuals as well as groups. It needs to grow from within and it is part of a collective commitment and a whole culture. Peace cannot be enforced by outsiders, but is made possible by creating opportunities for the population to enhance the process to peace.[96]

The basis for achieving all of this is to recognise equality between different states, cultures, ethical groups, religious groups, as well as the two sexes. The link between inequality and violence, including the link between gender inequality and violence, leads to the conclusion that inequality in society, including inequality between women and men is an obstacle to sustainable peace. As explained by UNESCO, "*equality between men and women is an essential condition of a culture of peace*".[97] It follows if real or "positive" peace wants to be achieved it is first necessary to overcome social relations of domination and submission,[98] because societies in which "*tolerance and respect for the rights of opponents*" are practiced, whether in the domestic or in the international sphere, they are less likely to resort to violence.[99]

Putting the knowledge acquired in this chapter together on the example of the Kurdistan Region, the region is currently dealing with a number of challenges, which are likely to hamper the achievement of sustainable peace. These have been well summarized by Nuria Tornas and Ana Villellas as part of their report in 2009. More immediate and outside risks, which might need to be fought against on a political and militaristic level in the short run, include the troubled relationship between Baghdad and Erbil and the issue of the disputed territories.[100] Furthermore there are a number of internal challenges, which are not likely to directly lead to armed conflict, and which are less visible because it especially affects people outside the political sphere and does not occur in public, but which have a substantial impact on human safety and structural violence and which are

---

[96] Flaubert Djateng, Christiane Kayser and Marie José Mavinga, *Our contribution to peace: a patchwork of complementary actions* (Berlin: Civil Peace Services, 2009) 7/8.

[97] Betty Reardon, *Education for a culture of peace in a gender perspective* (Paris: The Teacher's Library, UNESCO Publishing, 2001) 20.

[98] Caprioli, "Primed for Violence," 165.

[99] Ibid.p.163

[100] Nuria Tonias and Ana Villellas, *The Kurdistan Autonomous Region: Risks and Challenges for Peace* (Quaderns de Construccio de Pau, Escola de Cultura de Pau, July 2009) 7/8.

slowing down the peace process. These problems include an inadequacy in good governance and participation, human rights and women's rights. As derived from the results of this chapter, and as once more explained by Tornas and Villellas, these difficulties have to be tackled, in order to avoid conflict from forming beneath the surface.[101] The issue of women's rights in the region is thereby seen as especially challenging, since the relative stability of the region seems to stand in contrast with the high level of violence against women, and the level of legal advances and theoretical debates are contrary to the actual circumstances of the women in the region.[102]

The main political parties in the Kurdistan Region are very supportive of gender equality in public. The Patriotic Union of Kurdistan (PUK) considers itself as a "*political and pro- women's advancement party*" and, as part of its program seeks to "*promote the political, social, economic and cultural rights of women*".[103]

As noted by the current prime minister Nechirvan Barzani in November 2012, at the launch of a sixteen day campaign to combat domestic violence:

> "*At the Kurdistan Regional Government we are determined to protect women's rights and promote equality of opportunity.*"[104]

Such statements are still often criticized by opponents for being merely loose talk with no action. In order to answer the criticism, Barzani continued:

> "*This campaign is not a show for the media; it is rooted in the belief of the Kurdistan liberation movement and the Kurdistan Regional Government on women's rights.*"[105]

This thesis will analyse whether these statements are reflected in Kurdistan's politics today, and how the existence of gender inclusive strategies, or the lack thereof, influence the individual and social development of peace for the people in their local communities and in the region as a whole. Peace will be defined as "the

---

[101] Ibid.p.12

[102] Ibid.p.16

[103] Patriotic Union of Kurdistan, Leadership Council, "Program" http://www.pukpb.org/en/program (Accessed on 20.2.2013)

[104] RUDAW "Kurdistan Regional Government, PM Barzani kicks off campaign protecting women's rights, combating domestic violence" (2 December 2012) http://www.krg.org/a/d.aspx?s=010000&l=12&a=46004 (Accessed on 22.1.2013)

[105] Ibid.

well-being of all". But before analysing the specific strategies and their impacts in detail, the current situation within the Kurdistan's Region will be discussed, in order to enhance the understanding of the Kurdistan's Region current situation:

B.   Kurdistan's History – The Long Path to Autonomy

Understanding the past is vital for understanding the present and for imagining the future. Knowledge of past difficulties within a region, as well as its cultural foundations and the unique experiences of the people, is important for appreciating current events and hence for finding solutions to present problems and foreseeing potential complications.[106] For this reason the following subchapter will provide a short background on the history of the Kurdistan Region and its people.

Kurdistan, the "Land of the Kurds", stretches across the north of historical Mesopotamia.[107] The Kurds have a very vaguely estimated population of between twenty and forty million people, of whom about 5,6 million live in Iraq[108], which is about 15 to 20 per cent of the Iraqi population.[109] As a consequence, the Kurds are often described as the world's largest nation without a state.[110]

The Kurds see themselves as the native inhabitants of their land and as ethnically distinct from the Turks, Persians and Arabs.[111] Their language, customs, and traditions are distinct as well as their clan history, which comprises over 800 tribes in Kurdistan.[112]

Kurdish society is based on family and tribes,[113] with the Kurds having embraced a variety of religions, with the majority today being Sunni Muslims. However, they

---

[106]John Paul Lederach and Jenner Janice Moomaw (ed.), *A Handbook of International Peacebuilding, Into the Eye of the Storm* (San Francisco: Jossey-Bass A Wiley Imprint, 2002) 75.

[107] Michael Kelly, "The Kurdish Regional Constitution within the Framework of the Iraqi Federal Constitution: A Struggle for Sovereignty, Oil, Ethnic Identity and the Prospects for a Reverse Supremacy Clause" *Pennsylvania State Law Review* 114(3) (2010): 710.

[108] Anja Flach, *Frauen in der kurdischen Guerilla, Motivation, Identität und Geschlechterverhältnis in der Frauenarmee der PKK* (Köln: PapyRossa, 2007) 22.

[109] Hennerbichler, *Die Kurden*, 70.

[110] Wenona Giles and Jennifer Hyndman (ed.), *Sites of Violence, Gender and Conflict Zones* (London: University of California Press, 2004) 110.

[111] Kelly, "The Kurdish Regional Constitution," 710.

[112] Kerim, *The Kurds in Iraq*, 7.

[113] Incesu, *Die Stellung der Frauen in der kurdischen Gesellschaft*, 32.

also follow other Islamic believes, as well as the Yazidi belief, Christianity and Judaism.[114]

The ancient history of the Kurds and Kurdistan dates back several thousand years. Human skeletons were found from the time of the Neanderthals and the first village found in the regions was dated at 7000 B.C.[115].

The more recent history of Kurdistan was shaped by the incursion of different groups and empires which destroyed and reformed the region time and time again. From the 7th century until shortly before the collapse of the Arab Caliphate in 1258, Kurdistan was under Islamic occupation.[116] Shortly after being freed from the Arabs, Kurdistan was invaded by the Mongols during the 13th and the 14th centuries,[117] and from the 16th century to 1918 Kurdistan was forcibly divided between Iran and the Ottoman Empire.[118]

After the First World War and the fall of the Ottoman Empire, the British and the French split the Middle East in different mandates at the conference of San Remo in 1920. As a result, Turkey and Iraq were defined with their current borders, but there was no country for the Kurds. The western Kurdish part, previously occupied by the Ottoman Empire, was consequently divided between Syria, the transformed Ottoman Empire, Turkey, and the newly created state of Iraq.[119] What followed was a time of non-recognition of the Kurds as a people. While, the existence of the Kurds and their right to independence was still recognized in the Treaty of Sèvres[120] from 10 August 1920, the treaty never came into force. In the Treaty of Lausanne from 24 July 1923, the treaty of peace with Turkey, the Kurds were not mentioned. The next time the Kurds officially were internationally recognized was in the UN Security Council Resolution 688 from 5 April 1991.[121]

---

[114] Ibid.p.45

[115] Jaafar Hussein Khidir, *The Kurds and Kurdistan and Recent Political Development of IKR* (Wien: Dissertation, Universität Wien, 2002) 55.

[116] Ibid.p.61

[117] Ibid.p.63

[118] Giles and Hyndman (ed.), *Sites of Violence,* 110.

[119] Ibid.p.110

[120] See Articles 62, 63, 64

[121] Hennerbichler, *Die Kurden,* 424/425.

In the wake of these historic developments, today's Kurdistan is impossible to identify as one would identify a recognized state. There are no international boundaries to the territory, and even the internal ones are disputed. The region of the Kurds is divided between south-eastern Turkey, north-eastern Syria, northern Iraq and north-western Iran. The countries between which the Kurdish region is divided refuse to acknowledge the existence of a unified Kurdish geographical entity and, in the case of Turkey, reject the idea of a distinct Kurdish people and culture.[122] This division of the Kurdish land, created by the Allied powers, became the geographic fate of the land of the Kurds, which they have contested until today.

The consequence of their separation into different geographical entities, with different overlords, also led to the separation of the different Kurdish communities. While they had always ideologically held together against their common enemy, the overlord, they have arguably more and more drifted apart more and more in practice.[123] Even though all the Kurdish people are unified by the aim to achieve liberation, they are hardly united in any other way. They have different historical experiences, different cultural traditions, as well as religious differences and their dialects also vary greatly. The differences between the northern and southern Kurdish dialects, Kurmanji and Sorani, are so different, that they are often not mutually understood by native speakers[124].[125] Furthermore an important divisive factor in Kurdish society is the inherent tribal structure. Members of a certain tribe believe in a common descent and are often loyal to a traditional chieftain; rivalries exist between different tribes.[126] I followed there has not been a unified struggle for independence, but rather separate nationalist movements.[127]

Whether as unified or separate movements, the Kurds have, throughout their history, fought against the forced assimilation by the occupying powers. They

---

[122] Gareth Stansfield, *Iraqi Kurdistan. Political development and emergent democracy* (London: RoutledgeCurzan, 2003) 27.

[123] Hennerbichler, *Die Kurden,* 428.

[124] JN Postgate (ed.), *The Languages of Iraq, Ancient and Modern, The British School of Archaeology in Iraq* (Cambridge: Cambridge University Press, 2007) 139.

[125] Martin Van Bruinessen, *Kurdish Ethno-Nationalism Versus Nation-Building States, Collected Articles* (Istanbul: The Isis Press, 2000) 26/27.

[126] Ibid.p.27

[127] Kelly, "The Kurdish Regional Constitution," 721.

aimed at achieving self-determination through revolts and the struggled for the maintenance of their national culture and language.[128] Until now they have only been partly successful.[129] This fight for independence became the predominant feature of Kurdish history, which shaped all other issues in the regions.

Turning to historic developments directly relevant to the Kurdish community in Iraq, it can be observed that the wish of the Iraqi Kurds to have their own country, separate from Iraq, is as old as "Iraq" itself,[130] but was never achieved. While Britain supported the Kurds during the First World War, they later rejected the idea of an independent Kurdistan, in in view of their own strategic interests.[131] The period from 1918 to 1991, was marked by an unstable relationship between the Iraqi Kurds and 'the others', which was replete with promises made, but not kept, and a consequential flaring up of violence.

During the period of British administration in Iraq, the Kurds took up their fight for independence under Sheikh Mahmud Barzani (1881-1956), but without success.[132] The general inability to create a Kurdish country at any time in history, is principally due to two main reasons. On the one hand there was the internal separation of the Kurds as discussed above, and on the other, the political influence of the outside forces which opposed Kurdish interests.

The new state "Iraq" was founded intentionally with difficult power-relations inside the country. Sunnis, Shias, and Kurdish were forcibly incorporated into a geographic entity, arguably in order to facilitate control from outside.[133] The fight for independence following the First World War, saw a lack of political interest for an independent Kurdistan. However, the Kurdish determination led to active hostilities. The British bombing the Kurds and their use of chemical weapons against them in the 1920s is reminiscent of the later conflict with the Saddam regime.[134]

---

[128] Giles and Hyndman (ed.), *Sites of Violence,* 110.

[129] Jabar and Dawod (ed), *The Kurds, Nationalism and Politics,* 11.

[130] Walter Posch und Nathan Brown, *Kurdische Unabhängigkeitsbestrebungen und die irakische Verfassung* (Wien: Schriftreihe der Landesverteidigungsakademie, 03/2004) 9.

[131] Ibid.p.13

[132] Ofteringer und Marco, *Kurdistan* (Berlin: Edition ID-Archiv, 1995) 10.

[133] Gerard Chaliand (ed.), *People without a country* (London: Zed Press, 1980) 159.

[134] Ofteringer und Marco, *Kurdistan,* 10.

In 1921 the British created a kingdom in Iraq under King Faisal, which existed until after the British left the country in 1932.[135] Throughout his reign, the Kurds struggle for recognition continued. When Mosul officially became part of Iraq, the League of Nations tried, through the Treaty of Ankara in 1926, to ensure that the Kurds' identity was respected and that they would become an autonomous region within Iraq with their own justice system, administration and official language.[136] However these aims were not achieved. Further, Iraq's admission into the League of Nations in 1932, it was on the condition that the government should introduce Kurdish as an official language, next to Arabic, in the areas which were predominately Kurdish. This condition was also not fulfilled.[137]

As a consequence of these failures, Kurdish nationalism in Iraq further flared up during the 1930s and 1940s. After the Second World War the Kurds continued their fight for autonomy, this time under Mullah Mustafa Barzani (1903-1979).[138] The resulting consequences were closely connected to the different political developments in Iraq at a national level.

On 14 July 1958 a group of revolutionary officers ended the monarchy and Iraq became a republic under general Abdel Karim Qasim.[139] It was under him that "national rights" for the Kurds were recognized[140] the first time,[141] as stipulated in Article III of the Iraqi Constitution of 1958, which stated that Arabs and Kurds enjoy equal rights.[142] Through this action, the Kurdish population in Iraq received a level of recognition far ahead of the Kurdish people in the neighbouring countries.[143] Nevertheless they did not achieve what they aimed for. While the Kurds were assured by Abdel Karim Qasim that they would receive more autonomy, the promise was not kept.

---

[135] Norbert Stanek, *Irak, Land zwischen Tradition und Fortschritt* (Wien: Druckkunst Wien, 1980) 25/27.
[136] Postgate (ed.), *The Languages of Iraq,* 141.
[137] Ibid.p.142
[138] Hennerbichler, *Die Kurden,* 520.
[139] Ibid.p.28
[140] See: Iraqi Constitution (art 3) of 27 July 1958.
[141] Chaliand (ed.), *People without a country,* 165.
[142] Posch und Brown, *Kurdische Unabhängigkeitsbestrebungen,* 15-25.
[143] Visser Reidar, "The Kurdish Issue in Iraq: A View from Baghdad at the Close of the Maliki Premiership" *The Fletcher Forum of World Affairs* 34(1) (2010): 78.

When the Ba'ath regime took over power in the 1960s the Kurds hoped that the new government would prove sympathetic to their autonomy but the reverse was true.[144] In 1961 war between the Kurdish region and Iraq flared up once again.[145] The rest of Iraq cracked down on the Kurdish North, which led to armed resistance in Kurdistan and to an armed conflict that lasted for thirty years, until the US-led Gulf War of 1991.[146] During that time several attempts were made to resolve the difficult relationship between the Arabs and the Kurds, but remained unsuccessful, such as the negotiations in Baghdad led by Jalal Talabani in 1963.[147] In 1966 the Bazzaz-Declaration promised a decentralisation of Kurdistan within Iraq, but as with earlier promises, this was only kept on paper.[148]

Under the Iraqi president Al-Bakr in 1970 the Kurds once again hoped for change and for some time it seemed that they would finally achieve their goal of autonomy. However in the mid-1970s, the US, Iraq and Iran, which had previously supported the Iraqi Kurds, changed their position, and allied against the Kurds, as reflected in the Algiers Accord from 1975.[149]

As a consequence, from 1976 onwards new battles between the Iraqi army and the Kurdish partisans, the Peshmergas, flared up, as well as struggles for power between different Kurdish groups.[150] As a consequence, since the 1970s, a considerable proportion of Kurds left the region and went into diaspora. Others were forced by the Iraqi government to leave districts like Kirkuk and Khanaqin, which are very rich in oil, and were replaced by Arab peasants.[151] It was the aim of the Ba'ath regime to crush the Kurds and they initiated an "arabization" process that continued until the end of the regime in 2003.

---

[144] Internationaler Verein für Menschenrechte in Kurdistan (Hrsg.), *Das Kurdische Volk – keine Zukunft ohne Menschenrechte* (Landesvertretung Niedersachsen: Dokumetation der internationalen Konferenz Bonn, 27. – 28. September 1991) 44.

[145] Hennerbichler, *Die Kurden,* 532.

[146] Khidir, *The Kurds and Kurdistan,* 116.

[147] Hennerbichler, *Die Kurden,* 539.

[148] Posch und Brown, *Kurdische Unabhängigkeitsbestrebungen,* 15-25.

[149] Mehmet Salim, und Ralf Kaufeldt, *Daten und Fakten zu Kurden und Kurdistan, Eine Chronologie* (Köln: Pro Humanitate, 2002) 96.

[150] Chaliand (ed.), *People without a country,* 203.

[151] Van Bruinessen, *Kurdish Ethno-Nationalism Versus Nation-Building States,* 25.

But this was not the first attempt to eradicate the Kurdish culture from outside. Since the fall of the Ottoman Empire, the Kurdish North has been greatly influenced by the Arab region of Iraq, and the Kurdish are said to have suffered from cultural genocide under the Baathist regime. Their language, identity and culture were banned. Children were not allowed to speak Kurdish in school, people were killed for speaking up and talking about the Kurdish situation in public.[152] Additionally, the arabization was promoted through the resettlement of Arabs on Kurdish land, as well as, for example, offering Iraqi Arab men money if they married Kurdish women.[153] Even after the creation of the "safe haven", the Iraqi government tried to further "arabize" for example by selling land in Kirkuk either cheaper or exclusively to Arabs.[154]

At the same time, throughout the rule of the Baathist regime, the Kurds suffered from campaigns of mass arrests, displacements and killings. From the early 1970s, Faili Kurds living in Baghdad and other cities in Southern Iraq were arrested. Additionally family members of Kurdish fighters, as well as people who had power in Kurdish society were arrested, sent to concentration camps or disappeared for ever.[155] In the later years of the Baathist rule, the Iraqi army went against the Kurdish rural areas, destroying villages, deporting the inhabitants and transferring thousands to concentration camps throughout the country.[156] As a consequence, Kurdish refugees settled all over the world, with the first wave departing in the 70s as noted above, and a substantial number leaving their home after the uprising of 1991.[157]

During the time of struggles the different countries with Kurdish communities supported the uprisings among each other's Kurds, whenever it suited their political plan. Iran supported the Kurdish movement in Iraq led by Mulla Mustafa Barzani

---

[152] Sonja Wölte, *Human Rights Violations against Women during War and Conflict* (Geneva: Women's International League for Peace and Freedom, Report of a Roundtable Discussion parallel to the UN Commission on Human Rights, 1997) 19.

[153] Al-Ali, *Iraqi Women,* 163.

[154] Internationaler Verein für Menschenrechte in Kurdistan (Hrsg.), *Das Kurdische Volk – keine Zukunft ohne Menschenrechte,* 44.

[155] Mustafa Al-Karadaghi (Publ.) *Kurdistan times, A Quarterly Political, Freedom and Democracy for Kurdish Nation* (No.1, Winter 1990) 194.

[156] Ibid.p.196

[157] Al-Ali, *Iraqi Women,* 39.

financially as well as militarily from 1963 to 1975. But once the Iraqi regime made concessions to Iran, Iran stopped supporting the Kurdish movement and obliged Barzani to give up. Similarly, during the Iran-Iraq war, Iraq supported the Kurdish movement in Iran, while Iran allied itself with the Iraqi KDP (Kurdistan Democratic Party).[158]

From 1979, the Kurds experienced the darkest time in their recent history. Under Saddam Hussein the Kurds, together with the rest of the Iraq's people were part of the eight year war against Iran[159], the invasion of Kuwait[160], the constant struggle between different ethnic groups,[161] as well UN sanctions imposed on the country.[162] Under Saddam, the Kurds were deported, had to flee and were massacred.[163] Apart from the normal consequences of war, the Kurds suffered from attacks with chemical weapons, one of the most destructive being the attack against Halabja in March 1988, where a whole village was destroyed.[164] But Halabja was only one part of the bigger "Anfal" campaign, during which Saddam bombarded several Kurdish regions with chemical weapons.[165] The Anfal campaign[166] consisted of eight military offensives by the Ba'athist military machinery over six months, in spring and summer 1988. During the Anfal campaign chemical weapons were systematically used against Kurdish military as well as civilian targets. About 3000 villages were destroyed, approximately 1.5 million people were displaced and there were mass executions of civilians. It is estimated that around 180.000 people died as a result of this campaign.[167]

---

[158] Van Bruinessen, *Kurdish Ethno-Nationalism Versus Nation-Building States*, 29.
[159] 1980-1988
[160] 1990
[161] Especially the Arabs against the Kurds
[162] BBC online, "Iraq timeline" (21 May 2011) http://news.bbc.co.uk/2/hi/middle_east/737483.stm (Accessed on 10.10.2011)
[163] Hennerbichler, *Die Kurden*, 600.
[164] Internationaler Verein für Menschenrechte in Kurdistan (Hrsg.), *Das Kurdische Volk – keine Zukunft ohne Menschenrechte*, 148.
[165] Hennerbichler, *Die Kurden*, 611.
[166] Robert Olson, *The Goat and The Butcher: Nationalism and State Formation in Kurdistan-Iraq since the Iraqi War* (Qosta Mesa: Mazda Publishers, 2005) 233.
[167] Kerim, *The Kurds in Iraq*, 25.

As a consequence of the weaker position of Saddam after the First Gulf War the Kurds tried to rise against the regime in 1991.[168] But as the revolution was not backed by the US or the international community, it was easily crushed and more than 100.000 people were taken into detention, many never to be seen again. A total of 20,000 people were reported killed as a result of the crackdown [169] and about 5000 villages were destroyed. As a consequence a huge exodus began. Until 1990 about 370.000 Kurds fled into Iran, over half a million Kurds took refuge in Turkey and 10.000 came to Western countries.[170] Additionally it is believed that in 1990 as many as 1.5 million Kurds were displaced inside Iraq and they were confined in prisons or refugee concentration camps throughout the country.[171] It was only through these operations, which caused the near destruction of the Kurdish culture, that their autonomy within Iraq was finally made possible in 1991.[172]

Following the first Gulf War and UN Resolution 688 from 5 April 1991[173], it was the US and Britain's declaration of a "safe haven" for the Kurds in northern Iraq, which allowed for a "territorialisation" of Kurdish nationalism. With the protection of the US and Britain the Kurds were able to create a Kurdish Regional Government (KRG) and to proceed with elections.[174]

The main Kurdish areas in the North of Iraq, Dohuk, Erbil and Sulaimaniya, were parted from the Central Government in Baghad (ICG) after the ICG was forced to withdraw from the area in 1991, and left control to the Kurds themselves.[175]

It was thus after 1991 that the Kurds could start practicing their culture again. Kurdish books were reprinted, new centres of education were established[176] and the Kurds started an autonomous political system. As a result of the elections in

---

[168] Ibid.p.34

[169] Ibid.p.36

[170] Tilman Zülch, *Völkermord an den Kurden, Eine Dokumentation der Gesellschaft für bedrohte Völker* (München: Luchterhand Literaturverlag 1991) 61.

[171] Al-Karadaghi (Publ.) *Kurdistan times,* 198.

[172] Posch und Brown, *Kurdische Unabhängigkeitsbestrebungen,* 27.

[173] Ibid.p.28

[174] Olson, *The Goat and The Butcher,* 234.

[175] Khidir, *The Kurds and Kurdistan,* 103.

[176] Postgate (ed.), *The Languages of Iraq,* 143.

May 1992, the Parliament, representing the legislative power of the Kurdistan Region of Iraq, was established in Erbil.[177]

But the early days of the newly established autonomous region of Kurdistan was not easy. The election results were contested and led to internal conflict between the different Kurdish factions, for about six years after the first elections.[178] From 1994 to 1998 renewed fighting between the two factions broke out, which left thousands of people dead on both sides. The fighting was such that Barzani and his KDP asked for the assistance of Saddam Hussein to fight the PUK, which had allied with Iran. As a consequence Saddam's troops entered the North of the country again and the fighting continued. In 1997 Turkey entered the war. It was only in September 1998 that Talabani and Barzani agreed to and signed a US-mediated power-sharing treaty, the Washington Agreement, in which they agreed to share power and revenue but not to allow Iraqi troops or the PKK (Kurdistan Workers' Party) into the region again.

It was during the civil war in the 1990s that KDP and PUK became the main powers in the region. Previously there had been several other entities such as the Socialist and the Communist parties, as well as various tribes, which all acted in their own interests fighting for or against the Iraqi regime, as well as against one another. During the 90s, the KDP and PUK gained basically total control by defeating other party or tribal leaders or by forcing them into alliances.[179]

This is a period of history many Kurds today avoid discussing. The population suffered under the civil war and many were discontent with the parties' fighting.[180] As a result, the civil population took part in limited and temporary social protests, which were according to Faleh Jabar and Hosham Dawod widely supported by the public, but to which the parties were indifferent. In 1994 and 1995 numerous peace

---

[177] Khidir, *The Kurds and Kurdistan*, 170.
[178] Olson, *The Goat and The Butcher*, 234.
[179] Jabar and Dawod (ed), *The Kurds, Nationalism and Politics*, 171/265.
[180] Interview CG, Vienna on 11/11/2012

demonstrations and strikes were conducted, but to no avail and fighting continued.[181]

In addition the civil population suffered under the imposition of the international sanctions on Iraq by the UN after the Gulf War. Saddam Hussein's food rationing system led to increased hardship for the local population, despite the new "freedom".[182]

As a consequence of the decades of war, the suppression by the regime, as well as the direct and indirect effects of the UN sanctions[183] the people suffered from a destroyed infrastructure. From technical facilities, to hospitals and educational institutions, everything was demolished.[184] Throughout the 1990s the value of the Iraqi currency fell and many people had to live from aid alone. There was insufficient food and people lived in poverty[185] within an administrative vacuum. Everything from security, to health care, education, governance, employment and human rights had to be restored.[186] Moreover, the Kurds still lived under the constant fear of Saddam returning to the region.

It was at this time that the Kurds had to redefine themselves, while suffering from a humanitarian crisis and while constituting part of a country, whose regime tried to exterminate them. Robert Olson argued that this time was a period for the two Kurdish groups learned to understand one another and to tolerate the other's demands.[187] This became a reality around the turn of the new millennium,[188] and was manifested in 2003, with the fall of Saddam Hussein.

Today Kurdistan has a pluralistic political system with over one hundred civil society institutions, many of which are women's organisations. There is free

---

[181] Jabar and Dawod (ed), *The Kurds, Nationalism and Politics,* 169.

[182] Denise Natali, "The Spoils of Peace in Iraqi Kurdistan" *Third World Quarterly* 28(6) (2007): 1112.

[183] SR 661, SR 687 and SR 1284

[184] Shereen Ismael, "The lost generation of Iraq: children caught in the crossfire" *International Journal of Contemporary Iraqi Studies* 2(2) (2008): 152.

[185] Ibid.p.87

[186] Ibid.p.102

[187] Olson, *The Goat and The Butcher,* 234.

[188] Hennerbichler, *Die Kurden,* 652.

education for all children.[189] The Kurdish region is reasonably stable and most secure in the whole of Iraq.

In recent years, the Kurds in Iraq have gained importance and international and internal attention, which would have been unthinkable of in previous decades. Kurdish is an official state language in Iraq, schools are taught in Kurdish and Kurds have the right to broadcast.[190] Universities have been established in the Kurdistan Region and books are published in Kurdish. Additionally there exists a variety of Kurdish newspapers and magazines and the government is planning to develop a Kurdish cinema.[191] Democracy is progressing in Kurdistan, with opposition movements slowly emerging which challenge the monopoly of the two political parties. The 'Goran' movement and the Kurdish Islamic Union (KIU) are the most important.[192] The Kurds are able to govern themselves through an electoral process which, while far from perfect, is moving in the right direction towards achieving the people's wishes. The President of Iraq, Jalal Talabani, is not only Kurdish but also the leader of the PUK, one of the two most important parties of the Kurds in Iraq. Consequently at present the times of Kurdish isolation as an unheard minority are gone, at least for the Kurds in Iraq.[193]

After 2003, and at the time of the drafting of the interim constitution of Iraq, known as the Transitional Administrative Law (TAL), the Kurds managed to present themselves as a united front, in comparison to the divided Sunni and Shia Arab factions. With the support of the Western constitutional law experts, the Kurdistan Region was established as an autonomous region with considerable rights under the Iraqi constitution.[194] Kurdistan today is recognized as a distinct federal region within Iraq[195] and it has the right to exercise executive, legislative and judicial powers in accordance with its own Draft Constitution. While this is not allowed to

---

[189] Woodrow Wilson International Center for Scholars, „Winning the Peace: Forum Explores Role of Women in Post-Conflict Iraq" http://www.wilsoncenter.org/index.cfm?fuseaction=news.print&news (Accessed on 10.1.2011)

[190] Postgate (ed.), *The Languages of Iraq*, 141.

[191] Ibid.p.155

[192] Al-Ali and Pratt, "Between Nationalism and Women's Rights," 344.

[193] Jabar and Dawod (ed), *The Kurds, Nationalism and Politics*, 258.

[194] Kelly, "The Kurdish Regional Constitution," 726.

[195] Constitution of Iraq 2005, Article 117

contradict the Iraqi Constitution, and except for *"those authorities stipulated in the exclusive authorities of the federal government"*,[196] the Kurdish parliament and its authorities have a great leeway in dealing with their own citizen except for the matters dealt with by the federal government, which include international dealings, national security policy, the formulation of fiscal and customs policy, the distribution of water and the use of oil and gas.[197] Additional the Kurds are able to exercise some influence over the whole of Iraq through their politicians in Baghdad.[198]

Dramatic progress can be seen in the Kurdistan Region, even though the region is still not economically self-sustainable, social problems exist and party support is still very important to ensure individual success.[199] In comparison to the rest of Iraq, Kurdistan today is not anymore suffering from violent deaths on an almost daily basis[200], and the region has used the time for reconstruction.

The current leading politicians have great aspirations for the future. In his inaugural speech on 5 April 2012, Prime Minister Barzani, stated that he will work to continue the political, economic and social development in the region, by devolving more powers to the provincial and district councils, as well as by respecting the opposition, tackling corruption, reducing party influence in governance, enhancing the rule of law, improving economic and social services, increasing transparency and reviving the agricultural sector. Further, he will work towards respecting all people within his jurisdiction by strengthening democracy and human rights, especially for women and children, *"by protecting them from domestic violence and empowering women through allowing them to assume better and more effective roles in the KRG."*[201]

Despite all the positive developments over the previous decade and the even more ambitious plans for the future, problems in the region, as well as between Erbil and Baghdad still persist, and cannot be forgotten. The Kurds claim that 40 per cent of

---

[196] Ibid. Article 121

[197] Ibid. Articles 109-115

[198] Natali, "The Spoils of Peace in Iraqi Kurdistan," 1123.

[199] Ibid.p.1125

[200] Iraqi Body Count, "Iraqi Deaths from Violence in 2010" (30 December 2010) http://www.iraqbodycount.org/analysis/numbers/2010/ (Accessed on 10.10.2011)

[201] Prime Minister Barzani, *Inaugral speech by KRG Prime Minister Nechirvan Barzani at the swearing in of the seventh KRG cabinet* (Erbil: inaugural speech, Kurdistan Parliament, 5 April 2012)

the whole Kurdish region of Iraq is still under Iraqi leadership, namely Kirkuk, Makhmour, Khanaqin, Mandeli, Sheykhan and Sinjar.[202] Furthermore discussions of the allocation of oil and gas resources between Baghdad and Erbil are still on the daily agenda. Additionally, elements of the population have been disillusioned in recent times. Many households still do not have electricity or running water 24 hours per day and have the feeling that only people linked to the political parties are able to get jobs and money. They feel that there is no rule of law, that the political leaders today are just as corrupt as in the past and that the system has not much changed. Opposition parties basically still do not exist and it is therefore questionable whether it is really possible to have any independent voices.

From first hand field research it could be observed that when the people are asked today if they are satisfied with the reconstruction process in their region, about half are very satisfied, while the others still have various criticisms. While everybody recognizes that a lot has happened in the region throughout the last years, many believe that too much is done on the outside, such as the construction of streets, malls, new houses, but that the transformation is not going "deep enough".[203]

Nevertheless there are certain aspects in the transformation process which people where especially happy about: Several expressed pride that Kurdistan is now seen as a "developed region" region from outside and that they do not have to feel "backwards" anymore[204]. Especially several people of wealthier backgrounds were of the opinion that the poorer people benefitted from the transformation process and that the divide between rich and poor is getting smaller[205], although this was disputed by the other side.[206] Other positive aspects included the achievement of reasonable stability.[207] Many were of the opinion that they "have reached their goal" in both being and feeling free[208]. Only very few people recognized as a

---

[202] Khidir, *The Kurds and Kurdistan*, 103.

[203] Interview BT, Erbil on 24/07/2012; Interviews BY and BZ, Sulaimaniya on 10/08/2012

[204] Interview BI, Erbil on 08/07/2012

[205] Interview AR, Sulaimaniya on 21/05/2012; Interview BD, Erbil on 25/06/2012; Interview BG, Erbil on 02/07/2012

[206] Interview BX, Sulaimaniya on 09/08/2012

[207] Interview AT, Sulaimaniya on 24/05/2012

[208] Interview BU, Erbil on 24/07/2012; Interview AI, Erbil on 16/04/2012

positive achievement that women were part of the development[209] and that legal developments had occurred[210].

While a number of people expressed the belief that transformation so far failed, they also feel that the politicians do not care enough about the region and its people[211], and that not everybody is benefitting from the improvements.[212] They feel that corruption is still rife, there is a lack of public services,[213] and that the "old ways" are still persisting.[214] Despite all of this, the most commonly held opinion was that people are happy with the transformation process, in comparison with what existed before. As explained by a clerk:

> *"If one compares it with the past, I am very happy. But there is still a lot to be criticized and there is a lot than can be made better, but Kurdistan is on the path of hope."*[215]

Especially when it comes to the poorer people, many had the feeling that more needs to be done.[216]

While the population appreciates that elections have taken place, that the infrastructure has improved and that they have enhanced opportunities for travelling and leisure time[217], many complained that they had the feeling that the changes are merely taking place on the surface.[218] People from the opposition had the feeling that there is no true democracy and that the opposition still has no chance.[219] The more open people explained that they felt that the mentality is still the same and that this should finally change.[220] However, many said that the situation had already improved.[221]

---

[209] Interview AL, Erbil on 25/04/2012
[210] Interview AE, Erbil on 09/04/2012
[211] Interview AU, Sulaimaniya on 28/05/2012
[212] Interview BN, Erbil on 17/07/2012
[213] Interview BT, Erbil on 24/07/2012
[214] Interview BP, Erbil on 21/07/2012
[215] Interview AH, Erbil on 15/04/2012
[216] Interview AW, Sulaimaniya on 01/06/2012
[217] Interview CJ, Vienna on 28/10/2012
[218] Interview BZ, Sulaimaniya on 10/08/2012
[219] Interview BQ, Erbil on 21/07/2012
[220] Interview BZ, Sulaimaniya on 10/08/2012
[221] Interview AF, Erbil on 09/04/2012; Interview AK, Erbil on 20/04/2012

Even the politicians suggested unofficially that they would like to see more happening:

> *"As representative of my country I am satisfied, but as a private person I would wish for more and that the reconstruction was quicker. For example not even the hospitals are reconstructed in the correct way (there are not enough good doctors). The biggest problem is corruption. There should be more control systems when it comes to corruption. But the control systems are very slowly getting better. For example there were already a few restaurants closed by the health authority because of a lack of hygiene, which would have never been possible to even think of a few years ago, because everybody was just bribed."[222]*

Ten years after finally laying down arms, the transformation process can be described as on-going. The current "peace" in the region is frail, and further development will be needed to ensure the quality and longevity of peace.

Coming from the general background to the more specific one of gender relations, the following sub-chapter is going to outline the influence of the different armed conflicts on the role of women in society as well as gender relations:

C.   Women During the Time of Conflict

When discussing the role of gender in conflict transformation, as with commenting on the region as a whole, it is of great importance to understand the past, in order to evaluate the present and assess the future. It is first necessary to know about women's positions during times of conflict, in order to understand what influences their current position and to derive realistic suggestions for the near future. This will be done by analyzing women's roles within conflict, to then lead to a discussion on women's standing within Kurdistan's society throughout time in the subsequent sub-chapter.

Women occupy different roles during and in the aftermath of armed conflict. They are victims and actors at the same time, fighting against war, promoting it, and suffering from it. The different actions against women and perpetrated by them during the time of conflict are influenced by society, just as they will, in return, influence society at the time of conflict transformation. It will be the aim of the

---

[222] Interview CI, Vienna on 26/10/2012

following chapter to outline and discuss the specific horrors women had to go through in the Kurdistan Region during the time of armed conflict, as well as the different actions they took and how these experiences continue to influence conflict transformation today.

1.   Women as Victims during Armed Conflict and Beyond

Both, men and women, suffer during conflict in numerous and far-reaching ways. However the nature of their suffering varies greatly and research shows that in comparison to men, women are disproportionally victimized.[223] The type of victimization has changed with the nature of the war. Major General Patrick Cammaert even suggests that *"it is now more dangerous to be a woman than a soldier in modern wars."*[224]

This is not to say that men and women are not both suffering equally strong from the effects of war, but, as stated by the Red Cross, rather than to prioritise one gender over the other when it comes to helping victims, it is vital to recognize the specific vulnerabilities of each group.[225] Men, women, children and the elderly suffer during and after armed conflict in different ways. While in Iraq for example the percentage of people suffering a violent death was much higher for men (approximately 90%) than for women (approximately 10%).[226] However there are certain crimes which are generally specific for women, such as rape, trafficking and sexual slavery, which impact on their physiology, psychology and general social well-being.[227]

As every conflict is unique, so also is the specific type of suffering unleashed on the civilian population.

---

[223] UN ESCAP, *Women and Armed Conflict*, 9.

[224] Major General Patrick Cammaert, former Deputy Force Commander, MONUC, Parliamentary Hearing at the United Nations, New York, 20-21 November 2008, Background document: Session II, "Sexual violence against women and children in armed conflict", http://www.ipu.org/splz-e/unga08/s2.pdf (Accessed on 13.9.2011)

[225] The International Committee of the Red Cross in Iraq, *Women in War* (March 2009) 1.

[226] Iraq: The Human Cost, "Widows in Iraq indicate scale of killing during U.S. war" http://mit.edu/humancostiraq/ (Accessed on 21.2.2012)

[227] UN ESCAP, *Women and Armed Conflict*, 9.

A 40 year old Kurdish woman, who is today very much engaged with women's rights activism and the PUK, described her own experiences and the suffering of her mother and grandmothers, as follows:

> *"In Kurdistan women always had to suffer more than men. Like men, the women suffered under the war, but additionally they suffered under the suppression by men. During the Anfal campaign for example many women were raped by the Ba'ath regime and then they were expelled by their own families, because they were raped. Women always supported men during the war. It was the most horrible for them to sacrifice their own children, but they did it. The women never stopped the men in fighting for law, freedom and the home land. And for this they are respected today."[228]*

It will be the aim of this section to elaborate and discuss the different ways in which women have been victimized and have been forced to suffer during armed conflicts in general and during the recent conflicts in the Kurdistan Region in particular. This should lead to a better understanding of their situation and their needs after the cessation of violent conflict.

Violence against women is a daily occurrence during armed conflicts. According to UNIFEM (the United Nations Development Fund for Women; now UN Women) half a million women were raped during the genocide in Rwanda in 1994. In Sierra Leone the number of war-related acts of sexual violence was as high as 60,000 among internally displaced women from 1991 to 2001.[229] According to the UN an average of forty women daily were raped in South Kivu, in the Democratic Republic of Congo, during the time of conflict and between 20,000 and 50,000 women were raped during the Bosnian war in the early 1990s.[230] Even though numbers in Iraq are difficult to extract, activists claim that thousands of Iraq women have been raped since the American invasion in 2003[231] and it is known today through victims'

---

[228] Interview CJ, Vienna on 28/10/2012

[229] UNIFEM, Facts & Figures on VAW, "Crimes against Women in Situations of Armed Conflict" http://www.unifem.org/gender_issues/violence_against_women/facts_figures.php?page=7 (Accessed on 12.09.2011)

[230] Parliamentary Hearing at the United Nations, New York, 20-21 November 2008, Background document: Session II, "Sexual violence against women and children in armed conflict", http://www.ipu.org/splz-e/unga08/s2.pdf (Accessed on 13.9.2011)

[231] Anna Badkhen, "Iraq: The Hidden Crime of Rape" (2009) http://www.pbs.org/frontlineworld/stories/pakistan802/video/video_index_baghdad.html (Accessed on 21.2.2012)

accounts that rape was used as part of the war machinery by Saddam Hussein[232], although numbers are still unclear.[233]

Acts of sexual violence are thereby being used strategically to deliberately destroy the lives of the enemy and to give them the feeling that they are unable to protect their families. Rape destroys the "self", and by destroying the sense of the self in an individual, in the long run, the perpetrator not only destroys the individual, but also the whole community, the "enemy" group, to which the individual belongs.[234]

A specific example against the Kurdish population was at the so called "Anfal campaign", carried out by Saddam's regime officially from February 23 to September 1988, with the aim of "eliminating" the Kurdish problem. During different stages of assault the Iraqi troops used chemical weapons against approximately 40 Kurdish villages, the largest being Halabja on March 16, 1988, which killed thousands of people and left many permanently blind. Many still suffer cancer, other illnesses and disfigurements as a result of the chemical weapons. In some villages, especially those which tried to defend themselves, the whole population was shot. However in most villages only the men were shot and the women, children and elderly were taken to relocation camps. An estimated 182,000 Kurds died as an effect of the campaigns.[235]

The women, children and elderly were pushed through different transitional camps, many ending in the prisons of Dibs and Nugra Salman in Southern Iraq, before being put in camp-like settlements, where they remained under military control until 1991.[236] Women who spoke out later on their experiences in camps told about soldiers raping and killing women in the prisons.[237]

---

[232] See e.g. *Al Anfal* Case no 1/C Second/2006, 183-188

[233] The reported incidences of violence against women in armed conflicts vary depending on how the person releasing these numbers distinguishes general violence from violence arising out of the conflict.

[234] Robin Chandler, Lihua Wang and Linda Fuller (ed.), *Women, War and Violence, Personal Perspectives and Global Activism* (Basingstoke: Palgrave Macmillan, 2010) 21.

[235] Jennifer Rosenberg, 20th Century History Guide, "Top 5 Crimes of Saddam Hussein" http://history1900s.about.com/od/saddamhussein/a/husseincrimes.htm (Accessed on 25.2.2012)

[236] Mlodoch, "'We Want to be Remembered as Strong Women, Not as Shepherds'," 65.

[237] Prese Agence France, "Kurdish women tell of rapes in Saddam's death camps" (10 October 2006) http://www.kurdishglobe.net/display-article.html?id=B974F5B0DD6838F6A2EA19DB49F25E11 (Accessed on 23.2.2012)

These events were later acknowledged by the Iraqi High Tribunal, as part of the *Al-Anfal* Case, where the crime of rape and other sexual violence was used as proof for *"causing serious bodily or mental harm to members of the group"*,[238] for *"deliberately inflicting on the group living conditions calculated to bring about its physical destruction in whole or in part"*[239] as genocide, for *"deportation or forcible transfer of population"*[240] and for *"torture"*[241].

As part of the investigation for the trial, victims and witnesses of sexual violence in detention facilities spoke out, as follows:

> *"In (Tupzawa) men were separated from women, and there they took my son, father, and mother; they still remain with an unknown fate. I stayed with my grandfather and grandmother who died in the detention facility. We were badly treated in the detention facility. And once while we were standing in line waiting for food an officer named (Ja'far Al-Halawi) tore the clothes of a pretty girl and asked for the presence of her parents and raped her in front of her parents and the people, and killed her after that, by shouting her in the head and then we were taken to (Nuqrat Al-Salman) detention facility. We were treated very badly; they separated men away from women and young women away from elder ones. In (Nuqrat Al-Salman) detention facility I was in a hall with six other girls, [NAME REDACTED] from (Kirkuk), ([NAME REDACTED]) from (Hawraman), ([NAME REDACTED]) from (Kuysinjaq) and there were guards and officers who used to enter the room and assaulted all girls in the room and their names are (Hajjaj), (Shawqi) and (Sakhr) who were (Hajjaj) guards. (Hajjaj) used to rape the girls in front of the other girls. He raped me and raped (Sazan). We shouted and resisted, and once I put my nails in his face, he hit me in the face and until now the marks of the wounds are still on my face and then we were moved to (Tupzawa) camp. I am presenting a complaint against Saddam Hussein, suspects and the officers who raped us."*[242]

This was also confirmed by other women, who added for example that *"in Dibis detention facility, they used to take the girls in order to rape them and return them after midnight [...]"*[243].

---

[238] See e.g. *Al Anfal* Case no 1/C Second/2006 p.503 (Ali Hasan Al-Mahid), p.851 (Sabir Abd-al Aziz Husayn)

[239] Ibid.p.509 (Ali Hasan Al-Mahid), p.647/8 (Sultan Hashim Ahmed)

[240] Ibid.p.542 (Ali Hasan Al-Mahid), p.684/704 (Sultan Hashim Ahmed)

[241] Ibid.p.553/8 (Ali Hasan Al-Mahid)

[242] Ibid.pp.183/184

[243] Ibid.p.187

And a housewife from Kalar County reported that

> "there was an officer named (Hajjaj) [in (Nuqrat Al-Salman)
> detention facility] used to rape women and I used to see him taking
> a girl named [NAME REDACTED] to his room raping her
> constantly"[244].

But women were not the only suffering through killings and rape. Women in Kurdistan, just as in other conflict zones became victims of sexual slavery, trafficking, forced marriage or forced domestic labour.[245] The numbers increased following the loss of the stability of the community, such as occurs amongst communities of refugees or internally displaced people (IDPs).

When armed conflict reaches the villages and cities it results in the migration of individuals, families or even whole communities.[246] The number of displaced people and refugees is generally being considerably higher for women than for men. In Iraq, according to the *Iraqi Red Crescent,* 70 per cent of all refugees are women and children under 12 years of age.[247] This process of migration often leads to more physical danger and sexual violence for women.[248] The status of a refugee or internally displaced person makes women and children even more vulnerable. They lose any power they might have had and are unable to represent themselves. They are seen as superfluous and are not accepted as a full member of society in their new environment. They become "secondary-citizens" which results in even less stability and consequently the possibility of further exposure to physical violence.[249] Women as refugees often need to feed their children by themselves without being able to get a job. As a consequence many of them are forced into illegal work, including prostitution, in order to feed the family.[250]

Throughout the decades of fighting, hundreds of thousands of Kurds became refugees, and many more became internally displaced people. As part of their

---

[244] Ibid.p.188

[245] Helena Carreiras and Gerhard Kümmel (eds), *Women in the Military and in Armed Conflict,* (Wiesbaden: VS Verlag für Sozialwissenschaften, 2008) 229.

[246] Navniate Chadha Behera (ed), *Gender, Conflict and Migration* (London: SAGE Publications, 2006) 25.

[247] Al-Zubaidi, *Der Streit um Frauenrechte und das Personenstandsrecht,* 3.

[248] UN ESCAP, *Women and Armed Conflict,* 11.

[249] Behera (ed), *Gender, Conflict and Migration,* 206.

[250] Enloe, "Cynthia Enloe speaks on Women in Iraq"

experience as refugees many Kurdish women had to live in the mountains for years or endure the hardship of refugee camps.

The consequences of the displacement of millions of people throughout Iraq can still be seen today. In 2011 the estimated number of internally displaced persons, or IDPs, in Iraq was 1.3 million.[251] In the district of Sulaimaniya alone in 2010 there were still an estimated 7000 internally displaced families, or over 40.000 individuals, living in the area, and Sulaimaniya is one of the few places in Iraq which still has IDP tent camps.[252]

In the displaced communities, as in society as a whole, it is generally the role of women to be the primary caretakers of their families and the home.[253] During war women tend to assume a much greater burden than men in the care of children, the elderly and the survivors as well as ensuring the provision of food, and maintaining the general social life.[254] In situations of armed conflict women are often forced to fight for their own and their family's survival, because the men are either away fighting or they are injured or killed. This was also the case in the Kurdistan Region.

The destruction of infrastructure as well as the destruction of healthcare facilities and the general economy has a major impact on family lives. It becomes more difficult and dangerous for women to provide household goods, and this eventually leads to malnutrition and starvation.[255] If women are forced to accept work in order to be able to feed their families, they are often badly remunerated. Since the formal sector often stops functioning, and since many women are not trained for a job, they often have to work in the informal sector.[256] However, work in the informal sector often increases the likelihood of violence or other abuse. Even after the

---

[251] Iraq: The Human Cost, "Widows in Iraq indicate scale of killing during U.S. war"

[252] IOM, *Sulaimaniya, Governorate Profile, IDP and Returnee Assessment* (February 2010) 1.

[253] Naomi Cahn, "Women in Post-Conflict Reconstruction: Dilemmas and Directions" *William & Mary Journal of Women and the Law* 12(2) (2006): 336

[254] Pankhurst, "The 'Sex War' and Other Wars," 159.

[255] UN ESCAP, *Women and Armed Conflict,* 10.

[256] Tsjeard Bouta and Georg Frerks, *Women's Roles in Conflict Prevention, Conflict Resolution and Post-Conflict Reconstruction, Literature Review and Institutional Analysis* (The Hague: Netherlands Institute of International Relations, Conflict Research Unit, 2002) 38.

cessation of conflict, the main employment chances for women continue in the informal sector, since the formal sector takes longer to recover.[257]

The struggle of women to provide their families with basic goods is further enhanced as a consequence of the higher percentage of women-lead households after wars. This is especially difficult for women in patriarchal societies, in which matriarchal households are traditionally unknown, and have little chance of assimilation into the social fabric. [258]

As a result of campaigns like the Anfal, there developed a large percentage of women-headed households, especially within the internally displaced persons population of the Kurds, as well as a high number of female refugees.[259] As a result of the events in the Kurdistan Region, female-headed households in the governorate of Sulaimaniya amounted to 18 per cent in 2000.[260] Throughout the whole of Iraq there are today an estimated 1 to 3 million women-headed households, or about 10 per cent of all households. This number is higher in Kurdistan (14%) than in the south and centre of Iraq (9.5%).[261]

Due to of Iraq's patriarchal system women are hardly able to live a life without an adult male relative, because they lack economic, physical and social protection and support.[262] It is normal in Iraq that young widows return to their in-laws and that older widows stay with their children, who are expected to provide for them and any young children. However as a consequence of the wars fewer and fewer families in Iraq are able to provide this safety net, or the women have no surviving male relatives to turn to, because they were all killed.[263] Even though widows receive help from the government, this is difficult to access, because of the

---

[257] Ibid.p.36

[258] Kerim, *The Kurds in Iraq,* 58.

[259] Ibid.

[260] Louise Waite, "How is household vulnerability gendered? Female-headed households in the collectives of Sulaimaniya, Iraqi Kurdistan" *Disasters* 24(2) (2000): 153.

[261] IFHS, *Republic of Iraq, Iraq Family Health Survey Report* (2006/7) 1.3

[262] ICRC Iraq, *Women in War,* 4.

[263] Ibid.p.5

complex process, as well as shortcoming of the administration and the usual problem of corruption.[264]

As indicated above, the victimization of and violence against women does not stop with the official cessation of armed conflict. The post-armed-conflict situation is even worse for some women than the time during armed conflict. Women are often unable to leave their houses, after the cessation of the official conflict, because of insecurity on the streets. This was the situation in Iraq, where the militias which appeared after the end of the official war were nearly all men. When they entered the neighbourhoods, security, especially for women, was not provided.[265]

Also human rights abuses of women often stay the same or can even get worse after the official end of armed conflict.[266] In 2009 Amnesty International reported on-going human rights abuses against the people in the Kurdistan Region of Iraq. These include allegations of torture and other ill-treatment against the *Asayish*, the official security agency in Kurdistan,[267] the holding of political detainees without charge or trial,[268] the lack of fair trials[269] and a still existing lack of freedom of expression.[270] When it comes to the specific issue of discrimination and violence against women, Amnesty International acknowledges the positive developments which have been taken place in the region, but argues that the execution of women's rights, such as the protection from violence, is still insufficient.[271] Women who fight for human rights are often subject to discrimination or violence themselves.[272] Many women in the Kurdish region still have restricted life choices, are vulnerable to violence and some are subjected to forced or early marriage.

---

[264] Ibid.p.6

[265] Enloe, "Cynthia Enloe speaks on Women in Iraq"

[266] Lori Handrahan, "Conflict, Gender, Ethnicity and Post-Conflict Reconstruction" *Security Dialogue* 35(4) (2004): 431.

[267] Amnesty International, *Hope and Fear, Human Rights in The Kurdistan Region of Iraq* (London: Index: MDE 14/006/2009) 9.

[268] Ibid.p.11

[269] Ibid.p.25

[270] Ibid.p.42

[271] Ibid.pp.31-38

[272] Ibid.p.39

Many girls only receive little or no school education and have limited employment opportunities.[273]

A further consequence of conflict is increased domestic violence. It has been observed that the increase of "manliness" during war and the decrease of a good lifestyle makes domestic violence more common during times of conflict.[274] There is a strong correlation between violence on the battle field and violence in the home later on.[275] Women face increased violence not only from enemy forces, but also from their own family members before and after conflict.[276] The Iraq Family Health Survey of 2006-2007 showed in this respect that over ten per cent of women in the Kurdistan Region had suffered from physical violence, over sixty per cent experienced controlling behavior by their husbands and nearly twenty per cent suffered from emotional violence.[277]

In Kurdistan the official number of killings within families rose after 1991. Some argue that this was due to the reinforcing of old tribal rules as well as fundamentalist Islam, while others are of the view that an increased awareness simply lead to enhanced acknowledgement of the killings in the public.[278] The so called "honour killings" did not only increase within the families, but were also inflicted by armed groups. According to King, the peshmerga fighters after 1991 killed Kurdish women who were suspected of having sexual relations with Arab men.[279] Furthermore, the Kurdistan Region is still struggling with widespread female genital mutilation, with up to 40 per cent of women and girls between

---

[273] Ibid.p.33

[274] Elisabeth Reht and Ellen Johnson-Sirleaf, *Women, War, Peace: The Independent Experts' Assessment on the Impact of Armed Conflict on Women and Women's Role in Peace-building* (New York: UNIFEM, Progress of the World's Women 2002, Volume 1, 2002) 16.

[275] Marc Engelhardt, *Starke Frauen für den Frieden, Die Nobelpreisträgerinnen Ellen Johnson Sirleaf, Leymah Gbowee und Tawakkul Karman* (Freiburg im Breisgau: Verlag Herder GmbH, 2011) 52.

[276] Tamar Mayer (ed.), *Women and the Israeli Occupation: The Politics of Change* (London: Routledge, 1994) 123.

[277] Nadja Al-Ali and Nicole Pratt, "Conspiracy of Near Silence, Violence Against Iraqi Women" *Middle East Report* 258 (2011): 34/36.

[278] Ibid.p.6

[279] Ibid.p.7

eleven and 24 years of age, having been subjected to such operations, according to a survey in 2009.[280]

Next to the physical victimization after the cessation of armed conflict, often women who suffered physically during war continue to be victimized in society after the cessation of armed conflict. The surviving widows of the Anfal campaign are tragic examples. Their social and legal status was unclear. They often stayed with their dead husband's families in order to be able to stay with their children. In the difficult circumstances of the time they were often considered a burden. In addition the knowledge of or assumptions concerning tabooed sexual violence they suffered stigmatized them and made them into a problem for the family's honour.[281] As elaborated by Karin Mlodoch, the women were expected to live in grief. They were expected to live a life without happiness as befits the role of victims. At the same time they had to be strong for themselves and to manage to feed their children with minimal support.[282] If women experienced sexual violence during the time of armed conflict and survive, they could seldom confide in anyone, and especially not with male relatives. They had to cope with the trauma themselves, because they were seen as having brought shame over the family.[283] Sometimes women could not even go back to their families or were rejected from their society, when it became known that they had been victims of sexual violence or that they were pregnant with or had an illegitimate child.[284]

As a consequence, the women themselves felt unwanted by society. This feeling was exacerbated by the lack of support provided by the state, even though the situation has improved since 2003. They now receive budgets to build houses, and the infrastructure, as well as provisions for health and education services in the areas affected. However these improvements have taken about 20 years to commence.[285]

---

[280] Al-Ali and Pratt, "Conspiracy of Near Silence," 36.
[281] Mlodoch, "'We Want to be Remembered as Strong Women, Not as Shepherds'," 74.
[282] Ibid.p.75
[283] Handrahan, "Conflict, Gender, Ethnicity and Post-Conflict Reconstruction," 435.
[284] Haleh Afshar, "Women and Wars: Some Trajectories Towards a Feminist Peace" *Development in Practice* 13(2/3) (2003) 182
[285] Ibid.p.78

Further psychological implications, which still affect society 20 years on, are the long-term impacts of surprise chemical weapons attacks on civilians, such as the one in Halabja. As a study by Jonathan Dworkin and others shows, post-traumatic stress disorder symptoms and poor general functioning, which are more likely for women and the elderly to occur, remain major problems in society, even decades after the traumatic events.[286]

These manifold experiences as victims outlined in this section have had a profound effect on the women's current needs and aspirations. As a result of their experiences during and immediately after armed conflict, personal security is of great importance for many women, often more so than personal freedom.

Additionally, as a consequence of the years of hardship and having to provide for themselves and their families many older women especially support the reestablishment of the 'old structure' of shared responsibilities, with the men working outside and providing for the family. However, others have become accustomed to managing everything alone as a result of the war. Many women either wish to or are forced to continue in this way and must be given the opportunity.

Finally, the different experiences during war, which ranged from extreme situations, such as the Anfal campaign, to the varying experiences of those women who were forced to flee, and those who stayed, have created a diverse society, where one element does not truly understand the other. And while some would prefer to forget the past and move on, it is important for others to maintain the memory.

It is therefore of great importance that the views and experiences of the whole society are included in future decisions of the region, while giving all citizens the chance to follow their lifestyle options. In order to alleviate the on-going victimization of women in society, so that the can also experience the feeling of peace, it is vital to ensure as far as possible their security in the public as well as the private domains.[287] For women peace can only begin once their security is

---

[286] Jonathan Dworkin et.al, "The Long-Term Psychosocial Impact of a Surprise Chemical Weapons Attack on Civilians in Halabja, Iraqi Kurdistan" *The Journal of Nervous and Mental Disease* 196(10) (2008): 774/775.
[287] Al-Ali, "Reconstructing Gender," 741.

ensured, their human rights are respected and they are no longer beaten in their homes and assaulted on the streets.[288] At the same time the work for personal freedom should not be forgotten.

2.   Women as Actors

But women are not only passive victims during war. They also play very active roles in supporting, as well as trying to end or prevent armed conflict. While men commit on average more atrocities during the time of war than women, and more men are fighting as soldiers and militants,[289] this does not follow that women are simply victims. They are also actors during conflict in a variety of ways. They join the military, participate in liberation movements[290], support the general militarization of their country or region[291], or fight for peace.

As explained by the wife of a Peshmerga fighter, who lives in exile today:

> *"War in Kurdistan has a very long and horrible history. And the women were always part of it. The women also lived as fighters and they supported their men. Of course they were also housewives and mothers. Actually the women only fought. They fought with arms and they fought without arms. The women had to live in the mountains. I myself stayed in the mountains for many months with one baby and pregnant. Can you imagine? There was nothing to wear, nothing to eat. The women were arrested just as the men. Women and men suffered exactly in the same way."[292]*

One way in which women 'fought with arms' was as soldiers:

Women have served in the Iraqi Army since Saddam's regime.[293] In addition women could join the "people's army" and in the first years of war tens of thousands of Arabic and Kurdish women availed themselves of this opportunity.[294]

---

[288] Moghadam, "Peacebuilding and Reconstruction with Women," 70.

[289] Galtung, *Peace by Peaceful Means*, 41.

[290] Giles and Hyndman (ed.), *Sites of Violence*, 34.

[291] Winfried Kurth, Ludwig Janus und Florian Galler (Hrsg), *Emotionale Strukturen, Nationen und Kriege* (Heidelberg: Mattes Verlag, 2007), 237.

[292] Interview CD, Vienna from 21/10/2012

[293] United States Forces - Iraq PAO, "Female Iraqi Soldiers explore roles, ethics at seminar" (22 February 2010) http://www.usf-iraq.com/news/press-releases/female-iraqi-soldiers-explore-roles-ethics-at-seminar (Accessed on 23.2.2012)

[294] Eva Salvesberg, Siamend Hajo, und Carsten Borck, *Kurdische Frauen und das Bild der kurdischen Frauen* (Münster: LIT Verlag, 2000) 160.

Nevertheless, the number of women serving as active fighters is still comparatively small.

Another area, in which women were actively involved were the guerrilla forces, that is in general non-state armed forces:

Kurdish women took part in conflicts and in the fighting as part of their national movements. They were involved in the Peshmerga forces, by fighting with and supporting the men and have thereby women have played an active role in the liberation struggle. An official Peshmerga Force for Women was established in 1996, which, while only comprising a few hundred women soldiers, nevertheless earned respect.[295] Many women who were Peshmerga now have prominent roles in one of the two parties.

Women had been encouraged to join the Peshmerga forces from the 1980s onwards. Most undertook administrative tasks, but they were also used for acting as a courier and to smuggle clothes, medication and weapons, especially in the cities, where, because of the enhanced involvement of women, they were omni-present and less noticeable than men.[296]

Women's participation in the active fighting influenced the conflict, as well as the women themselves. Reasons for their participation included political conviction, the desire to make themselves heard[297] but also the opportunity to lead a different life.[298] Through their active participation in the war machine, women freed themselves from their traditional roles. Their increased participation may therefore be seen as a twisted approach towards emancipation.[299] Many women became part of movements such as the PKK[300] or the Peshmerga forces to get away from the strict family structure and to enjoy more freedom.[301] According to Fatma Incesu

---

[295] The Guardian, "Time for revenge" (28 February 2003) http://www.guardian.co.uk/world/2003/feb/28/gender.uk1 (Accessed on 23.2.2012)

[296] Salvesberg, Hajo und Borck, *Kurdische Frauen und das Bild der kurdischen Frauen*, 163.

[297] Wölte, *Human Rights Violations against Women during War and Conflict*, 24.

[298] Flach, *Frauen in der kurdischen Guerilla*, 63.

[299] Ibid. p.26

[300] The Kurdistan Worker's Party, who have developed in Turkey, where they are seen as a terrorist organisation and whose members are partly based in Northern Iraq.

[301] Incesu, *Die Stellung der Frauen in der kurdischen Gesellschaft*, 72.

the PKK liberated women because they believed that men could only be beaten, if women achieved more power. They therefore supported women in all parts of the organisational structure.[302] In 1993 the women of the PKK inaugurated their own women's army. They saw it as liberating to be able to fight for themselves and they wished to achieve liberation for all women of society.[303] The issue of women's liberation is very important for the PKK. It is not possible to have socialism without the liberation of women.[304]

Women had similar reasons for participation in the Peshmerga forces in Northern Iraq, including the feelings of hate for the regime, and the need for revenge after their men had been tortured and murdered by Saddam Hussein.[305]

Despite these involvements, women as active fighters still only comprise a small fraction of the actual female population of a region. While the female fighters are made visible on pictures and through articles, there is another role of women in conflict, which is far more significant, but often not recognized or forgotten when considering *"actors"* of conflict, namely their support of war and of the militarization process from below. As explained by a social researcher at one of Kurdistan's universities: *"Women did not only have an important role in their bodily work, but that they were very important morally, in supporting ideas."*[306]

It is crucially important to remember the role military wives and mothers play in maintaining up the military system. It is they who keep the camps running, who make it possible for their husbands and sons to go to war and who help the state in caring for injured soldiers.[307] This is true around the world. In Iran for example, during the war with Iraq, widows and single women were paid to marry disabled or wounded soldiers, to free the state from having to care of them itself.[308] States or groups within states are only able to lead violent conflicts if there are men who are

---

[302] Ibid.p.77

[303] Ibid.p.83

[304] Ibid.p.18

[305] Taylor-Lind Anastasia, "Warrior Women" (2003)
http://www.bbc.co.uk/wales/southeast/sites/newport/pages/article_peshmerga.shtml (Accessed on 23.2.2012)

[306] Interview BT, Erbil on 24/07/2012

[307] Enloe, "Gender' Is Not Enough," 96/97.

[308] Afshar, "Women and Wars," 183.

willing to serve as soldiers and if there are women who are ready to support and take care of the home front by themselves.[309] If women and wives would not take care of the wounded soldiers, it would not be possible to wage war in the same way, because all costs would have to be borne by the state.[310]

Women, as wives, girlfriends, hostesses and prostitutes help to create stable diplomatic and military communities. Without them such communities would not be possible. It is they who care of wounded soldiers, work in factories to produce clothes, and bring food etc.[311]

At the same time women and families are used as a reason by men to go to war. Men are told that they need to fight and kill in order to maintain the "*socially constructed notions the woman embodies*".[312]

Women are often perceived to be the cultural custodians as well as the biological reproducers of a nation.

As the biological reproducers of the nation women are often put under pressure by the state to either have more children or fewer according to the national need. This pressure depends on the woman's membership to a specific national collective and can vary depending on the situation.[313] While the women who are fighting at the front are expected to not have any children, women at home are expected to give birth to as many as possible in order to produce more warriors and workers.[314] Women are giving birth so that their sons can be killed again and mothers of martyrs are celebrated to encourage them and other women to have even more children.[315]

At the same time women are cultural custodians of the nation. They are seen as symbolic "border guards", who can "*identify people as members or non-members*

---

[309] Mayer (ed.), *Women and the Israeli Occupation,* 132.

[310] Cynthia Enloe, The Clarke Forum, YouTube "Women and Men in the Iraq War, What Can Feminist Curiosity Reveal" http://www.youtube.com/watch?v=XXUCLahznqs (Accessed on 7.12.2011)

[311] Karen Beckwith (Review), "Bananas, Beaches & Bases: Making Feminist Sense of International Politics. By Cynthia Enloe" *The Journal of Politics* 53(1) (1991): 290.

[312] Cnythia Enloe (1988:20) in Afshar, "Women and Wars," 185.

[313] Nira Yuval-Davis, *Gender & Nation* (London: SAGE Publications, 1997) 22.

[314] Afshar, "Women and Wars," 183.

[315] Ibid.p.184

of a specific collectivity."[316] It is considered shame for the whole family if a woman forcibly or willingly engages with an enemy or somebody from a different ethnic, cultural, or religious heritage.[317] Women are seen to have an important role in maintaining the cultural traditions of an ethnic group or a country especially at a time of social instability. They are therefore associated with the future and through "proper" behaviour and "proper" clothing they embody the line which defines the collective's boundaries and ensures that the cultural heritage will continue. Hence women are also seen as representing collective honour and this in turn is used as a reason to legitimize the control and oppression of women.[318]

Furthermore it is the women who are giving birth to new heirs of an ethnic group or of the nation. They are the first to teach their children to identify with their family, as well as with a specific ethnic or religious group. Consequently it is partly due to women's teaching of loyalty to a specific group and their support of the patriarchal structure that men continue to go to war.[319] Women are expected to raise the next generation, who will again fight for their country again and to teach them the appropriate standards of their society. Thereby mothers convey to their children certain attitudes which can either support or work against the militarization of society.[320]

In the Kurdistan Region today, the different roles that women occupy during the years of conflict are generally highly respected. It is often be heard that, as with men, a woman's most important role is to dedicate herself to the service of her homeland.[321] Both, men and women, have played important and leading roles throughout the wars and thereby command respect.[322] When the people are asked exactly which role was women's most important and active role during conflict, they

---

[316] Yuval-Davis, *Gender & Nation*, 23.
[317] Al-Ali, "Reconstructing Gender," 741.
[318] Yuval-Davis, *Gender & Nation*, 45/46.
[319] Enloe, "The Women behind the Warriors," 24.
[320] Yuval-Davis, *Gender & Nation*, 2.
[321] See e.g. Interview BC, Erbil on 25/06/2012
[322] Interview AW, Sulaimaniya on 01/06/2012

most often respond that it was the women's support of the fighting from their homes.[323]

The Kurdish people therefore describe themselves as having worked "*together*"[324] or "*side by side*"[325] during war. Most men tend to expresss the view that the women "*supported*" the men,[326] while many of the women have the feeling that they did "*everything*".[327] As explained by one young woman who grew up as a child in Erbil during the struggle:

> *"The women did everything! They had to work when the men were away to feed their families and in addition they also had to help the Peshmergas. As a little child, they gave me the messages to bring it to other Peshmerga fighters on the other part of town. They wrote the messages on little pieces of paper, rolled them together and put a plaster around it. Then they put it into my mouth and told me where to go. I went through the whole town to the other person. It was dangerous. It would not have been good if somebody had found the message in my mouth."*[328]

Despite slight discrepancies between different views it can clearly be seen that the active role of women, especially in day-to-day life, including cooking for the men, helping the wounded and transferring messages, is clearly recognized.

It can be seen that women's roles during conflict vary greatly and their variety is countless. Apart from being victims or perpetrators, women during the time of conflict occupy important roles in society, as mothers, wives, employers and employees, and many more. While some of the roles occupied by women are gender specific such as their role of mothers and as victims to specific violence, while others are traditionally male such as becoming active actors during war, being employed and becoming main breadwinners.

Finally, many women play very positive roles, often unnoticed or in the background, working for peace. They work with NGOs, religious groups, sometimes at the political level or simply in their communities to actively oppose

---

[323] Interview AQ, Sulaimaniya on 19/05/2012; Interview BP, Erbil on 21/07/2012

[324] Interview BH, Erbil on 05/07/2012

[325] Interview AU, Sulaimaniya on 28/05/2012

[326] Interview BL, Erbil on 12/07/2012

[327] Interview CD, Vienna on 21/10/2012

[328] Interview CH, Vienna on 05/11/2012

war.[329] They use "motherhood" to protest against atrocities committed and many make efforts to impose more positive values on the military or the militarized society, by promoting activities such as sport, music or reading, rather than gambling, drinking and prostitution.[330] This will be elaborated further in the section on women's activism below.

Women's active role in supporting or fighting against armed conflict is greatly influential is shaping the next generation, and thus the country's future and should therefore not be underestimated or even forgotten, when it comes to considering plans for the region's development.

When it comes to women's personal development and the achievement of gender equality within society, personal and cultural identity as well as past national and international developments each play a part. This will be the subject of the following sub-section.

D.   Women and Gender Equality in the Kurdistan Region – Then and Now

Just under seventy per cent of people in the Kurdistan region when asked whether they thought that men and women were equal within society today, replied in the negative[331]. Most people were of the opinion that women are respected, but that they simply cannot yet do everything to the level expected of men[332], that they have their specific roles[333] and that the theoretical thinking about quality is different from the practice[334]. For some people this "inequality" is not necessarily bad and it has become a common point of discussion that there exist differences between Western and Eastern ideas of "equality" and that it should rather be about "being worth the same" than actually "being the same".[335] This opinion is criticized by some as being used as justification, especially by feminists and people who

---

[329] More detailed examples will be elaborated in the section on "women's movements"

[330] Nancy Gentile Ford (Review), " Maneuvers: The International Politics of Militarizing Women's Lives by Cynthia Enloe" *The Journal of Military History* 65(4) (2001): 1176.

[331] See e.g.: Interview AG, Erbil on 13/04/2012; Interview AH, Erbil on 15/04/2012; Interview AP, Sulaimaniya on 18/05/2012; Interview AQ, Sulaimaniya on 19/05/2012

[332] Interview AX, Sulaimaniya on 03/06/2012

[333] Interview BA, Erbil on 21/06/2012

[334] Interview AC, Erbil on 06/04/2012

[335] See e.g. Interview BA, Erbil on 21/06/2012

returned from Europe, and that there is no equality[336], with one man from a small village even explaining that *"we do not have respect for women"*[337] and others reporting that they do not believe that equality is even possible to achieve in Kurdistan.[338] Whatever particular position people might take, it was generally observed, that the Kurdish population does not perceive itself as a society of equal opportunity. While some people are of the view that women in Kurdistan have never been truly equal and should follow Europe towards a path of equality, others believe that the Kurdish women were equal in times gone by, but that changed as a result of wars, politics or religion.

When people spoke about their concepts of equality, opinions ranged widely and included the ideas that *"behind every great man, there is a great woman"*,[339] that women are intellectually equal, but not otherwise[340], that women are already equal,[341] and that women will never be equal in the region as the people do not behave accordingly.[342]

It will be the aim of the following section to close the circle of background information, by describing and analysing women and gender equality in the Kurdistan Region in the past and present. This will further deepen the understanding of the challenges faced in the conflict transformation process, for which the achievement of equality is vital.

Traditionally, Kurdish men and women had had their distinctive roles. Women worked in the fields and took care of the children and the elderly, while men tried to earn extra money, and dealt with business in the cities and in general with people from outside.[343]

Travellers around 1900 saw the Kurds as "monogamous" with a family, seldom exceeding three or four. They described the Kurdish women as having a

---

[336] Interview CG, Vienna on 11/11/2012
[337] Interview BS, Erbil on 24/07/2012
[338] Interview BJ, Erbil on 09/07/2012
[339] Interview BK, Erbil on 12/07/2012
[340] Interview AQ, Sulaimaniya on 19/05/2012
[341] Interview AJ, Erbil on 20/04/2012
[342] Interview BJ, Erbil on 09/07/2012
[343] Incesu, *Die Stellung der Frauen in der kurdischen Gesellschaft,* 16.

"remarkable" freedom and defined them as "brave", hardworking and beautiful.[344] The women were described as joining with the military, doing manual labour and keeping the family in order. The Kurdish women were said to be more open than their Turkish or Persian neighbours and adultery was said to be unknown. Additionally most marriages were said to have arisen from mutual attraction and there was an especially good understanding between the sexes.[345] The veil was said to have been unknown to the Kurds and the women did not hide their faces.[346]

Also today, there is a general tendency towards a solely positive picture of Kurdish women's situation in the past. Women are said to have lived on an equal footing with men, working with them on the farms as well as fighting with them for a free Kurdistan.[347]

According to several Kurds, Islam worsened the situation for women and made men superior. If one believes many Kurdish nationalists, women originally had equal rights in the tribal society, as evidenced by the existence of women tribal chieftains. However this equality was lost through the domination by Islam.[348] This belief is deeply rooted, especially in some of the more Westernized people. When one woman was told during the interview that some believed that Islam brought equality, she got very excited and said:

> *"Religion does not help the women. That is not true. Maybe it was true 1500 years ago, but not now. The men always say that the women are equal, but when it comes to the point that a woman really wants something, then they are always against it."*[349]

Another reason for the loss of equality within society is said to have been the process of industrialization.[350] The increase in urbanization was said to have been problematic for many in the tribal society. Women lost their status in the cities,

---

[344] Ely Banister Soane, *To Mesopotamia and Kurdistan in Disguise: With historical notices of the Kurdish tribes and the Chaldeans of Kurdistan* (Boston: Adamant Media Corporation, 2005; original: 1928) 396.

[345] Ibid. p.297

[346] Ibid. p.402

[347] Ruwayda Mustafah Rabar, "Kurdish women and their struggle for equality" (14 December 2010) http://www.ekurd.net/mismas/articles/misc2010/12/state4435.htm (Accessed on 23.2.2012)

[348] Shahrzad Mojab, *Women of a Non-State Nation, The Kurds* (Costa Mesa: Mazda Publishers, 2001) 100. See e.g. Interview AH, Erbil on 15/04/2012; Interview AO, Sulaimaniya on 13/05/2012

[349] Interview CH, Vienna on 05/11/2012

[350] Rabar "Kurdish women and their struggle for equality"

because they did not have the opportunities for work.[351] At least in theory women and men were respected as equals in the villages. While in practice women had no power over goods or property, they were able to acquire a certain status through hard work,[352] and the village structure made it possible for women to secure positions of power. According to Mustafa Gundogdu, a worker at the Kurdish Human Rights Project, there has always been a basis for equality of women in Kurdish society through participation in leadership and decision making. Even though in villages women and men were separated by their specific roles, women were not exploited. They held meetings and were part of the decision making as were the men.[353] But once these structures disappeared, the women's status fell as well.[354]

While Kurdish society has always been highly male-dominated, there were women in Kurdish history, who reached high positions and became political or military leaders of the communities. Many of these women became national symbols and are seen by many Kurds as the proof for the respected position of women in Kurdish society and the Kurds' superiority over their neighbours.[355] Women who reached the peak of the social pyramid and who became chiefs of their communities included Adela Khanum of Halabja[356], Khanzade Sultan[357], Kara Fatima Khanum[358], Perikhan Khatun[359] and Shemsî Khatun[360]. They all ruled different tribes in the Kurdish region at different times.[361] While all of these women occupied powerful positions, they only achieved these positions through the prestige of their families, through highly supportive husbands or through their husbands' deaths.[362] According to Martin Van Bruinessen it is not known whether a

---

[351] Incesu, *Die Stellung der Frauen in der kurdischen Gesellschaft*, 17.

[352] Ibid.p.16

[353] James Simon, "Kurdistan, Women in Iraq" (Video) http://www.youtube.com/watch?v=x4POLH2O208 (Accessed on 15.11.11)

[354] Elisabeth Hartwig, *Rural African Women as Subjects of Social and Political Change, A Case Study of Women in Northwestern Cameroon* (Münster: LIT Verlag, 2005), 160.

[355] Mojab, *Women of a Non-State Nation*, 95.

[356] Shahrizur, around 1900

[357] Harir and Soran (the districts to the east and northeast of Erbil), around 1630

[358] Marash (present day Kahramanmarash in southeastern Turkey), around 1850

[359] Mardin region in present Turkey, Raman tribe

[360] Omeryan Tribe

[361] Mojab, *Women of a Non-State Nation*, 98-100.

[362] Ibid.

Kurdish woman of "*humble origins*" ever rose to a high position by her own efforts. However there are examples of men who did.[363] Nevertheless in some districts of Kurdistan female rule was so common that it was explicitly referred to in the records of customary law by the Ottomans.[364] The female tribal leaders were highly respected and seen as leaders in their own right as evidenced by the people using their leaders' names, rather than the names of their husbands or fathers.[365]

Also in recent time there have been women who have played a leading role in Kurdish public life, including Mulla Mustafa Barzani's second wife, Hamayl Khanum, during the 1960s or as some of the women Peshmergas[366] as well as high level Kurdish female politicians, such as Leyla Zana in Turkey in the 1990s.[367] All these women were powerful and great leaders in their own right. However, as with female Kurdish leaders centuries before, they stepped into their situation through their families' relations and continued their struggle for power from there. It might therefore be concluded that once a woman reached a high status, through birth or marriage, her gender no longer mattered. While high birth may compensate for the female gender disadvantage, gender equality does not spread beyond special classes.[368] While strong women are seen as admirable in stories and folklore and while there are women with great influence in Kurdish society, gender equality is not a widespread characteristic of today's society.[369]

Nevertheless, Kurdish women are today generally described as free, especially by the Kurds themselves. They are said to play a more active part in political and social life than women in other Middle Eastern societies and they are often unveiled, the veil thereby often being a symbol, either of freedom or restrictions, depending on the people talked to.

Public views on equality reflect the fact that women have become a symbol of identity for a nation and its society. This can be especially seen in the Middle East,

---

[363] Van Bruinessen, *Kurdish Ethno-Nationalism Versus Nation-Building States,* 101.
[364] Ibid.p.98
[365] Ibid.p.100
[366] Ibid.p.105
[367] Ibid.p.107
[368] Ibid.p.101
[369] Ibid.p.103

where the issue of women's rights is part of an "ideological terrain" in which the society's culture and individuality, as well as autonomy are discussed. The situation of women may serve as an indicator to the rest of the world of local culture and as a boundary marker for other cultures.[370] Women's equality is often presented as a question of tradition versus modernism and of East versus West. Women are often used as a pawn in the struggle between the competing forces of East and West. The women are used as "us versus them". [371] In the Kurdish case certain sectors in society congratulate themselves on their openness between men and women in comparison with the Arabic, Persian and Turkish cultures around them. However other sectors of society aim to distinguish their culture, and therefore their behaviour towards women, from the West.[372] These differences in the portrayal of women as part of a political statement can be observed throughout history.

Before 1992 Kurdish women in Iraq were disadvantaged on several levels. Apart from economic hardship and their oppression as women, they were disadvantaged because of their ethnicity. After 1992 their situation was arguably raised considerably above that of Iraqi women elsewhere in the country.[373]

Despite the ethnic discrimination, Kurdish women also profited from positive legal developments affecting women throughout Iraq. Still today several men and women tell stories about the 1970s and 80s having been more open, especially when it comes to dress code. Women in Iraq have long been the regional pioneers of gender-equality, at least outwardly. Already in 1948 a woman became a judge and in 1959 Dr. Naziha Al-Dulaimi became the first female minister in the Arab world.[374]

After the creation of modern Iraq as a sovereign state, women's rights were first put on the political agenda after the military-led revolution of 1957 by Qasim. Under Qasim the family law was reformed. He replaced the Sharia courts, restricted

---

[370] Lila Abu-Lughod (ed.), *Remaking Women, Feminism and Modernity in the Middle East* (Princeton: Princeton University Press, 1998) 3.

[371] Nadje Al-Ali in Simon, "Kurdistan, Women in Iraq"

[372] Al-Ali and Pratt, "Between Nationalism and Women's Rights," 350.

[373] Kerim, *The Kurds in Iraq*, 59.

[374] Al-Zubaidi, *Der Streit um Frauenrechte und das Personenstandsrecht*, 4.

polygamy, empowered wives to initiate divorce and instituted equal inheritance shares. After the next coup, under Abdul Salem Aref, several of the new laws were reverted to the old ones, because of religious pressure. However many stayed.[375]

Women's rights and their status were further enhanced during the early times of the secular Ba'athist socialist rule.[376] During the 1970s changes in the law were made, which made it possible for judges to prevent fathers from forcing their daughters to marry early, to prevent a polygamous marriage of her husband without the permission of the first wife and to permit women to join the armed forces.[377] Furthermore it was made easier for divorced mothers to get custody of their children and reforms were made in the conditions in which women could seek a divorce.[378] According to the Iraqi constitution drafted in 1970, which was suspended in 2003, women were guaranteed equal rights with men.[379] Women enjoyed equal rights before the law, even though this was restricted through the patriarchal nature of Iraqi society[380] as well as through the situation of war in the country. However, the real situation of women always depended on the part of society and type of family they lived in. While wives and daughters of families close to the regime were certainly more able to benefit from the new legislations, than women from opposing factions, or from ethnic groups the regime worked against, at least in theory the general situation of women improved.

Also in practice measures were put in place in the second half of the previous century, which are generally used as measures for describing enhanced gender equality within a society, such as the support of women in education, employment and political participation:

---

[375] Nikki Keddie, *Women in the Middle East, Past and Present* (Princeton: Princeton University Press, 2007) 127.

[376] UNIFEM, "Iraq" (2007) http://www.utoronto.ca/wwdl/bibliography_war/UNIFEM%20-%20Iraq%20-%20women%20war%20and%20peace.htm (Accessed on 17.09.2011)

[377] Saeid Neshat, "A Look into the Women's Movement in Iraq" *Farzaneh* 6(11) (2004): 57.

[378] Keddie, *Women in the Middle East,* 128.

[379] See Article 19

[380] Freedomhouse, "Iraq" (2004) http://www.freedomhouse.org/template.cfm?page=173 (Accessed on 15.11.11)

In 1980 16 from 250 seats in the Iraqi Council were won by women. Five years later it was 33 seats, or 13 per cent.[381]

In 1979 legislation was passed which required all illiterate Iraqis between 15 and 45 to attend reading classes and in 1976 primary school attendance was made compulsory to all children between six and ten. As a consequence, female literacy in Iraq before 1991 was the highest in the region.[382] In the Kurdistan Region, which had been under partly autonomous administration since 1974, classes were conducted in Kurdish. This later changed into Arabic. It was the official aim of the regime to include the country's women in the modern society. But when women were later asked about the benefits of the reading and writing classes, many replied that since their lives did not change in any other way, they had no great use for reading and writing. It follows that the campaign was designed not so much to support the emancipation of women, but rather to further a system of manipulation.[383] Nevertheless it must be conceded that the capability of reading and writing can also be the first step for some to build their self-esteem and to move towards an independent life.

At the same time the percentage of women in university courses was reasonably high. By 1979 51 per cent of first-year medical students at Baghdad University, and 75 per cent of students in English translation were female.[384]

Additionally, especially in the 1970s and 1980s women were actively incorporated in the labour force by the government. Their participation increased during the years of the Iran-Iraq war in order to replace the male soldiers.[385] Women received opportunities in the civil services, maternity benefits and freedom from harassment in the workplace through employment laws. As a consequence women's employment rose.[386] In the 1980s approximately 15 per cent of factory workers, 16 per cent of government employees, 29 per cent of physicians, 46 per cent of

---

[381] Al-Ali, "Reconstructing Gender," 754.
[382] Ibid.
[383] Salvesberg, Hajo und Borck, *Kurdische Frauen und das Bild der kurdischen Frauen,* 158.
[384] Valentine Moghadam, *Modernizing women: gender and social change in the Middle East* (2nd Edition, Boulder: Lynne Rienner Publishers, 2003) 60.
[385] Al-Ali, "Reconstructing Gender," 745/746.
[386] Keddie, *Women In the Middle East,* 128.

dentists, 46 per cent of teachers and 70 per cent of pharmacists were women.[387] Working women had maternity leave and the jobs of pregnant women were protected.[388] Under Saddam Iraq accomplished nearly entirely inclusive primary school education for boys and girls and Iraqi women were permitted to run for political positions, to vote, to drive and to work in jobs traditionally done by men.[389] But these advances did not reach everyone. The enjoyment of rights depended very much on social class, as well as on political affiliation.

The Ba'ath party encouraged women to join the party and also to seek election to parliament. The Ba'ath regime, while prohibiting any other political movements, supported its own women's organisation, the General Federation of Iraqi Women (GFIW), which had an estimated one million Iraqi women as their members.[390] From 1975 onwards many women, especially those working for educational institutions and for the government, were forced to join the GFIW to protect their jobs. This was another way for the regime to enhance total control.[391]

Further positive legal developments for women occurred in 1978, when a new Personal Status Code was adopted, which outlawed forced marriage and made it easier for women to get divorced and to have custody over their children. While it took into account some of their demands, women activists were still not satisfied with the code, as it did not achieve any radical change for women.[392]

To further enhance the image of the secular regime of the Ba'ath party and to support women's equality also on an international level, Iraq was one of the first Muslim countries to ratify the CEDAW in 1986, despite reservations applied to Articles 2, 9 and 16, which addressed women's rights in the private sphere as well as the issue of nationality.[393]

But the reality of most women's lives under Saddam did not correlate with the advances made on paper. A lot was only *de jure* and women did not have true

---

[387] Neshat, "A Look into the Women's Movement in Iraq," 56.

[388] Moghadam, *Modernizing women*, 60.

[389] UNIFEM "Iraq"

[390] Al-Ali, "Reconstructing Gender," 754.

[391] Salvesberg, Hajo und Borck, *Kurdische Frauen und das Bild der kurdischen Frauen,* 160.

[392] Al-Ali, *Iraqi Women,* 140.

[393] Freedomhouse, "Iraq"

power. The only way for a woman, just as for a man, to get a higher status in Saddam's Iraq was to join the regime. While these women enjoyed more freedoms, others were tortured and raped either for being dissidents themselves or for extracting information from other dissidents[394] and Saddam's sons Uday and Qusay were symbols in Iraq for violence against women, by openly raping, molesting and beheading women.[395]

By allowing women more rights and freedoms Saddam ensured their support for the regime, as well as ensuring that there was always a sound labour force, despite absence of the men fighting.[396] Hence Iraq during the Ba'athist rule is a prime example of how the change in the status of women is used to achieve certain political goals. Saddam supported the women's movement at a time when he needed women to fill in the vacancies in civil society left by soldiers at the front as well as for economic development. A further aim was to shift the loyalty of women away from the tribes and ethnic groups, through recruiting them into state-controlled agencies and through public schooling. However, Saddam again removed women's rights, when he needed more jobs for the returning men and when he wanted to save his power by connecting with local tribes and trying to garnish support from clan leaders [397]

At the onset of the Iran-Iraq war, Saddam changed his policies accordingly. The picture of the perfect woman changed from a young, educated, working woman to a patriotic, mourning widow who was dressed in a black *'abaya*[398].[399]

From 1982 married women were not allowed to travel unless accompanied by their husbands and unmarried women needed written consent from their father or guardian to do so.[400] In 1986 all birth control devices disappeared from pharmacies in order to encourage women to give birth to the next martyrs.[401] During the Iran-

---

[394] Lucy Brown and David Romano, "Women in Post-Saddam Iraq: One Step Forward or Two Steps Back?" *NWSA Journal* 18(3) (2006): 54.

[395] Ibid.p.56

[396] Miriam Cooke, *Women and the War Stories* (Berkeley: University of California Press, 1996) 221.

[397] Kandiyoti (ed.), *Women, Islam and the State*, 11.

[398] A traditionally black loose over-garment, which covers the whole body, except for the head.

[399] Salvesberg, Hajo und Borck, *Kurdische Frauen und das Bild der kurdischen Frauen,* 160.

[400] Moghadam, *Modernizing women,* 60.

[401] Ibid.p.61

Iraq War women were expected by the government to have at least five sons to be a "Patriotic Mother".[402] Further legal reforms gained for women were reversed after 1991, as Saddam turned to tribes and religion, in an attempt to reinforce his power. As a consequence, in the 1990s penalties for honour killings were reduced from eight years to six months, wives' consent for polygamy was no longer needed and women's personal status and their standing in labour law and criminal justice were weakened.[403]

The following years of war destroyed parts of Iraqi society and Iraqi women lost their achievements, gained in the previous decades. While they had gained many freedoms and rights from the end of the Second World War to the beginning of the 1980s, the situation changed dramatically with the collapse of Iraq's economy in 1990-91 and the civil unrest that followed.[404] One big factor in these upheavals was the impositions of sanctions[405] by the UN in response to the Iraqi invasion of Kuwait in 1990 which were maintained for the next 13 years.[406]

In Iraq, the UN, through Resolution 661[407], put a total ban on trade and trans-border financial transactions. There was a list of over 300 banned goods, ranging from light bulbs, socks, and ovens to needles, nails and refrigerators. There was a ban on all items which would have made it possible for Iraq to be self-sustainable in agricultural production. The sanctions were so efficient that only one month after the passage of the first Resolution, in September 1990, the Security Council felt the necessity to adopt a new Resolution, 666[408], to ensure that the civilian population would survive.[409]

As early as 1991 the situation had become so precarious that the Security Council Sanctions Committee, established to monitor the implementation of the sanctions, sought to allow food and medical supply because "*humanitarian circumstances*

---

[402] Cooke, *Women and the War Stories,* 245.

[403] Keddie, *Women in the Middle East,* 129.

[404] Neshat, "A Look into the Women's Movement in Iraq," 58.

[405] The first one being put into place through resolution 661 on 6 August 1990.

[406] Yasmin Husein Al-Jawaheri, *Women in Iraq, The Gender Impact of International Sanctions* (London: I.B.Tauris, 2008), 1.

[407] United Nations Security Council resolution 661, adopted on 6 August 1990

[408] United Nations Security Council Resolution 666, adopted on September 13, 1990

[409] Buck, Gallant, and Nossal, "Sanctions as a Gendered Instrument of Statecraft," 76/77.

applied with respect to the entire civilian population of Iraq." As a consequence Resolution 687[410] was passed on 3rd April 1991 to exempt foodstuffs and medical supplies from the sanctions regime. In May 1996 Iraq accepted the "oil-for-food" arrangements, laid out in Resolution 986 from April 1995,[411] which exchanged oil for food.[412]

According to Kurdish sources, the Kurdistan Region suffered tremendously under the sanctions, which greatly affected peoples' lives. The Kurds suffered from the international embargo, since it was still part of Iraq. In addition Saddam put an embargo on them, since the region was no longer under state control and finally the neighbouring countries, Turkey and Iran, refused free access to the Kurdish region. It was further claimed that the international support from the UN, as well as international NGOs was not sufficient.[413] However, according to Arabic sources[414] the Kurdistan Region was better off than the rest of the country, since it received significant international humanitarian assistance and could more easily receive goods from neighbouring countries. Whichever version is true, it can definitely be said that the civil population over the whole of Iraq suffered greatly under the sanctions. They changed peoples' lives, as well as the whole society.

The various armed conflicts in the region, as well as the sanctions had a great impact on women's roles in society. Even though economic shortages and sanctions were tough on the whole of the population, they arguably hit women and children disproportionally. The food shortage caused damage to a whole generation of children, of whom many were at "severe nutritional risk."[415] During the sanctions, work in the public sector lost all its value with an average employee earning only about US$ 1,50 to 4,50 per month. As a consequence many women gave up their jobs because their work was not seen as worthwhile for the family anymore and because services previously provided by the state, such as transport

---

[410] United Nations Security Council resolution 687, adopted on 3 April 1991

[411] United Nations Security Council resolution 986, adopted on 14 April 1995

[412] Buck, Gallant, and Nossal, "Sanctions as a Gendered Instrument of Statecraft," 77.

[413] Mustafa Al-Karadaghi (Ed., Publ.) *Kurdistan times, A Biannual Political Journal, The Kurdish Nation has the Inalienable Right of Self Determination* (No.4, November 1995): 93/94.
Interview CG, Vienna on 11/11/2012

[414] Al-Ali, *Iraqi Women,* 205/206.

[415] Ibid.p.80

and kindergartens, closed down, which made it impossible for women to continue with employment.[416] While it was still possible for men to try to find employment in the private sector, many jobs such as taxi drivers or as sales men on the street were not acceptable options for women and they were pushed back into their "traditional" roles.[417] As a result of money losing its value, about 60 per cent of the population became dependent on monthly food rations, paid for by the oil-for-food programme.[418]

The wars, as well as the sanctions also resulted in fewer opportunities for women in education. Through the destruction of educational establishments women and girls were less able to receive education, because their mobility was reduced in comparison to boys' and they had no way of reaching other institutions. Additionally families no longer saw a reason for educating their daughters, because there were no job prospects.[419] Even though the situation is continuing to change the education level of women is still highly dependent on their place of residence, as well as their family background.[420]

Furthermore the destruction of the health care system followed the sanctions and especially women and children died from shortages of food, medicine and pure water.[421] The sanctions affected women, as well as men, differently depending on their places of residence, rural or urban, their ethnicity, Kurdish or Arabic, their religion, Shi'a, Sunni or Christian, and especially their social class. During the war and throughout the sanctions a broad and stable educated middle class became impoverished and gave way to a class of war and sanctions profiteers.[422]

As a result of the change in the economy and the never ending insecurity, the people's thinking changed. Families became more conservative, and while the parents of many young people today, especially from the middle-class, used to mingle relative freely between boys and girls, today's young people have problems

---

[416] Al-Jawaheri, *Women in Iraq*, 35.
[417] Ibid. p.37
[418] Ibid. p. 746
[419] Ibid. p.66
[420] Al-Ali, "Reconstructing Gender," 747.
[421] Keddie, *Women in the Middle East,* 128/129.
[422] Al-Ali, "Reconstructing Gender," 746.

meeting one other.[423] Girls fear losing their reputation and bringing shame to their families and hence have even less chance of marriage by doing something that might be considered "wrong" by some people, such as talking to men etc.[424] As a consequence women became more vulnerable and more dependent on their male family members. At the same time increasing numbers of women needed to survive independently, because they lost their husbands, sons, brothers and fathers in the wars,[425] with eleven per cent of Iraqi households headed by women in 2008.[426] It followed that women were often stuck in their houses, especially when violence on the streets started to rise. A lack of security, whether it is through police or military forces, or because of harassment by their own people, prevent women and children from leaving their houses and makes it impossible for them to lead an ambitious life in the public sphere.[427] The fear of violence results in women not feeling safe enough to take up employment outside their houses or to get involved in political decision making.[428] As an example, women's rights activists such as Yanar Mohamed who founded the Organisation for Women's Freedom in Iraq, received death threats and had to hide in order to protect themselves and their families.[429]

Women have not only suffered violence outside their homes, but domestic violence against women has also risen due to increased unemployment and the high levels of poverty. There is a lack of support for women survivors of violence and a weak legislative framework.[430] Violence against women by their male family members is still widely accepted in Iraq, including the Kurdistan Region, mainly because of prevalent social attitudes, the misinterpretation of religious scriptures and the weak political initiatives. Many women have learned to accept violence as part of being a

---

[423] Ibid.p.751

[424] Ibid. p.752

[425] Al-Jawaheri, *Women in Iraq*, 98.

[426] Nicola Pratt, "Iraqi Women and UNSCR 1325: An Interview with Sundus Abbas, Director of the Iraqi Women's Leadership Institute, Baghdad, January 2011" *International Feminist Journal of Peace* 13(4) (2011): 614.

[427] Nooriahan Akbar, Al Jazeera, "Opinion, Afghan women fight back against harassment" (13.07.2011) http://www.aljazeera.com/indepth/opinion/2011/07/201171113305407580.html (Accessed on 5.12.2011)

[428] Christine Chinkin and Hilary Charlesworth, "Building Women into Peace: the international legal framework" *Third World Quarterly* 27(5) (2006): 941.

[429] UNIFEM, "Iraq"

[430] Pratt, "Iraqi Women and UNSCR 1325," 614.

"righteous woman".[431] As a result of international pressure two family protection departments have been established in Baghdad. They are not active, but they can provide a basis for the future.[432]

On a national level, the situation has not much improved since the American invasion in 2003.

The public perception of gender equality is still highly ambiguous. After 2003, women were also not included in discussions of their security and peacebuilding at a national level.[433]

Even though officials from the US government met with women's groups to hear their views on Iraqi women in post-war Iraq, in practice the needs of women were hardly addressed at the beginning of the occupation. Women were not adequately included in leadership positions and they were not included in post-war reconstruction processes.[434] One of the reasons stated by the US for not further including women in the reconstruction of Iraq was that they did not want to violate Iraqi sensibilities. But as Safia Al-Souhail pointed out, they forced many changes on the country, so it is legitimate to ask why these changes did not adequately include women's rights. It may be argued that by ignoring women, the Coalition encouraged the development of the rule of conservative male authorities.[435] There were not many women included in the discussions concerning the creation of an interim government and ultimately only three women were made part of the interim Iraqi Governing Council in 2003: Aqila al-Hashimi, who was later assassinated, Sondul Chapouk and Raja Habib al-Kuzaai.[436] The following interim government of 2003-2004 comprised 31 ministers, of which only five were women.[437]

The 2005 Iraqi Constitution prescribes that 25 per cent of parliamentary seats must be occupied by women.[438] The success of this quota could be seen by the fact that

---

[431] Ibid.p.613
[432] Ibid.p.615
[433] Marjorie Lasky, *Iraqi Women under Siege* (CODEPINK/ Global Exchange 2006) 7.
[434] UNIFEM, "Iraq"
[435] Lasky, *Iraqi Women under Siege,* 11.
[436] UNIFEM, "Iraq"
[437] Fischer-Tahir, "Competition, cooperation and resistance," 1384.
[438] See Article 49(4) of the Iraqi Constitution 2005

in January 2005 women won 31 per cent of parliamentary seats. However when the government was formed there were only six female ministers out of thirty-six. Additionally at the drafting of the Constitution only nine women were included out of fifty-five members and only two women became part of the committee for constitutional amendments. In the parliament elected in December 2005 the percentage of women elected fell under 25 and only four women were appointed ministers.[439] Today the Council of Representatives for Iraq has 82 out of 325 seats occupied by women, which is 25.2 per cent which might arguably be less if the quota did not exist.[440] While the introduction of a women quota can be seen as a success, the constitution is nevertheless far from inclusive, which arguably results of the unequal representation at its creation. When the Iraq Constitution was drafted only a few women were part of the committee in charge and most of those women were conservative Shi'a from the United Iraqi Alliance. As a consequence secularist female activists' voices were hardly heard and their ideas scarcely incorporated.[441]

It was noted by women activists that because of the political bargaining between the male party leaders in parliament the support for women's quota in the 2009 elections for national as well as provincial council nominations had been watered down. Compared with party interests, women's rights are not seen as important anymore.[442]

In principle, opportunities for women's inclusion and gender equality are present. Iraq, and thereby also the Kurdistan Region, is part of all international human rights conventions, agreements and declarations, including the International Covenant on Civil and Political Rights 1966 (ICCPR), the International Covenant on Economic, Social and Cultural Rights 1966 (ICESCR), UN Security Council Resolution 1325 (2000), adopted by the SC at its 4213th meeting on 31 October 2000 (Res 1325)

---

[439] Pratt, "Iraqi Women and UNSCR 1325," 612.
[440] Inter-Parliamentary Union "IRAQ, Council of Representatives of Iraq" (31 July 2011) http://www.ipu.org/parline/reports/2151.htm (Accessed on 15.09.2011)
[441] Fischer-Tahir, "Competition, cooperation and resistance," 1390.
[442] Enloe, *Nimo's War, Emma's War,* 111.

and the Convention on the Elimination of All Forms of Discrimination Against Women 1979 (CEDAW).[443]

In addition all women in Kurdistan, as in the rest of Iraq, are assured rights under the Iraqi constitution. The preamble states that attention will be paid to women and their rights.[444] The Iraqi constitution further stipulates that all Iraqis are equal before the law not withstanding inter alia their gender[445] and that *"equal opportunities shall be guaranteed to all Iraqis"*[446]. Additionally the State guarantees social and health services[447], especially to women and children, and prohibits *"all forms of violence and abuse in the family, school and society"*[448]. But at the same time the Iraqi Constitution declares that all laws inconsistent with Islam will be invalid,[449] that individuals only have personal privacy as long as it does not contradict public morals[450] and that they *"are free in their commitment to their personal status according to their religions, sects, beliefs or choices"*.[451] Different women's groups have thereby pointed out that the current interpretation of women's rights in Islam by some judges might be disadvantageous to women.[452] In addition the Constitution sometimes contradicts itself[453], and many laws which contradict the Constitution have not yet been repealed.[454] Further, other laws which have been pronounced by the Constitution offer no or little protection in practice[455].[456]

Relative to the national level, women's legal status, as well as their political participation are said to have been improved dramatically in the Kurdistan Region:

---

[443] Draft of the Iraqi Kurdistan Region's Constitution 2009, Article 37
[444] Constitution of Iraq 2005, preamble
[445] Ibid. Article 14
[446] Ibid. Article 16
[447] Ibid. Article 29
[448] Ibid. Article 30
[449] Article 2
[450] Ibid. Article 17
[451] Ibid. Article 41
[452] Chinkin and Charlesworth, "Building Women into Peace," 945.
[453] See for example Article 41 and Article 14
[454] See for example Para 41 of the 1969 penal code and Article 29 of the Constitution
[455] See for example Article 37 on the prohibition of forced labour, slavery, the sex trade and the trafficking in women and children
[456] Freedom House, "Women's Rights in the Middle East and North Africa 2010 – Iraq" (3 March 2010) http://www.unhcr.org/refworld/docid/4b990123c.html (Accessed on 22.2.2012)

Politicians maintain that participation of women in politics as well as the progress towards gender equality is actively encouraged. According to Abubakir Ali (Kurdistan Islamic Union) 48 per cent of the party's members are women. There are women in the leadership committee and women are part of all centres, as well as in the parliament in Kurdistan and in Baghdad. A woman could well become party leader as well as the president of the KRG. The Kurdistan Islamic Union portrays itself as a reformist party which works to improve women's conditions. According to Abubakir Ali the roots of abuse of women in Kurdistan come from the current transitional phase, with its instability and its insecurity, in which the country is in at the moment.[457] Pshtiwan Sadek from the KDP also supports this picture. He states that the KDP is working towards abolishing the social and traditional culture concerning women and the party is developing women's rights. The government is tackling the issue of violence against women, even though he states that this issue is often exaggerated. In addition he underlines the fact that women have equal job opportunities. In Erbil about half of the school principals are women. Women are civil servants, nurses and teachers.[458] According to the politicians equality has already greatly improved and they are working on improving it even more. The extreme nationalists again believe that the Kurdish women are free and equal and have a strong and important role in their own society. They contend that it was due to Arab occupation that the women became unequal. While this might not be the whole truth, it shows that the perception of different people is very dependent on their general ideology. However, as will be seen further below, there is wide agreement that at this moment in time women and men in practice are not equal in Kurdistan although this is changing.

In 2001, the KRG amended articles of the Iraq Personal Status Code and the Iraq Penal Code, to limit polygamy and to enhance criminal responsibility for honour crimes. During the 6th Cabinet, the High Council of Women Affairs was established, together with the Women's Rights' Monitoring Board at the Council of of Ministers, in order to combat violence of women from above. In 2007, several Directorates to Face Violence against Women were established at the Ministry of the Interior, as

---

[457] Simon, "Kurdistan, Women in Iraq"
[458] Ibid.

well as in all major cities of the region. In 2011 a law to combat domestic violence was passed, as part of which specialist judges were appointed and specialist police stations established to investigate domestic violence in the region.[459]

The positive developments, described by the politicians have certainly occurred, but represent only one side of the coin.

The specific legislation deployed to enhance women's position has its focus very much on physical protection, and gender inclusive policies to increase wider social development or to ensure the women's psychological well-being do not yet exist. And the existing legislations are often not implemented well enough, as also recognized by the politicians.[460]

When it comes to the acquisition of power, in 2003 only two of 20 ministers in the Kurdistan Regional Government were women and their public involvement in the Kurdish region was and still is opposed by conservative male political actors.[461] Today (2013) only one of the 21 ministers, including the prime minister, is a woman.[462]

It is for reasons like these that according to many women's rights activists the improvements already achieved for women in Iraq and the Kurdistan Region are only superficial. In practice women are still not truly equal before the law and often lack adequate opportunities to go to court.[463] The Kurdish Human Rights Project is critical that women are unable to seek redress for gender discrimination because it is difficult to get access to remedies due to the social structure and the impact of the conflict.[464] Furthermore it is critical that politicians ignore the struggle for women's rights in favour of the "greater political struggle for Kurds". Women rights

---

[459] Kurdistan Regional Government, "Prime Minister Barzani's speech at launch of campaign to combat violence against women" (26 November 2012)
http://www.krg.org/a/print.aspx?l=12&smap=010000&a=45955 (Accessed on 22.1.2013)
[460] Ibid.
[461] Al-Ali, "Reconstructing Gender," 754.
[462] Ms Asos Najib Abdullah, Minister of Labour and Social Affairs (see: KRG, "Kurdistan Regional Government ministers" (2009) http://www.krg.org/articles/detail.asp?smap=04060000&lngnr=12&rnr=159&anr=32148 (Accessed on 21.2.2012))
[463] Kreutzer, Schmidinger (Hg.), *Irak, Von der Republik der Angst zur bürgerlichen Demokratie?* (Freiburg: Ca Ira-Verlag, 2004) 215.
[464] Kurdish Human Rights Project, *The Role of Women in Civil society, Conflict Prevention, Resolution and Reconstruction* (Helsinki: OSCE Civil Society Forum, 2-3 December 2008) 1.

are seen as secondary, which only need to be addressed later, once everything else is resolved; but this "later" most often never arrives.[465] In addition, as argued below, the actions taken by women, especially when it comes to public efforts in the transformation process, are often not supported and only partially acknowledged.

One example where the differences between theoretical and practical developments can be seen is the issue of domestic violence, including honour killings. While the Kurdistan Regional Government has removed the motive of honour as a mitigating factor in murders, activists interviewed in 2007 complained of an absence of prosecutions for killing female relatives.[466] Accurate statistics on the victims of violence do not exist, despite the interior ministry registering cases reported to the police, and numbers are not reliable, first and foremost because many cases are not reported to the police. For instance, the official number of self-immolations in 2009 was 400, although it is assumed that the real number is much greater.[467]

According to data published in 2005 by the Soran Qadir Coste of Norwegian People's Aid over 50 per cent of both married and unmarried women of Kurdistan state that they have experienced domestic violence.[468] It is said that in the whole of Iraq 59 per cent of women believe that it is justifiable for a husband to beat his wife. The research also showed that the percentage varied widely depending on the region. They ranged from a high of 85 per cent of women, in Dhi Qar to a low of 31 per cent in Sulaimaniya. In Baghdad, 67 per cent of women affirmed that they believed that it is their husbands' right to beat them. Although this variation is likely due to a number of factors, it may point to the success of the awareness campaigns run by different Kurdish organisations since the 1990s.[469]

However improvements cannot be seen in all parts of the region. Women's rights organisations are critical that women and children generally do not get adequate

---

[465] Ibid.p.2

[466] Al-Ali and Pratt, "Between Nationalism and Women's Rights," 345.

[467] Mona Naggar, "Women's Rights in Iraqi Kurdistan: time for a Rethink" (21.3.2011) http://www.ekurd.net/mismas/articles/misc2011/3/state4880.htm (Accessed on 15.11.2011)

[468] Fischer-Tahir, "Competition, cooperation and resistance," 1391.

[469] Ibid. p.1392

support or advice within the traditional structure of Kurdish society. There is substantial control by men, so that women tend not to behave in a way which might not be appreciated. [470] Many women, especially in rural areas, are often totally dependent on their male family members.[471] The percentage of illiterate women in the rural areas of Iraq's North lies at up to 50 per cent, while women in urban areas have a literacy rate of up to 90 per cent, depending on age.[472] There are full legal provisions for gender equality in employment, housing, etc. However, level of equality and freedom allowed to the woman very much depends on the family and social settings. Social pressure discourages women, for instance, living by themselves, getting specific jobs or having relationships before marriage. Only now can women seek to influence public opinion to change these traditions.[473]

To understand the situation many women in the Middle East, including Kurdish women, live in, it is crucial to understand the concepts of shame and honour within the families. The honour of the family, and in particular of its males, depends greatly on the good reputation of its females, which is dependent on their sexual purity. As a consequence contact between the sexes is always seen as potentially bringing shame to the whole family. If a woman in Iraq for example tries to emancipate herself and live apart her husband or seeks to live alone before marriage, she must be ready to fight. It is very likely that all people: family, friends and everybody who means something to her, will refuse to support her and she risks acquiring a bad reputation.[474]

Two very open girls from university explained it as follows:

> *"You have to know that girls are still discriminated even in their families. Boys would rather get computers or iphones or something like that, but girls wouldn't, because they think that they don't need it. Simply everything depends on the family. If you have a good family, you are lucky, if not it is a problem. Really everything in life depends on your family. In Sulaimaniya it is a lot*

---

[470] Simon, "Kurdistan, Women in Iraq"

[471] Flach, *Frauen in der kurdischen Guerilla*, 39.

[472] Inter-Agency Information and Analysis Unit, UNESCO, "Literacy in Iraq Fact Sheet" (September 2010) http://www.iauiraq.org/documents/1050/Literacy%20Day%20Factsheet_Sep8.pdf (Accessed on 5.10.2011)

[473] Freedomhouse, "Iraq"

[474] Simon, "Kurdistan, Women in Iraq"

In general women's positions in society are very dependent on their family's situation. The Kurdish society is clearly a patriarchal society, whether in the tribal, rural or urban social domain. The exercise of this patriarchal power over women depends very much on the social class, the religion, and the political ideology embraced by the family. In Kurdish society, like in many other traditionally patriarchal societies, the broad majority of women receive their status through marriage and motherhood, but not in their own right.[476] For example, while some Kurdish women have been members of parliament in Iraqi Kurdistan, Turkey and Europe since the 1990s, others continue to be violently punished by their husbands and families if they do as little as talk to another man.[477] And while girls and women in the Kurdistan University in Erbil celebrated International Women's Day on March 8, 2008[478], other women would not know that an International Women's Day exists.

When the people themselves were asked in which areas women need more support or help, they generally replied "in all".[479] They complained that the poor do not get enough social support or that it is not accessible.[480] About one third were not satisfied with the women's security situation and believed that more support

---

[475] Interviews AE and AF, Erbil on 09/04/2012

[476] Mojab, *Women of a Non-State Nation,* 104.

[477] Giles and Hyndman (ed.), *Sites of Violence,* 111.

[478] Andrea Boudreaux "International Women's Day" (Arbil, Iraq, March 8, 2008) YouTube http://www.youtube.com/watch?v=4ooRd33Vu8A (Accessed on 7.12.2011)

[479] See e.g. Interview BN, Erbil on 17/07/2012; Interview BO, Erbil on 18/07/2012; Interview AJ, Erbil on 20/04/2012; Interview AK, Erbil on 20/04/2012

[480] Interview AO, Sulaimaniya on 13/05/2012; Interview AW, Sulaimaniya on 01/06/2012

was needed in this area.[481] People with a connection to the West, especially, felt that more needs to be done in the legal area, as for example support for access to courts.[482] By contrast many people from the Kurdistan region did not really consider the legislature or system of courts as part of their life. Improved infrastructure was not considered important by the people. Many people and especially women still do not have a driving license, but have the option of moving around by public transport. In general, the people agreed that a lot has changed positively, especially when it comes to political involvement. Women receive much more support than previously but it is still lacking in many areas.[483] This having been said, it was unclear from where the support was lacking. The people who support the government explained that the lack of support did not come from the regulations or the government itself. It came from different sources which could include the corruption of minor officials or the lack of support by husbands for their wives.[484] The people who opposed the government maintained the exact opposite position.[485]

Clearly the situation of women in Kurdistan at the moment can be described as highly contradictory; a view held by several feminist scholars, such as Nadje Al- Ali. On the one hand the region is opening up and is presented as a success story. Education is flourishing and the number of women at school and university is increasing. At the same time the number of female suicides and honour killings[486] is very high. Domestic violence has increased and is higher than a few decades ago. There are large gaps between urban, middle class women and women from other levels of society as well as women from the country side.[487]

---

[481] See e.g.: Interview AN, Erbil on 03/05/2012; Interview AU, Sulaimaniya on 24/05/2012; Interview BB, Erbil on 24/06/2012

[482] Interview CF, Vienna on 16/11/2012; Interview CJ, Vienna on 28/10/2012

[483] Interview AX, Sulaimaniya on 03/06/2012; Interview AB, Erbil on 03/04/2012; Interview AD, Erbil on 08/04/2012

[484] Interview AP, Sulaimaniya on 18/05/2012; Interview BV, Sulaimaniya on 06/08/2012

[485] Interview AB, Erbil on 03/04/2012; Interview AH, Erbil on 15/04/2012

[486] „Honour Killings" are defined as "Acts of violence, usually murder, committed by male family members against female family members who are perceived to have brought dishonour upon the family" (Human Rights Watch, 2001)

[487] Simon, "Kurdistan, Women in Iraq"

These type of contradictions can be seen in many areas, when applied to the status of women. There are great discrepancies between city and country life as well as between the lives of different families. Women and girls, clothing and behaviour varies greatly; from very open to very conservative. For an outsider it is difficult to assess the exact level of freedom or state of equality women enjoy. While they are attending university and dancing at the Nawroz festival, there are hardly any women on the street after sunset and they are seldom seen on their own. While the government says it is trying to assist all people, the gaps between different segments of the population seem to be increasing rather than decreasing. While richer families and especially families returning from the West, raise their children, including girls, in a Western style, by sending them to international schools, and living in areas resembling European or American cities, girls and women from lower classes lack these opportunities. While individual people may have very open views and be very supportive of women's equality, it is still the general feeling that it is the men who take the lead and who make decisions for the women in their family, as well as society; i.e. it is the men who largely influence what is seen as acceptable and unacceptable for women to do. There are so many influences from all sides, especially through TV, with channels from around the world, through people having more opportunities to travel and through more tourists and returnees gradually arriving in the region. It seems unclear in which direction the development of equality for women will go.

As noted above women in Kurdistan are pushing for and also achieving reforms. However they still have to fight social, political and legal restrictions. Kurdish women are sometimes perceived as more open than the rest of the region, because they do not veil and they are financially better off and hence have to money to dress accordingly. This sometimes hides the fact that there are still many issues which need be addressed. The simple fact of dress does not always represent a woman's social or economic power or her education level. In Kurdistan, Islam is often used as scapegoat when women's inferiority is discussed, especially by the upper classes. However it is often the Islamic parties in government which give women more seats than the secular ones.

Similar perceivable contradictions can be observed in day-to-day life. While women are employed in good positions, many are still restricted in their choice of jobs and are expected to have jobs, which are seen as respectable for women, and allow them to be home by mid-afternoon. At the same time women now have many public places to socialize. For instance, the creation of shopping malls has enhanced the opportunities for women to socialize outside the house. However these are still few, and only suite people from a certain social and financial background. Even though women can be seen more and more in expensive restaurants and bars, there are no places for poorer women to go.

Reasons for this contradiction are inter alia a lack of the practical implementation of announced measures by the government, as well as the lack of certain parts of society to put their theoretical ideas and ideals into practice in their day-to-day life.

In conclusion, the status of women in society in Iraq and the Kurdistan Region has constantly developed and changed, in response to the surrounding political, economic and social situation. The status of today's women in Kurdish society can be said to be at a stage of transformation. It is still unclear which pathways will be taken by society and by the women themselves. The situation of women has improved in sympathy with the general betterment of the region. Nevertheless there is still a lot of work to be done at all levels. Despite the enhanced development of independent women's organisations, and despite the enhanced presence of international communities in Kurdistan since 2003 and the on-going legal improvements, research shows that violence against women at all levels, both domestic and employment is at an alarming level.[488] According to several women's rights activists it is due to religion, tribal practices and "backward" cultural attitudes that women's rights are still hard to realise in practice.[489]

Research shows that this situation cannot simply all be attributed to "society as a whole". When asked if they believed that men and women should be treated equal, nearly everyone replied positively. It has to be remembered that this does not

---

[488] Maamoon Mohammed Alsayid, *Combating Physical Violence Against Women in Iraqi Kurdistan, The Contribution of Local Women's* Organisation (Thesis, Universitetet Tromso, Centre for Peace Studies 2009) 26.
[489] Al-Ali and Pratt, "Between Nationalism and Women's Rights," 345.

mean that everybody truly believes in total equality. However, many also said that they wanted women to be equal in spirit, but not necessarily all have the same roles and functions. The sense of gender equality is very present, more than it is sometimes recognized by activists or officials.

The following three chapters will present a detailed analysis of how the government and decision makers have influenced gender developments in the region during the current transformation process. The analysis will cover the political, economic and social dimensions of these developments and how they are affecting both transformation within society and the building of sustainable peace at both a national and an individual level.

When analysing the different policies deployed, the reactions towards them, as well as their influences, this chapter has shown that several historical region-specific issues have to be considered, which can be summarized as follows:

As indicated in the second subchapter, Iraq and Kurdistan have had a long history of occupation and suppression. Because of this, the people and the country as a whole, need to re-establish or find their own identity. Whenever the situation of a country changes, the values of its people change with it. At the same time, the Kurds have had a very strong feeling of their ethnical identity, because of their separation from the other groups of Kurds in the region and the lack of their own country. The achievement of an independent Kurdistan may therefore be at the forefront of some people's minds when thinking of the issues of conflict and peace.

When it comes to internal change, people's minds today are affected by the lengths of the various conflicts which lasted for over a generation. There is a generation of children and adults who have never known a stable and peaceful time in their life and may therefore not cope well with the new situation. There is residual hatred and distrust between the different groups which exist in the country and who have done so much harm to one another in the past. At times of war, dictatorship and submission, the social values are different from those during periods of democracy, economic prosperity, and personal freedom,[490] which has an influence on what is seen as important at the time of peacebuilding.

In general there is a substantial divide between urban and country life in Kurdistan as in the whole of Iraq. This is especially visible when dealing with education and has to be taken into account when considering the increased participation of women. At the same time there are great difference between the people who have stayed in Kurdistan their whole lives and those who have returned after spending years or decades in exile, and these lead to antagonisms between people of different mind-sets.

When evaluating different people's opinions it is also important to keep in mind their different experiences during conflict. The Ba'athist regime which suppressed many of them was socialist. At first it promoted more openness towards Western values, including the equality between men and women. People who had bad experiences during the time of the regime, might not only turn against those who supported it, but also against the values the regime promoted. Consequently people might rather see a more conservative way of life as the solution, since the socialist alternative brought them destruction.

At the same time, religion is often used as a basis for exercising certain rights or behaviour against women. However religion can also play a very positive part in the development of a region and Islam is interpreted by many to support men's and women's equality. Notwithstanding the different ideas of religion, the role of religion in general is very strong in the development of Iraq, as well as the Kurdistan Region.

Because of the Kurdish ancient tribal culture the people grow up in with a very strong patriarchal tradition. This is not the case in all parts of the world. Domestically Kurds, as well as Arab Iraqis, live in a very divided society where women and men are quite strictly separated. Personal contact in public between men and women who do not have a family relation is not acceptable. This divide in

---

[490] Helmut Klages, *Wertedynamik, Über die Wandelbarkeit des Selbstverständlichen* (Zürich: Edition Interfrom, 1988) 40-45.

the society determines people's thinking as well as their opportunities, since roles are often already set at birth.

America has recently had a great influence on the whole country, which has lead some to strive for Western values, and others to despise them. This might influence moves towards women's empowerment which still seen by many as a product of the West. Many people in the Kurdistan Region feel that they have been left alone by the rest of the world for a very long period of time and therefore want to move away from any Western influence now. However many others try to cooperate with and follow the Western countries, with the aim of making their region internationally acceptable and competitive and of distinguishing themselves from the Arabs in the country.

Finally, true unity amongst the Kurds has never existed, and today's ruling alliance between the PUK and the KDP, might not always be accepted by the local population.

In conclusion it can thus be said that the situation of the Kurdistan Region, just as the situation of any region at a time of conflict transformation, is a complicated one. The possibility of a further conflict is an ever present threat because of the unstable situation in and around the Kurdistan Region, and the elimination of gender inequality as one root cause of the unstable situation inside the region, might be challenging as a consequence of the conflicting influences present. How exactly the government has dealt with this situation in the political dimension will be subject of the following chapter:

IV.   Gender, Women and Politics

"The fate of women is often indicative of the fate of whole societies."[491]

Post-conflict situations provide extraordinary opportunities to set new norms, introduce new laws, engage new leaders and build new institutions.[492] It is a time

---

[491] Al-Ali and Pratt (ed.), *Women and War in the Middle East,* 19.
[492] Addison and Brück, *Making Peace Work,* 104.

when everything is new and everything can be done.[493] It is possible to open up decision making for civil society, to support minorities, the under-privileged and to set the basis for gender balance, by introducing quota systems and by opening up the political sphere for all.

Despite these possibilities, it is a common perception that it is "warriors" taking over once more in the political sphere. From a gender perspective, it is men who negotiate for peace, men who make decisions on future political measures, and men who head the state institutions. While there exist some exceptions, this perception is largely true.

While it should be the focus at a time of transformation to give citizens rights they did not have during conflict[494] and to rebuild an acceptable standard of living for all, it can be seen that there prevails in general a very militaristic approach to peacemaking. This point of view often excludes women from contributing to reconstruction efforts on the rationale that they did not fight in the war. Armed conflict is thereby seen as a temporary breakdown of law and order, and once this "breakdown" is overcome, it is often the aim to return to pre-war conditions, as defined by the men in power.[495] As a consequence, women can hardly be found at the negotiation table after the end of armed conflict, their positions as high level politicians and decision makers are scarce, and while they are involved in grassroots level politics, their influence is often only minimal.

But is this true? Is there truly such a lack of gender balance? What difference would it make if the political sphere were gender inclusive? How is society influenced by enhanced equality at the top? And most importantly, what value does political gender balance, or the lack of it, have for the process of conflict transformation? These and more questions will be addressed in the following pages.

---

[493] Engelhardt, *Starke Frauen für den Frieden,* 147.
[494] Cahn, "Women in Post-Conflict Reconstruction," 344.
[495] Laura Shepherd (ed), *Gender Matters in Global Politics, A feminist introduction to international relations* (London: Routledge, 2010) 172.

Taking up the hypothesis that positive conflict transformation is tightly correlated to gender equality, it is the aim of the following chapter to discuss the influence of different political actions and forces on gender quality in the country, on society and consequently on the positive transformation of peace.

In order to do so, a short introduction will first be given on the current academic and world political views on the issues of gender, women and politics at the time of conflict transformation. This will lead to the specific example of Kurdistan, by focusing on three different types of political activities in the region: peace negotiations, parliamentary activities and grassroots activism.

Within the framework of the three subchapters it will be elaborated how women and gender have been included in the Kurdistan Region's politics, what the current possibilities for the inclusion are, i.e. national and international legislation, as well actions by the officials. The resulting impacts on society, on national development and on the transformation towards peace at a personal level will be reviewed as well as further steps which should be taken.

1.   A Theoretical Overview

"Representation of the world, like the world itself, is the work of men; they describe it from their own point of view, which they confuse with absolute truth" (Simone de Beauvoir)[496]

Today it is widely acknowledged by scholars and political theorists that the inclusion of women and the maintenance of gender equality in political decision making is important at the time of conflict transformation, in order to ensure that the outcomes will underpin positive future development.

As explained by Andrés Pastrana, President of Colombia[497], everybody who is willing to fight for peace is needed, in order to achieve its aim.[498] Individual women

---

[496] Tickner, *Gender in International Relations,* 1.

[497] 1998-2002

[498] Swanee Hunt, interviews with 15 Club of Madrid members on the importance of womens leadership in politics and peace processes, YouTube "Inclusive Security: The Importance of Women's Leadership in Conflict Resolution" (Club of Madrid's 2008 conference on Global Leadership for Shared Societies) http://www.youtube.com/watch?v=NgNgWBiI950 (Accessed on 10.10.2011)

may thereby have distinct resources and capacities,[499] which will be lost if not included in the process. In the words of Eleanor Roosevelt:

> *"Too often the great decisions are originated and given form in bodies made up wholly of men, or so completely dominated by them that whatever of special value women have to offer is shunted aside without expression"* [500]

Suthanthiraraj and Ayo, taking up the point, argued that women, as at least half of a national population, are an important resource which cannot be overlooked. Ignoring their capacities and their abilities in peace building would be counterproductive for their country. [501]

Mark Boyer, Brian Urlacher and others go even further, and argue that an increased number of women at decision making would necessarily bring a new outlook to peace making,[502] because of the different outlooks of men and women, which result from different experiences, as well as different views of their "self" and their position in society.[503] They base this conclusion on the fact that women's and men's lives, as well as the lives of different generations of women, are marked by different experiences which they bring with them at the time of transformation,[504]

This argument was also recognized by the former President of Tanzania, Benjamin Mkapa[505], according to whom women have to be heard, as it is only they who can fully appreciate the impact of political and legal provisions on women; and only through their participation is it possible to have a balanced legislation and implementation.[506] He reasons that women will speak out for their different

---

[499] Judith Gardam and Hilary Charlesworth, "Protection of Women in Armed Conflict" *Human Rights Quarterly* 22(1) (2000): 156.

[500] Tickner, *Gender in International Relations,* 1.

[501] Kavitha Suthanthiraraj and Cristina Ayo, *Promoting Women's Participation in Conflict and Post-Conflict Societies, How Women Worldwide are Making and Building Peace* (Global Action to Prevent War, NGO Working Group on Women, Peace and Security, Women's International League for Peace and Freedom, August 2010) 11.

[502] Mark Boyer et al., "Gender and Negotiation: Some Experimental Findings from an International Negotiation Simulation" *International Studies Quarterly* 53 (2009): 24.

[503] Ibid.p.27

[504] Mary Caprioli and Mark Boyer, "Gender, Violence and International Crisis" *Journal of Conflict Resolution* 45(4) (2001): 505.

[505] 1995-2000, 2000-2006

[506] Hunt, "Inclusive Security".

needs,[507] and may also speak out for other women's rights, which can lead to more general equality in all areas of living, including access to land, loans, elections, etc.[508]

According to Zuckermann and Greenberg, it is a pre-requisite for more economically sustainable and physically secure societies that the violent and dominating power relations, which are commonly associated with masculinity are broken.[509] This can be achieved through the inclusion of women in the political process, as shown by Caprioli and Boyer: By measuring percentages of women in parliament and the number of years that women have had the right to vote, a correlation between gender equality and violence in a country has been observed. As the percentage of women in the legislature increases by 5%, as state is nearly 5 times less likely to use violence against another country or different group of people.[510]

Such statistics are controversial, as it cannot yet be known the type of difference a stronger presence of women in positions of authority would make to the institutions of government and parliament, and in the long run to the country itself. Although the level of women is not yet great enough and has not existed for a long enough time to be certain of its influence, feminist scholars, such as Pankhurst, agree that the existing patterns of masculinity in institutions, as well as in the state as a whole, will not change without the increase of the participation of women as a precondition.[511] Such change could help diminish a country's propensity towards armed conflict.

While the necessity for the general inclusion of women has been supported for some time, feminist scholars have recently introduced a new topic for discussion. For example Al-Ali[512] has pointed out in order to ensure gender equality,

---

[507] Engelhardt, *Starke Frauen für den Frieden,* 63.

[508] Ibid.p.34

[509] Elaine Zuckermann and Marcia Greenberg, "The Gender Dimensions of Post-Conflict Reconstruction: An Analytical Framework for Policymakers" *Gender and Development* 12(3) (2004): 79.

[510] Caprioli and Boyer, "Gender, Violence and International Crisis," 514.

[511] Pankhurst, "The 'Sex War' and Other Wars," 168.

[512] Simon, "Kurdistan, Women in Iraq".

consideration needs to be given not only to the number of women, but also to which women are involved.

As a hypothesis it is proposed that a more inclusive representation at the decision making process during conflict transformation, will lead to a more balanced gender sensitive perspective and in turn to different decisions affecting the general development of the region. They include many issues influencing a woman's individual opportunities, her personal development and standing in society such as security, economic measures, and the rule of law and the building of infrastructure,[513] which will consequently influence women's individual possibilities, and thus their personal development, as well as their standing in society.

The development of increased gender equality thereby is said to not only have an impact on women, but it also influences the general population. They become more sympathetic to equality and develop, as argued by Caprioli and Boyer, a more favourable disposition towards diplomacy and compromise,[514] which will lead to lesser support of using military and violent measures as a first mean to solve conflicts.

It is clearly not sufficient that equality between men and women is appreciated. The equality of all humans, regardless of their religious, ethical or economic background, needs to be recognized, to make it unacceptable to use violence against any group. But as Erik Melander argues the values that define equal relations between men and women, such as respect, are the same values that need to be brought to bear on other relations in societies, such as between political opponents or ethnic minorities.[515]

As a consequence of international lobbying, resolutions, such as the UN Security Council Regulation 1325, were adopted over a decade ago, to publicly acknowledge and support women's and gender inclusion and awareness in conflict

---

[513] Suthanthiraraj and Ayo, *Promoting Women's Participation in Conflict and Post-Conflict Societies,* 17.
Galia Golan, "Viewpoints. The Role of Women in Conflict Resolution" *Palestine-Israel Journal* 11(2) (2004): 93.
[514] Caprioli and Boyer, "Gender, Violence and International Crisis," 509.
[515] Erik Melander, "Gender Equality and Intrastate Armed Conflict" *International Studies Quarterly* 49(4) (2005): 696.

transformation. Nevertheless it has been argued by many feminist scholars, like Suthanthiraraj and Ayo, that there has been unequal progress towards the empowerment of women and their full participation at the time of conflict transformation, especially at the political level,[516] and this has led to a reverse effect on development. This discrepancy between theory and practice will be an issue coming up time and time again throughout this study, and especially in the following subchapteron gender and women in peace negotiations:

A.   Gender and Women in Peace Negotiations

"No approach to peace can succeed if it does not view men and women as equally important components of the solution."[517]

Peace negotiation, understood as discussions with some or all of the conflict parties, whether government or non-government forces, which address armed conflicts, with a view to ending it[518], are used as a tool to initiate the process of peace. The outcome of these negotiations have the capability, if successful, to end the bulk of the existing violence and to build the foundation of positive conflict transformation.

Despite their importance for the whole population, most peace negotiations are not inclusive. While it is in theory agreed on that all parties who have an interest in a peaceful society should sit at the table of such negotiations,[519] this is most often not the case. It is not the representatives of all parts of the popoulation who are leading the negotiations, but rather the former fighters, as it is perceived that parties which have previously used violent tactics and possess weapons are in the best position to end violence.[520]

---

[516] Suthanthiraraj and Ayo, *Promoting Women's Participation in Conflict and Post-Conflict Societies,* 14.

[517] Ambassador John D. Negroponte, United States Permanent Representative to the UN in Cohn, "Feminist Peacemaking," 8.

[518] Christine Bell and Catherine O'Rourke, "Peace agreements or pieces of paper? The impact of UNSC Resolution 1325 on peace processes and their agreements" *International & Comparative Law Quarterly* 59(4) (2010): 950.

[519] Andrew Lavin, "Achieving Peace in Iraq through Negotiations: lessons learned from the Northern Ireland Peace Process" *Ohio State Journal on Dispute Resolution* 24(3) (2009): 578.

[520] Ibid. p.589

"All interested parties" most often focus on political parties, ethnic groups, or religious groups. However women, other representatives from the civil society, minority groups or people from different class backgrounds are hardly considered;[521] forgetting that the outcome of the negotiations should and will influence the whole of society and not just these groups. According to the UN, about 50 per cent of all civil wars since 1990 have ended with peace agreements,[522] but only 2.4 per cent of peace process signatories since 1992 have been women.[523] Considering that it is already during this time of negotiations that the bases of future state structure, legal provisions etc. are laid, which will influence the lives of the whole population of the region affected, it is arguably especially counterproductive to not have women included in negotiations, as sustainable peace can only be achieved when a holistic participation in peace processes is assured.[524]

The widespread ignorance of the consequences of under-representing women in the official peace negotiations and in the drafting committees for peace agreements is difficult to understand. This is especially so given the international focus on the connection between gender equality and world peace, as recognised by many countries through the UN over the better part of the last century.

From its foundation, the UN has been concerned with the elimination of armed conflict and the creation of gender equality. The preamble to the Charter states:

> "We the peoples of the United Nations determined to **save succeeding generations from the scourge of war**, which twice in our lifetime has brought untold sorrow to mankind, and to reaffirm faith in fundamental human rights, in the dignity and worth of the human person, **in the equal rights of men and women** and of nations large and small, and to establish conditions under which justice and respect for the obligations arising from treaties and other sources of international law can be

---

[521] Ann Jordan, "Women and Conflict Transformation: Influences, Roles, and Experiences" *Development in Practice* 13(2/3) (2003): 241.

[522] Christine Bell, *On the Law of Peace, Peace Agreements and the Lax Pacificatoria* (Oxford: Oxford University Press, 2008) 27.

[523] Centre for Humanitarian Dialogue, Vimeao, "Women in peacemaking – Africa" http://vimeo.com/8078047 (Accessed on 9.12.2011)

[524] Buchanan (ed.), *Women at the Indonesian peace table,* 8.

> *maintained, and to promote social progress and better standards*
> *of life in larger freedom [...]",*[525]

The commitment to equal rights between men and women was reaffirmed in Article 2 of the Universal Declaration of Human Rights from 1948, which stipulated a prohibition of discrimination on the basis of a distinction of any kind, including sex.

More recently, the UN, through Resolution 1325, expressed the need for women's inclusion in all levels of peace-building, by

> "Reaffirming *the important role of women in the prevention and resolution of conflicts and in peace-building, and* stressing *the importance of their equal participation and full involvement in all efforts for the maintenance and promotion of peace and security, and the need to increase their role in decision-making with regard to conflict prevention and resolution."*[526]

While the introduction of the resolution can be seen to having had a positive effect on the inclusion of women in general in peace negotiations, as will be seen below, the scope of inclusion and the increase of gender, as compared to sexual, equality, is deemed unsatisfactory.

Despite the theoretical support of women's inclusion in peace processes practical implementation of the resolution has remained slow, one reason being that there are no monitoring mechanisms in place and no people in place to ensure implementation and accountability. Further the achievement of women's inclusion and gender awareness are still treated as an aspiration rather than a requirement.

Hence while women are still hardly ever seen present at official peace negotiations, they often play an important role in the negotiations on the grass root level. [527] In many cultures, especially indigenous cultures, as in Nepal, the Philippines and many others around the world,[528] it has always been the women

---

[525] Charter of the United Nations 1945, Preamble

[526] UN Security Council Resolution 1325

[527] Sharon Bhagwan Rolls, "Women as Mediators in Pacific Conflict Zones", February 2007
http://www.isiswomen.org/index.php?option=com_content&task=view&id=436&Itemid=207 (Accessed on 14.09.2011)

[528] Stella Tamang, "Peace Teachers: The History of Tamang Women as Conflict Mediators And Why the Human Rights Movement Must Listen to Them" (2004)

who were responsible for the mediating and resolving of conflicts. These have included armed conflicts, as in the Pacific Islands (Fiji, Papua New Guinea and the Solomon Islands) where the mediation processes seldom extended beyond the grassroots level.[529]

As stipulated by many Kurds, also in Kurdistan, it was the women who had the role of resolving conflicts in society, especially in the past when the Kurds still lived in a more rural structure.[530] Concerning the current role of women in conflict resolution, opinions amongst the population are split between those who strongly believe that women should have a role "in everything", and those who believe that women had or have no role in the resolving of conflicts. However, the vast majority considered that women in general should contribute to negotiations. As will be shown below, parts of the Kurdish female population have been very active in contributing to peace and advancing women's rights at during the current conflict transformation even if such contributions are not fully recognised by society.[531] Despite their acknowledged capabilities, and their efforts to have their voices heard, women in Kurdistan, as in other regions, were mostly ignored once the peace negotiations reached an official level.

This lack of involvement and its consequences will be discussed in the following sections. Particular attention will be paid to the negotiation processes involving the Kurdistan region namely: the Washington Agreement, the Helsinki Project and the current negotiations between Erbil and Baghdad.

1.   Women's Involvement in Negotiations

Over the previous 20 years there has arguably been substantial progress in advancing women's participation in official peace building, although the process still remains slow. There is a growing literature on the necessity of women's participation, women are slowly being selected for peace building positions in the

---

http://www.culturalsurvival.org/publications/cultural-survival-quarterly/nepal/peace-teachers-history-tamang-women-conflict-mediator (Accessed on 14.09.2011)

[529] Rolls, "Women as Mediators in Pacific Conflict Zones"

[530] See e.g.: Interview AD, Erbil on 08/04/212

[531] Interview AF, Erbil on 09/04/2012; Interview AG, Erbil on 09/04/2012; Interview AY, Sulaimaniya on 04/06/2012

UN and other international and regional organisations, and a number of conflict-ridden countries have started to acknowledge women's right to input. Further, organisations such as the Center for Humanitarian Dialogue (HDC), work aim to increase the participation of women in peace processes and to include gender issues in the substantive discussions, by creating networks of female negotiators and mediators in Africa and Asia.[532]

The different efforts have borne fruit, for instance in several African States, such as Burundi, Guinea, Sierra Leone and Liberia, where women actively tried to contribute to the peace process.[533] Further, women have been an important force in initiating peace agreements in Liberia, where they participated in the Akosombo Peace Talks, as well as in Rwanda,[534] the Philippines[535] and many other countries. Women were also represented in the peace talks on Afghanistan in Bonn in 2001[536].

The increase of women's representation in the Kurdistan Region's negotiations in its recent history, has not been so successful.

While there is not yet an official peace agreement between the Kurdistan autonomous region and Baghdad or between the different Kurdish fractions, negotiations have taken place over the last decades, including the Washington Agreement and the Helsinki Project. Such initiatives are continuing with the aim of finding lasting solutions between the leaders of Erbil and between Erbil and Baghdad.[537]

---

[532] Center for Humanitarian Dialogue, *Promoting gender issues in peace negotiations.*

[533] Bouta and Frerks, *Women's Roles in Conflict Prevention, Conflict Resolution and Post-Conflict Reconstruction,* 34.

[534] Center for Humanitarian Dialogue, *Promoting gender issues in peace negotiations,* 48.

[535] Centre for Humanitarian Dialogue, Vimeao, "Women at the Peace Table - Nepal Roundtable meeting Sept 2010" http://vimeo.com/16426911 (Accessed on 9.12.2011)

[536] Valentine Moghadam, "Patriarchy, The Taleban and politics of Public Space in Afghanistan" *Women's Studies International Forum* 25(1) (2002): 29.

[537] See: Nick Williams, Los Angeles Times, "Kurdish leaders, Baghdad hold political talks WAR IN THE GULF" (21 April 1991) http://articles.baltimoresun.com/1991-04-21/news/1991111053_1_baghdad-kurdish-saddam-hussein (Accessed on 4.5.2012)
Investors Iraq, "High-level Kurdish delegation to visit Baghdad to resolve the crisis file and Kirkuk oil" (6 August 2008) http://www.investorsiraq.com/archive/index.php/t-81206.html (Accessed on 3.5.2012)

The current negotiations between Baghdad and Erbil generally involve representatives from the main political parties, including, from time to time, representatives from the opposition.[538] However representatives from other segments of society are excluded in the official negotiations, as are women. The stance taken by the KRG when it comes to putting together negotiation teams seems to align with the traditional view outlined at the beginning of this chapter, namely that it is the old fighters, or the male politicians in general, who are in the best position to "build peace". Considering that the percentage of female politicians in the KRG is constantly increasing there seems no obvious reason why women should not also be included in negotiations, especially considering the advantages outlined above. It would appear that the decision makers consider that issues raised at the negotiations not to require a specific gender input. They thereby fail to consider the potential consequences to their region of allowing a one-sided view to dominate the outcomes of their negotiations.

But the absence of more balanced presence in negotiations is not only due to the KRG itself, as gender equality was not only absent in negotiations within the region, but also when help from outside was sought. At the Washington Agreement, which was signed by representatives of KDP and PUK, and which was mediated by the US, no women were present. [539]

In addition, at the Helsinki Project, in which Iraq's main parties to the conflict tried to solve their differences with support from outside no women were present. This is

Alsumaria News, "Shoresh: Interview Kurdish delegation in Baghdad was a preliminary agreement to defer consideration of the contentious points" (18 June 2010) http://onedinar.forumotion.net/t17426-shoresh-interview-kurdish-delegation-in-baghdad-was-a-preliminary-agreement-to-defer-consideration-of-the-contentious-points (Accessed on 4.5.2012)
Ako Muhammed, "Problems with Baghdad are on the table" (29 October 2011)
http://www.kurdishglobe.net/display-article.html?id=314A361429F26BAE682565C7423632C3 (Accessed on 3.5.2012)
KRG.org, "President Barzani receives senior Iraqi officials for talks" (30 April 2012)
http://www.krg.org/articles/detail.asp?rnr=223&lngnr=12&smap=02010100&anr=43764 (Accessed on 4.5.2012)
[538] KRG.org, "President Barzani receives senior Iraqi officials for talks"
PUKmedia, "Kurdish delegation in Baghdad soon to discuss Separated Area" (3 October 2011)
http://northerniraq.info/forums/viewtopic.php?f=1&t=7608#p57349 (Accessed on 3.5.2012)
Alsumaria News, "Shoresh: Interview Kurdish delegation in Baghdad was a preliminary agreement to defer consideration of the contentious points"
[539] Mahmoud Osman, "The Washington agreement, the negotiations, the implementation and its prospects" (1 May 2001) http://kurdmedia.com/article.aspx?id=8013 (Accessed on 8.5.2012)

despite the fact that the smaller political parties were included, to ensure representation from the different fractions in Iraq, including Sunnis, Shias, Kurds, Turkmen, as well as Assyrians.[540] Delegates met twice near Helsinki (in 2007 and 2008), and in Baghdad in 2009 to discuss "The Helsinki Agreement & The Future of Kirkuk",[541] and at none of the meetings women were present.

It is noteworthy that the Helsinki Agreement was led by senior representatives from Northern Ireland as well as South Africa to share their insights from similar peace processes.[542] Nevertheless gender was not taken into account despite the fact that the Northern Ireland Women's Coalition (NIWC) had formed part of the negotiations to the Good Friday Agreement, and it is agreed, in retrospective, that the benefits that Northern Irish women gained in the aftermath of the struggle, would not have been possible if they had not been present at the negotiations.[543]

Further, it is notable that there was not one woman appointed to the nine member committee, charged in 2004, with drafting the interim constitution of Iraq and only 9 of 55 members of the final drafting committee were women.[544]

Finally in the Kurdistan Region, the general perception holds true that it is the 'old warriors' who retain power, rather than shared arrangements with new parties, and a more representative cross-section of the population, no matter who sets up the negotiations.

Interestingly, even though research shows that women were not represented in Kurdistan's delegations in negotiations, many of the interviewees among the general population had a different perception. When asked, whether women already participated in peace negotiations or more generally in official peace building efforts, the answer was very quickly yes, but when it came to naming

---

[540] Iraq Helsinki Project, "Invited Parties" http://iraqhelsinkiproject.org/Default.aspx?pageId=500702 (Accessed on 11.5.2012)

[541] Iraq Helsinki Project, "Background" http://iraqhelsinkiproject.org/Default.aspx?pageId=500694 (Accessed on 11.5.2012)

[542] Lavin, "Achieving Peace in Iraq through Negotiations," 576.

[543] Ibid.p.595

[544] Enloe, Nimo's War, Emma's War, 121.

some of these women, the people were unable to do so.[545] It is possible that they tended to reply positively on questions concerning the inclusion of women within their region, as to present a positive picture of their homeland to the European researcher. However is more likely that the increased presence of women in regional politics and the generally positive attitude towards the inclusion of women at all levels has lead to a misguided public perception of the extent of balanced representation at negotiations on a national level. It would appear that while knowledge of the matter is limited, the people at large believe that women are included in the process.

It is argued that the real lack of women's participation has serious implications on the region's future. Having only men at the negotiating table poses the question of how representative the negotiators really are of the whole population and if the outcome of the negotiations will adequately meet their hopes and expectations. The sole inclusion of former fighters in peace negotiations might be useful in putting an immediate end to a violent struggle. However women's participation in the negotiations is crucial for the future balanced development of the country as a whole.[546] Clearly those present at the talks and negotiations and the interests they promote, will have a significant effect on how the future of the country will be shaped and whether the peace will be sustainable.[547] In Kurdistan today, the descendants of the old warriors are in power. As the public demonstrations in 2011, as well as interviews with the people, showed, not everybody is happy about the existing political landscape and a shift in the population's political support, as well as a possible uprising are predicted by several scholars in the West.[548] Further, improvements in legislation affecting women and increases in their level of participation have taken place, but full gender inclusion has still not occurred. Arguably, these trends could have been have been counter-acted had the processes of negotiation been gender inclusive and involved civil society .

---

[545] See e.g.: Interview BR, Erbil on 22/07/2012; Interview CK, Vienna on 20/10/2012; Interview AA, Erbil on 03/04/2012

[546] Enloe, *Nimo's War, Emma's War,* 590.

[547] Kvinna till Kvinna Foundation, *Building Security,* 38.

[548] Schmidinger and Hennerbichler at the meeting of the Austrian society of Kurdish Studies in June 2012.

As noted above, the negotiations for peace agreements between warring parties define the power relations and identify priorities for action immediately after the conflict. It follows that if peace agreements are merely negotiated between traditional military regimes, they will dominated by the ideas of these military regimes, including most likely a traditional gender regime,[549] which mitigates against the development of full equality in the country. From this idea it follows that the higher the percentage of men in negotiation teams, the more male-dominated will be the vision of post-war society incorporated into the agreements.[550] Such one-sided agreement, will rarely contribute to a just society.[551] It can be argued that this happened in Kurdistan, where the representation at the negotiations was hugely unequal. As shown through different interviews in this thesis, people, are still largely unhappy with the progress towards equality within society. Although improvements have occurred, they not go far enough. While it is possible to argue that gender inclusive peace negotiations would not be the whole solution to these problems, they would have been a first step in the right direction; a step which was not taken.

Arguably, if women had been involved in the political process, they might have been able to introduce strategies which engender widespread support from other women and consequently change the social outlook. However, this view is not shared by all. Sumie Nakaya argues from the example of Guatemala and Somalia, that the inclusion of women in the peace process does not bring any structural changes. She shows that despite the inclusion of Guatemalan and Somali women in the peace negotiations, women in both countries are still sidelined and gender equality has not been achieved.[552]

Nevertheless, when women were part of the official negotiations, a pattern could be observed in the issues they sought to have included in the peace agreement. These issues included the establishment of rights for women to own property and

---

[549] Al-Ali and Pratt (ed.), *Women and War in the Middle East,* 18.

[550] Azza Karam, "Women in War and Peace-building, The Roads traversed, the challenges ahead" *International Feminist Journal of Politics* 3(1) (2001): 9.

[551] Center for Humanitarian Dialogue, *Peacemaking in Asia and the Pacific,* 16.

[552] Sumie Nakaya, "Women and gender equality in peace processes: from women at the negotiating table to postwar structural reforms in Guatemala and Somalia" *Global Governance* 9(4) (2003)

to receive inheritance, the creation of a system to penalise perpetrators of gender-based crimes, a specific quota for the inclusion of women in politics, actions to support the return of displaced women, assurances of equal treatment for men and women as well as the upholding of women's rights through statutes.[553] It may be argued that since these issues are exclusively the concern of women, they would not have seen as very important by male negotiators or even raised. This appears to be the case in the Kurdistan Region.

At the same time it needs to be acknowledged that even if a woman takes part in the negotiating process, she may still not advocate gender issues. The mere inclusion of women in the discussions will not guarantee that a gender inclusive approach will be taken. Not all women are sensitive to women's issues, or would help other women, just because they are women.[554] It follows that there is the need to include a much higher number of women in peace process, including women who speak out for gender issues.[555] Gender expertise requires specific experiences and skills, which are needed in the process, and which can be provided by women as well as by men.[556] Practical experience, for instance from the Center for Humanitarian Dialogue, shows that it is crucial to include gender awareness groups, women and/or men, who are sensitive to women's and gender issues.[557]

For peace agreements to be truly successful in the long run, they must reflect the aspirations of society as a whole, including those of women from different political parties.

As Andrew Levin rightly remarks, true benefits and national reconciliation in any society will only be achieved if negotiations are "fully inclusive". All people need to have an input in the transformation of their country, as this makes it possible to influence the development of the country or region as a whole, as well as the

---

[553] Ibid.

[554] Center for Humanitarian Dialogue, *Peacemaking in Asia and the Pacific,* 31.

[555] Ibid.

[556] Center for Humanitarian Dialogue, *Meeting report,* 17.

[557] Center for Humanitarian Dialogue, *Peacemaking in Asia and the Pacific,* 31.

development of the different people and groups of society individually.[558] Full inclusion is thus of crucial importance at the time of negotiations. And this includes women.

This view was shared by the majority of the Kurdish interviewees. Most of the people indeed stated that the involvement of more women in official peace talks would make a positive difference.[559] While many were unable to state a reason why, in their opinion, it would make a difference, and some were uncomfortable speaking about it[560], which raised the question if all of them truly believed that an increased participation of women is indeed necessary, others, especially the ones who were highly interested in politics, stated a variety of reasons why women should be present at the region's negotiation tables. The arguments for women's involvement thereby overarched any religious, social, age or sexual differences:

A 23 year old female student from a very religious family explained that in her opinion there is no doubt that more women need to be involved in official peace talks, in order to break the cycle of an exclusive "male society", and to work against patriarchy.[561] A 50 year old blacksmith added that, through inclusive participation, women *"can show that they have also got something to say"*.[562] And another student stated that women have to be involved simply to show them respect, for their role in society and for everything they have done until now;[563] women's inclusion thereby being used further the interests of women throughout the region, to make them more visible and to push them away from their traditional roles.

Additionally, a range of people, including teachers, politicians and NGO workers, were of the opinion that women are able to drive negotiations forward. They believe that women have more understanding for the emotional needs of other

---

[558] Lavin, "Achieving Peace in Iraq through Negotiations," 585.

[559] See e.g.: Interview BR, Erbil on 22/07/2012; Interview BK, Erbil on 12/07/2012; Interview BV, Sulaimaniya on 06/08/2012; Interview AJ, Erbil on 20/04/2012

[560] Interview BE, Erbil on 26/06/2012; Interview BG, Erbil on 02/07/2012; Interview BI, Erbil on 08/07/2012; Interview BJ, Erbil on 09/07/2012

[561] Interview BV, Sulaimaniya on 06/08/2012

[562] Interview BN, Erbil on 17/07/2012

[563] Interview BW, Sulaimaniya on 08/08/2012

women[564] and are better in solving "women's problems", which would improve the situation for women over the region, "*since there do not only exist male problems on this earth*".[565] Still others expressed the view that it is easier for women to have empathy[566] and that are more polite at talks[567] or that they are calmer than men[568], which would be positive in negotiations. Some interviewees considered that women think differently and forgive quicker than men and hence reconstruction would move forward more quickly. The inclusion of women in the peace talks would change the dynamics of the negotiations because men behave differently if women are in the room.[569] As explained by an old lady, it would be much better for women to be involved, since "*women would work for women, since men solely work for men*".[570]

However, not all interviewees agreed that positive change is possible. A more pessimistic view came especially from several educated middle-aged men, who were of the opinion that women's inclusion would not make any difference, since society itself is far too focused on men[571] and that it is firstly necessary to radically change society itself, which already has to start in Kindergarten, in order to produce a new culture which will then allow for women to assume positions of power and to also have influence therein.[572] The men thereby did not believe that the further inclusion of women in the peace talks might actually start this "culture of change".

The only person who openly stipulated that women should not be involved in peace talks was one village man, who was very much in favour of women's equality within their family, but who believed that there are certain things in Kurdish society which women cannot do by themselves and for which it is better to have men.[573]

---

[564] Interview AJ, Erbil on 20/04/2012
[565] Interview CI, Vienna on 26/10/2012
[566] Interview CK, Vienna on 20/10/2012
[567] Interview BQ, Erbil on 21/07/2012
[568] Interview BR, Erbil on 22/07/2012
[569] Interview CJ, Vienna on 28/10/2012
[570] Interview CD, Vienna on 21/10/2012
[571] Interview AN, Erbil on 03/05/2012
[572] Interview BK, Erbil on 08/07/2012
[573] Interview BS, Erbil on 24/07/2012

The majority of the Kurdish population consequently follows the traditional feminist position, namely that in general women should be included. However, it is not necessary to have specific requirements or target gender equality or class inclusion. This might reflect the fact that no women have until now participated in high-level negotiations. Hence, it is necessary as a first step to think about the concept of inclusion, before proceeding to the next step and consider gender equality.

Despite the fact that women are lacking from negotiations in practice, it would appear that many people are in favour of women's equal participation, and are aware of the benefits that such participation would bring to the region. That these ideas are not being implemented in practice, arguably leads to a loss both in potential national development, and an opportunity to increasing women's standing within society. Given the potential beneficial impact on development in the region and on society, and given the general support within the population it seems surprising that the KRG has refrained from including women in peace negotiations. Had the KRG had already invited women take their place at the negotiation table, the region would now be one step closer to achieving true gender balance within negotiations and the consequential benefits outlined above.

We cannot yet quantify what impact a significant percentage of women at peace negotiations, such as 40 or 50 per cent, might have, since it has never happened and the impact of the few women who had been involved in peace talks is questionable, since their influence was not great enough.[574] Therefore it is only possible to surmise what influence women might have had. Considering the arguments by Suthanthiraraj, Ayo, Bayer, Urlacher and Hunt elaborated above,[575] namely that women are needed in political decision making as an individual resource, that women can bring a new outlook to peace building through their different experiences and that women's participation will most likely result in a more balanced legislation, which will be beneficial to civil society, it may be

---

[574] Center for Humanitarian Dialogue, *Peacemaking in Asia and the Pacific,* 12.

[575] Suthanthiraraj and Ayo, *Promoting Women's Participation in Conflict and Post-Conflict Societies,* 11.
Caprioli and Boyer, "Gender, Violence and International Crisis," 505.
Hunt, "Inclusive Security"

concluded that the KRG and the people in power, have passed over a chance for national and personal development for their people. Further, it seems self-evident that the earlier the positive transformation is started, the earlier the benefits will be seen. Consequently, even if the lack of gender consideration at the early time of negotiations does not set society back, it results in another lost opportunity to work for positive peace, and could prolong the conflict.

However, choosing the make-up of the negotiating teams is only one way of controlling the impact of the outcomes on society and on the region as a whole. The other way, which is more likely, but not necessarily under the control of the people at the negotiations, is through the contents of the ratified negotiation agreement:

2.   Gendering the Contents of Agreements

The impact of the enhancement of gender inclusion on agreements reached during the negotiations depends as much on qualitative factors as on quantitative numbers.

Apart from not being present in person at the peace negotiations, 'women', in the sense of gender considerations within the negotiated documents, are also seldom included in the peace agreements themselves resulting in the loss of opportunity to fight underlying issues of discrimination in society's structure. As elaborated by feminist scholars, such as Antonia Potter, peace agreements need to be written in a "gendered way". The word "women" has to be included, as the words used in the peace agreement will later either shut off or open up vital spaces for the implementers.[576]

The inclusion of women's issues in peace agreements can be the starting point for achieving general legal and political gains for women.[577] Since a peace agreement often has the status of a quasi-constitution or is even the basis for a future constitution, it is vital for future development that the document include rights for

---

[576] Antonia Potter, *Opinion, G is for Gendered: taking the mystery out of gendering peace agreements* (Geneva: Center for Humanitarian Dialogue, April 2011) 16.
[577] Bell and O'Rourke, "Peace agreements or pieces of paper," 946.

and concerning women.[578] But rather than considering gender issues, as it is "called upon" by the international community, through Resolution 1325,[579] the contents of peace agreements often focus solely on issues such as disarmament and demilitarisation, while ignoring or down playing other issues which pose equal threats to civilians. Specifically measures concerning women and security are often considered "fine tuning"[580], overlooking the fact that the contents of the peace agreement will have a lasting effect on the future governing of the country.

It has been observed that the lack of the consideration of gender issues and women's roles in societies in peace agreements often results in a loss for the future development of the country, as well as in a loss of possibility to increase gender equality. As observed by Swanee Hunt, former US Ambassador to Austria, a reason for the failure of the Dayton Peace Agreement in Yugoslavia in 1994 was the lack of women's involvement in the negotiations, as well as the lack of consideration of the general, as well as gender related impact of the agreement on society. The limited mind-set that the men brought to the table, most of whom were soldiers with no legitimacy as peacemakers, led to further problems for the population,[581] which could have been avoided by including a balanced representation of society. This was also recognized by Mr Zlatko Lagumdzija, Prime Minister of Bosnia and Herzegovina,[582] who developed the view, from his experience with the Dayton Agreement, that the outcome of peace agreements, would be better for everyone, if a true representation of society were involved in their negotiation including fifty per cent women.[583]

Similar mistakes have been made all around the world. A quantitative and qualitative assessment of several of the world's peace agreements' references to women, as conducted by Christine Bell and Catherine O'Rourke, shows that only an average of 16 per cent of all peace agreements contain references to women,

---

[578] Ibid.p.948

[579] Resolution 1325: *"Calls on all actors involved, when negotiating and implementing peace agreements, to adopt a gender perspective."*

[580] Agneta Soderberg Jacobson, Kvinna till Kvinna Foundation, *Security on whose terms? If men and women were equal* (Stockholm: 2009) 16.

[581] Swanee Hunt, "The Critical Role of Women Waging Peace" *Colum. J. Transnat'l L.* 41 (2002-2003): 560.

[582] 2001-2002

[583] Hunt, "Inclusive Security".

although this number has increased from 11 to 27 per cent since the passing of Res 1325. However while the quantitative assessment of peace agreements confirms a positive development, the qualitative assessment shows that the references to women are often poor in quality, sometimes contravening CEDAW provisions and only rarely illustrating good practice.[584] The assessment showed that most agreements which mentioned women did so in the context of women as victims, as well as women in politics. Only a few mention women in a legal context or specifically provide for the promotion of women's organisations and infrastructure.[585]

In the case of the principal agreements reached between the two main parties in the Kurdistan Region, as well as agreements between Erbil and Baghdad, not even the above mentioned inclusions can be found.

The main provisions of the Washington Agreement of 1998 between the KDP and the PUK included the formation of an interim joint government, the normalization of main towns, to the equal development of the PUK and the KDP areas and the end of the PKK presence as well as that of the Iraqi forces. The vagueness of the different clauses, as well as continued disagreement between the parties made the implementation of the agreement difficult. As with other peace agreements, the Washington Agreement merely involved the two conflicting parties. There were no other Kurdish parties or people involved, which meant that no other view points from the Kurdish society were represented and many issues of potential importance to the civil population and might have even solved certain matters, were not heard.[586] There was not a single clause within the agreement dealing with gender relations or any other aspect of social development.

The same is true of negotiations between Kurdistan and the rest of Iraq. Three main topics were raised time and time again between the two forces: Oil and gas law; the implementation of Article 140 of the Iraqi Constitution, which concerns the resettlement of displaced persons, as well as the people's right to determine their

---

[584] Bell and O'Rourke, *Opinion*, 7.

[585] Ibid.pp.10-14

[586] Osman, "The Washington agreement, the negotiations".

own national and ethnic affiliation, especially when it comes to Kirkuk, and finally issues concerning the Peshmerga forces.[587] While other topics, such as the provision and delivery of basic required services for all citizens, were discussed in the negotiations,[588] the above named issues certainly took priority. As with the Washington agreement, gender was not considered in any way.

Again the Helsinki Agreement, which was drafted as a consequence of the Helsinki Project and aimed to define *"general principles of joint national action"*, did not include the issue of gender. While the agreement ensures the commitment to peaceful negotiations, and to opposing international interference, respecting human rights and ensuring participation and equality of all, it thereby merely focuses on sectarian, ethnic and political differences, but not on gender.[589]

As explained above, the lack of gender consideration at this early stage of conflict transformation is likely to have had an aversive effect on the region's subsequent development, even though it cannot be proven. One indication of a detrimental development in the Kurdistan Region is that a more extensive adoption of gendered legislation only began in recent years, more than a decade after the establishment of the "safe haven".

It follows from the arguments above that the Kurdistan Regional Government, as well as political parties or in general parties to conflict, would be well advised to consider enhanced gender inclusion in future agreements, in order to ensure representation of the whole of society and to enhance the possibility of positive conflict transformation within society.

It must be conceded that the lack of gender inclusion in negotiations does not seem to be detrimental to the region's standing within the international community, as in truth other members of the international community do not put a great

---

[587] Zia Sharifi, "Kurdish lawmaker: Our delegation will visit Baghdad soon to discuss the implementation of the Convention on the remaining Arbil" (23 November 2011)
http://www.investorsiraq.com/archive/index.php/t-164761.html (Accessed on 3.5.2012)
Muhammed, "Problems with Baghdad are on the table".
Investors Iraq, "High-level Kurdish delegation to visit Baghdad to resolve the crisis file and Kirkuk oil".
[588] KRG.org, "President Barzani receives senior Iraqi officials for talks".
[589] Iraq Helsinki Project, "Helsinki Agreemen t" (28 April 2008)
http://iraqhelsinkiproject.org/Default.aspx?pageId=500699 (Accessed on 1.3.2012)

emphasis on the inclusion of women. However, the author argues that there is likely to be a slowing of positive gender development within society, as negotiated agreements can provide an impulse for future progress.

At the same time, it cannot be forgotten that, while reaching an agreement on specific factors might mark the initial point for an official end to the conflict, it does not resolve all problems. New procedures must be put in place and new institutions established in order to assure that the peace accords are observed and that on-going social tensions and inequalities will be mitigated. In order to achieve this, the work for peace, which includes the recognition of diverse social identities and their capacities, has to be integrated into the development of the state.[590] One way of doing so is by fully including representatives of all society in high level politics, including parliament:

B.   Gender, Women and Parliament

A positive influence from state representatives is vital in all societies, and especially so at a time of peace building, since it is this time, which will be decisive on whether new conflict will erupt, or lasting peace will be achieved.

Through their roles as representatives and their influence on national affairs, members of parliament and other high officials have an important role in developing the state and influencing the lives of its citizens.[591] According to the people interviewed for this study, the majority believed that it is the responsibility of "the government", "the ministries" or "the politicians" to take the primary role in questions of war and peace. Young women and those at university especially, but also many of the more socially disadvantaged people, were of the opinion that the most important drivers of the reconstruction effort had been the politicians. Regardless of whether or not they are feminist or sexist, or even whether or not they support the ruling parties, the people believe that the policy makers are the driving force in the transformation process. They see it as the government's role to

---

[590] Ho-Won Jeong, *Understanding Conflict and Conflict Analysis* (Thousand Oaks SAGE, 2008) 241.
[591] Cynthia Enloe, "Police and Military in the Resolution of Ethnic Conflict" *Annals of the American Academy of Political and Social Science* 433 (1977): 138.

set a new agenda for the achievement of peace building, thus giving the authorities the power to craft the state according to their beliefs or desires.

In the construct of a state, it is the state representatives, who form the structure and "being" of a state. Consequently if the high-level representatives of a nation or region are principally derived from a selected ethnic, social or gender groups, the state institutions will reflect those groups. In terms of gender balance most states today would thus be described as "masculine".[592] While many countries around the world have achieved a substantial percentage of women in parliament, no country has a female representation, reflecting the female percentage of their general population.[593] And there are only two countries in the world have more than fifty per cent women in their parliaments.[594]

Femininity or gender equality are thereby often still not seen as "fitting" a state structure. It is frequently seen as unacceptable to have certain gender relations represented in politics, including open homosexuals and "female" women, and there is only a specific type of person who is accepted in politics.[595] There is only the ones who "fit the picture".[596] As a consequence of this uniform representation, the policies deployed by mainstream politicians will reconstruct certain types of gender relations, which will have a lasting impact on the development of society.

On the other hand if balance and awareness on issues such as gender and ethnicity are achieved at a high political level, they will in the long run be reflected in society. If the state works towards equality for its entire people, notwithstanding sex, social class, ethnicity, religion etc. and if a situation is achieved where people regard themselves as a whole community based on the principles of justice and fairness, violent conflict is unlikely, and the people will be one step closer to positive peace. For this development to occur, it is necessary to move towards

---

[592] Laura Sjoberg, *Gender and International Security, Feminist Perspectives* (London: Routledge, 2010) 38.
[593] As'ad AbuKhalil, "Toward the Study of Women and Politics in the Arab World" *Spring Feminist Issues* (1993): 4.
[594] Rwanda: 56,3% (elections: 2008); Andorra: 53,6% (elections: 2011); see: Inter-Parliamentary Union, "Women in National Parliaments" (31 August 2011) http://www.ipu.org/wmn-e/world.htm (Accessed on 10.10.2011)
[595] Tickner, *Gender in International Relations,* 6.
[596] Ibid.p.37

equality between different social groups in politics, including women in high-level politics. As explained by Moghadam and Sadiqi, the emergence of women as political actors as well as as voters leads to the *engendering* and *feminization* of the public sphere in the country as well as to a *democratization* through the participation of all citizens.[597]

This was also the opinion of several representatives of Kurdistan's civil society. They held the view that progress towards the equality of women in political positions creates more balance in society; and that a society is not able to develop itself and move forward without the involvement of women in all levels, including positions of power.[598]

It will be the aim of the following subchapter to discuss the above theory with reference to the Kurdistan region. Special attention will be paid to if and how enhanced sexual and gender inclusion in parliament influences the development of a more balanced society and the process of conflict transformation.

1.   Supporting Women's Inclusion

The Kurdistan Region today provides the basic framework to enhance sexual equality in decision making positions. In theory all women have the opportunity to become part of the decision-making force and women also have the public support from current male politicians to raise their numbers in high-level politics. But while the support for sexual equality is on the rise, it will be seen that the support for high-level political inclusion does not cover women from all elements of society. Consequently, women are still an unequally represented decision-making force in politics, despite their general inclusion.

As a signatory to the CEDAW, as well as to Resolution 1325, Iraq, and the Kurdistan Region, agreed to

> *"take all appropriate measures to eliminate discrimination*
> *against women in the political and public life of the country and,*
> *in particular, to ensure to women, on equal terms with men, the*

---

[597] Moghadam and Sadiqi, "Women's Activism and the Public Sphere," 3.

[598] See e.g. Interview BL, Erbil on 12/07/2012; Interview BH, Erbil on 05/07/2012; Interview CJ, Vienna on 28/10/2012

> *right [...] to participate in the formulation of government policy*
> *and implementation thereof and to hold public office and perform*
> *all public functions at all levels of government"*[599];

as well as to

> *"ensure increased representation of women at all decision-*
> *making levels in national, regional and international institutions*
> *and mechanisms for the prevention, management and resolution*
> *of conflict".*[600]

These commitments were introduced into national legislation, through the inclusion of Article 20 into the Iraqi Constitution, which stipulates that

> *"Iraqi citizens, men and women, shall have the right to*
> *participate in public affairs and to enjoy political rights including*
> *the right to vote, elect, and run for office."*

More explicitly, women are ensured a minimum of 25 per cent representation as members of the members of the Council of Representatives.[601]

The Kurdistan Region went even further by enshrining in its Draft Constitution that women have a minimum of 30 per cent of seats reserved for them in the elections of the regional parliament, local councils as well as municipalities.[602]

In addition to the fixed quota for female MPs, the Kurdistan Parliament dedicated one of its standing committees to the area of women's rights.[603] The Women's Protection Rights Committee, which was founded in 2005, has eleven female members and is given the opportunity to contribute to policy making through the right to participate in and comment on decisions concerning women in parliament.[604] While the committee gives the women of the region an important platform to lobby for their rights, it does not yet ensure gender inclusion, as the

---

[599] The Convention on the Elimination of All Forms of Discrimination Against Women 1979, Article 7(b)

[600] UN Security Council Resolution 1325

[601] Constitution of Iraq 2005, Article 49

[602] Draft of the Iraqi Kurdistan Region's Constitution 2009, Articles 41(2) and 106(2)

[603] KRG, "The Kurdistan Parliament"
http://www.krg.org/articles/detail.asp?rnr=160&lngnr=12&smap=04070000&anr=15057 (Accessed on 15.10.2012)

[604] Alsayid, *Combating Physical Violence Against Women in Iraqi Kurdistan*, 31.

impact of the committee is limited when it comes to decision making which does not explicitly concern "women".

Furthermore, in 2011, the Supreme Council for Women's Affairs was established with the aim of addressing political, economic, social and cultural rights of women in the region,[605] and in 2012 a new monitoring body to protect women's rights, the Women's Rights Monitoring Board, was created,[606] which has as its aim to bring together representatives of several key ministries, such as the Ministry of Justice, the Interior, Labour and Social Affairs, Planning, Health, Education, Higher Education and Religious Affairs, to coordinate and improve gender politics in the region.[607]

Clearly big steps have been taken in recent years to ensure the enhanced presence of women in parliament, which provides the possibility, as argued by Zuckermann and Greenberg,[608] of initiating the necessary steps towards breaking with the old power relations and incorporating their own outlook into policy. Further, as argued by feminist scholars like Hunt, Posa, Al-Ali or Pratt,[609] measures such as the female quota for political representation is vital to secure long-term goals including opening the way for more women in leadership positions.[610]

Steps have not only been taken at the legal level. Authoritative figures have sought to enhance the public recognition of women's role in high level politics. Recently, well-known politicians have started promoting the idea of women's inclusion in public. As part of this movement, the President of the Kurdistan Region, Masoud Barzani, congratulated women on International Women's Day 2012 and underlined the proposition that the political leaders are defenders of women's rights and promoters of women's participation in political processes and social

---

[605] KRG-DFR, "Swedish rights training programme" (4 October 2011)
http://dfr.krg.org/a/d.aspx?l=12&a=41303 (Accessed on 9.5.2012)
[606] Rudaw, "New monitoring body established to protect women's rights" (13 August 2012)
http://www.krg.org/a/d.aspx?a=45015&l=12&r=73&s=02010200&s=010000 (Accessed on 11.7.2013)
[607] Unrepresented Nations and Peoples Organisation, "Iraqi Kurdistan: Condemning Femicide" (14 September 2012) http://www.unpo.org/article/14855 (Accessed on 03.08.2013)
[608] Zuckermann and Greenberg, "The Gender Dimensions of Post-Conflict Reconstruction," 79.
[609] Swanee Hunt and Cristina Posa, "Iraq's Excluded Women" *Foreign Policy* 143 (2004): 43.
[610] Al-Ali and Pratt, "Women in Iraq," 19.
See also: Heinrich Böll Stiftung, *Gender Politics Makes A Difference,* 13.

development.[611] Also Dr. Fuad Masum, who heads the Kurdistan Alliance bloc in the Iraqi Council of Representatives, announced on International Women's Day that he "*wished women to occupy sovereign position in the Iraqi state in the near future*".[612]

Such statements are criticized by their opponents as being 'mere talking' and as showing off in public rather than implementing in practice.[613] However, based solely the increasing numbers of women in parliament over time, the politicians have kept their promises. Between 1992 and 2005 there were only eight female members of parliament (MPs) out of a total of 111. The number increased to 24 in the second parliament from 2005 to 2009, and in the session of 2011 41 MPs were women, which counts for 37 per cent of the seats.[614]

The support of political actors for the issue also had an impact on society. The supporters of the two main political parties recognise and appreciate the work of their leaders.[615] In particular many highly educated men and women expressed the view that it is important for women to aspire to work in parliament or for politics in general. As explained by a lawyer: "*Women today have an important role in Kurdistan. Their quota of participation is 25% with all the new decisions in the state,*" to which an 18-year old pupil added: "*Today women in Kurdistan work as teachers or lawyers or members of parliaments. Those are their most important roles.*" People from all parts of the political spectrum maintained that their party contributed most to reconstruction. If they wished to be polite, they said that both,

---

[611] PUKmedia, "President Barzani congratulates Kurdistan Women" (9 March 2012) http://pukmedia.co/english/kurdish-women/179-president-barzani-congratulates-kurdistan-women (Accessed on 4.5.2012)

[612] PUKmedia, "Dr. Masum: We wish woman to occupy sovereign position in Iraq" (8 March 2012) http://pukmedia.co/english/kurdish-women/178-dr-masum-we-wish-woman-to-occupy-sovereign-position-in-iraq (Accessed on 4.5.2012)

[613] Interview BW, Sulaimaniya on 08/08/2012; Interview BY, Sulaimaniya on 10/08/2012

[614] The Kurdish Globe, "Statistics suggest women's role is "weak" in government, politics and civil society" (1 October 2011) http://www.kurdishglobe.net/display-article.html?id=9EDBB488AE5FA5A57B17A5F41D521667 (Accessed on 21.2.2012)

[615] Interview AA, Erbil on 03/04/2012; Interview AE, Erbil on 09/04/2012; Interview AM, Erbil on 27/04/2012; Interview BV, Sulaimaniya on 06/08/2012

Talabani and Barzani, did a lot for conflict transformation and social development in the region[616], including working for gender awareness.

On the KDP side, especially Nechirvan Idris Barzani, the grandson of KDP founder Mustafa Barzani and prime minister between 2006 and 2009 and from 2012, was seen especially as the driving force in reconstruction, and in the recognition of women's rights. To underline this point, one man told the following joke:

> *"One man says to another: Before, everything was horrible and my wife could not even leave the house. I did not really like that and I am happy for her to have more freedom now, but it is getting a bit much. Now she is coming home at 2 o'clock in the morning and because of Nechirvan I cannot even ask her where she was..."*[617]

While the joke is without doubt an exaggeration, it is an acknowledgment by Kurdistan society, or part of it, of the political efforts supporting women's issues.

Further actions to place the issue of enhanced gender inclusion on the public agenda included organising and funding various conferences, which put "Kurdish women" in the centre of attention:

In March 2007, a conference was held on *Kurdish Women for Peace and Equality*, which showed the recognition of the importance of the issue by the officials.

In 2009, the ministry of higher education sponsored the World's Women for Life first international women's conference in Erbil. The conference was attended by several high-level politicians, and addressed the difficulties faced by the Kurdistani women's movement.[618]

On 27 and 28 January 2011 a conference was held in Erbil on "*The Role of Women in Peace-Building, Reconciliation and Accountability in Iraq*", which was organised with the support of the Kurdistan Regional Government, the Iraqi Council of Representatives, the Kurdistan Parliament-Iraq and the Government of Italy. The

---

[616] See e.g. Interview BS, Erbil on 24/07/2012; Interview BW, Sulaimaniya on 08/08/2012; Interview CE, Vienna on 21/10/2012

[617] Interview CI, Vienna on 26/10/2012

[618] Soraya Fallah, World's Women for Life, "Press Release Resolution and Suggestion" (29.08.2009) http://www.wwfl.org/Persian/ (Accessed on 16.10.2012)

conference gathered more than 300 political figures, including high-level representatives from Iraq, the Kurdistan Region, the UN, the Arab League, the Organisation of Islamic Conferences as well as international experts from across the world.[619] The recommendations from the conference covered most of the women's issues in the public arena and[620] included commitments for further provisions and regulations for the enhanced involvement of women and for gender equality in the political field.

And in 2012, 200 women delegates met for the second National Conference on Kurdish Women in Erbil, which was organized under the leadership of Amina Zikri MP. The main goal was to *"integrate Kurdish women into Kurdistan's political process"*.[621]

While the holding of these conferences is certainly a positive sign, their effects on the local population are as yet unclear. They are not widely known about by the population, and their contents are subject to criticism. For instance an observer at the 2007 Conference remarked that the conference only reflected a fraction of the women's voices and while it celebrated the achievements of Kurdish women, it did not concentrate on the challenges they faced[622] and there was no place for open and critical debate.[623] Certain issues, such as the side-lining of women's rights in order to receive further political support, were not discussed[624] and consultations with Kurdish women were not sufficiently taken into account.[625]

These criticisms reflected those of several women's activists. They suggest that the government is putting on a show when it comes to women's rights and only allow them, as long as there is no disadvantage to the politicians themselves, or as

---

[619] No peace without justice, "International Conference on "The Role of Women in Peace-Building, Reconciliation and Accountability in Iraq"" (Erbil, 27-28 January 2011) http://www.npwj.org/MENA/International-Conference-%E2%80%9CThe-Role-Women-Peace-Building-Reconciliation-and-Accountability-Iraq%E2%80%9D (Accessed on 1.10.2011)

[620] The subject of women and religion and the state for example could not be brought to a conclusion

[621] Christian Chung, Rudaw, "Conference in Erbil Focuses on Women's Role in Politics" (27.05.2012) http://www.rudaw.net/english/kurds/4780.html (Accessed on 16.10.2012)

[622] Nadeen El-Kassem, "International Conference on Kurdish Women for Peace and Equality, March 8, 2007, Erbil, Southern Kurdistan" *Journal of Middle East Women's Studies* 3(3) (2007): 105.

[623] Ibid.p.106

[624] Ibid.p.107

[625] Ibid.p.108

long as they do not break any boundaries and that the government is not truly caring about gender equality.

Also the higher percentage of female MPs is not seen as wholly positive, as explained by an Austrian political scientist:

> *"There exist a few "token women" in political positions. But they are not independent and nearly exclusively deal with so called "women's issues", as for example social and family matters, but not for example with security subjects. In their self-perception the Kurds believe to be very progressive, but in reality this is not really the case."[626]*

The reality of the 30 per cent quota is sometimes criticised as simply being used as an indicator of the region's model development. This criticism is directed towards politicians and representatives of civil society, who emphasise the opportunities for women through the quota, while not considering necessary further advances. This could also be observed when asking the people, if they can think of any prime examples of female politicians in recent times. They were either unable to name anybody, or they referred to women like Hero Talabani, the wife of the current president, Bayan Sami Abdul-Rahman, daughter of the former deputy-prime minister Sami Abdul-Rahman, or Hamail Barzani, the late wife of Mullah Mustafa Barzani and mother of Massoud Barzani, who could all be classified as "token women" as all are connected to an influential male leader.[627]

Despite the lack of further considerations on gender issues, actions, such as the introduction of the quota, has had an effect on society. For example, as argued by Caprioli and Boyer[628] the growing acceptability of the concept of women in leadership positions, if continued, is likely to lead to more sympathy for gender equality within society as a whole. When surveyed, nearly three quarters of people signaled that they would support having even more women in positions of power.[629] However the respondees noted that the women must have the necessary

---

[626] Interview CB, Vienna on 04/12/2012

[627] See e.g. Interview BZ, Sulaimaniya on 10/08/2012; Interview AA, Erbil on 03/04/2012; Interview CH, Vienna on 05/11/2012

[628] Caprioli and Boyer, "Gender, Violence and International Crisis," 509.

[629] See e.g. Interview AK, Erbil on 20/04/2012; Interview AR, Sulaimaniya on 21/05/2012; Interview AS, Sulaimaniya on 23/05/2012; Interview AT, Sulaimaniya on 24/05/2012

abilities and be suitable for the position.[630] The supporters of women's rights were especially of the opinion that there should be no discrimination and that there should be just as many women as men in high positions.[631] There was a small number of people questioned who did not think that women should be in positions of power. They felt that men were better in politics, or that politics is *"not a woman's role"*.[632] Among the people who opposed women's equality in politics, prejudices persisted including: women are too emotional,[633] or women are not capable because of biological factors. A young teacher, who was described by one of her former pupils as extremely smart and loved by all her students, announced that "*there are differences, because men are more intelligent than women. Anyway all the scientists are men*".[634] In addition there were a few people who stated that they are happy to see women in high positions, as long as they are not too high and who were of the opinion that the very high positions are better preserved for men.[635]

Nevertheless, despite the persistence of some gender-related prejudices, the vast majority of both women and men, believed that there should be more women in positions of power, at least in theory.

Reality showed that several people simply articulated their ideals or what they thought was expected from them, since it could be observed that the people do not take upon themselves the prerequisites needed in order to achieve those ideals in practice. As with peace negotiations, there is a great discrepancy between theory and practice when it comes to the realization of gender equity in politics.

Even with those who truly support the idea of women's inclusion in parliament, many distinguish between "women in general", and women from their own families.

---

[630] Interview AE, Erbil on 09/04/2012; Interview AL on 25/04/2012; Interview AU, Sulaimaniya on 28/05/2012

[631] See e.g. Interview BH, Erbil on 05/07/2012; Interview BL, Erbil on 12/07/2012; Interview BN, Erbil on 17/07/2012

[632] Interview AI, Erbil on 16/04/2012

[633] Interview CE, Vienna on 21/10/2012

[634] Interview BU, Erbil on 24/07/2012

[635] Interview AH, Erbil on 15/04/2012; Interview AW, Sulaimaniya on 01/06/2012; Interview BF, Erbil on 29/06/2012; Interview BK, Erbil on 12/07/2012

As explained by two female students at one of Kurdistan's most prestigious universities:

> "Women cannot really be involved in politics, because they have no say. Everything in this regard only looks good on the outside at the moment. Nearly no families would accept their daughter to become a politician. It is not a respectable job. She would have to stay out late and be in the eyes of the public. Women even have to fight for a representative position at a university. I am a representative at the university, and it was so hard. The people told me that I am bringing shame to my family and that I will get a bad reputation. Additionally the guys think that women are not capable, and that they should only be in the kitchen. Even here at uni most guys' mentality is against women. If you have a discussion it usually ends with, that's the way it is because you are a woman."[636]

This lack of actual support for getting women into positions of power makes it nearly impossible to achieve gender equality. This has led to a lack of gender balance in Kurdistan politics; and the introduction of the quota has arguably not changed this situation greatly up until now. As remarked by Gareth Stansfield in an interview with James Simon, there have been efforts to put women into high positions in the KRG and women had always had prominent roles in the parties. The government is moving to empower women, but it is questionable whether this happens in practice, since women in public life are still just part of the patriarchal system.[637]

A number of conclusions can be drawn from the above discussion. The increase of numbers of women in parliament is certainly positive for the outside perception of the region. At the same time it has a positive influence within the region, by enabling public discussion of enhanced inclusion of women in politics. However it is questionable whether the increased numbers have already had an effect on women's personal lives. There is certainly still a long way to go to ensure that the inclusion into decision making becomes a reality for women from all parts of society. The practical impossibility for many women to become engaged in politics arguably hampers a more gender inclusive transformation and development of the

---

[636] Interviews AE and AF, Erbil on 09/04/2012
[637] Simon, "Kurdistan, Women in Iraq".

Kurdistan region It also hampers individual opportunities for the development of women from all levels of society, as will be more fully elaborated in the following section:

2.   Searching for Gender Equality

Assessing women's participation is not solely a matter of counting how many women are working in an environment. Considerations of which women are able to participate, the nature of their participation and how much power they have through their participation are crucial. The mere inclusion of a higher number of women in the political process is not enough to ensure achievements for women's equality. This is supported by the UNDP's *Gender Inequality Index*, which shows that the mere percentage of seats by women in national parliaments does not correlate with the development status of the countries.[638] As yet there is often so much concentration on getting more women involved that the further steps are forgotten.[639]

Not all women are feminists and not all women support their fellow female citizens. This could also be seen through the interviews conducted. Although the majority of women spoke in favour of supporting women in high positions,[640] there was a considerable number of women, who did not trust their fellow female citizens to lead the country and to support development.[641]

Furthermore, it has often been seen in the past that female politicians from a certain party or group would rather vote for their demands, than build a bridge to other women.[642] Women cannot be expected to work together and to function as a coherent group. Just as with men, women are not a homogenous group and many are loyal to their political party and think of their own interests first. While some women bring their distinctive style to politics described, by Mary Robinson, the

---

[638] UNDP, Human Development Reports, "Gender Inequality Index and related indicators" (2011) http://hdr.undp.org/en/media/HDR_2011_EN_Table4.pdf (Accessed on 09.12.2011)
[639] Cohn, Kinsella, and Gibbings, "Women, Peace and Security Resolution 1325," 136.
[640] See for example Interview AK, Erbil on 20/04/2012, Interview AI, Erbil on 16/04/2012, Interview AT, Sulaimaniya on 24/05/2012
[641] See for example Interview BU, Erbil on 24/07/2012, Interview CE, Vienna on 21/10/2012
[642] Kaniyoti, "Reconstruction & Women's Rights in Afghanistan," 20.

former president of Ireland[643], as *"less hierarchical and more enabling"*[644], others behave exactly as their male counterparts.[645]

Behaviour within a power structure depends upon the unique attitude of the woman, as well as her personal development. For instance, Cynthia Enloe asserts that women behave differently if they rise from a women's basis. If women have a women's, or at least a mixed base, such as the previous prime minister of Norway, Gro Harlem Brundtland[646] or the previous president of Chile, Verónica Michelle Bachelet Jeria[647], they are more conscious of women's realities and needs and consequently support women more. However if women simply advance through patriarchal system they will not make a difference to the country.[648]

Hence if gender equality is to be achieved, it is necessary to go further than merely include women as a whole in politics. There needs to be a consideration of how women can impact the most on the political process. As explained by the Heinrich Böll Stiftung, *"distinctions like social or ethnic origin, religion, or sexual orientation have to be taken seriously in any gender-equitable and feminist politics"*, as it will only then be possible to build truly emancipatory political strategies.[649] Involvement should thereby not only be restricted to an elite, or one type of women, but available to a spectrum of women, including those who have been directly affected by conflict. Additionally a representative for women should be included, as inter alia argued by Azza Karam, so that the women's views are heard as well, and not only the opinions of the various parties.[650]

Peace-building strategies, including political development strategies, usually do not address these challenges and either see women as a single group or take them to

---

[643] 1990-1997

[644] Hunt, "Inclusive Security"

[645] Caprioli and Boyer, "Gender, Violence and International Crisis," 507.

[646] 1981, 1986-89, 1990-96

[647] 2006-2011

[648] Enloe, "Women and Men in the Iraq War".

[649] Heinrich Böll Stiftung, *Gender Politics Makes A Difference*, 5.

[650] Azza Karam (ed.), *Women in Parliament: Beyond Numbers* (Stockholm: International IDEA Handbook Series 2, 1998) 9.

be genderless members of other groups.[651] This trend could also be observed in the Kurdistan Region.

As explained by Nadje Al-Ali in Iraq today, as in the Kurdistan Region, the challenge is not with having women involved in politics, but the challenge rather lies with the type of women who are involved and the way in which they are involved. She emphasises that the participation of women in every party, whether Islamic or communist, is a positive development, but that numbers are not everything. Just because women have a say does not mean that they will support women's issues; some women rather hinder than support women's rights. This can be seen in the Iraqi parliament, where the quota system is in place, but the women having a seat do not support women's rights. They are often the wives, daughters or sisters of conservative male politicians, who merely support the decisions of their male party members but who do not stand up for women. It will still take some time for women to insert their own opinions into the political discourse.[652]

Also in the Kurdistan Region it is widely criticized in this regard that the women who manage to become involved in high-level politics only manage to do so through personal relations, such as existing family ties, but not merely through their ability. The ruling families and the families which enable their own women to enter politics are said to be very similar in education and background. Several amongst the people interviewed had the feeling that the lifestyles of their leaders are not shared by the local population.[653] Consequently the women in parliament are not representative of the whole population. It follows that it is still not possible to have a truly balanced outcome, and this hampers development for all.

Women from less advantageous backgrounds often have no possibility of accessing high level politics. There are social-economic obstacles hindering the involvement of women from lower class backgrounds including lack of adequate financial resources, limited access to the profession of choice and the dual burden

---

[651] Pankhurst, "The 'Sex War' and Other Wars," 162.
[652] Simon, "Kurdistan, Women in Iraq".
[653] See e.g.: Interview AD, Erbil on 08/04/2012; Interview AO, Sulaimaniya on 13/05/2012

of professional and domestic obligations.[654] Furthermore culturally enshrined gender roles are also hindering including the pre-determined roles assigned to women and men, the consequential lack of support for women running for elections, as well as the lack of confidence in themselves.[655] Two men who are themselves closely connected to the political system, explained that while government supports women to enter high-level politics, it remains the public view is that it is better for women to stay at home and take care of the family and the children.[656] It can thus be seen that government's inclusion of women into parliament has until failed in making it easier for the majority of women to become involved in decision making. As a consequence, the population as a whole accepts that women in general can be part of the process, but they do not include themselves, as they do not identify themselves or the women of their families as being of the same standing as women seeking election.

The men further noted that is still the men who decide which women are suitable and what is considered to be a good position for a particular woman. In reality this means that they are often supported once they or somebody from their family achieves a certain position in society, but not otherwise.[657] The government itself thereby arguably only supports a certain types of women to participate in high level politics. It is usually women who have relatives in high positions or who have received a certain type of education, but not women who represent other elements of society. This leads to a loss of experiences within the decision makers, as well as a lack of balanced representation, and thus identification with all parts of society. Consequently the influence female parliamentarians might have on the general population, who do not feel connected could be impeded. At the same time the limited mind-set and experience in dealing with different social groups, is possibly reflected in issues brought before parliament by the MPs, and the resulting legislation. Both the issues discussed and the ultimate legislation are likely to be different, and more in line with the needs of the population as a whole, when considered or enacted by MPs representing all social groups.

---

[654] Karam (ed.), *Women in Parliament: Beyond Numbers*, 30.
[655] Ibid.p.32
[656] Interview AH, Erbil on 15/04/2012; Interview BM, Erbil on 13/07/2012
[657] Ibid.

But a lack of equal representation is not the only problem women in Kurdistan's parliament have to face. Women do not have sufficient power even if they have significant numbers, and this leads to even less gender influence on the output of the political process. As feminist scholars like Al-Ali or Naggar elaborate, it is not enough to have 30 per cent of women in parliament, if they not appointed to other official positions. Women should be present at all levels, and gender awareness needs to be incorporated at all levels.[658]

This was also the view of some of the Kurds surveyed, who explained that it is not worth having women in these positions, if this does not bring a certain power with it.[659] They added that the reasons for having women in positions of power include the maintenance of women's rights, because *"women are sometimes better in certain things than men are"*.[660] Further it gives women the possibility to *"free themselves"* from oppression,[661] which is all only possible if they also have certain power associated with the position.

In Kurdistan as in many other countries, the increase in numbers of women in parliament does not necessarily mean an increase in their power. The feminist critics of the current ruling party, as well as, unofficially, some party members, maintain that it is a problem with Kurdistan's politics today that it is the old warriors who are still mainly in power and who do not allow others, especially women, to get through with their demands. This often prevents the current women establishing themselves, and having their voices heard and their ideas implemented.[662]

The limited power given to women, can already be seen reflected in the positions they have acquired: After the Kurdistan elections in July 2009 only two have the roles of heads of a parliamentary bloc: Sozan Khala Shehab for the Kurdistan List and Kwestan Muhammad for the "Change" List.[663] In addition, women in the KRG have never held senior positions such as speaker or secretary. Of the 19

---

[658] Centre for Humanitarian Dialogue, "Women at the Peace Table - Nepal Roundtable".
[659] Interview CA, Sulaimaniya on 13/08/2012
[660] Interview BH, Erbil on 05/07/2012
[661] Interview BN, Erbil on 21/07/2012
[662] Interview AB, Erbil on 03/04/2012
[663] Fischer-Tahir, "Competition, cooperation and resistance," 1385.

permanent parliamentary committees only one, the Women's Rights Protection Committee, is chaired by a woman.[664] Finally there is currently only one female minister, Ms. Asos Najib Abdullah, who heads the ministry of Labour and Social Affairs.[665]

Women often face a variety of obstacles when it comes to their inclusion in politics. Problems continue once they are on top, as they are arguably not given the power needed. Such women often only engage with the so called 'women's issues', like the family, children or women's affairs in general, which is, while very important, not enough.[666] Furthermore, through the prevalence of a "masculine model" in politics, women can only be successful if they comply with the standards laid out by men. If they are unwilling to do so, reduced party support, in the form of limited financial support or limited access to political networks, will often be the result.[667]

Women MPs themselves point out that their actions have been extensive, but they are fighting a constant battle to have their proposals approved by parliament. As explained by Hazha Sleman, the current head of the Women Committee, at the 2012 parliamentary discussions on the budget, the women committee presented a proposal to allocate funding for the High Women Council, as well as for the directorate of counter violence against women. In addition, the women urged parliament to allocate a budget to fund women who had lost their husbands. However the government did not implement any of the proposals.[668]

Similar problems emerge with legislation. The female MPs have already been successful in promoting legislation such as law against domestic violence, against polygamy. However, the problems of women's under-representation in other decision making and the lack of implementation of laws which exist for women,

---

[664] The Kurdish Globe, "Statistics suggest women's role is "weak" in government, politics and civil society".
[665] KRG, "Ministers Profiles, Ms Asos Najib Abdullah - Minister of Labour and Social Affairs" http://www.krg.org/articles/detail.asp?lngnr=12&smap=04090200&rnr=136&anr=32574 (Accessed on 15.10.2012)
[666] Suthanthiraraj and Ayo, *Promoting Women's Participation in Conflict and Post-Conflict Societies*, 37.
[667] Karam (ed.), *Women in Parliament: Beyond Numbers*, 22.
[668] Warvin, "Regional Parliament Denies Women Demand, Endorses Budget" (24.06.2012) http://www.warvin.org/drejaE.aspx?=hewal&jmara=335&Jor=4 (Accessed on 15.10.2012)

remain. This situation was publicly criticized by Hazham Sleman, when it came to the prohibition of 'women provocation'.[669]

In order to fight the problem of being not being heard, Kurdish female MPs met with met with delegates from the British parliament to share relevant skills and experiences in order to work more effectively for the needs of women in the country. They decided to set up a women's lobby group, aimed at achieving greater influence on a number of issues in parliament.[670] However, the practical implications of this initiative are unclear.

The lack of women's power within parliament is well known within the region and has already been raised on the agenda, although with limited success. In their recommendations, the participants of *The Role of Women in Peace-Building, Reconciliation and Accountability in Iraq*" conference in Erbil in January 2011, for example asked for an upgrade of the State Secretary for Women's Affairs to a full State Ministry. They also requested enhanced inclusion of women within the party's leadership structure; an enhanced involvement of civil society in political decision making, and called for the establishment of a 'National Council for Women', consisting of organisations and 'leading personalities'. However these recommendations have not yet been put into practice.[671]

The failure to incorporate true gender equality into the political sphere or society, lead to the people having the feeling that women's inclusion and gender balance are unnecessary in the state structure, as well as private decision making, as the current experience shows that it does not bring any fundamental change.

Through the interviews it could be observed that despite all the efforts of female MPs to promote women's issues and to enact legislation for women, there is little impact on the general population.

---

[669] Dawan Hadi, Aknews, "No one arrested for women provocation in Kurdistan Region, says MP" (23.08.2012) http://www.aknews.com/en/aknews/3/322800/?AKmobile=true (Accessed on 16.10.2012)
[670] WFD, "UK MPs share experience with women counterparts in Kurdistan Parliament" (28.02.2012) http://www.wfd.org/wfd-news/latest/news.aspx?p=109549 (Accessed on 16.10.2012)
[671] No peace without justice, "International Conference on "The Role of Women in Peace-Building, Reconciliation and Accountability in Iraq"," 2/3.

Kurdish people, especially from the upper class with close ties to Europe, are critical that women do not have enough power. However, many are also of the opinion that it is the women's own fault. They criticize the women for being not active enough, for only complaining and for not using all the opportunities. Women who had already achieved positions of power were criticized for not trying hard enough to move even further forward due to laziness and a fear of confrontation. They were further criticised for supporting the unjust system and slowing down the process towards equality.[672]

Also amongst the Kurds in Kurdistan, there were several who did not consider women yet have a true role in politics or decision making, *"because they simply don't manage to 'prove their presence' in society"*.[673] Several interviewees were of the view that the existing women politicians are simply part of the already existing political machinery and would rather wish them to be more independent and to do more work on their own, as explained by several interviewees.[674]

At the same time it should be conceded that the women, who are currently facing the challenges of parliament every day have assumed pioneering roles, which will make it possible for other women in the future to follow their paths. However it follows from the arguments above that it is not sufficient simply to 'let them be', as has arguably happened in the Kurdistan Region until now. Rather it is necessary to grant the female MPs including those in favour of gender equality certain power but also to make them accountable. Only in this way will women's political effectiveness be enhanced.[675]

This opinion was supported by a young housewife, who was generally very in favour of women's equality, but explained that there is no equality when working with men. Women have no say and therefore they cannot achieve a lot in high positions.[676]

---

[672] Interview CE, Vienna on 21/10/2012; Interview CF, Vienna on 16/11/2012; Interview CJ, Vienna on 28/10/2012

[673] Interview BN, Erbil on 17/07/2012

[674] Interview BI, Erbil on 08/07/2012; Interview CA, Sulaimaniya on 13/08/2012

[675] Anne Marie Goetz and Shireen Hassim (ed), *No Shortcuts to Power* (London: Zed Books, 2003) 73.

[676] Interview AY, Sulaimaniya on 04/06/2012

In conclusion it can be observed that progress has occurred in the Kurdistan region when it comes to women's participation in parliament. However the impact of this development has not yet had an extensive influence on equity and positive conflict transformation within society. The implementation of a quota, and the continuous growth of the number of female representation in parliament, has been a positive move and has certainly given the KRG a platform to shine from. However considering the Kurdistan Region's standing within the international community and bearing in mind the current attitudes towards women in the West, the lack of inclusive representation, as well as the lack in power granted to the female representatives has resulted in their influence for social change being smaller than otherwise might have been. While the current developments have made gender equality in parliament in principle acceptable, a lot more still needs to be done to achieve this aim in practice for society as a whole. While legislation has been introduced and Kurdish officials have supported the inclusion of women in parliament, the focus has been on numerical balance. True gender equality is far from being achieved.

This is reflected in society, where the majority of people talk in favour of women's involvement, but they do not see themselves as being part of this involvement. While there is certainly still a long way to go, the KRG's efforts to include women at all need to be recognized. While women's aspirations are yet to be fully realised, their integration into parliament has been a big step forward and puts the KRG into the forefront of governments with a high percentage of women in decision making posts. This has certainly had an impact on the region's development.

To now go one step further and to ensure that representatives from the whole society are involved in politics, there needs to be an environment which gives the general population the opportunity to participate.[677] Work has to be done inside and outside of parliament to make it more accessible and a more positive place for women to have impact and for gender equality to flourish. This will enhance the impact of parliamentary institutions on society as a whole. To ensure that politics becomes gender inclusive, other aspects of life have to become gender inclusive

---

[677] Suthanthiraraj and Ayo, *Promoting Women's Participation in Conflict and Post-Conflict Societies,* 10.

as well, and accessible for all, such as education and the economy.[678] This will be discussed later in the thesis.

The political landscape of a country or region is not only influenced by high ranking officials. Other forces, such as grassroots activism within the region or international policy making can play a decisive role in the forming of a state. This 'other political activism' will be subject of the following subchapter.

C.   Other Political Activism

"We cannot achieve democracy and lasting peace in the world unless women achieve the same opportunities as men to influence developments at all levels of society".[679] (Thorbjom Jagland, Nobel Peace Prize Committee Chairmain, 2011)

While official peace building and high level politics have an important role to play in the development of a country or region, positive conflict transformation cannot be achieved by officials alone. As explained by several of the interviewees *"every force is needed in order to build up a country"*, including the people themselves. People can be the driving force in initiating political developments and without the population at large, no development initiated by the officials can be brought to fruition. As explained by a woman NGO worker:

> *"Of course also the people were a driving force. The people really support the security forces. The people hold together now. There are also attempts of suicide bombings in Kurdistan, but they could be prevented, because of the people."*[680]

Just as with the security situation, it is the people who influence which laws will be passed, ensure that laws will be observed and for example that equality is put into practice. It is at this "local level" that women come most often into play, who, through their unique position in society and during the time of armed conflict, have knowledge, which can and should be used by all stakeholders, who aim at supporting the building of peace in the region.

---

[678] Addison and Brück, *Making Peace Work*, 106.

[679] BBC online, "Nobel Peace Prize recognises women rights activists" (7.10.2011) http://www.bbc.co.uk/news/world-europe-15211861 (Accessed on 7.10.2011)

[680] Interview CJ, Vienna on 28/10/2012

As the previous chapters showed, women, especially from lower classes and less advantaged families, only seldom have access to formal peace politics. They are typically left out of the official peace negotiations and the formal work of the reconstruction of society and the value of their knowledge and experience is not recognised. Only a very limited number of women have managed to participate in formal peace talks and in the signing of peace accords[681] and equality between men and women is far from achieved. However this does not mean that women remain inactive. They often work for peace at the grassroots level. Their activities can be in social groups, religious groups and the community in general. It is in these groups that women, as well as men, raise their voices, work for democracy and thereby support the population's political influence on the developments, which will impact on their lives.[682]

All around the world there are women who stand up for themselves, for fellow women and for peace in their country, even in the most dangerous of circumstances. Women fight for their laws[683] and for their recognition[684], in order to improve the situation for themselves, their families and their whole country. Additionally women participate in wars, revolutions, protests, rebellions, social change and peace building[685] and organize groups and networks to fight militarization, prevent violence conflicts and to achieve sustainable peace.[686] Examples of their fighting for equality as well as peace throughout the world are countless.

For instance, during the Chechnyan war, the Russian Committee of Soldiers' Mothers demanded that their sons be sent back home and Yugoslav women protested in front of the National Army barracks in 1991 so that their sons be

---

[681] Bouta and Frerks, *Women's Roles in Conflict Prevention, Conflict Resolution and Post-Conflict Reconstruction,* 33.
[682] Ibid.p.10
[683] Heather Sharp, „Women challenge Jordan Nationality Law" (14.10.2011)
http://www.bbc.co.uk/news/world-middle-east-15306228 (Accessed on 16.10.2011)
[684] Karen Zarindast, „Afghan MP forced to stop hunger strike after 13 days" (14.10.2011)
http://www.bbc.co.uk/news/world-south-asia-15318141 (Accessed on 16.10.2011)
[685] Afshar, "Women and Wars," 178/9.
[686] Cockburn, "Gender Relations as Causal in Militarization and War," 139.

brought back home.[687] In 2010, 20.000 women and men from the Congo and other countries, peacefully marched against war and gender violence.[688] Sudanese women marched through their town naked to draw attention to the kidnapping of their children for use as soldiers.[689] Also in Sri Lanka women organized themselves during conflict to protest the killings and disappearances of their sons.[690] In Afghanistan youth groups and women's groups organize marches against street harassment.[691] The 'Women in White' in Liberia organized non-violent protests for peace by standing on a field for weeks to remind people of the importance of change and by making themselves heard by calling for a sex strike.[692] During the uprising in Libya women helped to smuggle ammunition for the revolutionary forces.[693] Women in Israel and Palestine are working for peace through organisations such as the *Jerusalem Link, Bat Shalom* or the *Women in Black.*[694] Women of Venezuela and Iran are striving toward a fundamental grassroots-driven transformation of politics and power in their countries.[695] And during the uprising in Egypt it was women, as well as men, who organized protests via Facebook, who camped on Tahrir Square and who fought the police[696] and it was the women who went on the streets after pictures were released of a woman having her clothes ripped off and being kicked by soldiers while lying on the ground.

---

[687] Bouta and Frerks, *Women's Roles in Conflict Prevention, Conflict Resolution and Post-Conflict Reconstruction,* 32.

[688] Global Fund for Women, "Top 10 Wins for Women's Movements", http://www.globalfundforwomen.org/impact/success-stories/top-10-wins-for-womens-movements (Accessed on 14.9.2011)

[689] Hunt, "The Critical Role of Women Waging Peace," 568.

[690] Asoka Bandarage, "Women, Armed Conflict and Peacemaking in Sri Lanka: Toward a Political Economy Perspective" *Asian Politics & Policy* 2(4) (2010): 659.

[691] Nooriahan, Al Jazeera, "Opinion, Afghan women fight back against harassment".

[692] Engelhardt, *Starke Frauen für den Frieden,* 79.

[693] BBC online, "Tripoli underground: Handbags, dinghies and secret emails" (3.12.2011) http://www.bbc.co.uk/news/magazine-16001247 (Accessed on 6.12.2011)

[694] Magda Maria Seewald, *Bewaffnet mit Schwäche, kämpfen sie für den Frienden. Die Auswirkungen der Geschlechterverhältnisse im Israel-Palästina-Konflikt auf die Friendensarbeit von Frauen,* (Wien: Dimplomarbeit, Universität Wien 2003) 121,140,126.

[695] Sanam Naraghi Anderlini, *Women building Peace, What They Do, Why it Matters* (London: Lynne Rienner Publishers 2007) 34.

[696] Naib Fatma, Al Jazeera, "Women of the revolution" (19.2.2011) http://www.aljazeera.com/indepth/features/2011/02/2011217134411934738.html (Accessed on 5.12.2011)

Furthermore there have been a number of women who sacrificed a part or the whole of their lives to work for their country or for their fellow women. Tawakkul Karman left the comfort of her home to stand up for a change in Yemen and to give confidence to other women and young people to do the same.[697] Chanu Sharmila, "the Iron Lady of Manipur" (India), has been in police custody in a hospital room for over ten years, being force-fed via nasal tubes as part of her act of civil disobedience to draw attention to an on-going conflict in India.[698] Leymah Gbowee made it her life's mission to make Liberia a better place and to help women overcome their traumas.[699] Further, politicians like Aung San Suu Kyi and Benazir Bhutto gave their life, or part of their life, to stand up for their people.

The countless acts of women's peace activism were recently recognized with the awarding of the Nobel Peace Prize in 2011 to three women rights activists for their work for women's rights, their safety and their full participation surrounding conflict situations: Ellen Johnson Sirleaf, Leymah Gabowee, and Tawakul Karman. In explaining the reasons for their choice the Nobel Prize Committee stated that it hopes that the prize will help end the discrimination against women.[700]

It can thereby be seen that the peace movement and the feminist movement are often intertwined, with many women not only being fighters for peace, but also supporters of the wider women's movements and of equality with men.[701]

Through their various actions, women have achieved enhanced gender equality. Only in 2010, the UN General Assembly established UN Women, the UN Entity for Gender Equality and the Empowerment of Women, which is a superagency headed by an Under Secretary General. Several Middle Eastern countries such as Libya, Palestine, Tunisia and Yemen have changed their national laws to grant women equal treatment under the law.[702] In 2011 the citizens of Morocco accomplished after months of protesting succeeded in having their constitution

---

[697] Engelhardt, *Starke Frauen für den Frieden,* 140.
[698] Center for Humanitarian Dialogue, *Peacemaking in Asia and the Pacific,* 67.
[699] Engelhardt, *Starke Frauen für den Frieden,* 64.
[700] Ibid.p.9
[701] Neissl, Eckstein, Arzt und Anker (Hrsg), *Männerkrieg und Frauenfrieden, Geschlechterdimensionen in kriegerischen Konflikten* (Wien: Promedia, 2003) 8.
[702] Global Fund for Women, "Top 10 Wins for Women's Movements".

reformed. Reforms included reinforcing women's equality to men under the constitution. Through protests in Egypt, the courts banned virginity tests carried out by the army on women. In addition, women have achieved increased political participation, with quotas in parliament having been put into place in about 100 countries of the world.[703] And these were only some of the victories achieved for women and by women.

These worldwide developments have also taken place in the Kurdistan region. Over the previous decades women have engaged in grassroots activism supporting peace and women's rights. Despite many challenge, they have succeeded in enhancing gender equality to a certain extent.

The following section presents a short overview of the historical movements by women in the Kurdistan region as well as discussing current actions on the ground. The aim is to address the question of how these movements for equality influence social development and whether they have the potential to progress positive conflict transformation, and gender equality at all levels.

1.   The Kurdistan's Women's Movement – A Historical Abstract

"Women are not just victims of violence. They are often the driving force for peace."[704]

Women's movements in the Kurdish regions have their origins in the early 20th century. In 1913 the *Women's World* (Kadinlar Dunyast), a journal to promote the equal status of men and women, was published and in 1919 the first Kurdish women's organisation, *The Society for the Advancement of Kurdish Women* (Kurd kadinalri Teali Cemiyeti) was established in Istanbul.[705]

Early in the history of their movement, women activists used the struggle for their ethnic group as a basis to enhance not only the rights of the general population,

---

[703] Sandra Grey and Marian Sawer, *Women's Movements, Flourishing or in abeyance?* (New York: Routledge, 2008) 106.
[704] Ambassador Stephan Tafrov (Bulgaria): original language French in Cohn, "Feminist Peacemaking," 8.
[705] Alsayid, *Combating Physical Violence Against Women in Iraqi Kurdistan,* 24.

but also their own. In Kurdistan, as in other similar regions, the women's movement was closely interwoven with the nationalist movement throughout its history. Nationalism and the fight for autonomy, although not always unproblematic, have provided many women with a platform to pursue a more public role.[706] The struggle as such was two-fold: on the one hand against the old social, economic and religious order and on the other hand against the oppression by European and other colonialists.[707] During the 1940s and 50s women were actively involved in the struggle for more rights as part of the revolutionary movement against the British influence as well as against the Iraqi monarchy. They were involved in humanitarian assistance, welfare work and also participated in strikes, demonstrations, and underground political activism, from all sides of the political spectrum.[708] Women, especially from the upper-class, were active in women's branches of charitable organisations, such as the Child Protection Society, or the Red Crescent Society.[709]

More and more women's organisations were created throughout the region during the second half of the 20th century, often associated with political parties. For example the League of the Defence of Iraqi Women's Rights (*Rabitat al-difa' 'an huqu al-mora'*)[710], was founded in the early 1950s by female members of the Iraqi Communist Party. The League gained wide influence and was arguably most influential in changing women's legal rights, including for example contributing to the passing of the unified personal status code in 1959.[711] In addition the Kurdistan Democratic Party, the Daawa party and the Ba'ath Party founded different women's organisations. However all of them, except for the General Union of Iraqi Women, established by the Ba'ath party, fell prey to the conflict.[712] As a consequence, it was virtually impossible for years to achieve any improvements, which lay outside the will of the ruling party.

---

[706] Enloe, "The Women behind the Warriors," 24.

[707] Golley Nawar Al-Hassan, "Is Feminism Relevant to Arab Women?" *Third World Quarterly* 25(3) (2004): 529.

[708] Al-Ali, *Iraqi Women*, 79.

[709] Ibid.p.85

[710] The name was changed in 1961 to the Iraqi Women's League (*Rabitat al-mara' al-'iraqiya*)

[711] Al-Ali and Pratt, "Women's organizing and the conflict in Iraq since 2003," 76.

[712] Fischer-Tahir, "Competition, cooperation and resistance," 1383.

When it was no longer possible to continue the fight from inside, other ways had to be sought. As a result of the great flows of refugees, who settled in other countries around the world, as well as the inability to operate effectively within the region, the Kurdish women's and peace movement continued the struggle outside their territory. Several organisations including the Kurdish Human Rights Watch and the Kurdish Women's Association, were first set up in America, as in this case, or Europe, to fight for Kurdish rights from outside.[713] The above-mentioned organisations are now present in Kurdistan as well.

The establishment of the safe haven in the North of Iraq enabled women's groups and organisations to mushroom out of the region after 1991. The safe haven once again enabled Kurdish women, who had been active in political parties for a long time, to increase their involvement through participation in women's organisations, women's unions, and groups not affiliated to political parties.[714] The civil society was once more allowed to become involved in party politics and to establish civil society associations. As a consequence dozens of organisations working actively for women in the region began appearing throughout Iraq's North during the 1990s. With money from the Oil-for-Food Programme for example about 400 centres were established for women. Classes were held teaching them how to read and write, as well as training workshops, etc.[715] The NGOs and women's organisations provided opportunities for women not only to acquire new skills but also to step out of their traditional roles and to take position on political issues.[716]

While it was the hope of activists that women's rights would come to the fore once the Kurdistan Region established its own government, this did not entirely happen.[717] In 1993 for example, several women's organisations presented a petition to parliament with over 30,000 signatures, demanding an improvement in

---

[713] Al-Ali, *Iraqi Women*, 40, 42.
[714] Al-Ali and Pratt, "Women's organizing and the conflict in Iraq since 2003," 76.
[715] UNIFEM, "Iraq".
[716] Sharoni, "The Myth of Gender Equality," 26.
[717] Dr Nadje Al-Ali in Simon, "Kurdistan, Women in Iraq".

the legal status of women. However the proposal never made it through to parliament, as the factions in power refused to have it discussed.[718]

While the influence of the Ba'ath party had disappeared, new political and societal forces influenced the independent work of the women activists. Before the first elections in May 1992, a women-only committee was established and commissioned with working on family law and drafting alternative legislation. The committee consisted of women from all the main political parties in Kurdistan, including the KDP, PUK, the Communist Party, the Democratic Independent Party of Kurdistan, and the People's Party of Kurdistan, and received wide public support. Nevertheless the proposal failed and the old law remained. The new powers in the region tried to recreate a society of tribalism, in which women's initiatives were regarded with suspicion[719] and women's issues were marginalized during the phase of reconstruction. Other issues, such as federalism or the question of oil were always more important.

Despite these challenges, women nevertheless managed to achieve certain power and to contribute to progress in gender equality. Local Kurdish women's rights movements lobbied successfully for the reintroduction of women's rights in the legislature and raised the awareness of women's rights and gender issues in general.[720]

Apart from becoming more active in the struggle for women's rights, Kurdish women also actively encouraged a peace movement to stop civil war from erupting between the KDP and the PUK in 1994.[721] On May 23, 1994, Kurdish women organized a Peace March from Sulaimanyia city to the Kurdish parliament in Erbil to ask the political leaders to end their conflict. They called themselves representatives of all the mothers, wives and sisters of the men being killed and the representatives of those desiring freedom, as well as representatives of half of

---

[718] Jabar and Dawod (ed), *The Kurds, Nationalism and Politics,* 168.
[719] Al-Ali and Pratt, "Between Nationalism and Women's Rights," 341.
[720] Kerim, *The Kurds in Iraq,* 57.
[721] Mojab and Gorman, "Dispersed Nationalism," 66.

society. They begged the politicians to stop the hatred and the selfishness and finally end the killing.[722]

In the Kurdistan region, as with other countries around the world individual women took the fight for their people into the public domain. This was difficult and also dangerous during the war. Nevertheless there were still some women who stood up for their beliefs, despite the danger. One young woman who lost her life in her fight for Kurdistan and who is still a martyr among many Kurds is Leyla Qasim. Others included Nesreen Berwari who was the minister of public works in the provisional Iraqi government as well as the minister of reconstruction and development for the Kurdistan Regional Government, Songul Chapouk, who represented the Turkoman population on the Iraqi Governing Council and who founded the Iraqi Women's Organisation in Kirkuk, which trains women in computer skills, literacy and agriculture;[723] and Ala Talabani, who was a former vice president of the Kurdistan Women's Union and who returned to Iraq in 2003 to cofound Women for a Free Iraq and the Iraq Women's High Council[724] and many more.

Today women continue to be very active in the struggle against violence and for equality. After the demonstrations in Sulaimaniya in 2011 as part of the Arab Spring and the consequent violent response by the government, women activists joined together and created the 'Sulaimaniya's Women's Group' to demand an end to the violence and a dialogue between the parties. Together with other protesting groups, they put pressure on the parties to dialogue and build peace in the region.[725] Women have also been active in their struggle for enhanced equality. In 2008 for example women activists actively worked for a unified law against polygamy.[726] In addition there was a week-long campaign to raise awareness on

---

[722] Al-Karadaghi (Ed., Publ.) *Kurdistan times,* 93/94.
[723] Hunt and Posa, "Iraq's Excluded Women," 42.
[724] Ibid. p.43
[725] Kvinna till Kvinna Foundation, *Building Security,* 34/35.
[726] Ariz Askari, "A question of scruples" *soma, An Iraqi-Kurdish Digest* 49 (2008): 6.

violence perpetrated against women, to speak for equality and to highlight the government's commitment to women's rights.[727]

It can be observed that throughout the previous century Kurdistan's women have been very active in standing up for themselves as well as their region. How this has influenced women's actions today and what consequences these actions have for the development of the region, as well as for the development of gender equality within society will be subject of the following section:

2.   Grassroots Political Activism Today

a)   *The Possibilities*

After long years of suppression, the Kurdistan Region and its population today have more autonomy than ever before. The Kurdistan Parliament is free to make its own laws in all areas, which are not exclusive to the federal government, including laws on the rights of women.[728] However, it is not only the officials who have more freedom to make changes, but also the people at large who now have the right to make themselves heard and to influence the dealings of their region.

As Article 25 of the International Covenant on Civil and Political Rights stipulates:

> *"Every citizen shall have the right and the opportunity, without any of the distinctions mentioned in article 2 (namely without distinction of any kind, such as race, colour, sex, language, religion, political or other opinion, national or social origin, property, birth or other status) and without unreasonable restrictions:*
>
> *a) To take part in the conduct of public affairs, directly or through freely chosen representatives."*

The Iraqi Constitution supports this right by stating in Article 20 that

> *"Iraqi citizens, men and women, shall have the right to participate in public affair [...]."*

While the Kurdistan Region Draft Constitution does not explicitly guarantee the right of the population to take part in the conduct of public affairs, it provides the

---

[727] Jen Sagerma, "Yes to gender equality" *soma, An Iraqi-Kurdish Digest* 49 (2008): 7.
[728] Draft of the Iraqi Kurdistan Region's Constitution 2009, Article 4

people with the right to freedom of expression (Article 18), the right *"to submit a complaint or petition with the authorities of the Region, who may not refuse to accept it"* (Article 21). Further, it guarantees the people the right to *"form and to freely join professional associations, unions, organisations and federations"*. (Article 26)

Through legislation, people have the right to participate in the country's affairs, to speak up for any issue, including for example women's involvement and equality. It consequently rests upon the people to have their voices heard; to use the new freedom; to speak up for change to long standing laws and traditions which prejudice sections of the population; and to express their ideas for the future development of the region.

b)   The Actions

Many women in Kurdistan today use the above-mentioned rights and are actively involved in their region's affairs, by supporting civil society projects and by campaigning for the promotion of peace, as well as equality. They are involved in different local and international NGOs and women's rights organisations, such as those which have mushroomed in Northern Iraq since the end of armed conflict.[729] These organisations are involved in a broad range of activities, such as charity work, the protection of human rights, the strengthening women's political rights and political understanding as well as working on commercial projects.[730] They also deal with aspects of women's lives such as rights advocacy, legal literacy, income generation, health and education and thereby provide an important basis for articulating and dealing with women's needs and play a part in the enhancement of equality and in influencing the transformation process.

The specific actions of women as part of different political actions was described by one of the interviewees as follows:

> *"Officially only men take part in peace building, but women work for women, but quietly, in the background. There are many*

---

[729] Such as the Kurdish Human Rights Watch, Kurdish Human Rights Project etc.

[730] Bouta and Frerks, *Women's Roles in Conflict Prevention, Conflict Resolution and Post-Conflict Reconstruction*, 33.

foreign and local organisations in Kurdistan today, which are nearly only lead by women. Individual women did a lot. The wife of Talabani for example campaigned a lot for women." She continued that *"since the 1990s women work together a lot, but it is still a problem that many women are not brave enough to take a step forward. It is a big problem that the honour of the family is so important and that it is so amazingly important to not bring shame to the family. The women have to assert themselves more. As a start, especially in the family."*[731]

Despite the critical tone from certain parts of the population, it is clear that women are once more very active at the grassroots level. This is also reflected in the actions of many Kurdish NGOs and women's organisations. The various organisations have made a great effort in trying to reform masculinity and gender relations and to contribute to state-building through making themselves and their needs heard in the political arena.[732] Their actions have been wide ranging:

Civil society and women's rights groups have been very active in contributing to the drafting of the regional constitution. According to WomensNews, hundreds of documents, lists and letters were collected from women's organisations who have sent in their suggestions from 2005. In this way they tried to increase their influence on the constitutional committee, only one member of which was a woman, Pakhshan Zangana, from the Communist Party.[733]

Actions by NGOs supporting women's rights also included the drafting of a 'Charter for the Rights and Freedoms of Women in the Kurdish Regions and Diaspora' by the Kurdish Human Rights Project and Kurdish Women's Project after years of consultations with women across the region. The Charter was presented to the Kurdish National Assembly and was followed up with a training manual to facilitate its implementation at grassroots level[734].[735]

---

[731] Interview AC, Erbil on 06/04/2012

[732] Mojab and Gorman, "Dispersed Nationalism," 66.

[733] Cyrille Cartier, "Iraqi Kurdish Women Voice Hopes for Constitution" (25 April 2006) http://womensenews.org/story/the-world/060425/iraqi-kurdish-women-voice-hopes-constitution (Accessed on 8.5.2012)

[734] The charter never became legally binding

[735] Kurdish Human Rights Project, *The Role of Women in Civil society*, 5.

In addition women's organisations drafted a proposal of a bill of rights for women, as presented by the Khatuzeen Center for Women's issues. This includes the elimination of discrimination against women, equality before the law, the eradication of all forms of violence against women, the elimination of harmful practices, political rights and the right to education.[736] While unlikely to pass in the near future, the proposed bill of rights was another way for women to express themselves and make their views public.[737] Women activists are currently working to enhance women's involvement in political decision making, by calling for qualified women to be offered high positions.[738]

In the long run the various efforts have borne fruit. On June 21, 2011 parliament approved the Family Violence Bill, which bans female genital mutilation; criminalizes violence against women; criminalizes forced and child marriage as well as the psychological abuse of girls and women and makes it easier for alleged victims to press charges.[739]

In August 2011 the KRG passed the Anti-Domestic Violence Law, in an effort to deal with the issue of violence against women. This was the first law of its kind in Iraq. It defines domestic violence as *"any act, word or threat against members of a family that might lead to physical, psychological or sexual damage and violation of rights and freedoms."* The law also prohibited female circumcision, the prevention of female education, forced marriage, and corporal punishment against children. A special anti-domestic violence court has already started its work, although this still needs to be enhanced. According to Pakhshan Zangana, Secretary General of the Supreme Council of Women's Affairs, *"if the law is dealt with consciously, then it will bring peace to families and help strengthen social relationships in society."[740]*

---

[736] Bill of Rights for Kurdish Women, Articles 1 - 5

[737] Cartier, "Iraqi Kurdish Women Voice Hopes for Constitution"

[738] The Kurdish Globe, "KURDISTAN: Kurdish Women Seek More Participation in Government" (4 February 2012) http://www.peacewomen.org/news_article.php?id=4629&type=news (Accessed on 21.2.2012)

[739] Human Rights Watch, "Iraqi Kurdistan: Law Banning FGM a Positive Step" (July 25, 2011) http://www.hrw.org/news/2011/07/25/iraqi-kurdistan-law-banning-fgm-positive-step (Accessed on 15.09.2011)

[740] Salih Waladbagi, The Kurdish Globe, "Anti-domestic violence law in Kurdistan" (3 April 2012) http://www.kurdishglobe.net/display-article.html?id=2465D8372C87030A2C08D36A5B17ABD2 (Accessed on 8.5.2012)

Furthermore the Kurdish parliament has banned forced marriage and marriage for minors and has restricted polygamy. Legislation also does not allow for the sentence for a conviction of honour killing to be reduced.[741] The Draft Constitution of Kurdistan stipulates that discrimination, as well as violence and abuse are also prohibited in the family, and that the government shall provide shelter to protect women *who have lost family security because of social reasons.*"[742]

Finally, according to Judge Mohammad Amin Al-Shirfani and Kurdish MP Karim Bahri Bradoust, it was due to the continuous demands by different women's groups, who requested amendments of the laws for women's rights, such as the restriction of polygamy, that the personal status law was amended by the Kurdistan parliament in favour of women's rights.[743]

Despite these successes, implementation of the provisions is not consistent and women are still suffering from honour crimes and other forms of discrimination.[744] Even though the simple existence of the law can be seen as a success, it was not widely promoted by the officials to the public out of fear of a confrontation with conservative forces. As a consequence the public perception of violence against women is not changing as quickly as it might.[745] The legislative changes, while absolutely vital for future development of the legislations, as well as development of the region as a whole, have until now not had the direct effect on many women's lives, as they are still not often lived in practice and especially women from lower classes of society are not aware of the legislations. As shown by the interviews, women especially from lower classes of society are generally not aware of the legislation. Even if they were aware, many women would not use their rights in practice, so as to not put shame on their families.

---

[741] Naggar, "Women's Rights in Iraqi Kurdistan".
[742] Draft of the Iraqi Kurdistan Region's Constitution 2009, Article 27(4)
[743] Layla Al-Zubaidi, *Amendments to the Personal Status Law in Iraqi Kurdistan strengthen women's rights* (Interview, Heinrich Böll Stiftung, 8 July 2009)
[744] Al-Ali and Pratt, "Between Nationalism and Women's Rights," 342.
Christian Peacemaker Teams, *Kurdish Activists' Observations of Women's Rights in Iraqi Kurdistan between March 2012 and March 2013 and their hopes for the future* (Women's Rights, 2013).
[745] Abdulrahman Suaad and Vormann Arvid, " Iraqi Kurdistan: Free yourself from FGM – A new approach: Eye see Media" http://www.mesop.de/2011/11/08/iraqi-kurdistan-free-yourself-from-fgm-%e2%80%93-a-new-approach-eye-see-media/ (Accessed on 16.11.11)

In order to enhance the implementation of this legislation and to promote further ideas, women activists at the grassroots level are actively speaking out about legal concerns, and are supporting change in society more directly.

They go on the street to publicly campaign for the equality of women, to let the public hear their voices and they work to enhance the women's knowledge of their rights,[746] as it happened for example on 8 March 2013, on International Women's Day.[747] Support services are provided for misused women to cope with trauma, by, for instance, the Women's Union of Kurdistan, the Independent Women's Organisation and the Women's Shelter Center in Sulaimaniya,[748] and women's shelters are provided to give women the possibility to seek refuge, if their families suspect them of having relationships outside of marriage, which can put their lives in danger.[749] NGOs work to prevent future violence against women, for example by campaigning against female genital mutilation (FGM) and by talking to people from different villages and explaining to them the dangers of FGM, as done by "Wadi".[750] Other actions include the caring for women inmates, who have been imprisoned for prostitution or adultery, to work on perspectives for the future, and to help the women to return to their families, as done by Khanzad. In addition, women's centers have been created for example in Halabja, Kifri and Biara, where women are given the opportunities to attend classes, to inform themselves of their rights, to attend computer, sewing or hair dressing courses and to visit the libraries. In Halabja the first coffee house for women was created.[751] And this is only a small fraction of the actions taken.

These targeted initiatives all have the potential to empower the population, to support exchange of knowledge and to push forward the movement towards equality. However their practical impacts on women's personal development and on gender equality within the family is disputed by the people themselves. Opinions

---

[746] Ariz Askari and Lawen Sagerma, "Injustices have been committed" *soma, An Iraqi-Kurdish Digest* 49 (2008): 1.

[747] Christian Peacemaker Teams, *Kurdish Activists' Observations*, 6.

[748] Mojab, "Kurdish Women in the Zone of Genocide and Gendercide," 24.

[749] Naggar, "Women's Rights in Iraqi Kurdistan".

[750] Abdulrahman and Vormann, " Iraqi Kurdistan: Free yourself from FGM".

[751] WADI, "Drei erfolgreich geführte Frauenzentren in Halabja, Kifri und Biara" http://www.wadi-online.de/index.php?option=com_content&view=article&id=79&Itemid=16 (Accessed on 16.11.11)

are very dependent on personal experience. While some interviewees received new employment or training opportunities through the NGOs and feel 'empowered', others are ignorant of the different initiatives. Some feel that the NGOs are not helping them, but only following their own agendas and that nothing is changing within the families.[752]

Nevertheless arguably much has already been achieved through these efforts. The grassroots activists have managed to change legislation, to put sensitive issues, such as FGM and honour killings, on the public agenda, and to provide local women with the opportunity to enhance their skills and knowledge. However the fight to make the peoples voices heard and to enhance gender inclusion in the region is not an easy one. Challenges are being encountered which come from outside, as well as from inside the region, which hamper the success of some of the grassroots movements.

The activists have had to fight forces from all directions, including tribal leaders, religious clerics, conservative attitudes in society, and even Parliament[753] in order to be able to live the rights, which are in theory already theirs. This is especially so for gender equality.

In Iraqi Kurdistan the issue of true democracy, in the sense of full public participation, is a highly disputed. While Kurdistan officials, as well as politicians from outside have long declared Kurdistan to have the most democratic system in the region, this has been contested by many academics and political activists. They maintain that the power sharing between the KDP and the PUK does not give the people opportunity for real choice in open elections. Genuine competition does not exist, as opposition parties or independent candidates have reported threats and intimidation[754] and voices of opposition in the population are still not accepted.

---

[752] See e.g. Interview AZ, Sulaimaniya on 06/06/2012; Interview BB, Erbil on 24/06/2012; Interview BD, Erbil on 25/06/2012; Interview BF, Erbil on 29/06/2012

[753] Enloe, *Nimo's War, Emma's War*, 114.

[754] Scott Carpenter and Michael Rubin, Washington Post "Kurdistan's Troubled Democracy" (18 April 2009) http://www.meforum.org/2121/kurdistan-troubled-democracy (Accessed on 25.2.2012)

It is said that the KRG, counter to its own public statements, is taking measures against any organisation or person who works against the parties' interest. Despite the official rhetoric, namely that the government is fighting for women's rights and is supporting women in the region the reality is often different. Women and women's organisations have been continuously suppressed and harassed by the government, if they did not work in the way preferred by the officials. For example, the Independent Women's Organisation (IWO) in Sulaimaniya, had to close down in 2000, because of pressure from the government.[755] Even though this situation has arguably improved today, the old values have not yet been eradicated. For instance, in 2006, when thousands of people demonstrated in Sulaymania to express their unhappiness about the current lack of energy and jobs, the women's organisations which linked themselves to the demonstrators had their funding cut. Additionally many women's activists are still harassed if they speak against the government.[756]

The consequent ambivalent progress towards women's political activity, as well as the influence of the government on the women themselves and the NGOs, were described by an interviewee, who was herself very active in a political women's organisations, but has lived in Europe for the majority of her life, as follows:

"Women rather fight for peace than men. Men only want revenge and more violence. That is not good for Iraq. Today the old fighters dominate the country: the Barzanis, the Talabanis… This is not good for the country. Everything is really politicised. There is nothing like real NGOs. In Kurdistan the women have been integrated since the 70s. There are many women at university, they have the right to vote and they have access to different institutions. But there is no true recognition of women and there is no equality. In the previous elections for example not even the women voted for the other women. The women are not trusted. Without the quota there would not be any women in parliament. But the women managed to achieve legal reforms, like for example the family law. Because of that men are not guardians of the women legally anymore. There are also men who fight for

---

[755] Al-Ali, *Iraqi Women*, 207.
[756] Dr. Nadje Al-Ali in Simon, "Kurdistan, Women in Iraq".

*women's rights. But there are still so many counter movements,
especially from the Islamists."*[757]

Taking the above allegation that *"there is nothing like real NGOs"* as a starting point, it is clear from various interest groups, especially scholars who are affiliated with the west, that the role of NGOs and of other non-governmental activities in Kurdistan and their role in the transformation of conflict are not seen wholly positive. NGOs and women's organisations, as with other organisations, are said to be corrupted or to not have the desired influence. While the local actions can be seen as a development of the civil society and a sign of the emergence of true democracy, it can also be interpreted as a new form of imperialism, dependent on the NGO's ideology, which might be linked to forces in the region or to their funding.[758]

In Kurdistan today, three different movements have developed on the ground: the "local", the "international" and the "party affiliated".

The number and names of civil society organisations are countless. They include for example the Kurdish Women's Rights Watch (KWRW), which supports and promotes women's rights in the Kurdish community[759], the People's Development Association (PDA), which realizes projects concerning human rights[760], the Kurdish Human Rights Watch (KHRW), which *inter alia* focuses on the equal participation of Iraqi women in the new democracy[761], Wadi which supports programmes and projects for self-help and for the empowerment of human and women's rights[762], and WEO, the Women Empowerment Organisation, which aims to enhance women's political, social, economic and cultural participation.[763] Other organisations include Asuda, an organisation for combating violence against women, the Rewan Women's Centre, the Al-Amal, Breeze of Hope Organisation,

---

[757] Interview CJ, Vienna on 28/10/2012

[758] Islah Jad, "The NGO-isation of Arab Women's Movements" *IDS Bulletin* 35(4) (2004): 34.

[759] Kurdish Women's Rights Watch, front page, http://www.kwrw.org/ (Accessed on 16.11.11)

[760] People's Development Association, front page, http://www.xelik.org/En/Default.aspx (Accessed on 16.11.11)

[761] Kurdish Human Rights Watch, "About us", http://www.khrw.org/?page_id=2 (Accessed on 16.11.11)

[762] WADI, front page, http://www.wadi-online.de/ (Accessed on 16.11.11)

[763] Women Empowerment Organisation, "WEO Profile", http://www.weoiraq.org/ (Accessed on 17.10.2012)

and the National Center for Gender Research in Sulaimaniya,[764] just to name a few. Further, the PUK, as well as the KDP, have their own women's unions, which they support. The unions organize seminars and training programs, have issued their own newspapers, and are supporting women victims and encouraging women to join politics [765].[766] While they all try to work for civil society's inclusion in decision making and the enhancement of equality in their own way, they are all criticized for working against their people and the development of equality, for different reasons.

For instance the group of women's organisations founded by one of the political parties is heavily critiqued for being influenced from outside. Such NGOs are said to merely support the party policies and to find excuses for work not being done.[767]

In addition, the close relationship of many women's organisations with the political parties is criticized of not being consistent and inclusive. The relationship might backfire on the women one day, as political protests and growing dissent in Iraqi Kurdistan slowly starts undermining the KRG. To the extent that they ally themselves with the government, they risk being linked to a corrupt regime, which will make it impossible for them to continue their work.[768] It is also claimed that the strong political affiliations of many women's rights activists with the two main political parties result in further inequality, as women could achieve high positions in women's rights organisations because of their membership of a specific party and not because of their abilities.[769] At the same time Kurdish women activists who are linked to a main political party still view others with suspicion resulting in a separation of women who would otherwise fight for the same cause.[770]

Nevertheless their work should not wholly be condemned. At the end of the day the aim of grassroots organisations is to work for the whole population. Affiliated organisations can most directly influence the political parties, because they rather listen to them than to others. While their work is appreciated by many, such

---

[764] Al-Ali and Pratt, "Between Nationalism and Women's Rights," 340.
[765] KDP, "Kurdistan Women Union" http://www.kdp.se/?do=women (Accessed on 15.10.2012)
[766] Alsayid, *Combating Physical Violence Against Women in Iraqi Kurdistan*, 31.
[767] Ibid.
[768] Al-Ali and Pratt, "Between Nationalism and Women's Rights," 352.
[769] Kreutzer, Schmidinger (Hg.), *Irak, Von der Republik der Angst zur bürgerlichen Demokratie?*, 217.
[770] Al-Ali and Pratt, "Between Nationalism and Women's Rights," 344.

organisations are criticized by independent women's activists for not pushing the boundaries, when it comes to social change. The ones which are truly pushing the boundaries are independent organisations, but their influence is limited as they do not receive funding.

The influence of organisations depends very much on the money available to them, as well as on any political support. For this reason, civil society organisations, which are funded by or affiliated with an international organisation or a local or foreign government, have many more resources and hence power than the others.

It follows that, while some of the small local organisations are trying very hard, their influence is often limited, especially at a national level. They do not have the funding and the capacity to realize large scale projects or to be heard by policy makers. In addition, their work is often not well known to the population and some are criticized by the people, especially when it comes to sensitive issues, such as FGM, because they are thought to *"work as Kurds against the Kurds"*.[771] Nevertheless they play a vital role, as they originate from the people themselves, and their work can serve as an opportunity and a role model for other citizens to get involved. While they might be criticized for their work in specific areas or the way they are conducting their work, they cannot be criticized for being influenced from outside or wanting to imperialize.

In comparison with local organisations, the international institutions as well as institutions from outside the country are often considered to have a high status. Work of the international NGOs is often positively received by the population and it is considered prestigious to work for one of these NGOs.

The international bodies have funds and are in the best position to remain independent of the local regime. However, as seen by some, there is a problem of latent imperialism. They are criticized for prioritising their own agendas ahead of the will of the people.

---

[771] Interview BC, Erbil on 25/06/2012

Organisations such as the Iraqi Women's Democracy Initiative,[772] and the Kurdish Human Rights Watch,[773] today organize programmes and workshops to build the capacity of Iraqi women in media skills, leadership, political participation, constitutional rights etc. With funding from the US, the START Social Development Organisation project was launched to empower women and enhance their skills,[774] through the International Republican Institute (IRI), a taskforce on discrimination against women, as well as to enhance the democratic process in the Kurdistan Region and the whole of Iraq.[775] There is a view that these democratisation initiatives, which are mainly funded from outside create a new type of imperialism. Certain ideas are promoted among those participating, while at the same time marginalizing the women's movements which come from within the country.[776] Movements which do not conform with the picture of the 'correct' democratization process are excluded.[777] Furthermore there has been criticism that it is always the same women who are supported, who appear at conferences and in the media and who act as representatives outside the country[778].[779] However, they are not representative of the majority of women in the region.[780]

Further criticism occurs when external funding leads to debates about authenticity and independence of the NOGs. The accusation of imposed imperialism and Westernization seems valid to a certain degree when considering the record. For example, it was announced in 2004 that the US would provide a $10 million grant to NGOs for a "Women's Democracy Initiative". These grants were the distributed among seven, US chosen and US-based, organisations, including Kurdish Human

---

[772] Iraqi Women's Democracy Initiative, "Fact Sheet, Women's issues" (30 April 2010) http://www.state.gov/s/gwi/rls/other/2010/141080.htm (Accessed on 27.2.2012)

[773] Kurdish Human Rights Watch, "Women's' Programs" http://www.khrw.org/?page_id=90 (Accessed on 25.2.2012)

[774] KRG, "START Social Development Organisation concludes pilot women's skills programme" (11.10.2012) http://www.krg.org/articles/detail.asp?lngnr=12&smap=02010100&rnr=223&anr=45529 (Accessed on 15.10.2012)

[775] International Republican Institute, "Taskforce on Discrimination Against Women Launched in Iraq" (27.01.2012) http://www.iri.org/news-events-press-center/news/taskforce-discrimination-against-women-launched-iraq (Accessed on 17.10.2012)

[776] Nadeen El-Kassem, "The pitfalls of a 'democracy promotion' project for women of Iraq" *International Journal of Lifelong Education* 27(2) (2008): 138.

[777] Ibid.p.139

[778] These include Dr. Maha Alattar, Tamara Quinn and Zakia Hakki

[779] El-Kassem, "The pitfalls of a 'democracy promotion' project for women of Iraq," 140.

[780] Ibid.p.144

Rights Watch.[781] Through these grants the beneficiaries became far more powerful than many other women's organizations, while staying loyal to the granting bodies.

However, not only NGOs from other countries, but also the Kurdish people themselves are responsible for Western trends in Kurdish affairs. Millions of Kurds have lived in Western societies in exile and on returning to Kurdistan bring with them the values acquired during their time in exile. Those returning are often very eager to contribute to regional developments and have often substantial means to do so, which is welcomed by the public officials.[782] However during their exile, their way of thinking and acting has changed. The experiences of the people returning can be used positively, by taking the best values of both cultures and unifying them.[783] Nevertheless, people from the diaspora sometimes evoke resentment which might have negative consequences for local movements.[784] Often women, and men, returning from exile, are not warmly welcomed, because they are perceived as having left the country at a time of suffering, of being ill informed of the realities within the country,[785] and, as with the international NGOs, of wishing to imperialize.

Many of the initiatives taken for women, while very positive, are certainly influenced by Western thought. While this pervasive Western influence is seen as negative by those who believe that the organisations are trying to impose Western values and to eradicate the local culture, it is welcomed by others. According to Nadje Al-Ali pressure from outside helps to push governments, in this case the Kurdish government, in a positive direction for women's rights.[786]

In order to deflate such criticism, and to support lasting development, it is important that women's organizations especially, are built up by the locals themselves

---

[781] Al-Ali and Pratt, "Women's organizing and the conflict in Iraq since 2003," 77.

[782] Alasor Roni, Ararat News and Publishing, "Minister Falah Mustafa: Kurdish Diaspora is an important asset for our future" (15.10.2012)
http://www.krg.org/articles/detail.asp?smap=02010200&lngnr=12&rnr=73&anr=45562 (Accessed on 15.10.2012)

[783] Mustafa Gundogdu in Simon, "Kurdistan, Women in Iraq".

[784] Al-Ali, "Reconstructing Gender," 743.
Interview AO, Sulaimaniya on 13/05/2012

[785] Al-Ali and Pratt, "Women in Iraq," 21.

[786] Simon, "Kurdistan, Women in Iraq".

without mirroring Western counterpart organizations. At the same time it is vital that the antipathy against the West, or indeed against any power, is not be used to prevent women from establishing themselves.[787]

One organisation which is arguably capable of promoting gender equality at the grassroots level as well as at the very top, without being linked to a particular regime, is the UN:

The UN, as the representative of the international community, and a neutral party, has the ability and capacity to support positive conflict transformation. However despite some initiatives, it is criticized for not doing enough.

The UN is actively involved in the region. The United Nations Assistance Mission for Iraq (UNAMI), which was established on 14 August 2003,[788] works in all the eighteen governorates of Iraq through such entities as the International Labour Organisation (ILO), the Office of the High Commissioner for Human Rights (OHCHR), the UN Entity for Gender Equality and the Empowerment of Women (UN WOMEN), the UN Development Programme (UNDP), and the UN Educational, Scientific and Cultural Organisation (UNESCO)[789]. These bodies undertook the task of supporting free elections in Iraq, of assisting the drafting of the constitution, of advising the Iraqi government in developing effective civil and social services, of contributing to the delivery of reconstruction and humanitarian assistance, as well as promoting the protection of the rule of law and human rights in Iraq, including the rights of women.[790]

With reference to women and gender inclusiveness, different UN agencies, such as the United Nations Democracy Fund (UNDEF), support and fund projects for peace and democracy building in the whole of Iraq, including the North. They aim

---

[787] Kurdish Human Rights Project, *The Role of Women in Civil society*, 757.

[788] UNAMI, "Facts and Figures" http://unami.unmissions.org/Default.aspx?tabid=2835&language=en-US (Accessed on 8.5.2012)

[789] UNAMI, "UN in Iraq, Frequently Asked Questions" http://unami.unmissions.org/Default.aspx?tabid=3431&language=en-US (Accessed on 8.5.2012)

[790] United Nations Security Council Resolution 1546 (2004), adopted by the Security Council at its 4987th meeting, on 8 June 2004.

to promote knowledge of human rights and fundamental freedoms to ordinary men and women.[791]

In November 2006 UNIFEM conducted a workshop "Towards Iraqi Gender Sensitive Constitution" in Amman, which included representatives from the Al – Tawafoq Iraqi Front Coalition, the Hewar National Iraqi Front, National Iraqi List and UNIFEM's partners from the Civil Society Organizations. The aim of the workshop was to discuss the main points relevant for a gender-balanced constitution and one which guarantees human rights for women.[792] In the same month, UNIFEM conducted a workshop in Amman for women parliamentarians of the Kurdish region and representatives from the Kurdish alliance from parliament in order to establish women blocs within the main political parties.[793] UN Women also provided grants for certain programmes, for example a project by Asuda, for the promotion of education for girls in Sulaymiyah.[794] And international pressure has arguably played a part in supporting the introduction of the quota and supporting more gender-friendly legislation.

While these actions are positive, if successful, the level of support is still limited. The level of involvement of the UN in women and gender matters in the Kurdistan region remains low. According to the Inter-Agency Information and Analysis Unit (IAU), there were only 5 UN Women Project activities in the whole of Iraq, three from the governorate and two on a national level.[795]

In addition to project support, the UN, provides the member states and citizens with international provisions, which are intended to enhance positive development. These provisions, such as the CEDAW and Res 1325, can empower citizens in their dealings with officials.

---

[791] UNDEF, "News from the Field: Human rights education and promotion in Northern Iraq" (11 February 2008) http://www.un.org/democracyfund/XNewsIraq_ConcordiaProject.htm (Accessed on 9.5.2012)
[792] UNIFEM, "Towards Iraqi Gender Sensitive Constitution" (November 2006) http://www.unifem.org.jo/pages/articledetails.aspx?aid=1083 (Accessed on 8.5.2012)
[793] UNIFEM, "Establishing Women's Caucus within the main Political Blocks of the Iraqi Parliament" (November 2006) http://www.unifem.org.jo/pages/articledetails.aspx?aid=1082 (Accessed on 8.5.2012)
[794] Asuda – Combating Violence Against Women http://www.asuda.org/ (Accessed on 17.10.2012)
[795] IAU, *Iraq – UN Women Project Activities by Governorate* (June 2011)

As part of their commitment for gender equality, the United Nations Assistance Mission for Iraq organized a roundtable discussion in 2011, bringing together representatives from the KRG, the Kurdistan Parliament, civil society organisations, women activists and UN agencies. At this meeting, different speakers also urged the UN to do more to implement Res 1325, on a national level, as well as on the grassroots level.[796]

As explained by Sundus Abbas, the UN has failed to implement Res 1325 thoroughly in its mission, particularly when it comes to the protection of women refugees and women being trafficked and kidnapped.[797] Not enough is being done to support the women's actions and to help implement Res 1325, through for example raising awareness of the resolution's existence.[798]

This is supported by Yanar Mohammed, who is of the opinion that the Iraq government has not complied with Res 1325, while at the same time claiming to be fair to women. As explained by Mohammed, Res 1325 calls upon all parties to fully respect international law concerning the rights of women, including *inter alia* the CEDAW[799], and it calls on all parties to protect women and girls from gender-based violence.[800] However, in Iraq today women's movements are not supported, killings of women take place for reasons of honour, there are no government facilities to support the victims, women are being trafficked. Further, under the 2005 constitution domestic violence is legal, polygamy is allowed, abortions are illegal and economic rights, such as inheritance, are unequal.[801]

---

[796] Sabah Abdulrahman, UNAMI, "UNSC Resolution 1325: Fostering the role of women in peace and security in Iraq"
http://unami.unmissions.org/Default.aspx?tabid=2792&ctl=Details&mid=5079&ItemID=3512&language=en-US (Accessed on 16.10.2012)

[797] Nicola Pratt and Sophie Richter-Devroe, "Critically Examining UNSCR 1325 on Women, Peace and Security" *International Feminist Journal of Peace* 13(4) (2011): 497.

[798] Oriana Ramirez, Operation 1325, Power to women in Peace Processes, "Women's Organisations Cooperating in Realising Resolution 1325, Expand collaboration between international missions and women's organisations" (25 November 2011) http://operation1325.se/en/nyheter/expand-collaboration-between-international-missions-and-women-s-organisations (Accessed on 23.2.2012)

[799] See Paragraph 9

[800] See Paragraph 10

[801] Yanar Mohammed, Organisation of Women's Freedom in Iraq "[Despite UN resolution 1325] Women of Iraq Left All Alone" (24 November 2010) http://www.global-sisterhood-network.org/content/view/2557/59/ (Accessed on 23.2.2012)

Res 1325 indeed provides a framework for women who are engaged in peace activism and it has helped to successfully frame their demand of the introduction of a women's quota in parliament. However as argued by Sundus Abbas, concerning the situation in Iraq,[802] not enough is done by the government and the UN to implement it.

Since the UN's mandates included assistance in drafting of the constitution as well as promoting women's rights, it is clear that women's rights were once again not high on the international agenda.

In addition hardly anybody in the general population is aware on any practical programme implemented by the UN. The people therefore do not consider the UN as a force in supporting their needs.

In general many of the local people interviewed were not aware of grassroots actions by and for women, or simply did not consider them a source of influence. This is despite all the work of different organisations at all levels, and from all sides. About one third of the interviewees were of the opinion that women have had no role in the peace building in Kurdistan or only a very small one.[803] While some people criticized the leading political parties for not letting women participate and for not using the abilities of the whole population,[804] hardly anyone took account of grassroots activism. Such activism *per se* is not seen as a true political movement and it is widely believed that its influence is minimal.[805]

While it was recognized by some that women participate in the transformation process by fighting for women's rights, this participation is seen as "trying" for development and peace, rather than being effective or successful.[806] There was

---

[802] Pratt and Richter-Devroe, "Critically Examining UNSCR 1325 on Women, Peace and Security," 497.

[803] See e.g. Interview AF, Erbil on 09/04/2012; Interview BU, Erbil on 24/07/2012; Interview BA, Erbil on 21/06/2012

[804] Interview AV, Sulaimaniya on 28/05/2012; Interview AS, Sulaimaniya on 23/05/2012; Interview AT, Sulaimaniya on 24/05/2012; Interview BT, Erbil on 24/07/2012

[805] Interview AL, Erbil on 25/04/2012; Interview AM, Erbil on 27/04/2012

[806] Interview AR, Sulaimaniya on 21/05/2012

only one very enthusiastic feminist student who stated that the women have the ability to succeed in achieving peace.[807]

By comparison, many believed that women are not able to fully participate in any political action or peace building efforts, as they have their roles in the families to fulfill[808] or because they are suppressed by the patriarchal structure or the authorities.[809]

As a young woman from university explained:

> *"What role do you expect the women had after the end of the war? Both, men and women could not talk out. They were not free to express their opinions (against the political parties) and they were not involved. So women could not really contribute to peace. They had no chance."[810]*

There were only two women who thought of women's roles as a means to prove themselves in different environments; to show other women the right path; or to fight for women in general.[811]

A possible reason for the lack of a 'feeling of connection' to the grassroots movement by the people at large, is that the grassroots sector in the Kurdistan Region suffers from a perceived lack of effectiveness. By comparison, NGOs have the ability to reach women from all backgrounds, urban and rural, and to give them an opportunity to enhance their skills and to provide them with their own space to develop. However, it is argued that these opportunities are often not taken. As Shahrzad Mojab explains, there is often a huge gap between the programmes implemented and funded and the actual poverty and marginalization experienced by a significant percentage of the population. The people involved in NGOs and women's organisations, are often urban-based and middle-class and are said to therefore not be in touch with other parts of society.[812] As argued by Simpson, some gender-specific NGOs merely support women of a certain social class,

---

[807] Interview BV, Sulaimaniya on 06/08/2012

[808] Interview AG, Erbil on 13/04/2012; Interview BM, Erbil on 13/07/2012

[809] Interview CA, Sulaimaniya on 13/08/2012

[810] Interview AM, Erbil on 27/04/2012

[811] Interview AT, Sulaimaniya on 24/05/2012; Interview BR, Erbil on 22/07/2012

[812] Al-Ali and Pratt, "Women's organizing and the conflict in Iraq since 2003," 78.

namely the 'class of civic activists' but ignore policies towards the underprivileged women who are not connected with this 'new elite'. The NGOs are consequently criticized for helping some privileged women to be more equal to some privileged men, but not working for more equality in general.[813] As explained by one female student, who was herself closely connected to women's rights organizations and NGOs, the NGO training programmes are very good, but they are only for educated women, women who already know their rights. However they should rather be designed for people from an economically less advantageous background, who do not know their rights and who might not have the opportunity to find out about them.[814] Nevertheless there are also organisations who have a broad membership and who have branches all over the country, including cities as well as the country side.[815]

Just as the structure and work of the different organisations and movements are ambivalent, so are the outcomes of their efforts. It is arguably the greatest problem in the region as a whole the level of *de jure* and *de facto* compliance with core international standards as well as their own legal provisions, and activities is not the same, especially when it comes to women's rights. While women have equal rights to participate in politics and other decision-making positions, they in fact still often lack true power in these positions in practice.[816] The same discrepancy between the legal provisions and their practical realisation for many women is true for health care[817], education,[818] as well as labour and economic rights.[819] Equality is far from achieved, especially when it comes to practical day-to-day life.

While activism from different sides has contributed to the passage of more gender sensitive legislation and the partial raising of awareness of the issues in society, as well as the creation of programmes for women, and while individuals are benefiting, the achievements are not leading to a 'big movement' throughout the

---

[813] Eifler and Seifert, *Gender Dynamics and Post-Conflict Reconstruction,* 37.

[814] Interview BY, Sulaimaniya on 10/08/2012

[815] Al-Ali and Pratt, "Women's organizing and the conflict in Iraq since 2003," 78.

[816] Iraq Legal Development Project, *The Status of Women in Iraq: Update to the Assessment of Iraq's De Jure and De Facto Compliance with International Legal Standards* (American Bar Association 2006) 12.

[817] Ibid.pp.36,41

[818] Ibid.p.129

[819] Ibid.p.162

population. Within the ever widening circle of the different movements and organizations, there is no clear structure and insufficient cooperation. The people speak with different voices, although this was said to have been improved by activists in 2013, who stated that the sense of collaboration between the different groups is growing and that there are in general more people becoming politically active.[820]

While a multitude of individual and scattered actions will achieve something, it will take much longer to achieve a larger aim, including the aim for equality. It is still unclear in which direction the current situation will take.

The lack of a unified movement, as well as the lack of people's awareness and the recognition of the existing activities, slows the process towards equality and positive peace. The people have the feeling that they are not in a position to influence policy making, and consequently remain passive. In addition the different criticisms of the imposing and imperializing nature of the movements makes many people vary of them. This can even lead to certain groups within society acting against the movements, in order to take a stand for their own culture.

Nevertheless, despite the criticism of certain activities at a local, as well as an international level, and despite not knowing just how far the influence of the different movements goes, they all have some role to play in the process of conflict transformation. As noted above the problems of conflicts are multidimensional and it can therefore be argued that a more multidimensional approach towards peacebuilding can only be positive.

Women raising their voices for equality, reminds others in the population of the importance of the issue. It gives other women the strength to support their struggle and pushes policy makers to take action in the long run. Speaking out also encourages the NGOs to provide a platform for people who might not otherwise be able to get involved. According to an Austrian women's rights activist, who is closely involved with the grassroots level actions in the Kurdistan region, the NGOs and women's organizations give the women more opportunities and help to create

---

[820] Christian Peacemaker Teams, *Kurdish Activists' Observations*, 3.

freedoms. As such they partly help to raise the living standard of some women and, if they work together with people from different ethnic groups, can enhance the feeling of solidarity. All of these factors contribute to positive peace.

In order to move the process towards positive peace even further, it is important that the different grassroots movements put behind their differences and start working together; that they concentrate their work only on the needs of the people; and that they make themselves heard even more clearly amongst the population. All women need to be made aware of the importance of politics for their own lives and that they need to be encouraged to participate. Just because women are not in public does not mean they do not have an opinion that needs to be heard.[821] The civil society has to be made aware that if they lack the political will, knowledge, or confidence, they are unable to influence their own lives and the country's development.[822] By renouncing the women's ability to speak up and by separating the domains of politics and civil society, the people indirectly reduce the power of their own voices.

As a general conclusion on the gender policies deployed at a political level it can be said that while a lot has happened in the previous ten years, their potential influence on national development and the enhancement of gender equality within society is far from exhausted.

When it comes to negotiations between different parties, and especially with factions from outside the region, women and gender considerations are not on the agenda; and it is said to be merely the old warriors who take charge. This has arguably changed within national politics. With the thirty per cent quota, women have achieved a break in the gender divide, which previously characterised power relations. Women are starting to be seen as an individual source for the region's development. On the downside, the increase of women in parliament arguably did not lead to a true gender balanced perspective as only certain fractions of the population have access to the political sphere. While not diminishing the positive

---

[821] As Cynthia Enloe showed, even beauty salons can become political spaces: Enloe, *Nimo's War, Emma's War*, 21.

[822] Buchanan (ed.), *Women at the Indonesian peace table*, 12.

achievements of the current politicians, this hampers development by not ensuring a truly balanced point of view in politics. While the increase of the number of women in parliament is seen from the outside as positive for the region, on a local level, the influence has not yet been great enough due to the lack of equal representation. The increase in female representation has led to increased sympathy for gender equal politics within society. However, this sympathy is often theoretical and not in practical and it is often not transferred into day-to-day life.

While developments in parliament can be seen to influence society as a whole in a similar way, the influence of grassroots activism within society differs from individual to individual, and is very much dependent on personal experience. From a national point of view, the existence of the grassroots sector itself promotes the democratic development within the region. However, the great differences between the different forces and their lack of cooperation, including also from the government side, hampers their influence on national development. As noted above it is still unclear what the true effect of the NGO and grassroots movements are on society as a whole.

It can thus be seen that while broad opportunities have been widely opened up, positive peace in general and gender equality in particular are far from achieved. But it is not only politics and political activism, which can influence national development and the attainment of peace for individuals. One further factor to consider is the power of economy:

V.   Gender, Women and the Economy

"The greater the role of women in the political and economic aspects of society, the less likely that the state will engage in militarized interstate conflict.[823]"

A rising economy is connected with prosperity and development, not only on an economic level, but also on a social and personal level. Positive economic development for every country and region is seen as vital around the world, as the economic situation of a country or region influences the region's standing in the

---

[823] Patrick Regan and Aida Paskeviciute, "Women's Access to Politics and Peaceful States" *Journal of Peace Research* 40(3) (2003): 289.

international community, as well as the citizens' quality of living. A stable and balanced economy enriches society, while an unstable and unbalanced economy is often an underlying factor for an outbreak of conflict and an eruption of violence, as the increasing discontent with the economic situation leads to the rising of frustration and consequently to either emigration[824] or conflict. Hence the state of the economy is partly responsible for an increase or decrease in the potential for conflict. In conflict ridden regions economic development can, in principle, contribute to the prevention of reignited armed conflict and the support of a positive peace building process.[825] However this is not an easy process.

The economies of countries in post-conflict situations are often characterized by high levels of unemployment, poverty and disrupted markets.[826] Only when this situation is ameliorated and people consequently experience a rise in their quality of living and of economic prosperity that they will tend to think about maintaining peace rather than pursuing further conflict. Further, the people will tend not support extremism, but politicians who can ensure further economic growth.[827] Experience shows that every region in a post-war situation, which wishes to decrease conflict potential in the short, as well as in the long term, needs to concentrate on economic growth and the stabilisation of its economy.

For example since the decrease in violence within the Kurdistan Region, it has been the government's high priority to secure rapid economic growth in order to prove themselves to the international community, as well as to improve their citizens' standard of living. While in the past the region's economy was destroyed through the internal and external conflicts, as well as through imposition of sanctions, today, signs of economic prosperity are visible everywhere. New roads are being built, houses are being constructed, there is a rising number of new exclusive residential areas, and people spend their leisure time in newly constructed malls. The region's politicians express pride in the impressive

---

[824] Jens Stilhoff Sörensen, *State Collapse and Reconstruction in the Periphery, Political Economy, Ethnicity and Development in Yugoslavia, Serbia and Kosovo* (New York: Berghahn Books, 2009): 248.

[825] Richmond, "Peace and Development," 437.

[826] Michael Pugh, "Normative Values and Economic Deficits in Postconflict Transformation" *International Journal* 62(3) (2007): 480.

[827] Michael Bhatia, "Postconflict Profit: The Political Economy of Intervention" *Global Governance* 11(2) (2005) 206

economic development of the recent years. Economic prosperity is seen as the key to international standing and peace and economic reconstruction is generally seen as one of the most important measures to ensure future development.

The interviewees were also of the opinion that one of the driving forces behind the reconstruction of their region was the economy, trade, and the financial power. People from all backgrounds, young and old, men and women, rich and poor, religious and non-religious, agreed that the power of physical reconstruction, but also peace building, lies with money, as well as with the workers.[828]

However, as will be discussed throughout this chapter, in order to truly ensure positive development and sustainable peace, the positive economic development needs to be accessible to and felt by all people. Despite the correlation between the economy and peace in a region, it has to be remembered that peace does not automatically appear with a higher GDP. The success in the reconstruction of a country will depend closely on the nature of the post-conflict economy. While a war economy can destroy a country, a "peace economy", including open markets for all, anti-corruption policies and the participation of ordinary people is able to rebuild a country.[829] As such the economy cannot be seen as an isolated domain. It is interconnected with political and social developments, where each influences the other.[830] Without positive social development, such as the decrease of violent conflict between different groups within society, or the creation of an educated people, positive economic development will not be achievable. At the same time, without positive economic development violent conflict is more likely to occur, and education is less supported. A similar correlation can be seen between the economy and politics.

In the Kurdistan region it is argued by many interviewees that the politicians have as yet been unable to synchronise economic and social development for all parts of society. Not everybody is benefitting from the region's economic prosperity to the same extent and there is a need for enhanced social services and a fairer

---

[828] See e.g. Interview BX, Sulaimaniya on 09/08/2012; Interview BQ, Erbil on 21/07/2012; Interview AZ, Sulaimaniya on 06/06/2012; Interview BF, Erbil on 29/06/2012

[829] Pugh, "Normative Values and Economic Deficits in Postconflict Transformation," 485.

[830] Stilhoff, *State Collapse and Reconstruction in the Periphery*, 27.

distribution of wealth. The fight against corruption and the fostering of national resources is needed to ensure that no further conflict will arise.[831] It is also here that women and gender equality come into play.

Women play a crucial role in a country's economy, as consumers, employees or entrepreneurs. In today's Western world it is generally accepted that the successful inclusion of women in the economy will support the development of social equality and will help to eradicate poverty. However, even today there is not a single country in the world, where women share totally equal economic rights with men or have the same access to resources as men.[832] In order for women to play a part in the economic cycle, they need to have the opportunities for employment or to establish their own businesses. This will enable them to feed their families, to contribute to a rise in the economic prosperity of the country, as well as to further their own personal development.[833]

But is this true? Is women's economic inclusion and empowerment necessary for national productivity? And if it is, how does this 'empowerment' reflect on women's personal state of peace?

As clearly laid out by the World Bank Development Report of 2012[834] gender equality in the economy benefits development and raises productivity especially at the national level. By contrast a lack of usage or a 'misallocation' of women's skills comes at an increased economic cost. At the same time women's personal empowerment, increases with financial power, as it gives them the opportunity to manage their lives more independently and thus provides them with confidence.[835]

Despite this knowledge there is often a lack of consideration of women's inclusion, and the links, argued by True, between macroeconomic policies, trade

[831] See e.g. Interview AR, Sulaimaniya on 21/05/2012; Interview BP, Erbil on 21/07/2012; Interview BT, Erbil on 24/07/2012

[832] Jacqui True, *The Political Economy of Violence against Women* (Oxford: Oxford University Press, 2012) 5.

[833] Bhatia, "Postconflict Profit," 220.

[834] The World Bank, *Gender Equality and Development* (Washington: World Development Report, 2012) 3.

[835] Ibid.p.94

liberalisation and the effects of financial crises on different forms of violence against women are overlooked.[836]

The aim of this chapter is to analyse how the Kurdistan region's macroeconomic, employment, and business policies and and the inclusion of women's and gender issues therein can influence progress towards gender equality, as well as positive conflict transformation on a national and a personal level. The discussion will cover the resulting impact on women's personal development and peace within the families and society and how this influences economic development in the region which is considered to be a driving force for positive conflict transformation. Firstly a short overview will be presented on the existing literature on the economy, gender equality and peace and the various academic views encountered. This will be followed by an outline of the legal opportunities for women in today's Kurdistan's economy and by a discussion on the KRG's macroeconomic policies and their influence on gender equality and positive conflict transformation within the region. The role of business and employment will be analysed with reference to women's empowerment and economic prosperity, and the resulting influence on the propensity for conflict within society. This will lead to the conclusion that the sought after positive development has only been realised for select groups of the population resulting in a loss of human resources for the region, and little or no progress towards gender equality.

1.   A Theoretical Overview

Apart from promoting general development, economic measures can influence the transition from conflict to peace. A whole area of academic research namely 'peace economics', seeks to define the right policies to optimise this transition. According to Walter Isard in 1994 they are,

> *"generally concerned with: (1) resolution, management or reduction of conflict in the economic sphere; (2) the use of economic measures and policy to cope with and control conflicts whether economic or not; and (3) the impact of conflict on the economic*

---

[836] True, *The Political Economy of Violence against Women*, 5.

<blockquote>
behavior and welfare of firms, consumers organisations, government and society"[837]
</blockquote>

For example, measures to adjust women's participation in the labour force, is a way to decrease unemployment, reduce poverty and diminish conflict potential within society.

Concerning the correlation between women's inclusion and economic development, the official position of the international community is clear:

<blockquote>
"Gender equality, poverty eradication and sustainable development are intrinsically linked. These linkages cut across the social, economic, environmental and governance dimensions of sustainable development. Acknowledging how development challenges and responses affect women, as well as women's vital contributions to economic progress, is essential for the success of sustainable development and poverty eradication policies and practices. Initiatives that engage women as full stakeholders have proven to enhance sustainable livelihoods of local communities and national economies.[838]"
</blockquote>

Many feminist economists agree that the inclusion of women in economic reconstruction following an armed conflict is vital for the country's economic, social and political development and criticise the international community for not implementing its official position.[839]

Jacqui True argues that women's participation in national or regional economies and labour forces is crucial, especially after war, due to the under supply of male workers as a consequence of death and disappearance as well as a lack of incoming migration.[840] She argues further that economic opportunities and economic security are closely linked to political participation. True continues that gender inequality in the economic and social arenas, leads reduced economic security. As a result, women are less available to participate in public decision making, and this limits their contribution to long term policy development, which is

---

[837] Raul Caruso, "On the Nature of Peace Economics" Peace Economics, Peace Science and Public Policy 16(2) (2010): 1.

[838] UNDP, Powerful Synergies, Gender Equality, Economic Development and Environmental Sustainability (Report, September 2012) 3.

[839] True, The Political Economy of Violence against Women, 85.

[840] Ibid.p.88

vital for the region.[841] It follows that women's economic empowerment is the basis for their political empowerment.[842]

This view is supported by Günseli Berik and others, who assert that inequality in income, as with economic inequality in general, leads to reduced political and social power, which is detrimental to the national as well as to the women's personal development. One way of counteracting this trend is through macroeconomic policies. Feminist economists, such as Günseli Berik, Yana van der Meulen Rodgers or Stephanie Seguino, maintain that macroeconomic policies, when directed to human well-being rather than the traditional goals of price stability and growth rates, would have a beneficial effect on peace building at all levels.[843]

For macroeconomic measures to benefit all, the perspectives of the whole population need to be considered. Feminist academics, such as Anne Tickner have asserted that 'knowledge' is not universal, but rather dependent on the person sharing the knowledge. In today's world most 'knowledge' coming from high decision makers is male and based on male experience.[844] With this idea in mind, feminist economists, such as Brigitte Young and Christoph Scherrer have concluded that, in general, the mainstream theories underpinning policy development in finance, trade and macroeconomics are 'male' and mostly based on a traditional understanding of gender roles.[845] To counter this tendency, the Platform of Action stressed the necessity to incorporate *"a gender perspective in budgetary decisions on policies and programmes"*.[846] However, many feminist academics also note that, in the political sphere, not all women are in the same situation and it depends very much on which group are being considered.[847]

At a personal level, economic development arguably impacts women in a very different way than men. As reported by the Heinrich Böll Stiftung, jobs in general

---

[841] Ibid.

[842] Ibid.p.89

[843] Günseli Berik, Rodgers Van der Meulen and Stephanie Seguino, "Feminist Economics of Inequality, Development, and Growth" *Feminist Economics* 15(3) (2009): 2.

[844] Anne Tickner in Brigitte Young and Christoph Scherrer (eds.), *Gender Knowledge and Knowledge Networks in International Political Economy* (Baden-Baden: Nomos, 2010) 9.

[845] Ibid.

[846] United Nations, *Beijing Platform for Action* 1995, Chapter VI: Financial Arrangements, para 345

[847] Al-Ali in Simon, "Kurdistan, Women in Iraq".

have enabled some women to gain more independence although many of the jobs for women are still too often badly paid. This leads to further restrictions for women, as they are unable to earn enough to support themselves. As a result women worldwide comprise about sixty per cent of the working poor,[848] which, according to the Arab Human Development Report leads to women's disempowerment and should be opposed.[849]

According to Agneta Soderberg Jacobson, the job market is only one reason for inequality in outcome for women's economic efforts. Unequal distribution of resources in families exacerbates this trend and makes it possible for the women in a family to be poor, while their husbands and sons are not. According to Soderberg Jacobson, issues such as inheritance, property ownership and the right to work are of particular importance for women and their personal development especially after armed conflicts.[850]

At the same time women contribute greatly to families', communities' and national economy, especially in the country side, without having their work acknowledged or remunerated. This was also acknowledged by the *Arab Human Development Report 2005: Towards the Rise of Women in the Arab World,*[851] which noted that the true extent of women's participation in social and economic activities in Arab society is not recognised and that women are not adequately rewarded for their participation.[852]

Feminist economists point out that non-marketed activities, such as household work are not regarded as economic activities and are thus not included within macroeconomic policy. This is criticized, as paid and unpaid labours are clearly tightly interrelated. When public spending decreases, especially in areas such as social services, unpaid work, which is mainly carried by women, automatically increases. For instance Diane Elson claims that the decrease of social welfare

---

[848] Heinrich Böll Stiftung, *Gender Politics Makes A Difference*, 52.
[849] UNDP, *Arab Human Development Report 2005, Executive Summary*, (2005) http://www.arab-hdr.org/publications/contents/2005/execsum-05e.pdf (Accessed on 28.11.11) p.10
[850] Soderberg Jacobson, *Security on whose terms?*, 14.
[851] Abu-Lughod, "Dialects of Women's Empowerment," 83.
[852] UNDP, *Arab Human Development Report 2005*, 6.

spending affects the entire economy, as it leads to a forced reallocation and arguably also a reduction of human capabilities.[853]

Consequently in order to enhance national economic development, as well as women's individual situation, the recognition of non-marketed activities on the economy, as well as the impacts of the associated economic policies, are of vital importance.

As argued by Brigitte Young and Christoph Scherrer, whatever way is preferred, whether women rather work in the formal economy, while the state is undertakes social services, or work full time in the home, it is imperative to see 'homes' as areas of economic productivity and acknowledge the work accomplished therein, in order to *"reveal the hidden costs of economic reconstruction"*.[854]

As argued by Maria Floro and Hella Hope, how and to what extent trade and financial policy reforms improve or reduce gender equalities, are not always measurable or even apparent. However it is clear that income and employment patterns influence a household member's authority and control over resources, as well as on his or her decision making role.[855] As noted by Jacqui True there is a connection between gender based abuse and violence and a woman's lack of, or reduced access to, productive resources such as income, employment, land, property, technology, credit, and education.[856]

This opinion is not shared by all. The findings of the World Bank, suggest that it is not always clear, whether, on a personal level, increased economic productivity by women leads generally to a greater or lesser standing in the family and in society for women. While it is argued that women with their own income have more power, less dependency, and experience less domestic violence, it is also observed that higher paid women especially are seen as a threat to the male status. This leads to

---

[853] Young and Scherrer (eds.), *Gender Knowledge,* 59/60.

[854] Young and Scherrer (eds.), *Gender Knowledge,* 60.

[855] Isabella Bakker and Rachel Silvey, *Beyond States and Markets, the Challenge of Social Reproduction* (Milton Park: Routledge, 2008) 40.

[856] True, *The Political Economy of Violence against Women,* 17/18.

an increased work load of women in comparison to men, and thus to more conflict.[857]

While there is a general tendency, especially among Western feminist academics, to view women's increased participation in the formal economy as a wholly or mainly positive development, it has been pointed out that the resulting increase in women's independence is seen by some men as a direct challenge to their dominance. This can lead to violence against women, as well as social unrest. Masculine identity has traditionally been built around the man's role as the main breadwinner. As this identity is challenged, the perceived loss of status by some men can result in the outbreak of conflict in the private, as well as the public space.[858] According to True, this could be observed in several countries, such as Pakistan or Bangladesh, where violence against women increased, at the same time as the percentage of women obtaining paid employment and higher education increased.[859] While the economic empowerment of women might lead to further personal conflict and tensions within society, as a result of a loss of identity felt by men, nevertheless it is debatable whether this is a short or long term development.

In conclusion the current prevailing opinion of the international community, as well as the majority of feminist scholars, that economic empowerment of women is vital for the country's development. It is important to widen the categories of recognised 'economic activities' to include household work. At the same time opinions on the effects of economic 'empowerment' on women's personal 'peace' are split. While it is generally agreed that the access to assets are vital, pushing women into employment, especially when badly remunerated, is crticised by several economic feminists. Nevertheless it is generally agreed that is vital to open up economic opportunities for women, especially after the end of armed conflicts. This will support positive conflict transformation and provide women with the possibility for further personal development as demonstrated in principle in the Kurdistan Region.

---

[857] The World Bank, *Gender Equality and Development*, 153/171.
[858] True, *The Political Economy of Violence against Women*, 39.
[859] Ibid.pp.18/19

2.   Legal Foundation

The importance of the economy to the Kurdistan region is already apparent from the highest law of the region. In its draft constitution the current government enshrined that

> *"The Kurdistan Region shall adopt a competitive legal market economy, which encourages and embraces economic development on modern foundations, as well as public and private investment. Monopolies shall not be allowed, except as regulated by law."[860]*

When it comes to the equality between male and female citizens in the economic sphere, Iraq, and thus the Kurdistan Region, by becoming a party to the ICESCR, agreed to:

> *"[...] ensure the equal right of men and women to the enjoyment of all economic, social and cultural rights [...]"[861].*

These rights were reiterated in the Kurdistan Draft Constitution, where it states in article 20 that

> *"Men and women shall be equal before the law. The Government of the Region must seek to remove all obstacles hindering equality in all spheres of life, and in civil, political, social, cultural and economic rights. The Government of the Region guarantees that all shall enjoy their rights, as stipulated in this Constitution and the international charters signed by the State of Iraq.[862]"*

When it comes to specific economic rights, every Iraqi citizen has the right to own property[863] and to conclude a contract, unless restricted to do so by law[864].

Also concerning the right to work, Iraq, including the Kurdistan Region, have, through their acceptance of the different international covenants, including the ICESCR, the CEDAW, the ILO Convention on Equal Remuneration for Work of Equal Value from 1952, the Convention on the Abolition of Forced Labour from

---

[860] Draft of the Iraqi Kurdistan Region's Constitution 2009, Article 15
[861] International Covenant on Economic, Social and Cultural Rights, Article 3
[862] Draft of the Iraqi Kurdistan Region's Constitution 2009, Article 20, Third
[863] Iraqi Constitution 2005, Article 23, Third
[864] Iraqi Civil Code No. 40 of 1951, Article 93

1857 and the Convention on Discrimination in Employment and Occupation from 1958,[865] have agreed to

> *"recognize the right to work, which includes the right of everyone to the opportunity to gain his living by work which he freely chooses or accepts, and will take appropriate steps to safeguard this right.[866]"*

and to

> *take all appropriate measures to eliminate discrimination against women in the field of employment in order to ensure, on a basis of equality of men and women, the same rights.[867]*

Additionally they have agreed to

> *"take into account the particular problems faced by rural women and the significant roles which rural women play in the economic survival of their families, including their work in the non-monetized sectors of the economy, and shall take all appropriate measures to ensure the application of the provisions of the present Convention to women in rural areas".[868]*

The indiscriminate right for equal opportunities of employment is also enshrined in the Iraqi Constitution, as well as in the Draft Constitution of the Kurdistan Region. However the Iraqi Constitution limits the right to work wherever this would not ensure a "dignified life" for the worker. While certainly honourably in its motive, this qualification is open to interpretation, especially when considering the issue of gender.

> *"Work is a right for all Iraqis in a way that guarantees a dignified life for them".[869]*

> *"Everyone shall have the right to work in a profession or an occupation to which he or she freely consents.*
> *Every worker shall have the right to equal pay for equal work. The relations between workers and employers shall be regulated by law and founded on economic bases, while taking into account the rules of social justice".[870]*

---

[865] International Trade Union Confederation, *2012 Annual Survey of Violations of Trade Union Rights – Iraq* (6 June 2012) 1.

[866] International Covenant on Economic, Social and Cultural Rights, Article 6

[867] The Convention on the Elimination of All Forms of Discrimination Against Women 1979, Article 11

[868] Ibid, Article 14

[869] Iraqi Constitution 2005, Article 22

[870] Kurdistan Region Draft Constitution 2009, Article 24, Fourth and Fifth

The equal rights to work, including equal pay for equal work, are endorsed in national law in the Labor Code of 1987, which

> *"[...] guarantees the right to work, under equal conditions and with equal opportunity, to all citizens who are able to work, without any discrimination on the basis of sex, race, language or religion [...]"*[871]

and additionally ensures

> *"the principle of equality of remuneration for the same type and the same quantity of work performed under identical circumstances."*[872]

But since there is no law, which determines minimum wages, it is difficult to determine whether women are paid the same as men.[873]

In addition to the provisions of equality, the Iraqi Labor Code provides for the protection of women workers. It prohibits the employment of women in *"arduous work or work which is harmful to health*[874]*"*, assigning work to pregnant women work, which is likely to endanger their health or the health of their fetus[875], and obliging women work at night, with certain exceptions.[876] Furthermore the act ensures maternity leave[877], as well as sick leave for any child under the age of six,[878] with 62 days of the maternity leave being fully paid under the act[879], and any additional time being subject to the consent of the employer.[880] Finally, the provisions of the act do not apply to women who

> *"are engaged in a family enterprise in which only family members work and which is under the authority and supervision of the woman's spouse, father, mother or brother."*[881]

---

[871] Iraq Labor Code, Act No. 71 of 1987, Article 2

[872] Ibid. Article 4(2)

[873] UNDP – Iraq, *Women's Economic Empowerment, Integrating Women into the Iraqi Economy* (March 2012) 10

[874] Iraq Labor Code, Act No. 71 of 1987, Article 81

[875] Ibid. Article 82

[876] Ibid. Article 83

[877] Ibid. Articles 84-86

[878] Ibid. Article 87

[879] Ibid. Article 84

[880] Ibid. Article 86

[881] Ibid. Article 89

Apart from the fact that the Labor Law of 1987 could be interpreted in a way that precludes women from certain types of jobs, and is not applicable to all women, one of the greatest problem of the act is that the people are not aware of its existence or its provisions. According to a monitoring report, initiated by Harikar NGO in 2011, on the implementation of the Iraqi Labor Law 71 of 1987 in Dohuk, approximately 75 per cent of workers were not aware that the labour law existed in the region or what it entailed. This resulted in the law not being implemented appropriately.[882]

The labour laws are of great importance, as they can open up the labour market to the whole population and ensure equal treatment. One provision is of particular importance for many women in the Kurdistan at present, since only about 17 per cent of women are officially 'working'. It relates to a functioning social security system.

By becoming a member of the ICESCR, Iraq agreed to

> *"[…] recognize the right of everyone to social security, including social insurance."*[883]

This right to social security was also enshrined in the Kurdistan Draft Constitution, which states that

> *"Everyone shall have the right to social security, especially in cases of motherhood, sickness, unemployment, injury, disability, old age, displacement, and loss of one's means of livelihood in circumstances beyond one's control"*[884]

Different social security and welfare laws in Iraq and the Kurdistan Region ensure social security to every citizen during his lifetime, as well as his survivors after death.[885]

---

[882] Rasheed Bakhtiar Ahmed, Hussein Delshad Arif, *Implementation of Iraqi Labor Law 71 of 1987 in Dohuk Governorate* (Dohuk: Monitoring Report, Hawar Printing Press – Dohuk 2012) 25.

[883] International Covenant on Economic, Social and Cultural Rights, Article 9

[884] Kurdistan Region Draft Constitution 2009, Article 24, Third

[885] Social Welfare Law No. 126 of 1980, see: Institute for International Law and Human Rights, *Women and the Law in Iraq* (Washington: December 2010) 82.

The different laws provide for workers' pensions and social security in the public[886] and the private spheres.[887] In all cases old age, disability, survivors' benefits and maternity leave are covered.[888]

As part of the survivor's benefit, the surviving spouse, underage children and any other dependents of the breadwinner are entitled to a share of the insured person's old-age pension.[889]

In addition all vulnerable families, who are on a very low income, or no income at all, as well as widows and divorcees with minor children, are entitled to a family welfare allowance[890], which provides these families with a monthly cash benefit by the state.[891]

As with the labour law, the different social security schemes in Iraq and the Kurdistan Region, provide an important safety net and benefit society in general. However they are in need of improvement, as they are not applicable to all in the same way, and even where they are, it is not always possible in practice for the citizens to benefit from the provisions.

As explained for example by the Institute for International Law and Human Rights, which analyzed "Women and the Law in Iraq" in 2010, the Workers' Pension and Social Security Law offers a comprehensive scheme, under which workers are protected, but they exempt those employed by their close relatives, those in temporary employment, domestic servants and those working in agriculture[892] from the protection of the law. According to the institutes, these are all employment sectors, which are dominated by women workers.[893]

In addition, as argued by the UNDP, the Iraq laws often fail to establish equal provisions in the economic sector for both genders, as a result of their flawed

---

[886] Civil Pension Law No.33 of 1966

[887] Workers' Pension and Social Security Scheme under Law No. 19 of 1971

[888] Amjad Rashid, Julian Havers (eds.), *Jobs for Iraq: An Employment and Decent Work Strategy* (International Labour Organisation 2007) 75.

[889] Worker's Pension and Social Security Law No.112 of 1969, Article 39

[890] Social Welfare Law No. 126 of 1980, Article 3

[891] Rashid and Havers (eds.), *Jobs for Iraq*, 79.

[892] Workers' Pension and Social Security Law No. 112 of 1969, Article 3

[893] Institute for International Law and Human Rights, *Women and the Law in Iraq*, 87.

interpretations.[894] Furthermore, too many people are still not aware of their rights,[895] or are not able to receive the benefits applicable to them. For too many people, the benefits are not adequate for their needs.[896]

Finally, there are certain provisions, such as child support by the divorced father, which are in need of reform, in order to ensure economic security for all.[897]

In conclusion, despite a few points of criticism, the legal provisions for inclusiveness and fair treatment in the work place, as well as for social security and the general support of the population within the economy are in place, although not always implemented as illustrated with some examples below. However, when it comes to economic inclusion, legal provisions alone are certainly not sufficient. National level macroeconomic policies are also important:

A.   Influencing the Economy from a National Level– Macroeconomic Policies

"[We] recogn[ize] that women's poverty and lack of empowerment, as well as their exclusion from social policies and from the benefits of sustainable development, can place them at increased risk of violence, and that violence against women impedes the social and economic development of societies and states, as well as the achievement of the internationally agreed development goals, including the Millennium Development Goals"[898]

Macroeconomic policies can shape society. Through the adopted measures it is possible to decrease or increase equality, and lead the country towards economic or social development. Through the budget the government can support or oppose specific national policies or projects.

Adequate macroeconomic financing is supremely important for stability and prosperity in the region at a time of peacebuilding. During such a period especially, the macroeconomic policy should be designed to ensure positive development by

---

[894] UNDP – Iraq, *Women's Economic Empowerment,* 7.

[895] Institute for International Law and Human Rights, *Women and the Law in Iraq,* 82.

[896] UNDP – Iraq, *Women's Economic Empowerment,* 7.

[897] *"By law, divorced Iraqi men are only required to provide alimony or financial payments to their ex-wife for a three month period after the divorce."* See: UNDP – Iraq, *Women's Economic Empowerment,* 22.

[898] UN Economic and Social Council 2010 Resolution 45/4 Women Economic Empowerment

raising the standard of living of the population through reduced unemployment, ensuring a low inflation rate, reducing poverty, ensuring economic growth and uplifting society's well-being in general.[899]

It is in the hands of the major economic players, namely the international investment and trade organisations, as well as the different governments, to influence employment and income patterns,[900] as well as to provide for social security, the enhancement of education and general economic opportunities for the citizens. The major economic players should endeavour to ensure that these possibilities are equally accessible to every citizen notwithstanding their ethnic group, class or gender. It therefore lies partly in the hands of the government whether or not women have the opportunities to enhance their incomes and consequently also their authority.

With reference to macroeconomic policies and gender, it is still the prevalent view among feminist scholars, such as Tina Johnson, that the formulators of policy at the World Bank, the IMF and national ministries of finance too often view their domain gender neutral.[901] At the same time it is known that women and men are affected differently by macro-economic policies because of their different economic roles in society.[902] Cutbacks in the expenditure for health services or the civil service sector for example mean that women are less likely to be able to find a job and to help provide for their families.[903] It is argued that macroeconomic policies are often implemented without due consideration for their effects on the primary and secondary incomes of citizens, especially those with few economic and social resources. [904] It is consequently argued that in order for the policies to be beneficial

---

[899] Hashim Al-Ali, "Towards establishing a viable macroeconomic and medium-term fiscal framework integrated approach for the Iraqi economy" *International Journal of Contemporary Iraqi Studies* 6(2) (2012): 196.

[900] Bakker and Silvey, *Beyond States and Markets*, 40.

[901] Tina Johnson (ed.), *Small Change or Real Change? Commonwealth Perspectives on Financing Gender Equality*, (London: Commonwealth Secretariat 2008) 10.

[902] Zuckermann and Greenberg, "The Gender Dimensions of Post-Conflict Reconstruction," 73.

[903] Ibid.p.74

[904] Johnson (ed.), *Small Change or Real Change?*, 10.

to the development of the country, as well as to the majority of its citizens, gender differences as well as differences in classes need to be considered.[905]

Despite this knowledge, peacebuilding processes often do not support the creation of economic opportunities for women. Women remain side-lined, even though a high percentage of them have become heads of households after war, and that their economic participation, and the recognition thereof, would greatly contribute to the economic uplift of the war-struck region. They are often not provided with the opportunities to become economically active, either through employment or through recovering income-generating property, as governments often fail to anticipate the need for legal reform, when it comes to women's rights to assets and economic opportunities in general.[906]

In the Kurdistan Region it is the official position of the government that women's economic participation as part of the reconstruction efforts has to be seen as increasingly important for the region's development, as well as for progress towards gender equality. However, as argued by representatives of the people, this position has not yet been fully implemented. On this basis the participants of the conference on *"The Role of Women in Peace-Building, Reconciliation and Accountability in Iraq"*, which took place in Erbil in January 2011, for example crafted the following recommendations:

> *"48. Social security and employment laws should be reformed in an effort to facilitate and encourage the participation of women in public life, including by:*
>
> *(a) The provision of better working conditions for women*
>
> *(b) Extending and increasing social security with rises in oil revenue*
>
> *(c) Include provision for prioritising the applications of women*
>
> *49. Train women and those supporting their families so as to aid them in their search for employment*
>
> *50. Investment, banking, and labour laws should be reformed to encourage women to enter the formal economy and private sector,*

---

[905] Ibid.

[906] True, *The Political Economy of Violence against Women*, 83.

including the oil sector, including by giving the applications of women priority when allocating loans and investments

51. Job creation programmes for women should receive more funding and attention, as opposed to a focus only on welfare programmes. This should include a job creation programme for women with limited education

52. Ensure the neutrality of all State institutions, as these are required to represent and provide services for all of Iraq without any discrimination.

53. Give women priority in job applications in cases where she is equally qualified to competing male candidates"[907]

They were not alone with their recommendations. The participants of the *"International Conference on Kurdish Women for Peace and Equality"* asked for

"creat[ing] job opportunities for women to be independent financially of their husband and other members of the family, because economic independence of women will result in self-confidence and lowering the abuse against them."[908]

Decision makers are responding to the ever increasing lobbying for gender equality within the economy. For example, in October 2012, the first Women's Economic Empowerment Conference was held in Baghdad, and was attended by inter alia the Head of the High Council of Women's Affairs in the Kurdistan Region. The Deputy Prime Minister Shaways stated that it was the aim of the conference to work to 'kick-start' further support for women in accessing more and better jobs.

The conference itself was initiated by the UNPD Iraq, together with UN Women, ILO and IOM, which shows the importance to international organizations of demonstrating support for women in the economy. They recognise the correlation between national or regional development and a gender inclusive economy, as well as between a gender inclusive economy and international recognition. This was expressed by Ms. Jacqueline Badcock, Deputy Special Representative of the UN Secretary-General for Iraq in Development and Humanitarian Affairs, by stating

---

[907] No Peace Without Justice, *The Role of Women in Peace-Building, Reconciliation and Accountability in Iraq, Outcomes and Recommendations* (Erbil , Kurdistan-Iraq, 27-28 January 2011)

[908] The Kurdish National Congress of North America, *International Conference on Kurdish Women for Peace and Equality, Resolution and Suggestions* (Press Release – March 20, 2007) para.11

that "*without including women, a country will never be able to have a strong economy, a key to its development.*"[909]

To what extent the recommendations of the Conference are being put into practice by the KRG and the resulting impact on development, will be subject of the following sections:

1.   The KRG & Economic Measures for Conflict Transformation

In the Kurdistan Region, the main political parties at the moment have three main economic goals, which are all translated in the PUK's aims and objectives, namely to support the redevelopment of agriculture, as well as to encourage private sector industries and to build up domestic as well as international trade, as part of the economic policies.[910]

The increase of 'internationality' is thereby one of the KRG's main foci for the economic sector at the moment. The KRG aims to work with regions around the world to improve its economic standing and make Kurdistan's economy highly internationally competitive.[911]

Together with the international organizations active in the region, the KRG also aims to strengthen the private sector, and to create a shift in the balance of employment from the public to the private sector.[912]

---

[909] Juliette Touma, UNDP Iraq, *Women's Economic Empowerment Conference held in Baghdad* (UNAMI Newsletter, Issue 27, October 2012) 6/7.

[910] Patriotic Union of Kurdistan, Leadership Council, "Program".

[911] See for example: KRG, "Kurdistan Investment Board Chairman visits Austria and Slovakia to discuss investment and trade opportunities" (January 2013)
http://www.krg.org/a/print.aspx?l=12&smap=010000&a=46083 (Accessed on 22.1.2013)
Law No.4 of 2006, Law of Investment in Kurdistan Region – Iraq

[912] See for example: ILO, "Private Sector Development Programme" (IRQ/08/01/UNQ, 2009-2011) (03 April 2012) http://www.ilo.org/public/english/region/arpro/beirut/what/projects/iraq/irq_08_01_unq.htm (Accessed on 22.1.2013)
Stephen Rimmer and Mohammed Al-Ani, *Supporting Private Sector Development in Iraq* (World Bank, MENA Knowledge and Learning, Quick Notes Series, Number 48, November 2011)
Zebari Abdel Hamid "Amendments Act of retirement and social security conference in Arbil" (30.10.2011)
http://onedinar.forumotion.net/t37184-amendments-act-of-retirement-and-social-security-conference-in-arbil (Accessed on 27.01.2013)

Finally, it is the current government's aim to rebuild the agricultural sector, which is of great importance to the region. Apart from the fact that the people feel closely connected to the land which they see it as their cultural heritage, agriculture still one of the most important sectors in Kurdistan's economy, behind the oil and gas sector.[913] In the past, the Kurdistan Region has been largely built upon the agricultural sector, which was destroyed through the years of wars and sanctions. According to the Minister of Agriculture, Serwan Baban, the production of foodstuff, such as red meat, oat, corn, milk, sunflower, tomatoes and various fruits was less than half of that required for self-sufficiency in 2011. Hence the aim of the Agricultural Ministry is to raise the agricultural productivity of the region. The minister plans to rebuild village life and support the farmer, in order to ensure that Kurdistan can be largely self-sufficient once again.[914]

From a gender perspective these different objectives lead to a variety of potential opportunities for the economic empowerment of women at a personal level. The enhanced internationalization of the economy might benefit big businesses directly, as well as indirectly by facilitating more interaction with the rest of the world, through business travel, study, training, or simply tourism. However, such benefits flow to only a small fraction of the population in general, and to an even smaller fraction of women. Through first-hand experience of the life of young Kurdish women today, the author observed that even if they had the opportunity to go abroad, only a small percentage would be permitted by their families to travel alone and only a similarly small percentage would be willing to defy their families' strictures in such a matter. It follows that while the internationalization of Kurdistan's economy, is certainly positive for the development of the region as a whole, its positive influence on gender equality is currently limited, although it is conceded that all available options are of value, as they may lead to enhanced gender inclusion in the future.

---

[913] USAID, *Kurdistan Region, Economic Development Assessment* (RTI International, Local Governance Project, Final Report, December 2008) 5.

[914] Lorin Sarkisian and Roni Alasor, Ararat News-Publishing, "Minister Baban: Kurdish agricultural production should be self-sufficient and untimely provide food security for the region" (26 October 2012) http://www.araratnews.eu/nuce.php?aid=627 (Accessed on 27.01.2013)

With reference to support of the private sector, both international organizations, and the government are committed to including women in microfinance projects and support them in running their own businesses.[915] While this might offer women the opportunity of increasing their family's income, it is questionable how far their businesses will be able to compete with the leading companies of the region, which benefit through the increased internationalization. At the same time, the increased support of private sector employees, mainly influences women's lives through the impacts on their husband's situation, as private sector employment is still principally a male domain. However appropriate legal and practical transformations of the sector may open it up for an increased female work force. While, a more thorough analysis of gender and the workforce will be provided further below, it should be noted that gender inclusion in the private sector is a highly disputed topic within the region as most of the employment is seen as socially unacceptable by society. Such perceptions on the one hand diminish women, but on the other hand limit the risk of women being exploited through labour as has happened in other regions, which focussed on rapidly boosting their economies. In summary, while an increased private sector is seen as positive for national development, it is highly questionable whether it leads to the advancement of gender equality in any way and so far does not seem to advance women's personal development.

Finally, the support for rebuilding the agricultural sector can have very positive effects on national development, as well as personal development including gender equality. The majority of rural women in the Kurdistan Region are working in agriculture. If the rebuilding of the agricultural sector includes a gender perspective and if women's traditional work is properly recognized, benefits would accrue not only to the national economy through rising agricultural production, but also to the farmer's personal lives and those of the female workers.

Hence while the current KRG's three main macroeconomic objectives may contribute to the development of the region as a whole, two of them will have little influence on gender equality. The impact of the third will largely depend on how it is put into practice. Exactly if and how the governing authorities have included

---

[915] World Bank, "Gender Dimensions of Private Sector Development, Capacity Building for Women in Business, The Example of Iraq" *PSD Gender Notes* 1(1) (2004): 1-4.

strategies for enhanced gender inclusion in the national economy, and its effects on national and personal development, will be the subject of the following section:

### 2.	Budgeting for Gender Equality

Given the Kurdistan Region's current very advantageous economic position, the region has every opportunity at this point in time to influence society's development, including progress towards gender equality in the economy from above.

Iraq's economy, including that of Kurdistan, is largely based on the oil industry. According to the national budget for 2011, 95 per cent of anticipated government income is from oil revenues.[916] While the oil industry as such does not provide much employment, the income from oil exports can be used to advance other parts of the national economy. Hence the importance of budgeting should not be underestimated. Currently, much of the oil money is invested in the public sector, which accounts for 60 per cent of the full time employment in the country as a whole.[917]

The people in the Kurdistan Region are aware of the resulting opportunities. Many see the oil as a curse, because of the sufferings of the past. However, they also see oil as a pathway to security since they are of the opinion that trading with other nations will enhance development and reduce the likelihood of armed hostilities. With oil income streets and houses can be rebuilt, jobs can emerge and economic activity generated through a range of investments.[918]

The size of the national or regional budget and the way the money is disbursed is an essential tool to achieve the above. The annual budget largely determines the economic well-being of segments of the population. As argued by feminist economists it is consequently vital to insert gender awareness into budgetary talks,

---

[916] UNDP – Iraq, *Women's Economic Empowerment,* 10.

[917] Ibid.

[918] Interview BX, Sulaimaniya on 09/08/2012; Interview BM, Erbil on 13/07/2012; Interview BO, Erbil on 18/07/2012

so that the whole of the population is able to profit from the macroeconomic policy making.[919]

As argued by Young, Tickner and Scherrer,[920] it is detrimental to gender development if macroeconomics are solely defined by men. Contributions from all parts of the population are needed to ensure that the policies can benefit everyone. From this perspective, the Kurdistan Region is not in an optimum position. Since the annual budget is approved by the high level political representatives, decisions on how to distribute public resources are not based on considerations of gender equality. Hazha Sleman, the current head of the Women Committee, explained that at the 2012 parliamentary discussions for budget, the women's committee tried to enhance the gender perspective in Kurdistan's budget, and presented a proposal to allocate budget for the High Women Council, as well as the directorate of counter violence against women. In addition the women urged parliament to allocate a budget for funding for women who had lost their husbands, but the government did not implement any of the proposals.[921] One of the consequences is that the national budget is not spent in a gender equal way, or with gender considerations in mind. In Young and Scherrer's view is detrimental to the region's and its people's development.[922]

In 2009 UNDP Iraq initiated a project to support the KRG in its budget execution, control, policy and planning, with *inter alia* the aim to "*improve policies stratefies and relation institutional developments that are sensitive to [...] gender equality and pro poor economic growth.*"[923] While the project showed up that the KRG's problems included that there were no regional and sectoral strategies and policies linked to budget planning[924] and that further detrimental factors include lack of transparency and accountability, no monitoring, weak reporting and low

---

[919] Young and Scherrer (eds.), *Gender Knowledge,* 29.

[920] Anne Tickner in Young and Scherrer (eds.), *Gender Knowledge,* 9.

[921] Warvin, "Regional Parliament Denies Women Demand, Endorses Budget".

[922] Anne Tickner in Young and Scherrer (eds.), *Gender Knowledge,* 9.

[923] UNDP Iraq, *Budget Execution Support in the Kurdistan Regional Government* (Project Document, April 2009) 1.

[924] Ibid.p.11

credibility,[925] there was no clear proposal on how the measures proposed to counter these challenges will have a positive effect on gender equality.

Still in 2011, the usage of the budget in the region is unclear. The allocated budget for the Kurdistan Region was $11.8 billion (USD), which was divided among on-going long-term projects, provincial development projects and new projects. Most of the money for new projects went into power generation and improvements in electricity distribution, while part of the long-term project money contributed to the insurance and pension fund, and to pay for and create more government jobs. While $21 million were assigned to the creation of jobs and small loans, $170 million were given to the political parties in the region.[926]

Also in 2012 the budget was about $12 billion, which only passed under a wave of criticism. According to the opposition, the budget is not sufficiently transparent. Further criticisms include the following: the budget was mainly allocated to operating costs, with under one third set aside for investment; the amounts allocated for the regional leadership, the intelligence services and the security apparatus were too high; and there was a presumed deficit.[927]

Next to the public spending for politics and security, the KRG has included measures to benefit the poorer people on the ground individually, even though, as argued by critics, the percentage of the budget allocated is far from adequate.

In order to reduce poverty, the government is working to decrease the unemployment rate in the region. The Ministry of Labour and Social Affairs initiated the project 'Jobs for Everyone', through which it gives about 150.000 Iraqi Dinars, approximately 130 US Dollars, to business owners for each job they create. At the same time vocational training centres were opened to train workers, and the government supported the pension fund for private sector employees, so that the

---

[925] Ibid.p.13

[926] KRG, "Council of Ministers finalises 2011 Kurdistan Region draft budget" (3 March 2011) http://www.krg.org/a/d.aspx?l=12&s=02010100&r=223&a=39080&s=010000 (Accessed on 22.1.2013)

[927] Sangar Jamal, Niqash, "Iraqi Kurdish State Budget Passes – Eight Months Late, Against Strong Opposition" (12 July 2012) http://www.niqash.org/articles/?id=3085 (Accessed on 22.1.2013)

private sector becomes more attractive for the citizens.[928] Furthermore, the annual budget also provided for a so called 'marriage loan', which is available to newly-weds on low incomes, and which was increased from $850 to $2.125 in 2011.[929] Finally, the government supports small loan projects. As part of one of these projects, any citizen between sixteen and 35 years of age, who is unemployed can apply for a tax-free loan between 1 and 15 million Iraqi Dinars (approximately $860 to $13.000) which has to be paid back within five years.[930]

While some of the measures described above can, in principle, foster development and gender equality, there is no clear gender strategy visible from outside. It is not clear that women's skills are considered or that specific provisions are in place which make it necessary to consider the gender effect of the budget spending. The general lack of transparency of the annual budget leads to lost opportunities for economic improvements for the whole population, and thus for the region as a whole.

This point of view was also shared by several representatives of the civil society. When people in the Kurdistan region were asked whether women are economically supported in the region today, the univocal reply was that the women who are most supported by the state are those already working, and especially those who are working for the public authorities and are themselves politicians or politically active in one of the two main parties.[931] Therefore it was the opinion of the interviewees that women needed more support to reach the employment market especially when it comes to the private sector.[932] They had the feeling that it was hard for anybody to get a job, but especially for women, without the necessary connections.[933] In addition a number of men had the feeling that many women were not treated well in their workplace.[934] Comparable numbers of men thought

---

[928] Eli Doosky, Kurdish Globe, "Government works to reduce Kurdistan unemployment" (10 May 2011) http://www.krg.org/a/d.aspx?s=02010200&l=12&r=73&a=39943&s=010000 (Accessed on 22.1.2013)

[929] KRG, "Council of Ministers finalises 2011 Kurdistan Region draft budget".

[930] Doosky, "Government works to reduce Kurdistan unemployment".

[931] See e.g. Interview BO, Erbil on 18/07/1012; Interview AZ, Sulaimaniya on 06/06/2012; Interview BB, Erbil on 24/06/2012; Interview BC, Erbil on 25/06/2012; Interview BP, Erbil on 21/07/2012

[932] Interview BQ, Erbil on 21/07/2012; Interview BG, Erbil on 02/07/2012; Interview BK, Erbil on 12/07/2012

[933] Interview BF, Erbil on 29/06/2012; Interview AI, Erbil on 16/04/2012

[934] Interview BQ, Erbil on 21/07/2012; Interview AN, Erbil on 03/05/2012

that women should be further supported because a great work force is needed to build up the country.[935]

By and large, the interviewees felt that support is lacking and that there are no social provisions and help for citizens in general, and women in particular, who do not work for the state.[936] While it can be seen as positive that working women are supported, it has to be remembered that the vast majority of female population, about 83 per cent, in the region are not working and therefore feel that they receive little or no financial support.

While all the prerequisites are there, it appears that budgetary measures are not being used to the fullest extent to improve people's lives within the region. If they are, it is not apparent from outside, as a consequence of a lack of transparency.

There has been widespread discussion of including women into the economy and of the benefits to their personal development and the regional economy of progress towards gender equity. Unfortunately such discussions are not yet reflected in the annual budget. This was also supported by women's rights activists in the region, who put as one of the government's necessary points of action in 2013 to address gender equality in the national budget.[937]

3.   National Strategies – Putting Theory into Practice?

In response to issues such as discussed in the previous section, the country as a whole has developed two National Development Strategies, from 2007 to 2010, and from 2010 to 2014:

As part of its National Development Strategy in 2007, the country set itself the task to "*transform Iraq into a peaceful, unified federal democracy and a prosperous, market oriented regional economic powerhouse that is fully integrated into the global economy*",[938] by 'strengthening the foundations of economic growth', through a stable macroeconomic strategy, improving the performance of the oil

---

[935] Interview AE, Erbil on 09/04/2012; Interview AQ, Sulaimaniya on 19/05/2012; Interview BA, Erbil on 21/06/2012

[936] Interview AP, Sulaimaniya on 18/05/2012; Interview AV, Sulaimaniya on 28/05/2012; Interview AY, Sulaimaniya on 04/06/2012

[937] Christian Peacemaker Teams, *Kurdish Activists' Observations*, 8.

[938] IAU, *Iraq, The National Development Strategy (2007-2010)* (March 2007) i.

sector, and diversify the economy,[939] by 'revitalizing the private sector', by 'improving the quality of life', and by 'strengthening good governance and improving security'.[940]

The National Development Strategy of 2007 included measures which arguably benefit the country as a whole, such as the strengthening of the private sector, the banking sector, the improvement of the infrastructure, as well as human development goals, such mitigating poverty, achieving education for all, ensuring access to water and decent housing and controlling corruption.[941]

With respect to gender equality, the Development Strategy included in its goals to increase the representation of women in decision making,[942] to support women entrepreneurs through technical resource networks,[943] to increase women's employment[944], to enhance women's education,[945] to expand micro finance programs especially for women,[946] as a measure to decrease poverty, and to support women within the public health system.[947] While it was not explained in detail how this will be achieved, it is clear that gender equality is seen as vital when it comes to human development. By comparison, general macroeconomic or financial policies were seen as gender neutral.

As indicated throughout this thesis, the objectives set out in the Development Strategy of 2007 have been partially realised in the Kurdistan Region. The numbers of women involved in decision making has increased, employment opportunities for women have been created, micro finance programs targeting women have been established, and the number of women in higher education is rising. Nevertheless the impact on the entire population, as well as on national development, arguably remains low, as the different measures principally target one segment of the population, namely upper class women.

---

[939] Ibid.pp.ii-iv
[940] Ibid.pp.v/vi
[941] Ibid.p.62
[942] Ibid.p.vii
[943] Ibid.p.53
[944] Ibid.p.60
[945] Ibid.p.61
[946] Ibid.p.63
[947] Ibid.p.80

The National Development Strategy 2010-2014 in comparison gone much further and concentrated on improving the financial sector, agriculture and water resources, infrastructure, public services, issues of social status, environmental sustainability, the private sector and good governance.[948]

Apart from raising the GDP and diversifying Iraqis economy, the Development Strategy also has as an objective to reduce the poverty rate by focusing on rural development and creating job opportunities, especially for the youth and for women. The strategy includes providing adequate health and educational services for so called 'vulnerable groups', which include women.[949]

Women are thereby seen as outsiders, who do not play an economically active role, a situation which needs to be changed in order to "*make women capable*". The strategy is to provide women with adequate education, health services and social security, as well as with the opportunities to obtain resources and to become aware of their rights.[950] Gender issues are clearly being considered, but within limits. There is no consideration of gender issues when it comes to infrastructure, the environment or industry. As already noted, women appear to be seen as outsiders in their own country, at least when it comes to the national economy. While there is definitely a real intent to raise the overall educational levels and the standard of living of the people, it remains questionable if any underlying problems leading to the above issues will be addressed by government.

From the allocation of the anticipated investments under that development plan, it is clear that the government currently prioritises the industrial sector, followed by construction, oil, electricity, and the agricultural sectors. Education has the lowest allocated investment, and social services are not being considered under this plan.[951] It may therefore be argued that the strategies for more gender inclusion are rather considered in principle rather than implemented in practice and it is not apparent that this will change greatly in the near future.

---

[948] Ministry of Planning – Republic of Iraq, *National Development Plan for the Years 2010-2014* (Baghdad 2010)
[949] Ibid.p.18
[950] Ibid.pp.134-136
[951] Ibid.p.18

In conclusion it is clear from the actual policies and planned strategies elaborated above, that efforts for transformations have been made, which benefit the population and development of the country as a whole. However, when it comes to the impact of economic measures on social and gender transformations, still more is discussed in principle than implemented in practice. This also affects the peace building and the conflict potential within the region.

As Hashim Al-Ali pointed out in 2012, "*Iraq could be considered a unique example for macroeconomic and fiscal management irrationality in recent times.*"[952] Iraq, and especially the Kurdistan Region, is one of the regions of the world, with access to enormous economic resources, especially oil and gas, and a well-educated people, especially those returning from the diaspora. Nevertheless Iraq, including the North, although arguably less so, is characterized by high rates of unemployment, poverty, a low quality or lack of public services and low productivity. According to Hashim Al-Ali this situation can be attributed to mismanagement in public finance, and "*the absence of a realistic and proactive socio-economic development strategic vision based on well-articulated, actual needs and priorities.*"[953]

Also USAID Iraq concluded in its Economic Development Assessment of the Kurdistan Region conducted in 2008 that the Kurdistan has the possibility for a bright economic future in industry, agriculture, as well as tourism, but the current lack of information and transparency from the Government's side, as well as the absence of a modern banking system, a lack of suitable infrastructure, and the absence of an educational system, which works to meet the demands of the market economy, hamper Kurdistan's development.[954]

As noted above, macroeconomic policies have can change relations between different social groups. This has to be taken account, as otherwise it is likely that inequalities will be established through the policies, including gender-based inequalities, which would in turn limit probable benefits to disadvantaged

---

[952] Al-Ali, "Towards establishing a viable macroeconomic and medium-term fiscal framework," 202.
[953] Ibid.p.203
[954] USAID, *Kurdistan Region, Economic Development Assessment*, 1.

households.[955] It follows that if legal rights to make land and housing transactions, as well as equal rights in marriage, employment and mobility, are not secured after conflict, many poor women, and especially those who lost their close male relatives through war, will not be able to rise from poverty.[956] Next to providing equal opportunities, the state needs to finance, through its macroeconomic policies, equal outcomes. It is not sufficient to merely allow women the access to income generating activity. It is vital to ensure equity within these activities, as women, who are in disadvantaged employment situations, will most likely also suffer when it comes to quality health service, education, food security, water, or housing,[957] and this will affect their family and consequently also society.

As explained by Zuckermann and Greenberg from the example of the World Bank, too little attention has been focused on the connection between gender and macro-economic policies. While the World Bank produces extensive and prominent gender studies, it fails to incorporate them into investment strategies.[958] The same is arguably true for the Kurdistan Region, but while the World Bank's employees do not suffer greatly under the lack gender inclusive investment strategies, the development potential in the Kurdistan Region is impaired through the lack of socio-economic, including gender, considerations, which could lead to a rise in conflict potential in the future.

B.   Women, Gender and the Labour Market

Another factor which is said to be greatly influential on the social fabric, as part of economic development, is the employment level and the type of employment made available to the population.

When it comes to women and employment, opinions around the world are split. While some are of the view that it is a woman's place to do the housework and to take care of the children, others insist on the importance of women working, in order to ensure their equality within society, as well as their country's economic progress. It has been argued that every available working person is needed and

---

[955] Bakker and Silvey, *Beyond States and Markets*, 38/39.
[956] True, *The Political Economy of Violence against Women*, 84.
[957] Ibid.p.85
[958] Zuckermann and Greenberg, "The Gender Dimensions of Post-Conflict Reconstruction," 73.

that equality in the labour market increases personal as well as regional development, and thus fosters peace building. The involvement of women is vital as it is often they, who are in the best position to acquire new skills and keep the country or region running, while the men were fighting.

Times of war and conflict change the social fabric of a region. During the time of conflict women are often forced to enter the work force and to acquire new skills. This can happen in their home country as well as in refugee or internally displaced camps, or in the diaspora; everywhere where labour is in short supply. Additionally women often become more involved in politics, and other occupations previously dominated by men,[959] as a consequence of men no longer being available to fulfil these posts. As argued by Sorensen, it is these new skills and abilities acquired by women, which are needed in post conflict times to rebuild the country.[960]

However rather than embracing these opportunities, contrary developments are often observed. While gender roles often change during the time of armed conflict and become more open or fluent, the opposite is often true after the arms are laid down.[961]

After the time of war male unemployment is usually very high and it is seen as an important political goal to provide employment opportunities for men, even if this means that women lose their jobs. Women's unemployment is not seen as a political threat. Women are merely seen as reverting what is "natural" and consequently no intention is paid to their employment.[962] As a consequence, women can be forced to resign their jobs or accept lower wages than the men returning from conflict.[963]

---

[959] UN ESCAP, *Women and Armed Conflict,* 12.
[960] Sorensen, *Women and Post-Conflict Reconstruction,* 5.
[961] Bouta and Frerks, *Women's Roles in Conflict Prevention, Conflict Resolution and Post-Conflict Reconstruction,* 39.
962 Cynthia Enloe, Connecticut College, Lectures, YouTube "Cynthia Enloe speaks on Women in Iraq" http://www.youtube.com/watch?v=BUVPm0vJINA (7.12.2011)
[963] Bouta and Frerks, *Women's Roles in Conflict Prevention, Conflict Resolution and Post-Conflict Reconstruction,* 39.

This is especially problematic for women who retain sole responsibility for their households.[964] The impoverishment of a large part of society is an inevitable consequence of war. On an individual level, if the breadwinner loses his or her employment or if a wife is widowed it is difficult for the whole family. It is often next to impossible for women to find work and an income, and they and their children then become dependent on other family members or on some form of social services.[965] At the same time the impoverishment of society and its effects makes it difficult for the war torn region as a whole to recover economically, which in turn leads to further conflict potential. Consequently, it is questionable whether the country can afford the loss of women's formal economic activity at a time of peace building.

In addition, a severe lack of employment opportunities especially for males has had detrimental consequences on the social construct. Men who face unemployment and poverty, especially after returning from fighting or displacement, often succumb to alcoholism and drug abuse resulting in a rise in domestic violence and prostitution.[966] Consequently it is necessary to be careful that women's control of resources and their successful efforts to generate income do not create a backlash against them.[967]

These are only few of the challenges related to the employment situation after the end of violent conflicts, and they cannot be taken lightly. As UNDP early warning reports show, jobs are the top priority in the reconstruction of countries, after physical security.[968] Only after people can once again feed their families and the country has a sufficient workforce and expertise to build up a necessary infrastructure, will the population feel that the conflict is over.[969] While it is important to employ men, for all the reasons mentioned above, missing out on the opportunity to further employ women in the formal sector could have devastating

---

[964] Ibid.

[965] Chandler, Wang and Fuller (ed.), *Women, War and Violence,* 118.

[966] Lidauer (ed.), *Women in Armed Conflict,* 9.

[967] Sanam Naraghi Anderlini and Judy El-Bushra, *Post Conflict Reconstruction* (Inclusive security, Sustainable peace: A toolkit for advocacy and action) 64.

[968] Pugh, "Normative Values and Economic Deficits in Postconflict Transformation," 481.

[969] UNDP, "Gender Inequality Index and related indicators".

impacts on the post-conflict reconstruction.[970] The following sections will discuss how the Kurdistan Region has reacted to these male and female employment issues, how many women are currently employed and in which type of employment, how this affects the women's individual and the wider national development and whether the adopted strategies are a step towards positive peace.

1. Including Women into the Workforce – Raising the Numbers

As a prosperous economic region, the Kurdistan Region today does not face the same problems as other poorer regions, recently emerging from conflicts. As discussed above, it is one of the government's major goals to make Kurdistan economically competitive, also in the international sphere, and to use all available resources including the contributions from women to achieve this goal. As a consequence the government is providing women, especially at a professional level, with every opportunity to join the labour force.

With reference to the specific advancement of women in society, it is relevant that the only female minister in the current KRG cabinet is the Minister for Labour and Social Affairs, Asos Najib Abdullah. While some of the interviewees were of the view that she is *"just as the others"*,[971] the general feeling towards her is very positive. She is said to have been working hard to improve the social security situation, especially when it comes to the elderly and disabled.[972] She is currently focussing her work on reducing unemployment, especially amongst the young by providing training programs and offering micro loans to young graduates. As part of their programme specifically for women, the Ministry of Labour and Social Affairs, runs and supports the women's shelters of the region. It was one of Asos Najib's

---

[970] Ibid.

[971] Interview BI, Erbil on 08/07/2012

[972] Mufid Abdulla, The Kurdistan Tribune "Asos Najib Abdullah: an exemplary KRG minister" (20 October 2012) http://kurdistantribune.com/2012/asos-najib-abdullah-exemplary-krg-minister/ (Accessed on 27.01.2013)

Interview BD, Erbil on 25/06/2012; Interview BE, Erbil on 26/06/2012

aims to improve the quality of the shelters and also to raise awareness amongst the women regarding their rights.[973]

As discussed above, labour laws in the region ensure equal access to work, for men and women[974], and also ensure equal remuneration[975], as well as special provisions for women's workers.[976] Women have the opportunity for maternity leave, there are kindergartens in the region and some companies even provide a space where children can be looked after.

Apart from ensuring their legal rights, the KRG is working to further increase the employment rate through for example the establishment of training centres,[977] or the hiring of female employees in the public sector. According to Rudaw, the number of women employed by the government is steadily rising. In 2011, 4000 of 7600 people newly employed by the government in Sulaimaiyah were women, raising women's participation in the public sector in that city to 41 per cent. It should be noted that the majority of women working for the government are still employed in the education and health sectors and it is still difficult for women to gain promotion,[978] which impedes the attainment of a level of gender equality beyond simple numbers. The effects of this will be discussed in the next section.

The recent economic boom in the Kurdistan Region also provides new job opportunities in the private sector including the new malls where women are particularly wanted. It is arguably easier for women to find jobs in certain areas, as there are fewer women looking for jobs than men and some employers specifically seek to hire women, for example in stores for women's clothing. However, it is still the case that in almost every company the employment opportunities are biased against women, as are the level of the positions offered.[979]

---

[973] Najiba Mohammed, Rudaw "Kurdistan Govt To Introduce New System To Shelter Threatened Women" (16 November 2010) http://www.rudaw.net/english/culture_art/3298.html (Accessed on 27.01.2013)

[974] Iraq Labor Code, Act No. 71 of 1987, Article 2

[975] Ibid. Article 4(2)

[976] Ibid. Articles 81-89

[977] Doosky, "Government works to reduce Kurdistan unemployment".

[978] Nawzad Mahmoud, Rudaw, "Steady Rise in Women Civil Servants" (06 May 2012) http://www.rudaw.net/english/kurds/4707.html (Accessed on 27.01.2013)

[979] Najib Muhammad, "Iraqi Kurdistan's private sector prefers female employees" (15 May 2010) http://www.ekurd.net/mismas/articles/misc2010/5/state3838.htm (Accessed on 27.01.2010)

Finally, in order to support women's economic inclusion hundreds of projects throughout Iraq, and dozens in the Kurdistan Region, have been conducted by NGOs, as well as government organisations, including vocational training, awareness raising, income-generation and food and non-food distribution.[980] According to UNDP, the projects provided women with opportunities for economic empowerment as many were very keen to increase their skills and experience. The projects can also impact on the women's mind-sets, can provide them with more confidence, and build hope for a better future.[981] However the projects suffer from inadequate or unreliable funding and from difficulties in accessing certain groups of women.[982]

While the in principle opportunities for women to work in Iraq and the Kurdistan Region are given, the reality looks different. Women do not avail themselves of all of the opportunities either out of personal choice, or through social circumstances.

Unlike elsewhere in the world, Iraq's and the Kurdistan Region's greatest challenge for the national economy does not necessarily lie with excessive unemployment rates, but rather with economic inactivity. According to the Iraq Household Socio-Economic Survey, conducted by the Iraqi Government, with help from the KRG and the World Bank, the economic activity rate in the Kurdistan Region in 2007 i.e. the percentage of the general population engaged in formal economic activity, amounted to 69.7 per cent for men and 12.9 per cent for women, an average of only 40.3 per cent. The unemployment rates were similar between men and women, with 5.8 per cent of economically active men being unemployed, and 7.2 per cent of women.[983]

In 2012, according to the Kurdistan Region Statistics Office, the level of unemployment was 6.0 per cent, with 4.6 per cent of men being unemployed and 12.6 per cent of women. In addition, the survey revealed that the level of unemployment is higher in the rural areas than in the cities and that the level of

---

[980] UNDP – Iraq, *Women's Economic Empowerment,* 15/16.

[981] Ibid.p.23

[982] Ibid.p.25

[983] Central Organisation for Statistics and Information Technology, Kurdistan Region Statistics Organisation, The World Bank, *Iraq Household Socio-Economic Survey, Volume II: Data Tables* (Tabulation Report, Volume II, IHSES-2007) 290.

unemployment correlated with the level of education, with illiterate women having the highest level of unemployment, at 16.3 per cent.[984] According to the Kurdistan Region Statistics Office, there are several reasons for women's very low rate of economic activity (14%) in comparison to men's (67.3%) including the following. Firstly, women have 'specialized' in household work and there is no need for them to work outside the home, and secondly, the number of women looking for jobs is generally low, even if they do not have to work at home.[985]

At the same time it should be noted that the percentage of economically active women has slowly but steadily risen again since the fall of Saddam Hussein, although numbers are still low. According to UN data 12.5 per cent of the adult female population in Iraq was part of the labour force in 2000. This number slowly rose to 13.5 per cent in 2005 and 14.1 per cent in 2008.[986] By comparison, in 2008 52.6 per cent of the UK female adult population participated in the labour force.[987]

The low percentage of the economically active population, resulting from the very low percentage of women participating in the formal labour force, arguably impedes on Kurdistan's international competitiveness and general economic development, as only less than half of the population's human resources are being used.

With reference to the influence on women's personal development and empowerment opinions are split. As explained in the theoretical section above, and as noted by the Heinrich Böll Stiftung,[988] while increased participation in the labour force can increase women's independence, it can also lead to further restrictions and inequality.

While it is possible that it is the women's free choice to not work, and thus their 'economic inactivity' ensures their personal freedom and peace, it is very unlikely

---

[984] Kurdistan Region Statistics Office, *Labour Force* (Fact Sheet 3, September 2012) 1.

[985] Ibid.p.2

[986] UNdata, "Iraq", http://data.un.org/CountryProfile.aspx?crName=Iraq (Accessed on 16.09.2011)

[987] Undata, "United Kingdom", http://data.un.org/CountryProfile.aspx?crName=United%20Kingdom (Accessed on 16.09.2011)

[988] Heinrich Böll Stiftung, *Gender Politics Makes A Difference*, 52.

that the majority of Kurdish women prefer to work in informal employment or to be housewives. As explained by a young woman, who is herself currently not working:

> *"The women in Kurdistan really want to work. Basically everyone wants to work. That is clear, because they want to be independent from the men. Can you imagine what it feels like when you have to ask a man for everything? Whenever you want clothes, for every book, you have to go to your husband or father and ask them for money."*[989]

She further maintained together with other women interviewed, that concerning employment, women meet opposition from all different directions, including the government, society, and their own families. This makes it almost impossible for them to work, should they so wish. Hence the measures adopted by the government to increase the numbers of female employees are not sufficient as there has not yet been a huge increase in women taking up employment.

This shows once more that the current measures are insufficient to give women genuinely equal opportunities for employment. Rather it is necessary to consider the surrounding circumstances and view the generating of employment through a gender lens. It will later be argued that success will contribute to ensuring peace for individuals, as well as for the region, by ensuring prosperous economic development for all.

If and to what extent gender equality is manifested in Kurdistan's labour force, how this is working out in practice and what influence these initiatives or the lack thereof are having, will be subject of the following section:

2.   From Work to Gender Equality?

When it comes to the current employment situation in the Kurdistan Region in general, feelings are very mixed. While one side believes that region is currently full of opportunities and proudly talk about the different high-paid job opportunities in the Region,[990] the other side has the feeling that they are unable find any job,

---

[989] Interview AP, Sulaimaniya on 18/05/2012
[990] Interview CF, Vienna on 16/11/2012

and if they do, they cannot feed their families. This side believes that the few jobs left are taken by migrant workers South East Asia or Africa.[991]

At the same time many of the companies complain that the Kurdish population is not willing to accept hard manual work anymore and that they have no option but to employ migrant workers. They claim that the local population has become accustomed to government jobs, where they receive all the salary and social security for fewer working hours than private employees.

There is in general a large discrepancy between the different types of labour as well as a wide range of earnings. This results in the privileged classes raising the prices, while the lower class have the feeling that it is not worthwhile for them to accept jobs with low salaries, as they will not be able to appropriately feed their family.[992]

With respect to working conditions and prospects for women, the situation in the Kurdistan Region is highly variable as it is with education, social life and any other aspects of living. As noted by the World Bank, women in today's world have a better chance of equal employment, since the importance of physical strength in the workplace is declining, while the importance of cognitive skills is on the rise.[993] However this is true only for that extremely small percentage of women in Kurdistan who have the benefit of higher education and can choose whether or not they wish to be employed and in which area. Women from other parts of society either do not have any possibility to work, or must work under harsh conditions. The latter is true for women from low income families. Support to offer them employment by the government is much lower than for women from the upper class, and at the same time many of them, who either want or have to work, are forced to deal with great social obstacles, as they are either expected by their families and social surroundings to not work at all or they are expected to only execute certain types of professions.

---

[991] Interview BS, Erbil on 24/07/2012; Interview BJ, Erbil on 09/07/2012

[992] Nabard Hussein, Rudaw, "Conflicting Unemployment Rates in Kurdistan" (07 March 2012) http://www.rudaw.net/english/kurds/4502.html (Accessed on 22.1.2013)

[993] The World Bank, *Gender Equality and Development,* 272.

In general, the types of jobs and positions seen as acceptable by society are very clear cut. While some occupations are considered to be 'shameful' and unacceptable, others are regarded very highly.

In addition more conservative families oppose women working in a "male environment". The women are then either forced to not work at all or to choose a different work place.

Hence women who want to work and have an adequate education are often not able to accept their preferred employment. This diminishes their freedom of choice and leads to a waste of human resources for the region. However this is not the case for all parts of the population:

In Iraq, including the Kurdistan Region, there have long existed opportunities for a certain class of professional women, especially those whose families belonged to the upper class and had political influence. Chandler describes Iraq before the first Gulf War as a

> "prosperous, modern, secular state with universal education and one
> of the best healthcare systems in the region, where most women
> were well educated, many working in professional fields as doctors,
> lawyers and engineers."[994]

Today, it may be observed that the majority of women in employment are either professionals or working in agriculture. By comparison, the majority of men work in services or sales and in crafts and related trades.[995] In addition it may be observed that women mainly work in the public sector (over 78%), while equal numbers of men work in the public and the private sector.[996]

There are barriers for women seeking access to the private sector, as this is not seen as 'acceptable' by the wider society. Even within the public sector, not all types of positions are distributed equally between men and women. According to the Kurdish newspaper *Rudaw* female leaders and high-ranking civil servants were decreasing in 2011, because they were being replaced by men. The *Rudaw*

---

[994] Chandler, Wang and Fuller (ed.), *Women, War and Violence,* 126.
[995] Central Organisation for Statistics and Information Technology, *Iraq Household Socio-Economic Survey, Volume II,* 308.
[996] Kurdistan Region Statistics Office, *Labor Force,* 3.

investigation has found that of 27 female mayors, municipal chiefs and general-directors in the Sulaimaniya province, only ten still hold their posts. It is said that this development is due to the tribal thinking and the fact that women are not sufficiently supported in public positions and their abilities appreciated.[997]

The situation is particularly problematic for women with low skill jobs in private companies and factories. They are they are not highly regarded by society and have to work long hours for a low wage and are not adequately protected by workplace regulations.[998] At the same time, such work does not offer the same benefits as the public sector, although efforts are being made to change this situation. It follows that the choice of work is limited.[999]

Despite all the challenges when it comes to women practically being part of the labour force, the population's theoretical views on the issue were very different ones:

Many interviewees stated that next to that of the family, a woman's most important role in Kurdish society is that of a worker or employee,[1000] although it was made clear what was thereby seen as acceptable.

With respect to women as workers, it was most often understood that they should be state employees in the ministries, administrative bodies or schools, but not work in the private sector. While interviewees from all walks of life were of the opinion that it was a woman's most important role to work, a significant number of men expressed the belief that it was the most important role of a women in Kurdistan to work specifically as a state employee.[1001] People also stated that it was the most important roles of women to work in hospitals[1002] or as lawyers[1003] or on cultural

---

[997] Nawzad Mahmoud, "Female Leaders Decline in Kurdistan" (Rudaw, in English – The Happening, 21.09.2011) http://www.rudaw.net/english/kurds/3993.html (Accessed on 1.10.2011)

[998] Trades Union Congress, "Women in Iraqi Kurdistan – demanding their rights at work and at home" (19 May 2010) http://www.tuc.org.uk/international/tuc-17949-f0.cfm (Accessed on 29.01.2013)

[999] UNDP – Iraq, *Women's Economic Empowerment*, 10.

[1000] Interview AF, Erbil on 09/04/2012; Interview AG, Erbil on 13/04/2012; Interview AK, Erbil on 20/04/2012; Interview AL, Erbil on 25/04/2012; Interview AP, Sulaimaniya on 18/05/2012

[1001] See e.g. Interview BQ, Erbil on 21/07/2012; Interview BT, Erbil on 24/07/2012

[1002] Interview BW, Sulaimaniya on 08/08/2012

[1003] Interview AX, Sulaimaniya on 03/06/2012

matters,[1004] thereby acknowledging the importance of work in general, but not accepting all types of jobs.

This way of thinking was also reflected in the children's wishes for future career choices, with the majority aiming at a career in medicine, engineering, teaching, or in general as a state employee. According to the Iraq Women Integrated Social and Health Survey (I-WISH), the vast majority of girls in between 10 and 14 in the region desired a career in education, i.e. working as a government employee, teacher, nurse, etc. While approximately 10 per cent aspired to become a public figure, another 10 per cent wanted to work in a different sector, and only 4.5 per cent wished to become house wives.[1005]

Clearly the general importance of economic activity for the rebuilding of the region is embedded in the people's thinking, with nearly half of the people questioned expressing the view that it is the women's most important role to support the physical reconstruction and peace building process, through being part of the work force.[1006] The concept of women working for the support of the region pervades all strata of society, as well as men and women. However, in practice they sometimes do not include the actual women in their family. Many people believe that women, just as men, should work to reconstruct the country, as everybody is needed, especially in the areas of engineering, doctors and teachers. Further they should engage in paid work more than they have done until now, but this should never go *"against the interest of the family"*.[1007] In practice this often means that women are not working after all or that they have only specific jobs.

Hence a woman's employment is still very dependent on the family and society as a whole, rather than her individual decision and consequently the opportunities for women are not equal to those for men, even if they are greater for women from more advantaged backgrounds.

[1004] Interview BX, Sulaimaniya on 09/08/2012

[1005] Kurdistan Regional Statistics Office, *Iraq Women Integrated Social and Health Survey, Knowledge and behavior of adolescent girls (10-14) age* (I-WISH, October 2012) 2.

[1006] See e.g. Interview AM, Erbil on 27/04/2012; Interview AS, Sulaimaniya on 23/05/2012; Interview BB, Erbil on 24/06/2012; Interview BD, Erbil on 25/06/2012

[1007] Interview AD, Erbil on 06/04/2012

Related to the differences in classes is the correlation over the region between economic activity and education. Research has shown that the participation of women in the labour force in Iraq is highly dependent on the level of education. While only about 10 per cent of women with primary education are employed or seeking a job, 30 per cent of women with secondary education and 80 per cent of university-educated women participate in the labour force.[1008]

The great divergences between women's participation in the labour force based inter alia on education levels have also been observed by international organizations, such as the IOM, according to which women face a variety of difficulties in accessing the labour market, such as a lack of qualifications, childcare responsibilities or constraints resulting from social norms.[1009]

The consequences of the strong concentration on government and professional jobs for women in the region are twofold. From a national point of view, it would preclude nearly half the population of participating in low skill jobs, which are needed as much as the professional jobs to realise the region's full economic potential.

Secondly it needs to be remembered that the public employment opportunities are only accessible to highly educated women. Consequently uneducated women only have very low chances of employment, which makes them automatically dependent on their husbands or other male relatives. This limits their personal development and has flow on effects nationally.

At the same time, Iraq and the Kurdistan Region are not following other countries around the world and advancing their economies by employing the vast cheap female labour currently available.[1010] This would arguably offer the women who are currently in dire straits, a higher personal quality of life, and thus generally reduce the potential for conflict.

The situation for women even in high skilled job is often worse than that for men. Their roles as carers of the families make it more difficult for them to accept the

---

[1008] IAU, *Iraq Labour Force Analysis 2003-2008* (January 2009) 3.

[1009] IOM-Iraq, *Female Headed Households* (Special Report 2011) 6.

[1010] True, *The Political Economy of Violence against Women,* 77.

stipulated working hours. Their remuneration is often less than that of men and they are seen as unfit by some to fill certain positions. This is especially so for women who have no immediate male relatives. Since women are not expected by the society to need to work, they do not have the same chances as men for employment and are often forced to accept low paid work in the informal sector where they are frequently exploited and remain poor.

Several women interviewees complained that the conditions in the work place are generally far from easy. They feel watched and some have the feeling that they always have to be careful so that nothing happens involving a man, which could ruin their reputation. As explained by a previous teacher, who later continued her studies:

> "When I was a teacher at a village school, I had to take the bus there every day. It was not possible to do anything right. The men who went with me always talked about me, and some told my family about what I was doing. Once I was in school, I always had to take care that the door of the class room was open at all times and that I always had a few children around me, so that some of my colleagues could not assume anything wrong."[1011]

Many men do not want their wives to work, because they do not see it as their role and because of possible connections with other men. Hence if a married woman finds a job that she likes, she cannot complain if she is treated badly, because her family would most likely make her quit.

As argued by Cynthia Cockburn, this situation is a result of the relationship between capitalism and patriarchy with each reinforcing the other.[1012] Capitalism has developed in the same patriarchal way as the rest of society. Skilled men are generally privileged over skilled women and many workplaces and workers' unions choose the patriarchal model, rather than accept the full inclusion of women and their skills into their organisations.[1013] In order for women to enhance their own and their country's prosperity they do not simply be appended to the job market. Often the whole social system needs to be changed, as to ensure equality in outcome.

[1011] Interview CH, Vienna on 05/11/2012
[1012] Cockburn, "On 'The Machinery of Dominance,'" 269.
[1013] Ibid.p.270

As emphasised by Günseli Berik, Yana van der Meulen Rodgers and Stephanie Seguino the equality in outcomes is just as important as the equality of opportunities. As observed in the Kurdistan Region, equal opportunities, for example equal access to the labour market, might not lead to equal outcomes, for example equal pay, working hours etc.[1014]

Working women encounter problems not only in the workplace, but also in their homes. In reality in most households still consider that women should stay at home and look after the family. Employment is often seen as a privelege which does not change their traditional role. In addition many work places do not provide adequate working conditions for women, such as flexible working hours, or part time jobs. It follows that many of the working women, while they also do not enjoy being housewives, feel under pressure because of the dual responsibilities. One young newlywed and pregnant woman explained outside the formal interviews, that while she has enjoyed working, she is waiting for the day that she can finally stay at home. The duties of a wife, in addition to the long hours at work and the additional physical challenges of pregnancy, are becoming too much to handle.

As noted above, women's employment in the current social structure might well lead to enhanced inequality for women on a personal level. However this does not need to be the case. Such trends can be addressed by the state, by providing access to child care, giving women more time through better infrastructure, improving parental leave policies, facilitating women's access to markets through technologies, or introducing flexible working hours.[1015] While some of these initiatives have been taken to a certain extent in the Kurdistan Region, they are far from sufficient and inclusive.

In conclusion the development of a truly gender equal work force in the region is still in the formative stage. The legal provisions are not sufficient for gender equality and while society agrees, in principle, with gender equality in the workplace, in practice, this compact seldom extends to the home and family. Apart

---

[1014] Günseli, Van der Meulen and Seguino, "Feminist Economics," 5.
[1015] The World Bank, *Gender Equality and Development*, 297.

from the consequences already noted above, this has several effects on individual, social and national transformation:

3. The Effects of Women's Employment Situation on Individual and Social Transformation

From the analysis above, two developments can be observed, which hamper women's personal economic development. One the one hand, the family and society, i.e. men, are still crucial factors in deciding which employment, if any, women may seek, and this greatly limits their possibilities. On the other hand, it would appear that the government is greatly supporting women in the work force, primarily to promote economic development in the region, but without necessarily considering their personal choices and empowerment. The support does not explicitly extend to gender equality.

The consequential limited contribution of women to the official economy and their limited choices of employment is arguably detrimental to the region's development and the conflict transformation process as a whole.

From a national point of view, the importance of women using their skills and participating in the labour market after the end of the conflict should not be underestimated. At the time of violence it is often the highly educated people with money from the upper and middle class who leave the country and it is only the poor with no other choice who to stay. Post conflict reconstruction is therefore more difficult as every skill is needed.[1016] Furthermore, as argued by the ILO, increasing employment rates are one way of facilitating peace. High levels of unemployment and limited economic opportunities are sources of dissent and social unrest, and thus feed the cycle of conflict and obstruct peacebuilding.[1017] It follows that the situation in the Kurdistan region, with female economic inactivity reaching over 80 per cent, is in a greater risk of returning to violence than a country with a lower percentage of economic inactivity.

From an individual point of view, the time of reconstruction is the best time to re-evaluate gender relations and to lay the foundation for sustainable peace within

---

[1016] Enloe, "Cynthia Enloe speaks on Women in Iraq".
[1017] Rashid and Havers (eds.), *Jobs for Iraq*, 1.

society. Working women can also act as role models and change the outlook of the next generation, with potentially long-lasting impacts on the development of the country. Positive economic development can thereby be used to enhance general equality amongst the population. This was also be opinion, especially of educated women interviewees, who stated that equality implies having women working in all sectors including the law, academia, security etc.

As discussed by the IOM, the exclusion of women from the labour force leads to their isolation from other groups in society and marginalization in day-to-day life.[1018] This could also be observed in the Kurdistan Region, where non-working women, who did not have a large tightly knit family, had great difficulties contacting and making friends with other women, except in the immediate neighbourhood. Many pursued scarcely any activities outside the house.

In addition the inability of women to work, especially when they are heads of households, puts a strain on their family members, who experience an increased financial burden.[1019] As noted by the Kurdistan Region Statistics Office, a household, comprising of an average of five people, in the Kurdistan Region spends an average of just under 1500 thousand Iraqi Dinars, approximately 1.300 US Dollars, per month,[1020] with an average of 55 per cent for food, and residency.[1021] Given that there are no minimum wages in Iraq and the Kurdistan Region and that the average wage for low skilled jobs falls much below the stated average spending,[1022] not every household with a single breadwinner is economically stable. The existence two breadwinners, enhances the chances of raising families out of poverty. This reduces the potential for conflict within society, and also offers enhanced opportunities to the next generation.

Furthermore employment and economic activity in general, can provide women with access to the public sphere. Work might also give women the opportunities to develop skills needed for political involvement and the confidence to stand up for

---

[1018] IOM-Iraq, *Female Headed Households*, 6.
[1019] Ibid.
[1020] Kurdistan Region Statistics Office, *Expenditures* (Fact Sheet 6, September 2012) 1.
[1021] Ibid.p.2
[1022] With interviewees explaining that a low-skilled worker could get as little as 300 to 500 dollars per month

themselves.[1023] Access to paid work has the potential to shift boundaries and to give women more power. If women earn their own money, they are economically independent or at least semi-independent. This increases their and their family's quality of life and gives them a say in how the money is to be spent.[1024] While this point is currently contested by several academics, it could be observed that, even if the women did not have a greater say in household budgeting, they cherished having their own money available.[1025]

These arguments are especially valid for those households which are headed by women. During and often also after armed conflict, women become main breadwinners for the family and heads of households. They assume all the responsibilities men had before going to war, in addition to their traditional chores. Since they have to carry all the responsibilities alone, the female-headed households and widows are often poorer than others and require special attention,[1026] although it has been shown that female-headed households cannot *per se* be said to be more vulnerable than male-headed households, but that they experience vulnerability in a different, gendered way.[1027]

In 2003 UNICEF (the United Nations Children's Fund) estimated that 60 per cent of households in the Iraqi city Basra were led by women. If this is true for most larger cities, it becomes apparent that the success of conflict transformation will be limited unless the government supports and empowers these women and their families. Clearly they will be unable to effectively support the reconstruction of their country if they have difficulties in obtaining enough food for their family.[1028] An estimated 1,5 million women lost their husbands in Iraq due to violence from 1980 to 2010. Many of them lost, not only their husbands but also their income. Widows without a supporting family and who are unable to provide for themselves end up living in

---

[1023] Regan and Paskeviciute, "Women's Access to Politics and Peaceful States," 293.

[1024] Naila Kabeer, "Gender Equality and Women's Empowerment: A Critical Analysis of the Third Millennium Development Goal" *Gender and Development* 13(1) (2005): 18.

[1025] See e.g. Interview AP, Sulaimaniya on 18/05/2012

[1026] Bouta and Frerks, *Women's Roles in Conflict Prevention, Conflict Resolution and Post-Conflict Reconstruction*, 36.

[1027] Waite, "How Is Household Vulnerability Gendered?," 167.

[1028] Helmut Krieger, *Gender und bewaffnete Konflikte, Irak* (Vienna: Vienna Institute for International Dialogue and Cooperation, 2007) 34.

camps with their children.[1029] Those women need the opportunity to earn their own money, in order to be able to feed their children and to give them a secure future. If the children do not see any future, they will not see any reason to support stability.

According to IOM there are currently between one to two million female headed households in Iraq, with a substantial percentage in the Kurdistan Region. Only two per cent of the female headed households assessed by the IOM are employed regularly.[1030] The women themselves ranked access to work as their most important need, as this would solve many of their other problems, such as insufficient food, or inadequate health services.[1031]

However, as already shortly noted above, paid work can also have negative impact on women's lives. Women do not merely need the opportunity to get any job. They need a job matching their abilities and the opportunity for choices in employment or business. As the *Gender Inequality Index* shows the simple fact of having more women in the labour force does not mean a higher level of development for the country or increased equality between the sexes because employment can often be used to exploit women.[1032] It is often not about the access to work, but rather about the nature of work. Even if women manage to obtain an acceptable job, the mere fact of earning money does not mean that they have a greater control over their lives. Even if women increase their time at paid work, their domestic chores are rarely renegotiated. They still bear the main burden for domestic chores and as a consequence gender inequality in the total amount of work seems to be intensified.[1033] Therefore one needs to ask whether the outside work is well paid and fulfilling or rather badly paid, and exploitive.[1034]

As expressed by Lakshmi Lingam: "*Women are being considered a 'resource' for globalizing capital,*"[1035]while the implications for them as individuals are not always taken into account. According to feminist researchers the mere integration of

---

[1029] Charlotte Ashton, BBC-online "Iraq women: Winners or losers in a war-torn society?" (16.11.11) http://www.bbc.co.uk/news/world-middle-east-15743078 (Accessed on 27.11.11)
[1030] IOM-Iraq, *Female Headed Households,* 1.
[1031] Ibid.p.5
[1032] UNDP, "Gender Inequality Index and related indicators".
[1033] Kabeer, "Gender Equality and Women's Empowerment," 21.
[1034] Abu-Lughod, "Dialects of Women's Empowerment," 88.
[1035] Bakker and Silvey, *Beyond States and Markets,* 72.

women into paid labour does not necessarily give them any advantages. They are integrated into a patriarchal system, which has the opportunity of exploiting them. The system needs to change, to make it more accessible for women, and to empower rather than exploit them.[1036] Measures can include more part time jobs, the possibility of a career within a part-time job and more flexible working hours, etc. The mere fact of employment is not by nature liberating. Women need to be allowed economic independence by the family as well as by society.[1037]

It has consequently been argued that women should not be forced to be 'pushed' into economic activities, as this will result in their suffering through double or triple burdens, and it might lead to even more inequality rather than the hoped for equality. Persuading women to become economically active may have negative consequences. It follows from this argument that it may be in a woman's interest to remain economically inactive. As argued by the researcher this way of thinking is exactly one of the problems. Several other feminist researchers, such as Carolyn Nordstrom maintain that women are already economically active, but this activity is most often not formally recognized.[1038] Hence it is necessary to make women's current economic activities visible and to provide the women in these situations with the opportunity of moving from economically invisible corners to economically viable activities with all the benefits enjoyed by the rest of the population.

The field research in the Kurdistan region confirmed that many interviewees that it was vital for women stay at home and take care of the family and the household. However, this was generally not seen as "work" or anything worth mentioning. When people described women as "not having a role"[1039] or not being of political or economic value, it generally meant that the woman stayed at home and looked after the family. According to the interviewees, also the government is not doing enough to recognise women's positions within the home.[1040] While this is not only a

[1036] Moghadam, *Modernizing women,* 67.

[1037] Abu-Lughod, "Dialects of Women's Empowerment," 89.

[1038] Carolyn Nordstrom, "Women, economy, war" *International Review of the Red Cross* 92(877) (2010): 162.

[1039] See e.g. Interview AG, Erbil on 13/04/2012; Interview BN, Erbil on 17/07/2012; Interview BQ, Erbil on 21/07/2012; Interview CA, Sulaimaniya on 13/08/2012

[1040] Interview AG, Erbil on 13/04/2012; Interview AH, Erbil on 15/04/2012; Interview BV, Sulaimaniya on 06/08/2012

Kurdish problem, the recognition of unremunerated work, especially by women, would be a big step towards achieving equality.

In conclusion improved access to the work force by women from all strata of society would likely benefit not only national development, but also individual development and gender equality, and would thus decrease the potential for conflict. At the same time it is necessary to change the employment system, to ensure a decrease in pressure on and violence against female workers. This will require further government regulations and interventions.[1041]

Furthermore, to improve women's opportunities and to ensure more equal gender relations, the barriers between the public and private sector employment conditions need to be broken down. Finally, so to give women's work in society a greater standing, volunteer work, household work, subsistence labour and reproduction have to be taken into account when discussing economic productivity.[1042]

If all of the above issues were resolved, the productivity of the region and the living standards of the whole population would rise. Further, the empowerment of women and a reduced potential for conflict inside the homes, would follow.

The positive utilisation of employment is only one way individual and national development can be influenced by the population as a whole. A second way is through of self-employment.

C.   Running Businesses to Achieve Equality

When driving through Kurdistan's bigger cities new businesses can be seen popping up everywhere, from factories, to beauty salons and shops. It has been part of the government's plan for the region's reconstruction to support the rising economic boom, through fostering business opportunities, especially on an international level.[1043] If and how this development has influenced the situation of women and gender equality in the region will be subject of this subchapter.

[1041] True, *The Political Economy of Violence against Women,* 80.

[1042] Tickner, *Gender in International Relations,* 93.

[1043] Kurdistan board of investment, http://www.kurdistaninvestment.org/ (Accessed on 14.07.2013) Kurdistan Regional Government, "Fact sheet: Doing business in the Kurdistan Region" http://www.krg.org/p/p.aspx?l=12&s=050000&p=302 (Accessed on 14.07.2013)

As with any other country in the world, there is a certain percentage of women in the Kurdistan Region, albeit small in comparison to their male counterparts, who make it to the top of the top. Some of these include Ghada Gebrar, who has been the CEO of Korek Telecom Iraq since 1st of August 2011,[1044] Talar Faiq, who is the director of Erbil International Airport, and as such the first female airport director in Iraq, and the only one across the Middle East,[1045] as well as Ferda Cemiloğlu, a Kurdish entrepreneur, who owns a construction company in Erbil, and is the Head of the Management Committee of the Kurdish Women Entrepreneurs Association, which provides micro credits and prepares vocational courses for women.[1046] According to these women, the opportunities in the region exist, but practical implementation is still problematic.

Talar Faiq is of the view that women in Kurdistan today have every chance to become successful, even though it is still a difficult for them reach the top CEO positions. According to her, making it to the top is about setting priorities. She notes that the situation of 'the woman at home' is slowly changing in the region, because middle class families can no longer thrive with one breadwinner, and because women speak up and no longer accept to merely stay at home.[1047] Ferda Cemiloğlu also believes that women in Kurdistan have everything it takes to become successful entrepreneurs, and observes that the number of female entrepreneurs registered at the Commercial Organisation has increased in the previous years. At the same time it is a problem for the region that many women are educated very well but do not take up professions once they finish their education. They choose to stay at home, or are content to become civil servants, but do not invest their knowledge in the private sector.[1048]

United States - Kurdistan Business Council, http://uskbc.org/ (Accessed on 14.07.2013)

[1044] Korektel, "CEO – Ghada Gebara" http://www.korektel.com/top-links/about-us/ceo (Accessed on 27.01.2013)

[1045] Rabar Ruwayada Mustafa, The Kurdish Globe, "'The opportunities are always there, but we need the right mindset for it' – Talar Faiq" (31 December 2012) http://www.kurdishglobe.net/display-article.html?id=DCA3483B1F76D860D6B9A36CDE2C203B (Accessed on 27.01.2013)

[1046] Solin Hacador, The Kurdistan Tribune "The Big Success of women Entrepreneurs is a Kurdish Princess" (24 December 2011) http://kurdistantribune.com/2011/big-success-of-women-entrepreneurs-kurdish-princess/ (Accessed on 27.01.2013)

[1047] Mustafa, "'The opportunities are always there".

[1048] Hacador, "The Big Success of women Entrepreneurs is a Kurdish Princess".

The reason for such a development was explained by a woman, who is currently living with her family in Europe, but who is intending to return to Kurdistan:

> *"I am intending on opening a shop for cosmetics in Kurdistan. The women would love that. My husband is not very fond of the idea, but I will do it anyway. As a woman one simply has to fight for everything. It is possible to achieve a lot, but one has to fight for everything."*[1049]

It follows that while the organisational and legal structures may be in place in the region, the social circumstances still prevent or impede many women from establishing their own businesses or achieving high-level positions in existing businesses.

While it is certainly not possible for all women in the region to reach the position of a CEO, the existing female CEOs can play an important role, not only in using their skills to support development in the region, but also in opening up possibilities for other women. Increasing gender equality at the top can be another way of supporting the development of equality in general, through role models facilitating changes on the ground. This has already happened, although only to a limited extent:

The Kurdish population seems very much in favour, at least in principle, of increasing gender equality at a higher level, with nearly three quarters of the interviewees indicating that they would support such a development.[1050] Nevertheless, in practice, the concept that men should be in leading positions is still embedded in society. Interestingly there were more women than men who clearly stated that they did not think that women should be in positions of power. Many such women were from well-off families, and would have the possibility of reaching positions of power. Especially noteworthy were young women with a high standard of education and otherwise vocal supporters of women's rights believed

---

[1049] Interview CH, Vienna on 05/11/2012

[1050] See e.g. Interview AP, Sulaimaniya on 18/05/2012; Interview AQ, Sulaimaniya on 19/05/2012; Interview AV, Sulaimaniya on 28/05/2012; Interview BC, Erbil on 25/06/212; Interview BD, Erbil on 25/06/2012

that they did not have the chance to achieve high positions or should not aspire to such positions.[1051]

Many of the younger men especially were of the opinion that while there should be few women in positions of power in order to have some balance, there should not be too many.[1052]

The general opinions of the interviewees demonstrated once more that the legal structures and framework which already exist are not yet embedded in people's thinking or put into practice.

But it should thereby not be forgotten that the vast majority of people surveyed believed that there should be more women in positions of power. These included both women and men, although the women, and especially young educated women, were in the majority. The men included middle aged and religious men.

The people interviewed, who were in favour of a higher percentage of women's inclusion, were of the opinion that a higher number of women in high positions would be positive for their personal, as well as the region's development. Their reasons included the following: in order not to forget women's rights;[1053] simply because there are currently not enough women in these positions;[1054] or because women as well as men should also have the chance to achieve high office,[1055] especially those with the same or equivalent education. At the same time they also reasoned that women are sometimes better than men in certain areas,[1056] that this creates more balance in society[1057] and that it is especially important for women to be in high positions, in order to free themselves.[1058] Finally it was argued that a

---

[1051] See e.g. Interview AM, Erbil on 27/04/2012; Interview AW, Sulaimaniya on 01/06/2012; Interview BG, Erbil on 02/07/2012; Interview AI, Erbil on 16/04/2012; Interview BF, Erbil on 29/06/2012; Interview BU, Erbil on 14/07/2012

[1052] Interview AF, Erbil on 09/04/2012; Interview AX, Sulaimaniya on 03/06/2012; Interview BK, Erbil on 12/07/2012

[1053] Interview BV, Sulaimaniya on 06/08/2012

[1054] Interview AK, Erbil on 20/04/2012

[1055] Interview AT, Sulaimaniya on 24/05/2012

[1056] Interview BH, Erbil on 05/07/2012

[1057] Interview AO, Sulaimaniya on 13/05/2012

[1058] Interview BN, Erbil on 17/07/2012

society cannot develop and move forward without the involvement of women at all levels including positions of power.[1059]

The prevailing opinion was that there should be more women in positions of power. This view was mostly qualified by the reservation that women should only have certain positions, if they have the necessary abilities and personal qualities. It was very important to the interviewees that women, as well as men, only advanced to a high position if they had the capability. For many, it was especially important that such people live according to the law and are not corrupt. They did not care whether there was a man or a woman on top, if they were qualitatively good. They did not support the notion of having somebody in the top position merely because he or she was a man or a woman.[1060] A middle aged teacher expressed this view as follows: "*In several areas women can have good roles, but not in others. The distribution is dependent on the ability of each person*".[1061] In this regard the people's opinions represented gender equal ideas at a very high level. By stating that it should be ability that counts irrespective of gender, social class, ethnic background or religious belief, the interviewees were supporting the concept of utopian gender equality.

With reference to the practical aspects of women's access to high positions, opinions were split. Some interviewees believed that no further development is necessary, as enough has already been achieved.[1062] Others disagreed including a 28 year old house wife who was of the view that women have little chance of achieving higher positions, as they have no say and are not accepted by men in the working environment. She added that a large number of men in positions of power will not readily change, *"as the society believes in this and women will only be let into these type of positions if the thinking of the whole society will change."*[1063] In addition it was noted that the concept of positive discrimination was

---

[1059] Interview CF, Vienna on 16/11/2012

[1060] Interview AZ, Sulaimaniya on 06/06/2012; Interview AU, Sulaimaniya on 28/05/2012; Interview BT, Erbil on 24/07/2012; Interview BW, Sulaimaniya on 06/08/2012; Interview BQ, Erbil on 21/07/2012

[1061] Interview BA, Erbil on 21/06/2012

[1062] Interview AI, Erbil on 16/04/2012

[1063] Interview AY, Sulaimaniya on 04/06/2012

not well received by many, who believed that everybody in the region should have the same opportunities.[1064]

Despite the above contradictory statements, the reality is that men and women are still seen by many as having their specific roles, and that it is not acceptable for everyone to aspire to every available post. To underling this point one young doctor explained in a half joking way that *"women should certainly be in positions of power, but only in the finance authorities, as women are better in dealing with money than men are."*[1065] It became clear through other remarks and by observing their lives that it was very important to many interviewees that every person "is on their respective place". While people then added that this place could be anywhere and that women could aspire to the same positions as men, provided they had the abilities, in practice it was most often the case that a "woman's place" was in the house and with the family.[1066]

While the interviews revealed an in principle positive attitude when it came to gender equality in higher positions, it could be seen that many women with realistic hopes for such positions, feel barred and do not achieve them in the end. This results in a loss of human resources for the region, and a resulting loss of potential development. One way to counter this situation was through the introduction and support for the microfinance sector:

1.   Raising Economic Productivity – The Microfinance Sector

As discussed previously, peace and economic development go hand in hand. Peace is a prerequisite for economic growth and investment, while economic development can help diminish the likelihood of social unrest and ultimately armed conflict. To support economic development it is not enough to improve employment opportunities in the public sector, or in private companies through foreign investment. Citizens need to have the opportunity to build up businesses themselves. In order for women to be economically independent and to generate their own living through business, they need, as a prerequisite, the secure right to

---

[1064] Interview AD, Erbil on 08/04/2012

[1065] Interview AN, Erbil on 03/05/2012

[1066] Interview AU, Sulaimaniya on 28/05/2012; Interview BM, Erbil on 13/07/2012

property,[1067] as well as access to either macro, or micro credit.[1068] Small businesses, especially in the rural regions, can provide women with more flexibility and with the ability to support their family, to develop themselves, and to contribute to national development. Further, the women are not dependent on an employer, do not need to keep fixed hours or travel far.

In Kurdistan it has been normal for women contribute to the household income by working at their own small business, generally from home. Several women explained that they sewed clothes or weaved carpets to earn some money for themselves and the family especially during times of war.[1069]

In order to start such a business, however small, capital is needed. Commercial banks often attach conditions to their loans, which numerous women in a post-conflict situation are unable to meet. They therefore cannot obtain a loan.[1070] Further, today's trade liberalization, especially on an international level, favours large and medium producers over small ones. In many countries women, especially from poorer backgrounds, do not have the same access as men to credit as well as modern technologies and marketing know-how. They are therefore not able to participate in the current market in the same way as their male counterparts.[1071]

In response to these difficulties faced especially by women, a new system has been developed, as an adjunct to the formal loan system, to provide the poorer population with the opportunity of acquiring loans and opening businesses: the system of micro-loans, as pioneered by Muhammad Yunus, Nobel Peace Prize winner of 2006. Through his program millions of Bangladeshis, mostly women, were able to start their own businesses. Today micro-credit projects are being funded across Asia, Latin America and Africa and they play an important role in the development of these countries.[1072] Many of the projects target especially women,

---

[1067] Addison and Brück, *Making Peace Work,* 107.
[1068] Ibid. p.115
[1069] Interview CH, Vienna on 05/11/2012; Interview CD, Vienna on 21/10/2012
[1070] Zuckermann and Greenberg, "The Gender Dimensions of Post-Conflict Reconstruction," 74.
[1071] Bakker and Silvey, *Beyond States and Markets,* 43.
[1072] Michael Kevane, *Women and Development in Africa, How Gender works* (London: Lynne Rienner Publishers, 2004) 160.

as it is said that these are most successful.[1073] Microfinance is seen as part of the solution to reduce poverty and to create and reconstruct job opportunities.[1074] In recent years microfinance has become increasingly important to the international community, and has been inter alia deployed to countries at a conflict transformation stage.

In Iraq there is a microfinance sector, which includes fourteen Microfinance Institutions (MFIs), which operate in all of the 18 provinces to provide financial services for the 7.1 million poor or low-income people in Iraq.[1075] Microfinance started in Iraq in 2003 and it is funded through US Government sources.[1076] In 2007 the Iraqi government established microfinance programs as well through the Ministry of Labour and Social Affairs and through the Ministry of Industry and Minerals.[1077] As noted above, one of the development strategies for the country is to expand micro finance programs, especially for women.[1078]

The number of active clients in 2010 was 75,182, of which an average of 16 per cent were women. Even though the interest rates are comparably high[1079] the availability of small loans to poor people gives them the opportunity to build up their lives in a way, which might not be otherwise possible.[1080]

According to Tijara the microfinance industry in Iraq has a priority to reach women, as they have high success rates in terms of repayment as well as a positive socio-economic impact on their families. In order to support the involvement of women, MFIs have actively hired female loan officers, which in 2010 represent 19 per cent of all such staff.[1081]

[1073] Engelhardt, *Starke Frauen für den Frieden,* 150.
[1074] USAID Iraq, *Provincial Economic Growth Program, State of Iraq's Microfinance Industry* (Tijara, June 2011) 15.
[1075] USAID Iraq, *State of Iraq's Microfinance Industry* (Tijara, June 2010) 5.
[1076] USAID Iraq, *Provincial Economic Growth Program,* 15.
[1077] Ibid.p.16
[1078] IAU, *Iraq, The National Development Strategy,* 63.
[1079] 12% to 18% per annum
[1080] USAID Iraq, *Provincial Economic Growth Program,* 18.
[1081] Ibid.p.38

Women have so far used the loans from the microfinance organisations to build sewing businesses[1082], frozen food businesses[1083], beauty salons[1084] and a kindergarten.[1085]

Despite certain success stories, the microfinance sector has still got some work ahead to release the whole entrepreneurial potential of Iraqi women due to women's often limited social and economic mobility within the region.[1086]

Micro-finance programmes are said to be positive, especially for poorer women. They are said to close the gender gap in areas such as holding custody of income, ownership of and control over assets, productive versus reproductive roles, gaining access to domestic and community economic/other resources; and indebtedness.[1087] Women additionally get more confidence in dealing with banks, markets and the public in general.

As argued by Stefan Lovgren, micro-credit projects help people to lift themselves out of poverty. They encourage social responsibility, through the repayments of the loan, and consequently strengthen the whole community and help prevent social unrest.[1088] Even though the banks charge relatively high interest rates, their repayment rates are over 95 per cent. One reason is that borrowers are placed into groups and if a member of the group does not pay, the others are liable for their debt and might suffer penalties. This joint liability leads to people working together and to a sense of commitment.[1089] The outcome of the work will result in better living standards, better health and improved opportunities for education[1090] and consequently less reason for conflict.

[1082] Ibid.p.20

[1083] USAID Iraq, *State of Iraq's Microfinance Industry,* 14.

[1084] Ibid.p.17

[1085] Ibid.p.47

[1086] USAID Iraq, *Provincial Economic Growth Program,* 38.

[1087] Johnson (ed.), *Small Change or Real Change?,* 54.

[1088] Stefan Lovgren, for National Geographic News, "Nobel Peace Prize Goes to Micro-Loan Pioneers" (October 13, 2006) http://news.nationalgeographic.com/news/2006/10/061013-nobel-peace.html (Accessed on 15.09.2011)

[1089] Kevane, *Women and Development in Africa,"* 160/161.

[1090] Ibid. p.166

Academics supporting microcredit projects are of the opinion that they enable women to improve their standing in their households, and thus gives them more influence and freedom.[1091]

At the same time, feminists and academics, critical of micro credits, argue that money is not sufficient to change gender relations. They claim that even if microcredit programmes are successful from the outside, in terms of loan repayment rates and growth of memberships, they do not challenge the existing social hierarchies. According to some researchers, such as Fernando and Heston, they even validate these hierarchies.[1092] It is argued that men may take the loans from the women, or that the women spend the money in the way wanted by the men. Kabeer even went so far as to suggest that the micro credits provide a 'safety net' for the poor, but do not help them to leave poverty behind.[1093] It is therefore questionable, whether microfinance projects really give the women more freedom or empowerment.

As part of the field research in Kurdistan, it was observed that none of the interviewees questioned on the subject had considered applying for a micro-credit loan, or knew anyone who had done so. The majority of the respondees were not even aware that these possibilities exist.

While the microfinance sector is certainly important in providing opportunities, the steps taken by the government and the different organizations have not yet been sufficient to make the sector accessible to the whole of the local population. In addition, while the microfinance sector might give the women involved certain opportunities, it should not be seen as a substitute for gender inclusion measures for national loan systems, or for medium or large companies. Banks as well as companies should be aware that their economic policies may intensify social tension and contribute to the potential for conflict.[1094]

[1091] Bakker and Silvey, *Beyond States and Markets,* 73.
[1092] Ibid.p.73
[1093] Ibid.p.75
[1094] James Boyce, "Aid for peace" *World Policy Journal* 15(2) (1998)

In conclusion, while the economy in general, and employment generating in particular, may support progress towards gender equality and positive peace, there is still insufficient progress in the Kurdistan Region. Basically only women from the higher classes of society have access to well-paid jobs, and not enough is being done to raise women's general economic activity. This leads to a loss of resources for the region, as well as reduced potential for personal development.

There is a problem that macro-economic measures are largely decided by the men in power, and thus lack a gender balanced point of view. The result is that the current economic system dose not serve the the majority of Kurdistan's women very well. This was apparent within society, where gender equal employment and economic activity were seen as positive in principle but not realisable in practice.

The various measures taken by the government, such as the appointment of a female Minister of Labour, the inclusion of gender issues in the national strategy plan, the employment of women within government institutions and the support of microfinance projects all look great on the surface and are cited by regional officials. However, progress towards female inclusion in the economy and the flow on benefits to national as well as the individual development of the people are far from exhausted.

Social perceptions on women and work seem hardly to have changed. While some women have made it to the top, others are struggling under a double or triple burden, or are unable to get any job at all, which could place their families in precarious situations.

The lack of support for all levels of society within the current economic structure is likely to have resulted in a substantial under-utilisation of the nation's human resources. That many women are unable to generate income risks impoverishment of certain parts of the population and enhances the possibility of future conflict.

As yet, the economic measures taken to redress gender inequality do not seem to be having a great effect. This lack of a gender inclusive economic system hampers development of equality in the private sphere. Many women wish to, or have to, generate their own income. However, the current system often makes this impossible, and places many of those, who must work in an even more restricted situation.

At the same time it is conceded that the necessary legal and administrative provisions for women's inclusion in the economic sphere exist, and that some women who were either supported by their immediate environment or stood up against the social mores, made it to the top. As with female politicians, these women can function as role models and lay the foundation for the future.

These women were able to struggle through a patriarchal structure and ensure their personal 'empowerment' on a greater scale. However a change of the system as a whole is needed, which improves the working conditions, gives women from all social backgrounds opportunities to work, provides women with enhanced rights to receive assets and recognizes the economic value of 'non-marketed activities'. Once this is achieved, positive peace will be one step closer.

One way to guarantee a basis for providing equal opportunities for women in the work force is to firstly provide them with equal opportunities in education:

VI. Gender, Women and Society – The Power of Education

"Education is a fundamental human right and it is decisive to the development of individuals (men and women) and societies" [1095]

Education can form people's minds and be employed as a tool to influence transformation in any way desired. While it offers the skills and knowledge necessary for economic development and the transfer of social and cultural values, education can also be used politically for the development of particular ideologies, from liberal ideas to extremism. [1096]

[1095] UNESCO Iraq Office, Literacy Network for Iraq, "Gender and Education for All" http://www.lifeforiraq.org/en/content/gender-and-education-all (Accessed on 09.01.2013)
[1096] Fiona Leach and Mairead Dume (ed.), *Education, Conflict and Reconciliation, International Perspectives* (Bern: Peter Lang, 2007) 21.

For instance, education has been used as a tool to indoctrinate and to fuel radicalism, chauvinism and militarism.[1097] Schools have been transformed into indoctrination centers, where children are made to sing patriotic songs, cite a dictator's speeches and salute his picture in school, as it was done under the Saddam regime in Iraq.[1098]

But just as education can fuel conflict, it provides all the tools necessary to achieve equality, development and peace. As explained by the World Bank:

> *"Education is one of the most powerful instruments societies have for reducing deprivation and vulnerability: it helps lift earnings potential, expands labor mobility, promotes the health of parents and children, reduces fertility and child mortality, and affords the disadvantaged a voice in society and the political system".*[1099]

Education can thereby support personal as well as national economic development, through providing people with the ability to work and consequently to feed themselves and their families, as well as to boost the country's economy.[1100] In addition, literacy and critical thinking provides people with the opportunity to enhance their knowledge, and hence to shape their personal outlooks and form their own opinions on all life matters. This empowers them to take part in political and other decision-making.[1101]

Positive or critical education can thereby lead to a broader understanding by people of people, which can in turn result in a lessening of discrimination, as well as ethnic, religious and cultural impediments. Education will in the long run lead to a more peaceful society and can therefore also have a profound influence on social equality. Many people, whether in conflict situations or not, grow up with certain prejudices which have either been created through particular experiences or which have been nourished by their immediate surroundings. In the extreme, prejudices

---

[1097] Clayton Thyne, "ABC's, 123's, and the Golden Rule: The Pacifying Effect of Education on Civil War, 19080-1999" *International Studies Quarterly* 50(4) (2006): 738.

[1098] Al-Ali, *Iraqi Women,* 120.

[1099] Thyne, "ABC's, 123's, and the Golden Rule," 735.

[1100] Alice Tuyizere, *Peace, Gender and Development, The Role of Religion and Culture* (Kampala: Makerere University, Fountain Publishers Ltd, 2007) 194.

[1101] Ibid.p.194

can lead to a willingness to kill people from another group, simply because of a wrong perception of that group. Education can be used to work against such prejudices. [1102] As discussed above, a society in which people believe in the idea of equality is less likely to start a violent conflict, than a society which does not believe in equality, whether such inequality is based on ethics, religion, or gender.[1103]

As already argued by Bertha von Suttner[1104], the achievement of more equality between women and men lies partly in education. Education can contribute to a more equitable relationship between the genders,[1105] through better understanding, as well as the provision of more equal opportunities.

Do all types of education lead to more equality? Can education do more harm than good? Is it truly possible to achieve peace through education? What is the impact on a woman's individual standing, whether or not she attended school?

As argued by academics, such as Naila Kafeer, increased participation of women in all levels of the education system will change their positions in society and consequently change society as a whole. Studies have shown that power relationships within and outside of the home change with the level of education. Educated women are less likely to suffer from domestic violence.[1106] Knowledge thereby goes together with power,[1107] and arguably has a positive influence on women's personal development. At the same time gender inclusive education is said to be greatly influential on the development of a region as a whole. The way an education system operates, whether it supports equal access to high quality education and training, and in which way it communicates particular values to the group taught, will influence whether conflicts between particular groups are ameliorated or inflamed.[1108] Education is therefore seen as a tool not only to decrease social tensions and prejudices, but also as a first step to improve

---

[1102] Ibid.p.4

[1103] See: Caprioli and Boyer, "Gender, Violence and International Crisis," 509.

[1104] Sandra Hedinger, *Frauen über Kried und Frieden* (Frankfurt/Main: Campus, 2000) 95.

[1105] Tuyizere, *Peace, Gender and Development*, 194.

[1106] Kabeer, "Gender Equality and Women's Empowerment," 17.

[1107] Hartwig, *Rural African Women as Subjects of Social and Political Change*, 144.

[1108] Leach and Dume (ed.), *Education, Conflict and Reconciliation*, 22.

economic development. As part of Iraq's National Development Plan for 2010 to 2014, it is planned to develop intellectual know-how to increase economic productivity, the employment rate and the GDP as well as to reduce differences between urban and rural areas. It is therefore tacitly acknowledged that access to quality education, particularly for vulnerable groups, which include women, is vital to ensuring participation in economic activities and consequently in the economic development of the country as a whole.[1109]

Considering the large number of relevant international conventions and declarations, including the Universal Declaration of Human Rights, the ICECSR, the CEDAW, the Convention on the Rights of the Child, the Millennium Development Goals and many more, it would appear that there is universal agreement at the international level for the need to achieve gender equality in education and to provide education for every child. Despite this clear intention, the international community has as yet only partially achieved equality in education.[1110] The majority of school drop outs and illiterate people around the world are still girls and women.[1111]

With respect to gender equality and gender parity Iraq, and thus also the Kurdistan Region, they lie within the lower range of countries in a world-wide comparison,[1112] and there is a growing demand for improvement.

As explained by UNESCO's World Data on Education report from 2011, education in Iraq has always been highly dependent on the leader's objective at that point of time.[1113] There have been times when religion was at the forefront or nationalism and other times when the education of women and girls have been more supported. According to the report, the overall aim of education in Iraq until the end of the 1990s was to construct an "enlightened" generation, who believe in God, are

---

[1109] UNESCO Iraq Office, *Literacy Initiative for Empowerment in Iraq 2010-2015* (Literacy Needs Assessment Report, UNESCO) 19.

[1110] Christopher Colclough, "Achieving Gender Equality in Education: What Does It Take?" *Prospects* XXXIV/1 (2004): 3.

[1111] Ibid. p.4

[1112] UNESCO, *World Atlas of Gender Equality in Education* (Paris: UNESCO, 2012)

[1113] UNESCO, *World Data on Education, Iraq,* "Principles and general objectives of education".

loyal to their country and dedicated to the larger Arab nation, but who also maintain a scientific approach to reasoning.[1114]

As part of the political shift in 2003, the education system needed reform to respond to the shift in society. The new curriculum framework, which was drafted with the support of UNESCO, aims at underpinning the faith in God, and respect for all, as well as putting the family back in the centre of attention and the foundation of society.[1115] Education was thereby used once more to convey the ideologies of the leaders and society to the next generation, as well as a tool to support the reconstruction of the country.

It is observed that little trust is put into education by the population at large. Only very few people were of the opinion that political education and an anti-war programme, from Kindergarten to University, is needed and would change people's outlook on war and consequently its likelihood.[1116] Only few of the interviewees were of the view that intellectuals are the driving force for change in the region and that a country can only be rebuilt on the basis of thought and reason and that this can only be achieved by the intellectuals.[1117] For instance, as explained by an elderly blacksmith, their know-how is needed to build up the region and also to educate the next generation, so that they will not make the same mistakes again.[1118] However, when asked about conflict prevention techniques, many more people believed in the power of politicians, than in the power of education.[1119]

The following chapter will discuss exactly how far education has come in the region and how it influences the development of gender equality and consequently conflict transformation as a whole. Firstly a more in depth review will be presented of the analyses of generations of researchers on the influence of the different forms of education on peace and equality. This will be followed by a discussion of legal

---

[1114] Ibid.

[1115] UNESCO, International Bureau of Education, *World Data on Education, Iraq* (IBE/2011/CP/WDE/IQ, 7th Edition 2010/2011) "Principles and general objectives of education"

[1116] Interview BI, Erbil on 08/07/2012; Interview CF, Vienna on 16/11/2012; Interview CI, Vienna on 26/10/2012

[1117] Interview AN, Erbil on 03/05/2012; Interview BE, Erbil on 26/06/2012

[1118] Interview BN, Erbil on 17/07/2012

[1119] See e.g. Interview BW, Sulaimaniya on 08/08/2012; Interview BS, Erbil on 24/07/2012; Interview AS, Sulaimaniya on 23/05/2012; Interview AM, Erbil on 27/04/2012; Interview CI, Vienna on 26/10/2012

options related to gender and education in the Kurdistan Region with more concrete and practical illustrations. These will include examples of children's schooling and higher education, gender equality and gender parity, i.e. equal access to education and the quality of education. From the analyses, conclusions will be drawn on how the different forms of education are currently supporting positive transformation within the region and which further developments will be needed to ensure full gender equality and sustainable peace. Finally, the adults' role in the development of the region will be considered from an educational perspective, by concentrating on the education of women through literacy programs and on women's roles as educators of the new generation. The different chapters will then lead to the conclusion that while education is certainly seen as a priority in the region and huge developments are currently taking place, which will undoubtedly lead to positive economic development, the current education system as constructed at the moment, supports social inequalities rather diminishes them. Education has therefore not led either to gender equality and hence the elimination of conflict potential in the private sphere, or to a reduction of conflict potential in the public sphere.

1.   A Theoretical Overview

"In many conflicts around the world, education is part of the problem, not the solution."[1120]

Reflecting on education as a separate factor influencing conflict and conflict transformation is an emerging field of study. It has been considered by several academics in analysing current situations, and options for the future, in conflict ridden areas of the world, such as Rwanda, Palestine and Nepal.[1121] Different academics ascribe to education various functions and roles, which all in one way or another influence conflict within society.

While the positive impact of education must always be recognized, it is also important for academics to point out the devastating effects that education can

---

[1120] Bush/Saltarelli quoted in Klaus Seitz, *Bildung und Konflikt, Die Rolle von Bildung bei der Entstehung, Prävention und Bewältigung gesellschaftlicher Krisen – Konsequenzen für die Entwicklungszusammenarbeit* (Rossdorf: TZ-Verlagsgesellschaft, 2004) 49.

[1121] Leach and Dume (ed.), *Education, Conflict and Reconciliation.*

have on the population. Klaus Seitz especially underlines the importance of not only seeing education as a measure to prevent or overcome conflict, but also as a tool, which can be used to support social differences and inequalities within a society and consequently increase the potential for conflict.[1122] Education has been used in the past, for example, to promote propaganda concerning national identity and has consequently exacerbated social tensions and fuelled violent escalations.[1123]

Seitz is only one of many scholars who argue that education and schooling is *"the primary vehicle through which society produces and legitimates inequality"*.[1124] As demonstrated by Svi Shapiro the education of children is influenced by factors such as race and wealth, or gender. She argues that schools pursue a "hidden curriculum", which gives more chances to some than to others, and consequently decides on the children's future life style long before their adult life.[1125] From a gender perspective, the formal education system is thus seen as reinforcing a traditional hegemonic masculinity, as explained by Davies, and discouraging greater gender equality.[1126]

When the inequality within the school system augments other conflict promoting factors, education in general and schooling in particular can have a role in creating and sustaining conflict, as shown by Sarah Parker and Kay Standing using the example of Nepal. By not addressing inequalities within society, whether social, ethical, religious or gender inequalities, schooling contributes to the alienation of certain elements of the population. This is a problem which cannot be solved by merely providing enhanced access to education. As emphasized by Parker and Standing, the solution involves creating a similar range of schools and quality of teaching. If parts of the population have access only to inappropriate educational facilities and poor teaching quality, violence at school will be high and the drop-out

---

[1122] Seitz, *Bildung und Konflikt*, 48/49.
[1123] Ibid.p.51
[1124] Ibid.p.82.
[1125] Svi Shapiro, *Educating Youth for a World beyond violence, A Pedagogy for Peace* (New York: Palgrave Macmillan, 2010) 83.
[1126] See Davies (2004) in Seitz, *Bildung und Konflikt*, 53.

rate even higher with the consequent impact on the children's future opportunities.[1127]

According to Salmi there are four different forms of violence in education: *"deliberate injury to the integrity of human life"*, such physical violence and weapons in schools, *"indirect violation of the right to survival"*, such as inequality in accessing education, or unequal chances in education, *"deprivation of fundamental political rights"*, such as the lack of democracy and the right of participation in school and *"deprivation of higher rights"*, such as the dominance of certain learning content over another, or the suppression of languages or points of views of ethnic minorities.[1128]

One may compare the forms of violence outlined above to the ones discussed by Galtung, which are said to determine the existence of peace within society. Thus Salmi's *"indirect violation of the right to survival"*, and the *"deprivation of fundamental political rights"* can be related to Galtung's "structural violence", while the *"deprivation of higher rights"* can be seen as equivalent to "cultural violence". Considering that these different forms of violence are present in many education systems and schools around the world, it may be concluded that in practice schools and other educational institutions are often counterproductive to the establishment of positive peace.

While the potential for education to fuel conflict needs to be understood, Seitz also recognises the other side of the coin. Through education the very strategies used to support the development of violent conflict may also be used to support peace. If schools and other educational institutions have a culturally and gender sensitive curriculum and encourage all students to support democracy and participation in community activities as well as to reduce physical violence within the student environment, they have the potential to decrease the use of violence within society. This can be done by providing scholarships for children from less advantaged families, to teach multiple languages and points-of-views, to teach critical thinking

---

[1127] Leach and Dume (ed.), *Education, Conflict and Reconciliation*, 53.
[1128] As explained in Seitz, *Bildung und Konflikt*, 52.

and to support political participation in a peaceful way.[1129] If social inequalities and exclusion within education can be ameliorated, the basis will be laid for establishing peace and preventing violent conflict.[1130]

On the basis of this hypothesis, several scholars have argued only through education can peace be established and future conflict prevented. This starts with the building of new schools after a time of violent conflicts. As argued by Clayton Thyne, education is an especially powerful influence following violent conflict, as educational investment provides a signal to the people that actions are being taken to improve their lives and to give them the tools needed to generate political, economic and social stability as well as to resolve disputes peacefully.[1131] Parents who see schools being built will be more positive about their children's future and young adults who have the possibility of attending adequate higher education will see a better future for themselves and be less likely to become involved in violence.[1132]

Scholars such as Eifler and Seifter further argue that it is of crucial importance for a long term change at a time of conflict transformation to make primary, secondary and university educational opportunities available to all, as well as to support adult learning skills.[1133] Education can then play a positive role in economic development, political decision making and social life in general, and thus increase understanding and reduce hatred against 'the other'. Education can be used as a tool to make people aware of past atrocities and to teach them to react differently should conflict reoccur.

A strong educational system is also critical for the maintenance of democracy, since it teaches people to participate as well as to respect others' views.[1134] As stated by Glaeser, Ponzetto and Shleifer, people are more able to participate in

---

1129 Seitz Klaus, Bildung und Konflikt, Die Rolle von Bildung bei der Entstehung, Prävention und Bewältigung gesellscahftlicher Krisen – Konsequenyen für die Entwicklungszusammenarbeit (TZ-Verlagsgesellschaft, Rossdorf 2004) p.56

1130 Ibid.p.59
1131 Thyne, "ABC's, 123's, and the Golden Rule," 733.
1132 Ibid.p.735
1133 Eifler and Seifert, *Gender Dynamics and Post-Conflict Reconstruction*, 85.
1134 Woodrow Wilson International Center for Scholars, „Winning the Peace".

democracies because education provides them with a better understanding of their country's politics.[1135] According to Thyne, schools teach people the social, legal, political and interpersonal principles, which are expected of them as "good citizens", as well as the consequences of not observing these norms. Schools bring together people from different backgrounds and origins and teach them to work together peacefully, while giving them the chance to succeed in life.[1136] In addition, in schools, children are taught values and respect for each other, as well as the right to speak and to listen. As a consequence the right for everybody to participate in politics can be one of the lessons learnt.[1137]

Finally it has been reasoned by Thyne that an educated population will be less likely to resort to conflict as a first option, since they are more likely to be able to express their grievances through peaceful means and to be able to distinguish between a bad government and a government which simply takes time to overcome a difficult economic situation.[1138]

Internationally it has been recognized that specific type of education should be used within the school curriculum as well as part of university courses to reduce the likelihood of conflict. Within the campaign for a *Culture of Peace*, the international community saw education as one of the highest priorities.[1139] Projects and initiatives have been started by UNESCO as well as regional organizations and national institutions to support this education for peace.[1140]

While these arguments for education as a tool for conflict prevention and for reconstruction have validity, it would be wrong to take them for granted within any education system, as they are dependent on surrounding factors. For instance, as explained by Semra Demir, for peace education to be successful teachers are

---

[1135] Edward Glaeser, Giacomo Ponzetto and Andrei Shleifer, "Why does democracy need education?" *Journal of Economic Growth* 12(2) (2007): 81.

[1136] Thyne, "ABC's, 123's, and the Golden Rule," 737.

[1137] Glaeser, Ponzetto and Shleifer, "Why does democracy need education?," 82.

[1138] Thyne, "ABC's, 123's, and the Golden Rule," 750.

[1139] Ratkovic and Wintersteiner (Eds.), *Yearbook Peace Culture 2010,* 20.

[1140] Majid Tehranian (ed.), *Bridging a Gulf, Peacebuilding in West Asia* (London: I.B. Tauris, 2003) 222.

needed, who are tolerant, socially sensitive and who have the adequate knowledge.[1141]

As with other aspects of society, the education system is in need of transformation before it can ensure a positive influence on the population. It is especially after the end of violent conflict, when change is necessary and wanted, that the education system can be revamped to support equality and positive conflict transformation.

In order to support positive development within society the concept of "peace education" has been developed. Peace education aims to create a culture of peace based on equality, justice, democracy, human rights, solidarity and tolerance and thereby diminish violent behaviour and conflict potential within society.[1142] Through peace education pupils will be taught to think critically and analytically and will thereby gain skills and knowledge which are a prerequisite to achieving the above aims.[1143]

Peace education is therefore designed to transform thinking which has previously supported oppressive societal structures and consequently the use of violence as a mean to resolve conflicts. Peace education aims to communicate skills like reflection, cooperation, listening and problem-solving, to create an attitude which fosters peace. Peace education is thereby not limited to a certain age group, but it is applicable to people from all paths of life and at all ages.[1144] To implement peace education, a reform of the old education system is needed.

In their 2003 CPR Working Paper "*Central: America: Education Reform in a Post-Conflict Setting, Opportunities and Challenges*" Marques and Bannon established several recommendations for a possible positive education reform in societies arising from violent conflicts. These were based on examples from El Salvador, Guatemala and Nicaragua and included the need:

[1141] Semra Demir, "An Overview of Peace Education in Turkey: Definitions, Difficulties and Suggestions: A Qualitative Analysis" *Educational Sciences: Theory & Practice* 11(4) (2011): 1740.

[1142] Ibid.p.1739

[1143] Ibid.

[1144] Susan Opotow, Janet Gerson and Sarah Woodside, "From Moral Exclusion to Moral Inclusion: Theory for Teaching Peace" *Theory into Practice* 44(4) (2005): 305.

- To establish a clear vision of the reform wanted, which is in consensus with society,
- To openly discuss sensitive topics, such as cultural discrimination,
- To initiate the practical steps for implementation as early as possible,
- To gain the support of the most important social actors,
- To depoliticise the education system,
- To decentralise the education system and to give parents the opportunity to participate, and
- To establish appropriate curricula.[1145]

As will be seen in the subsequent chapters, initiatives have been taken in the Kurdistan Region to create a reform closely following the recommendations of Marques and Bannon. While these reforms have led to visible progress, it is still arguable that education is not reaching its full potential within the region. There are two reasons, which are necessary to ensure that education is truly used to prevent rather than further conflict, in addition to those listed above, namely: the application of the reform uniformly across the whole population; and the implementation by all means necessary to ensure a cultural, religious, social and gender sensitive education including critical thinking.

As explained by Betty Reardon, critical education can filter religion, culture, politics and international dealings through a variety of lenses and thereby empower people to better able support prosperity in a country and maintain a situation free of violence. If people stop seeing things in black and white or simply "good" and "bad", they will be more open to others, and will consequently resist the urge to use violence as a first option. Education thereby gives the opportunity to develop ideas and facilitate a space for open thoughts, which will lead to a culture of peace.[1146]

[1145] Jose Marques and Ian Bannon, *Central Amercia: Eduation Reform in a Post-Conflict Setting, Opportunities and Challenges* (CPR Working Papers, Paper No. 4, April 2003) 20/21.

[1146] Reardon, *Education for a culture of peace in a gender perspective*, 40.

Clearly the quality of education is the key. The knowledge taught in schools and universities can start students questioning traditional thinking and fighting for change.[1147]

As stipulated by the ICESCR:

> *"that education shall be directed to the full development of the human personality and the sense of its dignity, and shall strengthen the respect for human rights and fundamental freedoms. They further agree that education shall enable all persons to participate effectively in a free society, promote understanding, tolerance and friendship among all nations and all racial, ethnic or religious groups, and further the activities of the United Nations for the maintenance of peace."[1148]*

Through critical education people can start anticipating and thinking about issues which have not yet emerged. As Cynthia Enloe shows, the militarization of the nation, and consequently also of women, often starts long before conflict arises. Militarism "creeps" into ordinary life. The army uses advertisements as recruitment techniques, and thereby influences people to join up.[1149] But militarization can be more hidden. Food can be shaped like weapons, films can be crafted to convey a militarized message, clothing design can reflect a militarized style and toys can come on the market which celebrate war.[1150] If people are made aware of these facts, they cannot be influenced so easily. Only if people experience critical and free education, will they be able to question political messages and cast a fully considered vote at elections and thereby influence the future well-being of their country.

The most important way of ensuring this critical education is by appointing appropriate teachers. With reference to Rwanda, John Rutayisire points out that it is especially challenging for countries arising from conflict to establish educational institutions which will eliminate injustices and discrimination. Teachers are crucial

---

[1147] Glaeser, Ponzetto and Shleifer, "Why does democracy need education?," 78.

[1148] International Covenant on Economic, Social and Cultural Rights 1966, Article 13

[1149] Enloe, "Women and Men in the Iraq War".

[1150] Ford (Review), " Maneuvers," 1175.

in the process as it is they who are the main medium through which different values are transmitted.[1151]

For instance, it is the teachers who communicate to their pupils discriminatory or harmonious attitudes towards the sexes. When it comes to gender relations, it has been established, that greater equality leads to an enhanced rate of development, and consequently to the positive transformation of conflict.

The use of education to promote peace, and the importance of gender equality in education as a prerequisite to this goal, are not new ideas. In 1999, as part of the Hague Appeal for Peace Conference, the Global Campaign for Peace Education (GCPE) was launched to support the development of peace education globally.[1152] Earlier in 1990, a World Declaration on Education for All was adopted in Jomtien, Thailand, and later confirmed in Dakar in 2000.[1153] It stated that

> *"The most urgent priority is to ensure access to, and improve the quality of, education for girls and women, and to remove every obstacle that hampers their active participation. All gender stereotyping in education should be eliminated."*[1154]

Arguably it follows that that if men and women both receive adequate education their situations will become more balanced, their mutual understanding will increase and the country will be less conflict prone. On the basis of Galtung's theory that violence is partly socially constructed,[1155] it may be assumed that in order to decrease the level of violence, a different social framework needs to be constructed. For example, if boys and girls are raised in the same way, the concept of manhood as it exists today will be redefined and replaced with the concept of equality, which will consequently lead to less use of direct violence.[1156]

[1151] Leach and Dume (ed.), *Education, Conflict and Reconciliation,* 118.

[1152] Global Campaign for Peace Education, "Campaign Statement" http://www.peace-ed-campaign.org/statement.html (Accessed on 08.01.2013)

[1153] UNESCO, World Education Forum, *The Dakar Framework for Action, Education for All: Meeting our Collective Commitments* (ED-2000/WS/27, Dakar, Senegal, 26-28 April 2000)

[1154] See World Declaration on Education for All 1990, Article 3(3) in UNESCO, *The Dakar Framework for Action,* 75.

[1155] Galtung, *Peace by Peaceful Means,* 42/43.

[1156] Ibid.p.46

This idea has also been taken up by scholars like Abu-Lughod, who argues that women's education is fundamental for a nation's development. If women as well as are well educated, the whole nation is educated and consequently development is advanced.[1157] As the UNDP's *Gender Inequality Index* shows development is highly dependent on the percentage of men and women having at least a secondary education: the higher the percentage of educated people, the higher the country's development.[1158]

Or as explained by UNESCO,

> *"a quality basic education is essential to provide girls and boys with the knowledge and skills necessary to take an active role in social, economic and political decision-making, to adopt healthy lifestyles and to become engaged citizens."*[1159]

According to Opotow, Gerson, and Woodside, peace education has been used as one of the pillars to diminish gender inequality. By revealing disparities between men and women, the oppressive structures leading to these disparities and the consequences of the continuation of these disparities, gender inclusiveness can increase and societies, as well as the individuals themselves, will be enriched.[1160]

Furthermore, it is recognized that education can have a positive effect on women's participation in political and other decision making. Using elections as an example, AbuKhalil points out that women in the Arab and other regions today are often still influenced by their fathers, brothers and husbands who cast their vote. Women will be less able to make an informed decision of their own if they are illiterate.[1161] If literacy and consequently the access to information increases, the possibility of making an informed political decision increases as well. That educated women can support development through having a voice in the community has also been recognized by the KRG. As put plainly by one KRG representative as part of a private interview: *"Equality can be achieved through education. Often girls only attend primary school, and because of that they cannot be involved in all areas."*

[1157] Abu-Lughod (ed.), *Remaking Women,* 102.

[1158] UNDP, "Gender Inequality Index and related indicators".

[1159] UNESCO Iraq Office, "Gender and Education for All".

[1160] Opotow, Gerson, Woodside, "From Moral Exclusion to Moral Inclusion," 309.

[1161] AbuKhalil, "Toward the Study of Women and Politics in the Arab World," 13.

But, as rightly stated by Lila Abu-Lughod, it is not sufficient to give women and girls merely the opportunity to access any education, but they are in need of high quality education, which is too often not the case.[1162]

In addition, according to Christopher Colclough several associated issues have to be considered when it comes to promoting gender equality in education. Firstly it needs to be acknowledged that educational inequality is both a consequence and a cause of wider gender-based discrimination within society. The "right environment" has to be provided a basis for girls and women to receive education, such as the reform of family law and the passing of more gender-equal legislation, including inheritance rights. Furthermore poverty has to be considered through a gender lens and measures need to be taken which allow families to survive while sending all the children to school. Finally the practices inside the classes need to be appropriate for girls. The curriculum, as well as the teachers, need to be gender-sensitive and girls need to be protected from violence within the schools.[1163]

The necessity of a "gender sensitive environment", not only as part of the pupil-teacher relationship, but also in the family, and in society as a whole, was recognized by UNESCO.[1164] In order to provide women and girls with a quality education and open the way to improved social and economic development, a strategy is needed to end discrimination within the education sectors and to promote gender equality. According to UNESCO, four dimensions have to be considered when implementing such a strategy: equality of access, equality of the learning process, equality of educational outcomes and equality of external results.[1165]

The following sections will focus on whether and to what extent the first two of these dimensions are present in the Kurdistan Region's education system, and the implications for society. The third and fourth dimensions will be discussed in the section on the economy.

[1162] Abu-Lughod, "Dialects of Women's Empowerment," 87.
[1163] Colclough, "Achieving Gender Equality in Education," 5-8.
[1164] UNESCO Iraq Office, "Gender and Education for All".
[1165] Ibid.

To conclude, while the negative consequences of education should not be forgotten, the opportunities of achieving positive development through critical education equally have to be remembered. Education has the potential to contribute to the development of both peaceful co-existence and gender equality.

2.   Legal Foundation

Today the Kurdistan Region of Iraq has every opportunity of providing their people with the best of education.

Through being a signatory to several international treaties concerning access to schooling and training programmes for men as well as women, Iraq, including the Kurdistan Region, has agreed to:

> *"recognize the right of everyone to education,"*[1166]

> *"take all appropriate measures to eliminate discrimination against women in order to ensure to them equal rights with men in the field of education,"*[1167] and

> *"to increase their voluntary financial, technical and logistical support for gender-sensitive training efforts, including those undertaken by relevant funds and programmes, inter alia, the United Nations Fund for Women and United Nations Children's Fund, and by the Office of the United Nations High Commissioner for Refugees and other relevant bodies."*[1168]

Concerning the education of their citizens, the national, as well as the regional, authorities in Iraq are supporting the same line:

According to Article 3 of the Iraqi Constitution of 2005 everybody has the right to be educated in their mother tongue, which gives all people in the Kurdistan Region the possibility to access education in their mother tongue.

Furthermore the constitution stipulates that:

> *"First: Education is a fundamental factor for the progress of society and is a right guaranteed by the state. Primary education*

[1166] International Covenant on Economic, Social and Cultural Rights 1966, Article 13(1)

[1167] The Convention on the Elimination of All Forms of Discrimination Against Women 1979, Article 10

[1168] UN Security Council Resolution 1325

is mandatory and the state guarantees that it shall combat illiteracy.

Second: Free education in all its stages is a right for all Iraqis.

Third: The State shall encourage scientific research for peaceful purposes that serve humanity and shall support excellence, creativity, invention, and different aspects of ingenuity.

Fourth: Private and public education shall be guaranteed, and this shall be regulated by law."[1169]

In the Draft Constitution of the Kurdistan Region, corresponding provisions state that

"First: The Government of the Region shall guarantee free education at the primary, secondary and university levels. The Government shall also guarantee vocational training and technical education. Education shall be compulsory until the completion of the primary level.

Second: The Government of the Region shall be in charge of the campaign against illiteracy.

Third: The family is the fundamental core of society. Therefore, mothers and children must be protected, and the economic exploitation of children must be prohibited.

Fourth: The government of the Region shall guarantee the establishment of special homes to protect and care for women who have, for social reasons, lost their family security.

Fifth: All forms of discrimination, violence and abuse in society, school, and in the family shall be forbidden."[1170]

In addition, in accordance with its responsibilities, the Kurdish government has set itself the task of supporting young people by providing the following opportunities namely: to enhance their skills, through education as well as in their leisure times; to enhance their moral and national values; to support their involvement in economic, social and educational projects; and to encourage their working together, as well as democratic practice.[1171]

[1169] Constitution of Iraq 2005, Article 34
[1170] Draft Constitution of the Kurdistan Region 2009, Article 27
[1171] Draft Constitution of the Kurdistan Region 2009, Article 55

Hence all people in the Kurdistan Region, regardless of their ethnicity, class or gender, have the right and even some obligation to access education. The aim is to offer a "moral" and "democratic" education, even though this is not always available in practice, as will be seen in the following subchapter:

A.   Children's Schooling

"A culture of peace will be achieved when citizens of the world understand global problems, have the skills to resolve conflicts and struggle for justice non-violently, live by international standards of human rights and equity, appreciate cultural diversity and respect the Earth and each other. Such learning can only be achieved with systematic education for peace."[1172] (Hague Appeal for Peace, Global Campaign for Peace Education)

Years of war and violent conflicts not only destroy buildings and infrastructure but also often destroy the morals and values of the population[1173] as well as an intellectual culture, a critical teaching environment and an open system of knowledge exchange. While houses can be easily rebuilt, it takes much more time and effort to rebuild the intellectual foundation of a whole nation. As already noted, an enlightened education policy can be used as a tool to achieve the aims outlined above, and thereby help to create a culture of peace.[1174]

During times of war high quality education for all is not considered a priority. The little education received by the population leading up to and during, armed conflict is most often marked by a manipulated account of culture and history, as for example in the Iraq of Saddam during the Iran-Iraq war.[1175] It follows that after the cessation of an on-going conflict, a high percentage of the population are uneducated. The few who attended schools and universities were most likely been manipulated to a certain extent through the education received. As the name

---

[1172] Hague Appeal for Peace, "Global Campaign for Peace Education, Campaign Statement" (2003-2005) http://www.haguepeace.org/index.php?action=pe (Accessed on 15.07.2013)

[1173] Al-Ali, "Reconstructing Gender," 751.

[1174] Reardon, *Education for a culture of peace in a gender perspective,* 26.

[1175] Cooke, *Women and the War Stories,* 230.
Nabil Al-Tikriti, "War, State Collapse and the Predicament of Education in Iraq." In *Education and the Arab World: Political Projects, Struggles, and Geometries of Power, World Yearbook of Education 2010,* eds. André E. Mazawi and Ronald G. Sultana (London: Routledge Press, 2009) 352.

suggests, change is needed at a time of "conflict transformation" and one way such change or transformation comes about is through education and knowledge exchange.

Also in the Kurdistan Region, the education sector was greatly destroyed and prevented from developing during the decades of armed conflicts. It is consequently the aim today to rebuild and enhance educational possibilities in the region, starting at school level. Still today, about 14 years after the end of the civil war in the region, pressures on the school system remain, with insufficient buildings, discrepancies between basic facilities in the rural and urban areas, and with challenges in making suitable facilities available to all pupils.[1176]

As a result of the wars and recent developments in health care and other social developments, the Kurdish society today is a very young, with about 37 per cent of citizens being under the age of 15.[1177] Education will play a vital role in the lives of this young generation but also for the region as a whole. As explained by Majid Tehranian, education is critical in shaping children's attitude. The values and skills children learn at school will influence how they will lead and shape their society and country in the future.[1178]

While the high percentage of young people in the region is an enormous potential for future development, it currently gives rise to the challenge of raising and educating them in a way which will lead to prosperity, development and peace for the region.

The various challenges have also been recognized by representatives of Kurdistan's society. They placed special emphasis on eliminating gender discrimination through critical education as part of their proposed Bill of Rights for Kurdish Women, by demanding:

> *"Commitment to modify the social and cultural patterns of conduct of women and men through public education, information, education*

[1176] Audrey Osler and Chalank Yahya, "Challenges and complexity in human rights education, Teachers' understandings of democratic participation and gender equity in post-conflict Kurdistan-Iraq" *Education Inquiry* 4(1) (2013): 191.

[1177] Kurdistan Regional Statistics Office, *Iraq Women Integrated Social and Health Survey.*

[1178] Tehranian (ed.), *Bridging a Gulf,* 224.

and communication strategies in order to eliminate the harmful cultural and traditional practices and all other practice which are based on the idea of inferiority or superiority of either of the sexes, or on stereotyped roles for women and men."[1179]

"Actively promoting peace education through curricula and social communication in order to eradicate elements in traditional and cultural beliefs, practices and stereotypes which legitimize and exacerbate the persistence and tolerance of violence against women,"[1180] and

"Elimination of all stereotypes that perpetuate discrimination between the female and male genders in the school system."[1181]

"Provision of equal access for women to enrolment in universities and institutions and eradication of all forms of discriminative requirements against women in those areas."[1182]

"Elimination of all stereotypes in textbooks and syllabus that perpetuate discrimination against women."[1183]

From the governmental side, the fall of Saddam Hussein in 2003, meant a turning point in education, especially in the Kurdistan Region, where Prime Minister Nechirvan Barzani at the time promised to improve teaching methods and raise education standards.[1184] The last ten years has seen development in education in the Kurdistan Region, initiated by the KRG with help from outside.[1185] However, as argued below, while improvements in access to education and in educational standards have been achieved for some, it will take a long time to ensure development for all, and the consequent reduced potential for conflict at all levels. Using the example of gender equality and gender parity, the approach the KRG has taken to raising the standard of education will be the subject of this sub-chapter. The question of whether these efforts meet the aspirations of the civil population, as expressed through the proposed Bill of Rights for Kurdish Women,

---

[1179] Bill of Rights for Kurdish Women, Article 1(6)

[1180] Ibid. Article 2(2)(d)

[1181] Ibid. Article 4(1)

[1182] Ibid. Article 4(5)

[1183] Ibid. Article 4(6)

[1184] Kurdistan Regional Government, "New School Year Starts" (22 September 2003) http://old.krg.org/news/index.asp (Accessed on 04.01.2013)

[1185] Ministry of Planning, "The Ministries of Planning, Education and Health announced the results of four RAND Projects to improve Region's health, Education and Economic Systems" (8 March 2011) http://www.mop-krg.org/index.jsp?sid=3&nid=52&y=2011&m=2&d=8&lng=en (Accessed on 04.01.2013)

will be raised by discussing both the access to and the quality of schooling in the Kurdistan Region.

1.   Access to Schooling

"Education is the most important process by which people can attain the values, attitude and behavioural patterns consistent with a culture of peace". [1186] (Ingeborg Breines)

Equal access to schooling for boys and girls constitutes a prerequisite for the support of gender equality through education. Equal access to schooling can provide pupils with equal access to education taught and consequently equal educational outcomes and chances in life. As such equal provision of education for women has always been a highly political subject,[1187] with those in power deciding whether girls should have equal access to schooling and consequently better opportunities to shape the future of their society and region.

In Iraq, including the Kurdistan Region, education for all remains a great challenge. According to IAU, in Iraq today the illiteracy among women today (24 %)[1188] is more than double that of Iraqi men (11 %).[1189] Additionally, there are great discrepancies between the rural and the urban population, with over 50 per cent of women between fifteen and twenty-four in rural areas being illiterate, but only 20 to 28 per cent of women in the same age group being illiterate in the cities.[1190] Girls are generally less than half of the children enrolled in primary education and according to UNICEF about 75 per cent of girls who started school dropout during or at the end of primary school.[1191]

This is a general problem, which has persisted since the wars, and is still not diminished. According to the *Iraq Household Socio-Economic Survey* from 2007, approximately 90 per cent of children attended primary school in the Kurdistan Region, but only about 45 per cent continued intermediate education, with the

---

[1186] Ratkovic and Wintersteiner (Eds.), *Yearbook Peace Culture 2010,* 12.
[1187] Colclough, "Achieving Gender Equality in Education," 4.
[1188] According to IAU in March 2012
[1189] Ibid.
[1190] IAU, *Women in Iraq Fact sheet* (March 2012)
[1191] UNICEF, *Girls Education in Iraq* (2010) 4.

percentage being higher in cities (51%) than in the rural areas (32%). The percentages are reasonably comparable between boys and girls in the cities, but with more boys (34%) than girls (30%) attending in the country side.[1192] In the Kurdistan Region secondary enrolments dropped to an average of 22 per cent, with more girls (29%) than boys (22%) attending in the cities, but with nearly twice as many boys (13%) than girls (7%) attending in the rural areas.[1193] Clearly access to education is generally dependent on geography, as well as class, and consequently not all children, and especially not all girls, are offered the same opportunities of education and consequently of life choices.

In comparison to the rest of the country, positive developments have taken place in the Kurdistan Region especially over the past ten years. Today the percentage of girls enrolled in primary school is the highest in Dohuk, Erbil and Sulaimaniya and the region also has the highest percentage of children in pre-school education.[1194] Nevertheless, the percentage of girls drop out before intermediate education is still very high in Kurdistan, although it is slightly less than the national average of 75 per cent, with 35 per cent of girls starting intermediate education in Sulaimaniya and 30 per cent in Erbil.[1195]

Illiteracy among the young generation remains high, and is generally higher for women than for men. According to the Kurdistan Region Statistics Office, 25.9 per cent of women between 20 and 29 are currently illiterate, compared with 11.1 per cent of men. In contrast only 8.4 per cent of girls between the age of 12 and 19 are illiterate compared with 5.5 per cent of boys. As pointed out by the Statistics Office, significant improvements have obviously taken place in the previous ten years, especially when it comes to female education, considering that the illiteracy rate for girls dropped 17.5 per cent over this period compared with 5.6 per cent for boys. The higher enrolment of children, and especially girls, according to the government, is linked to the increased awareness of the importance of girl's education by the people, as well as to improvement in the political and economic

---

[1192] Central Organisation for Statistics and Information Technology, *Iraq Household Socio-Economic Survey, Volume II*, 230/231.
[1193] Ibid.p.232
[1194] UNICEF, *Girls Education in Iraq*, 4.
[1195] Ibid.p.15

situation in general.[1196] This supports Thyne's argument stated above, namely that the provision of education after conflict is a sign of peace, which leads to families feeling more secure and sending their children to school again, which in turn leads to less potential for conflict.[1197] The statistics also support Colclough's contention that it is just as important to look at the surrounding circumstances, such as poverty reduction, as a pre-requisite to equal access to schooling. Only families who feel secure and have the financial means will send their children, and especially their girls, to school.[1198]

While developments have led to children, including an increasing number of girls, entering the school system, the greatest challenge for the Kurdistan Region at the moment seems to be retaining children at school. About 30 per cent of people from 12 to 29 years old have no official school certificate. Thirty two (32) per cent finished primary school, 22 per cent secondary school, 10 per cent high school. Only 3 per cent have graduated from an institute and another 3 per cent have achieved a bachelor degree or higher.[1199]

The most significant factor determining girls and women attendance at learning facilities are family attitudes and circumstances. Poverty, the journey to school, lack of security, displacement, the low quality of teaching and teachers, as well as the mixing of girls and boys are often factors preventing girls from attend school.[1200] According to the *Iraq Household Socio-Economic Survey* of 2007, which has still some relevance today, the two greatest challenges facing children in general, and girls in particular, wishing to attend schools, are the lack of appropriate facilities in their region, the lack of interest in schooling by their families or themselves and social reasons, which are more important for girls than boys.[1201]

Also according to a UNICEF survey conducted in 2008 throughout the whole of Iraq, the most decisive factor in girls' education is their families. The parents, and

---

[1196] Kurdistan Region Statistics Office, *Education* (Fact Sheet 2, October 2012) 1.

[1197] Thyne, "ABC's, 123's, and the Golden Rule," 733.

[1198] Colclough, "Achieving Gender Equality in Education," 5-8.

[1199] Kurdistan Region Statistics Office, *Education*, 3.

[1200] UNICEF, *Girls Education in Iraq*, 20-22.

[1201] Central Organisation for Statistics and Information Technology, *Iraq Household Socio-Economic Survey, Volume II*, 234.

especially the fathers, play a significant role in either pushing their girls to stay in education or preventing them from attending school. The family's attitude towards their daughters' schooling is often dependent on the family's income[1202], as well as one their attitude towards the role of girls once they reach puberty.

This has been supported by the people themselves, who asserted that the most important reason for girls to drop out of school or never attend school lies with the family.[1203] As some explained, the families are sometimes put under pressure by the local community, and in turn put pressure on their girls, who have no option but to obey.[1204] As one woman explained:

> *"One day a family friend came to my father, who was a very respected men in our neighbourhood, and he told my father that it would be better if my sister did not continue to go to school, as this was not proper. My father consequently took my sister out of school, but one year later this same man let his own girls go to school. My sister never concluded any education level, and she still feels sorry about that."[1205]*

A further reason lies with their treatment at school and the state of the schools themselves. Some of the schools are not well maintained and do not have adequate resources. Some are simply very far away from the children's homes and the girls are either unable or not permitted to travel to school.[1206] In addition to other problems, such as displacement or a lack of papers, another very significant factor in deciding whether or not girls attend school are the teachers. School children have complained that the behaviour of their teacher is unacceptable to them and that they do not explain the subjects in an way the children can understand. If together with all the other aggravating circumstances, girls have teachers who are unable to teach their subject, are insensitive to their needs or even themselves oppose the their education, it is more likely that girls will drop out of school.[1207]

[1202] UNICEF, *Girls Education in Iraq*, 20.
[1203] Interview BL, Erbil on 12/07/2012; Interview BP, Erbil on 21/07/2012; Interview AD, Erbil on 08/04/2012
[1204] Interview AJ, Erbil on 20/04/2012; Interview BE, Erbil on 26/06/2012
[1205] Interview AZ, Sulaimaniya on 06/06/2012
[1206] UNICEF, *Girls Education in Iraq*, 21.
[1207] Ibid.p.22

The treatment of girls by the teachers, especially in previous generations when it was normal to hit children, was a reason for them to leave school. As explained by a 33 year old woman from Erbil, the children were very scared of the teachers and some left school out of this fear. She continued that the general situation has improved today, but that it is still not perfect. She still knows of schools, where children are hit, but nobody goes to the police, because the people are scared. It is one of the consequences that some children leave school.[1208]

Another reason for the high dropout rate for girls, especially in the country side, is the inability to access schools above primary school level in their area. The government is trying to combat this problem by building new schools. According to Hero Talabani in 2008, there have been more schools built since 2003, than between 1958 and 2003 together[1209]. In 2003 there was a total of 2,986 schools in the governorates of Erbil and Duhok and 544,937 students were about to enroll at kindergarten, primary, secondary and vocational schools. Of these students 43 per cent were female (236,607) and 57 per cent male (308,330).[1210] In comparison, according to UNESCO there were a total of 5,323 schools in the Kurdistan Region for academic year 2008/9[1211]. Nevertheless, there is still a problem concerning the number of schools in the region, with many pupils having to rotate in school. For this reason the RAND cooperation, a research and analysis centre which works with the KRG on development strategies, proposed in 2011 the building of up to 200 new schools per year for the following ten years.[1212]

Despite efforts by the government to raise the numbers of schools, many people and especially those who were educated themselves had the feeling that not enough is being done for women's and girls' education in the region. They saw a problem particularly in the country side, where women only go to primary school. They often do not have the opportunity to proceed to higher education and

---

[1208] Interview BR, Erbil on 22/07/2012

[1209] Randa Jamal, UN Assistance Mission for Iraq, "Educational Reform in the Kurdistan Region of Iraq" (19 August 2008) http://reliefweb.int/report/iraq/educational-reform-kurdistan-region-iraq (Accessed on 04.01.2013)

[1210] Kurdistan Regional Government, "New School Year Starts".

[1211] UNESCO, *National Education Support Strategy, Republic of Iraq, 2010-2014*, 24.

[1212] Ministry of Planning, "The Ministries of Planning, Education and Health announced the results of four RAND Projects to improve Region's health, Education and Economic Systems".

consequently lack certain knowledge. Hence the gap between the different social groups is growing.[1213] At the same time in the city, while more and more international schools are built to teach the elite of the country, many local schools still have to accommodate different groups of children in the morning and in the afternoon, as there is not enough space. This results in a situation of inequality, where people from the upper class people have the feeling that the state is investing enough in education, while others, especially from the middle class, believe that this is not the case.

The statistics support the general feeling of the people, namely that there is still a great discrepancy between the education of different social groups as well as between men and women, and increasing the number of school buildings will not be sufficient to ensure equal access to education for the whole population.

While the situation has improved in today's Kurdistan Region, representatives from the Kurdish population showed that the problems, though ameliorated, still persist in the region.

It follows that equal access to schooling in general, and quality schooling in particular, is yet to be achieved in the Kurdistan Region. There is a discrepancy in school enrolments between children of different social classes, as well as between boys and girls. Consequently the attainment of gender equity is impossible. Even though the vast improvements in school enrolments need to be recognized, further work is still required to provide the whole population with the opportunity for quality education; a pre-requisite for all citizens to realise their full personal potential and to maximise human resources for the benefit of the region.

Girls need the opportunity to attend schools which are situated near them and have all the basic facilities. The families need to be made aware of the importance of educating their daughters and security of the girls in school must be assured. But the best school buildings count for nothing if there is nobody to teach the children constructively.[1214] Quality of the teaching is the most important when it comes to

---

[1213] Interview BB, Erbil on 24/06/2012; Interview BY, Sulaimaniya on 10/08/2012; Interview BZ, Sulaimaniya on 10/08/2012
[1214] UNICEF, *Girls Education in Iraq*, 25.

school, because with the profession of the teaching comes a great responsibility. The quality of schooling in the region from a region as a whole is the subject of the following section.

2.   Quality of Schooling

"There is a direct connection between violent conflict and intransigent, uncompromising worldviews."[1215]

While equal access to schooling is a vital step for achieving gender equality and diminishing social discrimination, gender equality in education is more than an equal number of boys and girls enrolling into school at all levels. In the view of UNESCO,[1216] and as explained by Colclough,[1217] gender equality implies equal chances to attend school, equal learning experiences and an equal outcome in society.

It will only be through equal learning experiences and their high quality that transformation will take place for all. If children are taught to place themselves into the shoes of another, and to see life through the lens of somebody who is different from them, whether ethnically, sexually, socially, or by age or religion, their understanding will broaden. They will first consider others as fellow human beings, before resorting to violent behaviour towards them.[1218] The classroom can be used as a space for children to learn self-respect and respect for others, to express their points of views and to resolve problems without violence. Hopefully these skills and knowledge will be applied outside the classroom and will consequently influence the children's dealings with the wider society and the world.[1219] From a gender perspective it is argued that high quality education for all has the potential to diminish violent behaviour within the household, as well as violence between the different social groups outside. This outcome is sought by teaching the traditional "stronger" party to value their "weaker" counterparts and not to misuse them.

[1215] Shapiro, *Educating Youth for a World beyond violence,* 26.

[1216] UNESCO Iraq Office, "Gender and Education for All".

[1217] Colclough, "Achieving Gender Equality in Education," 4.

[1218] Shapiro, *Educating Youth for a World beyond violence,* 28.

[1219] Tehranian (ed.), *Bridging a Gulf,* 224.

At the same time high quality education can empower the "weaker" party. From a gender perspective this means that women need to learn about their legal and religious rights and how to use them so as not to be restricted in their development and opportunities by men, by other women or by the state system.[1220]

High quality education is thereby crucial to the empowerment of women. For women to be able to make choices about their lives, they must be aware of the alternatives which exist for them. Education can help to clarify these alternatives, as well as to give women the opportunity to access different options.[1221] Education can empower girls and women and give them the right skills to be more productive, to enhance their status and to enable them see the world in a different way. However education can also be used to limit a woman's abilities and skills and to make it even more difficult for her to become employed or even to see the possibilities of work, if that is what she needs or wants.[1222]

In the Kurdistan Region the quality of education has suffered under the different wars and is still at the state of recovery. The education system in the region was subject to Ba'athist ruling until the 1990s, and until 2002 school material differed between the different sub-regions, controlled by the KDP and PUK respectively, which lead to a unified system only establishing after 2002.[1223] According to Hero Talabani, the problems of the educational system in the Kurdistan Region are connected to a lack of schools as well as an old curriculum, which has not been adequately updated over time.[1224] Other representatives from the political, international and civil society communities concur and have demanded or recommended the improvement of the quality of education in the region. For example, the outcomes of the 2011 conference on *The Role of Women in Peace-Building, Reconciliation and Accountability in Iraq*" in Erbil, included recommendations to

> *"Reform and develop school curriculums, including those of higher education, to avoid sectarian ideologies, and disseminate a culture*

[1220] Eifler and Seifert, *Gender Dynamics and Post-Conflict Reconstruction*, 85.

[1221] Kabeer, "Gender Equality and Women's Empowerment," 15.

[1222] Ibid.p.9

[1223] Al-Tikriti, "War, State Collapse and the Predicament of Education in Iraq," 354/355.

[1224] Randa Jamal, "Educational Reform in the Kurdistan Region of Iraq".

of partnership, pluralism, and to promote an inclusive national identity."[1225]

As a reaction to these shortcomings, the changing of the national school curriculum has come to the forefront in recent years.

Even before 2008, in response to the need for reform, the KRG introduced new text books and has reformed the curriculum for certain subjects. Reforms included the introduction of new material for teaching English, revising the curricula for Mathematics, Science and Social Economics, developing plans to improve the Kurdish language programs, History, Geography and other 'social' classes as well as to incorporate Arabic as a second language. In addition modern teaching methods were encouraged leading to more analytical thinking amongst the children.[1226]

As part of the 2009 curriculum reform, an emphasis on human rights education was introduced, but its implementation remained challenging as a consequence of a lack in trained teachers and textbooks lacking in quality.[1227]

Consequently, in 2011, "The new Iraqi Curriculum Framework" was drafted with help from UNESCO's International Bureau of Education. The document aims to define a common curriculum model, for the Arab as well as the Kurdish regions of Iraq, and to raise the quality of education by orientating the curriculum to provide education which *"promotes human rights, gender equality, intercultural understanding and sustainable development".*[1228] As stated in the document, it is the government's intention to develop a curriculum, which meets the needs of the labour market, addresses the developments on a local and international level, as well as the needs of the learners themselves and which raises a generation of moral persons, who reject radicalism, who believe in justice, freedom and democracy, who think critically and who have a perspective of lifelong learning,[1229]

[1225] No Peace Without Justice, *The Role of Women in Peace-Building,* Recommendation 41.

[1226] Randa Jamal, "Educational Reform in the Kurdistan Region of Iraq".

[1227] Osler and Yahya, "Challenges and complexity in human rights education," 199.

[1228] UNESCO, *World Data on Education, Iraq,* "The educational process".

[1229] Ibid.

while putting specific emphasis on the faith in God, love of the homeland, and also open expression and love to the environment.

The intention behind the reform demonstrates clearly that the new curriculum is aimed at supporting a culture of peace, while at the same time communicating values, which are currently seen as admirable by the leading parties and most of society.

According to UNESCO, gender equality and women's empowerment is also promoted through its work on curriculum reform and teacher training.[1230] However it is not clear how this is to be achieved, and it is thus arguable that there is currently not sufficient consideration of a gender perspective within the revised curricula and this may hamper the work towards gender equality.

Next to reforming the school curriculum UNESCO notes that the KRG, is prioritising the enhancement of the quality of teaching and administration, as well as to *"increase(ing) the role of the private sector in the education and increasing the number of quality schools in the region."*[1231]

In the Kurdistan Region today an emphasis on private education at an international standard is clear. The region is currently constructing a network of international schools, with the SABIS schools being in the forefront. In 2012 alone four new SABIS schools opened their doors, which raises their number of SABIS schools to seven. These schools implement the SABIS Educational System, are taught in English and aim to be a college-preparation for their pupils.[1232] In contrast to the Kurdish state schools, the international schools charge tuition fees at an average of 3800 US dollars per year, in addition to transportation, book and lunch and other fees.[1233] They therefore arguably develop an elite, which remains inaccessible to other parts of society. And while gender based divisions between children within these schools is diminishing, social and gender differences are increasing in

---

[1230] UNESCO, *National Education Support Strategy, Republic of Iraq, 2010-2014*, 49.

[1231] Ibid.p.10

[1232] SABIS, "About SABIS" http://www.pppkurdistan-sabis.net/fakhir-mergasori/general/fakhir-about-sabis (04.01.2013) and SABIS, "Project Overview" http://www.pppkurdistan-sabis.net/fakhir-mergasori/general/fakhir-project-overview (Accessed on 04.01.2013)

[1233] SABIS, "Fees Structure" http://www.iscerbil-sabis.net/fees-structure/ (Accessed on 04.01.2013)

society as a whole as development is occurring unequally. While those members of society who are provided with the best basis remain on top, the others are left behind. In addition to the SABIS schools, the Kurdistan Region is also the seat for other international schools, such as the British International Schools-Kurdistan[1234], the Cambridge International School-Kurdistan,[1235] the American International School Kurdistan,[1236] the Deutsche Schule Erbil (German School Erbil),[1237] and the Danielle Mitterrand MLF International French School, Erbil.[1238]

Many members of high-income families, especially returnees from the diaspora favour the existence of private schools, as they, according to them, they offer education of better quality to their children.[1239] Also the government is very supportive of the international private education developing in the region, as it is hoping to raise educational standard in the region through these schools. Many also believe that is the responsibility of private people and businesses to contribute to the financing of the education sectors, so that the government can focus on other areas. At the same time there is some awareness that the great differences between public and private schools will result in sever class distinctions, which raise the potential of conflict and should be therefore be opposed. [1240]

Large discrepancies between education in the cities and in the country side were noted especially by representatives of the urban population. According to two students from the University of Kurdistan Hawler, the lack of education for women in rural areas holds back the development of the country as well as of the people themselves[1241], as *"the women in the country side only live in their small worlds*

[1234] British International Schools, "Welcome to British International Schools in Kurdistan – Hawler" http://www.bis-kurdistan.co.uk/ (Accessed on 04.01.2013)

[1235] Cambridge International School-Kurdistan, "About CISK" http://www.cis-kurdistan.com/aboat-us/about-cisk.html (Accessed on 04.01.2013)

[1236] American International School Kurdistan http://ais-k.org/ (Accessed on 04.01.2013)

[1237] Deutsche Schule Erbil, "Willkommen" http://www.ds-e.org/ (Accessed on 04.01.2013)

[1238] Danielle Mitterrand MLF International French School, Erbil http://erbilfrenchschool.com/about.php (Accessed on 04.01.2013)

[1239] Interview AD, Erbil on 08/04/2012; Interview AO, Sulaimaniya on 13/05/2012

[1240] Rashadaddin Hawzhen, The Kurdish Globe, "Private schools provide better education in the region" (08 January 2011) http://www.kurdishglobe.net/display-article.html?id=1B11C0EEF9F7159B921BD87E606616E9 (Accessed on 05.01.2013)

[1241] Interview BL, Erbil on 12/07/2012; Interview AE, Erbil on 09/04/2012

and they don't know their rights, because they only go to primary school."[1242]
Additionally it was argued that the quality of some of the state schools is not comparable to that provided by the private schools. But as argued by Parker, Standing and others, equity in high quality schooling should be aspired to, as it would lead to improvements in the region's as well as the individual's situation and thus greater equality and less potential for conflict.[1243]

Concerning gender inclusion, research shows that schoolbooks still continue to promote traditional gender roles. Kurdish school books, especially in primary school, reflect the traditional roles of women as mothers, cooks and carers for the families. In subsequent years children learn about the great and strong women of the past, who led battles, saved people's lives and safeguarded the Kurdistan identity. However, they read like myths in the distant past rather than events relevant to today.

Svi Shapori[1244] argues that some of these obvious differences in education between girls and boys from the same 'level' may reflect a 'hidden curriculum'. However, such differences are generally not considered problematic by the Kurdish population. As explained by a mother, who also worked as a teacher in the region for several years, there is no obvious discrimination between boys and girls in the Kurdish school system, although it is common that the teachers support the traditional gender roles in front of their pupils, especially when it comes to the career choice. Girls are encouraged to become teachers or nurses, but they are taught that it is not acceptable for women to become engineers or lawyers or to study art.[1245]

One factor, which is seen as far more important than the child's sex, is the achievement of high marks. Successful pupils are supported by the teachers, while those who do not manage to achieve high marks by themselves are told to leave school. The situation is different when it comes to children from wealthy or well-known families. Indeed it is argued by some interviewees from less-advantageous

---

[1242] Interview AE, Erbil on 09/04/2012

[1243] Leach and Dume (ed.), *Education, Conflict and Reconciliation,* 53.

[1244] Shapiro, *Educating Youth for a World beyond violence,* 82.

[1245] Interview AL, Erbil on 25/04/2012

backgrounds that corruption inside the school system, when it comes to marks, especially in the final exams, is very high.[1246] The resulting differentiation between the sexes and between the different social classes leads certain groups within society to believe that they are unable to achieve their aspirations.

Further, when it came to critical education, it was noted by several locals that teachers simply do not have enough leeway, as their schedules are so tight that they are unable to truly meet the needs of individual students.[1247]

It has been argued that especially the so called "shift schools", which still exist over the whole region, and in which a high number of children are forced to rotate in school, do not allow quality to flourish.[1248] This is certainly true to a certain extent and new schools are needed in the region. However, it may be argued that the reaction to the problem of the rapid rise in the school population in a very short time, is currently also impeding the quality of teaching at these schools. For instance several interviewees from the civil society contend that that the quality of teaching is inadequate, especially in subjects like English, as the teachers themselves are lacking qualifications and experience.[1249] It was consequently the opinion of a large number of the people questioned for this thesis, that there needs to be further development in education.[1250]

The teachers themselves and the people working in the education sector, especially, were of the opinion that more focus should be on education and that more development is needed.[1251] While the exact nature of the recommended development depended on the personal experience, there was a focus on increasing literacy within the population[1252] and giving the children a better

---

[1246] Interview AJ, Erbil on 20/04/2012; Interview BJ, Erbil on 09/07/2012

[1247] Interview BL, Erbil on 12/07/2012; Interview BO, Erbil on 18/07/2012; Interview BP, Erbil on 21/07/2012

[1248] Interview BY, Sulaimaniya on 10/08/2012

[1249] See e.g.: Interview AD, Erbil on 08/04/2012; Interview AG, Erbil on 13/04/2012; Interview AP, Sulaimaniya on 18/05/2012

[1250] See e.g.: Interview BV, Sulaimaniya on 06/08/2012; Interview AR, Sulaimaniya on 21/05/2012; Interview AS, Sulaimaniya on 23/05/2012

[1251] Interview AS, Sulaimaniya on 23/05/2012; Interview BC, Erbil on 25/06/2012; Interview BT, Erbil on 24/07/2012

[1252] Interview BU, Erbil on 24/07/2012

opportunity to have higher education.[1253] Other interviewees were of the opinion that a necessary first step is to make further education (high school) compulsory for everybody[1254] and to support people's reading opportunities by opening more public libraries. This will give them more access to a wider variety of knowledge and better enable them to inform their own opinions.[1255] As explained by one girl from a low-income family, who herself did not get the best education: "*There are still many problems here. There should be more public libraries to educate the people*".[1256]

Several people had the feeling that, while Kurdistan is thriving on the outside, there is still a great need to change "*in the inside*", such as a change in morals and mentality. It was recognized that this "*change of the inside*" needs to include the entire society.[1257] Time and time again interviewees expressed the wish for a change in the mentality of all people, men as well as women, in order to have more openness in society, including awareness of the suppression of women.

The Kurdish women who have lived part of their lives in the West especially hoped that a reformed school system would be the first step towards more liberal thinking and towards openness towards women.[1258] In comparison, when people in the Kurdistan Region were asked on how this type of equality could be achieved, the term "enlightenment" came up time and time again. Society as a whole, women as well as men, have to be enlightened, so that their mentality changes and equality becomes possible.[1259] Surprisingly for the researcher, the people did not consider education or schools as a way to bring forward or achieve this enlightenment. While people who had a connection to the West were of the opinion that education should be used to achieve equality,[1260] Kurds who have lived their whole life in

---

[1253] Interview BT, Erbil on 24/07/2012

[1254] Interview BZ, Sulaimaniya on 10/08/2012

[1255] Interview BU, Erbil on 24/07/2012

[1256] Interview AV, Sulaimaniya on 28/05/2012

[1257] See e.g.: Interview AO, Sulaimaniya on 13/05/2012; Interview CA, Sulaimaniya on 13/08/2012; Interview BM, Erbil on 17/07/2012

[1258] Interview CF, Vienna on 16/11/2012; Interview CE, Vienna on 21/10/2012; Interview CK, Vienna on 20/10/2012

[1259] Interview AU, Sulaimaniya on 28/05/2012; Interview AV, Sulaimaniya on 28/05/2012; Interview BN, Erbil on 17/07/2012; Interview BP, Erbil on 21/07/2012

[1260] Interview CE, Vienna on 21/10/2012; Interview CK, Vienna on 20/10/2012

Kurdistan did not really consider this option. This may be due to the fact that people in the region had not experienced school as a place of critical exchange.

Only a very few interviewees noted that educating women is very important as this will give them the ability to do everything else. It was stated that "*already in kindergarten girls have to be taught to get involved. There are in general not enough well educated adolescents in Kurdistan today. Good education of all is simply a necessity*". [1261] Others believed that women need education to be able to teach their children at home.[1262] While it was recognized by the majority that the education of women is vital for economic or social reasons, the transformative capability was not seen.

In contrast, several men explained that in their opinion equality for the women has to start in the families and in the house and not in public. As explained by a 29-year old teacher:

> "*Equality has to start within the family. Women first have to establish equality in their families, so that they have a right to live, after that it is only possible to become truly equal*"[1263].

Following the idea of an education for peace, namely that, apart from having the possibility to achieve a more equalised society and to support positive conflict transformation, education should also be used in the future to already make children aware on how it is possible to prevent further conflict from happening and a new dictator from rising to power. This idea was brought up only by one person, a social researcher.[1264] Other conversations showed that people did not believe that society itself has to change, in order to prevent further violent conflict. Many were of the view that the existence of a state of peace or war is not the choice of the people, but rather imposed on them by a force from above.[1265]

[1261] Interview CI, Vienna on 26/10/2012

[1262] Interview AH, Erbil on 15/04/2012; Interview AI, Erbil on 16/04/2012; Interview AL, Erbil on 25/04/2012; Interview AR, Sulaimaniya on 21/05/2012

[1263] Interview BQ, Erbil on 21/07/2012

[1264] Interview BT, Erbil on 24/07/2012

[1265] Interview AJ, Erbil on 20/04/2012; Interview AM, Erbil on 27/04/2012; Interview AN, Erbil on 03/05/2012; Interview AQ, Sulaimaniya on 19/05/2012; Interview BD, Erbil on 25/06/2012; Interview BE, Erbil on 26/06/2012

Teachers, who are every day at the forefront in the education system, were of the same opinion as the rest of the population. When the teachers themselves were asked how development in the country could be improved or how gender equality could be enhanced, they did not see themselves or their schools as being able to do so. While they considered morality, understanding and involvement as core principles, they did not consider themselves or their schools at the forefront of pursuing these principles. While all the teachers interviewed considered that educated women had an easier life in society, the majority did not think that women should be especially favoured when it comes to education; rather that the situation at schools should further improve as a whole.[1266] At the same time only some would like to see further development in the education sector, relative to other developments.[1267] However one teacher put a special emphasis on improving the culture of reading in the region, which is still much lacking in her opinion[1268] and two others believed that it will be necessary to develop more well-educated people able to further advance the reconstruction efforts.[1269] Finally there was only one teacher who stated that political education will be necessary to prevent further conflict from erupting.[1270]

Considering that education will only have an impact that is broadly supported by society, the population in general and teachers in particular need to be made aware of the role education can play in fuelling or preventing private as well as public violent conflict. If the teachers are not aware of the role they are playing, they can fuel social inequalities rather than undermine them. Gender stereotyping by the school curriculum or by the teacher for example might show girls as passive and modest and might reinforce their inferior status and thus create a culture of low

---

[1266] Interview AK, Erbil on 20/04/2012; Interview AZ, Sulaimaniya on 06/06/2012; Interview BA, Erbil on 21/06/2012; Interview BC, Erbil on 25/06/2012; Interview BQ, Erbil on 21/07/2012; Interview BR, Erbil on 22/07/2012; Interview BU, Erbil on 24/07/2012
[1267] Interview AK, Erbil on 20/04/2012; Interview BP, Erbil on 21/07/2012
[1268] Interview BU, Erbil on 24/07/2012
[1269] Interview AZ, Sulaimaniya on 06/06/2012; Interview BA, Erbil on 21/06/2012
[1270] Interview BA, Erbil on 21/06/2012

self-esteem.[1271] Further, the division between various social classes in schools will most likely fuel conflict and extremism if not worked against.

Clearly much work will be necessary to provide high quality education in all schools in the Kurdistan Region. As a first step people should be made more aware of the important role school is playing in the development of a child, society and the region as a whole. While positive reforms are taking place on a national level, these do not seem to have already reached the population on the ground.

In the Kurdistan Region today great discrepancies exist especially between public and private schools, which split the population. While the one part of society has the feeling that development is underway, another part of the population feels that it is being left behind and does not have the same chances of succeeding, as their wealthier counterparts. The lack of high quality education for all arguably hampers the development of the region, and the feeling of distinction between the different social groups over time raises the potential for conflict.

On an individual level, while the school system as a whole, and the schools themselves do not openly discriminate between the genders, practice shows that especially in the schools for children from less advantaged families, the teachers and school in general often merely support or even deepen gender inequalities, which exist in society, and thus often do not have any empowering functions for women, and cannot be said to improve a peaceful and democratic development within the region, which schools would be able to support, as explained by academics, such as Glaeser, Ponzetto, Shleifer and Thyse,[1272] or as wished for by the drafters of the proposed Bill of Rights for Kurdish Women.[1273]

The numbers of new institutions, the increased enrolments of children, and especially girls and the reforms initiated at the political level, show that development of education in the Kurdistan region is taking place. Nevertheless, as reflected in the statements of several of the residents, as well as scholars, there is

---

[1271] Kabeer, "Gender Equality and Women's Empowerment," 18.

[1272] Glaeser, Ponzetto and Shleifer, "Why does democracy need education?," 81. Thyne, "ABC's, 123's, and the Golden Rule," 737.

[1273] Bill of Rights for Kurdish Women, Articles 1(6), 2(2)(d), 4(1) and 4(6)

still need for improvement in quality and gender inclusiveness, in order that education becomes a comprehensive force for fighting discrimination and supporting conflict transformation. Educational institutions should therefore be used to make people aware of the roles they play in their society and the consequences their day-to-day actions will have for the region as a whole. People should also be made aware of the role of education, as this is not happening at present.

While people in the region do not yet consider educational institutions to be leading forces in equalising society, and all had different ideas on what this leading force is or should be, one principle on which everybody agreed was, in the words of a young woman from Sulaymania, *"for both to be equal, this needs to be reality, not mere talking"*.[1274] If this has been achieved for the higher education sector will be subject of the following subchapter.

B.   Higher Education and Social Research

"Education is one of life's most important necessities. It is the only way for an individual to face the requirements of the modern age, its variables, the emergence of modern concepts such as human rights and, most importantly, to claim their right to education, culture, and health care." (Ministry of Education – Erbil)[1275]

As with a high quality basic education system, institutions for higher education as well as a thriving academic community, which encompass representatives of the whole community, are vital if the region is to flourish. University and other higher education being the peak of the education system, play a vital role in the development of society. Higher education can promote intellectual values within a region, and provide citizens with the skills to support development at an international level, and to create future leaders for a country. Universities can thus be at the forefront of development by training academics and highly qualified professionals to assist in economic, medical or technical progress. Institutions of higher education can also form the basis for knowledge exchange, which can

---

[1274] Interview BW, Sulaimaniya on 08/08/2012
[1275] UNESCO Iraq Office, *The Power of Literacy, Stories from Iraq* (IQ/2011/PI/H/1 2011) 3.

change a region's intellectual landscape. Students are often the first to demand social change.

In the Kurdistan Region today the development of higher education is seen as vital for the development of the region by all parts of society, the general population, as well as the authorities, although occasionally for different reasons:

Many amongst the Kurdish people interviewed, and especially those from the upper class and those who opposed the current ruling parties were of the opinion that a country can only be rebuilt with the force of thought and reason and this can only be done by the intellectuals. Their know-how is needed to build up the region and also to educate the next generation, so that they will not make the same mistakes again. [1276]

In comparison, higher education in the Kurdistan Region is seen by decision makers as the pathway to international recognition and especially to increased economic development in the region. As expressed by Dlawer Ala'Aldeen, former Minister of Higher Education and Scientific Research:

> *"These exciting developments are just the beginning. They must be underpinned by serious investment in human capacity and higher standards in the fields of science, technology and management."*[1277]

The reform of the higher education sector is thereby seen as an important step in the transformation of the region from a state of conflict to a state of peace, and from a marginal to a high level player in the international field. For this reason great efforts have been made in the region to develop the sector.

As a result of these efforts, the Kurdistan Region is currently undergoing a great transformation within higher education. As with the other sectors, the whole higher education infrastructure had been destroyed during the various wars over the previous decades. Before 1991, the education sector in the Kurdistan Region was administered by and dependent on the regime of Saddam Hussein. Until 2003, the

---

[1276] See e.g.: Interview AN, Erbil on 03/05/2012; Interview BE, Erbil on 26/06/2012; Interview BN, Erbil on 17/07/2012

[1277] Dlawer Ala'Aldeen, University World News, "A determined push for higher education progress in Kurdistan" (17 June 2012) http://www.universityworldnews.com/article.php?story=20120615064310850 (Accessed on 06.12.2012)

civil war within the region as well as its general isolation prevented education from flourishing and the quality of teaching from rising.

Since 2003, the KRG has been working hard to establish an internationally competitive higher education sector. New universities, including international universities, were established and professors from around the world are lecturing especially at the international universities. The Ministry of Higher Education and Scientific Research published "A Roadmap to Quality" in 2010, which aims to form the basis to "*reform teaching to ensure quality*", "*to promote scientific research and connecting the Region's scientists with their counterparts in international centres of excellence*", to "*invest in higher education and establish new universities*", to "*change the management structure of the universities and the institutes of technical education*", to "*institute administrative reforms*" and to "*protect human rights and establish social justice*".[1278] In addition the reform included modernization of the curricula, "*with an emphasis on self-learning, critical thinking, developing IT skills and learning international languages [...]*".[1279]

The wish for international recognition can be seen especially in the reformed 'new PhD pathway'. With reference to scientific research, the KRG has placed emphasis on "*connecting the scientific research community of the Kurdistan Region to the academic community in the rest of the modern world*". In order to produce experts who will make the Kurdistan Region competitive within international academia and the international marketplace, the new PhD pathway requires a four year PhD program, with a the second year spent abroad "*in a centre of excellence under the supervision of a collaborating scientist*". It aims to develop collaboration between academics in Kurdistan and colleagues around the world.[1280] In addition the KRG has endeavoured to bring "internationality" into the region, by supporting the opening of English-speaking and international universities in the region. However

---

[1278] Ministry of Higher Education and Scientific Research, *A Roadmap to Quality, Reforming the System of Higher Education and Scientific Research in the Kurdistan Region of Iraq, A Report on the Main Achievements, From 1st November 2009 to 1st September 2010* (Ministry of Higher Education and Scientific Research, Kurdistan Regional Government 2010)

[1279] Ala'Aldeen, "A determined push for higher education progress in Kurdistan".

[1280] Minister of Higher Education and Scientific Research, Kurdistan Region, Iraq, "A New PhD pathway in Kurdistan, Promoting Research and raising standards" http://www.mhe-krg.org/node/343 (Accessed on 06.12.2012)

their sometimes questionable quality is currently proving a challenge to the system, as explained by a member of the Education committee for the accreditation of universities within the region. Despite such challenges the efforts by the government to support higher education in the region have born fruits:

While in 1992, there was only one university operating, there are now nineteen state and state-recognised private higher education institutions in the Kurdistan Region[1281], which include universities and *"equivalent higher education establishments such as technical universities, comprehensive universities and specialised institutions at university level"*.[1282] The public universities include the Salahaddin University, the Hawler Medical University, the University of Duhok, Soran University, the University of Sulaimani, the University of Kurdistan Hawler, Koya University, the University of Zakho, the University of Raparin, the University of Halabja, and the University of Garmian. The private universities include the American University of Iraq – Sulaimani, the Sabis University, the Jihan University and the Ishik University.[1283] In addition, the number of students has risen dramatically. As an example, the University of Duhok was opened in 1992 with 214 students[1284] and in 2010 enrolled more than 11,000 students.[1285] The total number of students in institutions of higher education is currently around 100,000, with a female percentage of just under fifty per cent.[1286]

The rapid development in the higher education sector within the Kurdistan Region has also been welcomed and supported by other countries around the world. For example the *UK Higher Education International Unit of the Illuminate Consulting Group*, issued a report in 2009, which noted that the success of Kurdistan's higher

---

[1281] Ala'Aldeen, "A determined push for higher education progress in Kurdistan".

[1282] Kurdistan Board of Investment, "Education" http://www.kurdistaninvestment.org/education.html (Accessed on 06.12.2012)

[1283] Ministry of Higher Education and Scientific Research, "Universities in Kurdistan" http://www.mhe-krg.org/node/23 (Accessed on 06.12.2012)

[1284] University of Duhok, "The University" http://www.uod.ac/en/university (Accessed on 08.12.2012)

[1285] University of Duhok, http://www.uod.ac/en/ (Accessed on 08.12.2012)

[1286] Kurdistan Board of Investment, "Education".

education sector had already received praised in 2007, but which warned of challenges to quality.[1287]

The recent growth and reform of the higher education sector, including the challenges to quality will be discussed in the following section. Attention will be paid to the implications for gender equality in the sector and in the region and for peace building in general.

1.   Supporting Equality in Higher Education

In contrast to primary and secondary education, where number of boys at school normally exceeds that of girls, in the tertiary education sector women start to comprise equal, or even higher enrolments.[1288] This development can also be seen in the Kurdistan region. However, for higher education to benefit the whole of society, numbers are not enough. Higher education needs to be accessible to all, regardless of class, religion, ethnicity or gender.

In the Kurdistan Region the authorities placed support for development through higher education as a clear aim. As stated in the University Act, universities in the Kurdistan Region shall

> *"encourage academic research, cultivate talent, enhance culture, serve society and accelerate the development of the country. Universities shall be guaranteed academic freedom and shall enjoy autonomy as the laws and regulations allow."*[1289]

However, there is no specific stipulation in the national legislation for the support of women or of students from less advantaged backgrounds, unless they qualify under the exceptions of Article 25. These exceptions relate to students who received excellent grades in international fields or in written contests or to students with excellent sports achievements.[1290]

[1287] The Illuminate Consulting Group, UK Higher Education International Unit, *UK Higher Education engagement with Iraq* (Research Series/4, June 2009) 22.

[1288] The World Bank, *Gender Equality and Development,* 107.

[1289] University Act, Ministry of Higher Education and Scientific Research, Kurdistan Region Iraq, http://www.mhe-krg.org/node/28 (Accessed on 06.12.2012) Article 1

[1290] Ibid. Article 25:

"Students suffering serious trauma, children of foreign service personnel of the government, students receiving excellent grades in international field or written contests, students with excellent sports

Nevertheless, the official website of the Ministry of Higher Education and Scientific Research states that

> *"The University seeks to prevent discrimination on the grounds of race, colour, ethnic origin, nationality, religious belief, gender, sexual orientation, disability, age, marital status, family circumstance, citizenship, social and economic status, or any other individual differences."*[1291]

In addition ministerial regulations were issued to enforce equal opportunities, as well as gender equality.[1292] According to the Ministry, the concept of equal opportunity is an important element of the debate around undergraduate education. The universities aim to provide an environment which is free from discrimination, whether against students or staff, and in which all are treated solely according to their merits.[1293] From the outset, the KRG was aware of the importance gender equality in higher education to the social and economic development of their region and was hence supportive.

However, in general there is no official quota for gender balance in the different faculties. However, there are some exceptions, such as the college of nursing at the University of Duhok, which has established a quota of 25 per cent of places for male versus 75 per cent for female students. Admission to the different faculties at the universities is rather dependent on the final marks in high school, and is thus greatly dependent on achievements.[1294] While this can be seen as a way to ensure quality as well as equity and to ensure that only the best of the best are admitted to the courses, regardless of where these 'bests' came from, it may also be seen as discriminatory, as children who were from less advantageous backgrounds, or

---

achievements, veterans, overseas compatriot students, and Mongolian and Tibetan students shall not be limited by the previous paragraph in terms of quotas and means when entering universities to study for degrees. Regulations on the quota, means, qualifications, terms of transaction, composition of the student recruitment committee, principles of recruitment and other proceedings about the rights and responsibilities of examinees, shall be stipulated by the Ministry of Higher Education."

[1291] Ministry of Higher Education and Scientific Research, "Equal Opportunities" http://www.mhe-krg.org/node/27 (Accessed on 06.12.2012)

[1292] Ala'Aldeen, "A determined push for higher education progress in Kurdistan".

[1293] Ministry of Higher Education and Scientific Research, "Equal Opportunities".

[1294] University of Duhok, "Undergraduate Admission" http://www.uod.ac/en/undergraduateadmission (Accessed on 08.12.2012)

were not supported with their education, will be less likely to achieve the high marks necessary to enter the courses.

For the most able of their students, the KRG has initiated different mechanisms of financial support, so that the financial background does not have to play a role in accessing higher education. There are no tuition fees at the public universities and higher education is in general free in the Kurdistan Region. For students who live too distant from the university, the state also provides free dormitories although places are limited.[1295] The universities have in general established support facilities such as student homes and financial assistance, to enable students from all backgrounds to continue their education. Inevitably the nature and level of support varies.[1296]

Furthermore, as recognized by the former Minister for Higher Education and Scientific Research, Professor Dlawer Abdul Aziz Ala'Aldeen, the region is in need of more postgraduates in order to meet the demands of the Regions developing economy. [1297] To support PhD candidates, the state pays for salaries and allowances throughout their study.[1298] In addition, the KRG has developed the Human Capacity Development Program in Higher Education (HCDP), a scholarship programme for Master and PhD students, which aims at developing human capacities in the field of higher education. Through the scholarship programme, the KRG has sent thousands of students abroad to study for their master or PhD degrees at internationally renowned universities in North America, Europe, Australia, Asia or a neighbouring country. The aim of the programme is to train the young generation in order to ensure future development in the Kurdistan Region. The generous scholarship gives all students the opportunity to complete their postgraduate studies abroad. The program certainly supports the

---

[1295] Ministry of Higher Education and Scientific Research, "Higher Education in Kurdistan Region" http://www.mhe-krg.org/node/105 (Accessed on 06.12.2012)

[1296] See for example: University of Duhok, "Financial Aid" http://www.uod.ac/en/financialaid (Accessed on 08.12.2012) or University of Sulaimani, "Study" http://www.univsul.org/E_U_Xwendin.aspx (Accessed on 08.12.2012)

[1297] Dlawer Abdul Aziz Ala'Aldeen, Minister for Higher Education and Scientific Research, "Studying for Master's degree in Kurdistan Region, Reforming the Master's Degree in the Kurdistan Region: Enhancing Capacity and Quality" http://www.mhe-krg.org/node/117 (Accessed on 06.12.2012)

[1298] Minister of Higher Education and Scientific Research, "A New PhD pathway in Kurdistan".

internationalization of Kurdistan's economy, technology and politics. While there are a certain number of scholarship spaces especially allocated for sons and daughters of martyrs, there is no specific allocation of scholarships between male and female students. However it is made clear in the official introduction to the scholarship programme that everybody, men and women are needed and wanted for the programme.[1299] In addition, it is possible for students to receive individual scholarships from the university or from other countries.[1300] Consequently, higher education, at least in theory, is accessible to everybody.

Clearly some children from poorer families have an opportunity for a high quality education because of their abilities, which might not have been available if access were based on fees. However, many youngsters, who might be just as able as their peers, are not admitted to their chosen course, because of lower marks in school, as a result of lower quality teaching. The scholarships, especially at a PhD level, are not dependent on family income. However, since the long process for gaining admission is highly dependent on family support, it seems that the upper class is being advantaged, while the majority of the population is effectively excluded. This is especially true for women from lower income families, who will not get the support needed throughout their childhood and teenage years. Many women still suffer from cultural impediments and will never be in the position to access any of the support provided by the state.

Leaving aside the possibility of underlying hidden discrimination, especially when it comes to differences between social classes, it can be clearly observed that the government has made great efforts to expand the higher education system and to provide a system which includes a relatively high percentage of the population, and which is on the way to becoming competitive internationally. However, while the government publicly promotes the view that it supports the universal education, there are many in the civil society, who are rather of the view that the authorities

---

[1299] Ministry of Higher Education and Scientific Research, "KRG-Scholarship program Human Capacity Development" http://www.mhe-krg.org/index.php?q=node/249 (Accessed on 06.12.2012)
[1300] See e.g. University of Duhok, "Scholarships" http://www.uod.ac/en/scholarships (Accessed on 08.12.2012)

merely provide further opportunities for well-educated or intellectual women among the population.

It was the general opinion among the people interviewed that the government, next to supporting the ministerial employees, especially supports educated women within their system.[1301] Two men even went so far as to say that only the "modern" women, who live in the big cities, are supported by the State,[1302] although it has to be noted that this is not the official stance of the government.[1303]

The perception by the population that educated women are supported by the government can have the effect that "the educated woman" is seen as acceptable in society. Hence, to become an educated woman can be an aspiration or a path to follow, and this may lead to more women achieving higher qualifications to the benefit of region.

However, just as people recognised the government's support for highly educated women, they also noted its lack of support for mothers and house wives, a position which was shared by much of society.[1304]

The prevailing opinion amongst the interviewees was that the only women supported by society were the mothers and the housewives and this created a gap between the women leaving school and staying at home and the women who were highly educated. The women from each group felt unfairly treated. The housewives complained of not receiving any, especially financial, support by the government,[1305] while the students and working women talked about their struggle with society. Several students regretted that it was still necessary for girls to fight to be recognized in certain subjects and that their families were less sympathetic to

---

[1301] Interview BX, Sulaimaniya on 09/08/2012; Interview BC, Erbil on 25/06/2012; Interview AW, Sulaimaniya on 01/06/2012; Interview AJ, Erbil on 20/04/2012; Interview AK, Erbil on 20/04/2012; Interview AL, Erbil on 25/04/2012; Interview AJ, Erbil on 25/04.2012

[1302] Interview BP, Erbil on 21/07/2012; Interview AN, Erbil on 03/04/2012

[1303] Interview AB, Erbil on 03/04/2012

[1304] Interview AU, Sulaimaniya on 28/05/2012; Interview AG, Erbil on 13/04/2012; Interview BV, Sulaimaniya on 06/08/2012

[1305] Interview AI, Erbil on 16/04/2012; Interview AV, Sulaimaniya on 28/05/2012; Interview AY, Sulaimaniya on 04/06/2012; Interview BG, Erbil on 02/07/2012

them during their student years than to their brothers.[1306] For these students it is not sufficient that women are allowed to study at university, as they often have to overcome great obstacles within society to do so. Many felt pressured to become a good wife and a good mother, which meant that they could either not continue their education or not use their education in a relevant position in the work force.[1307]

According to the Kurdistan Region Statistics Office, the young generation has high expectations. Forty-two per cent of girls between ten and fourteen believe that the highest level of education girls should achieve is a bachelor degree or higher.[1308] This contradicts the reality that currently three per cent of the whole population under 30 received a bachelor degree or higher.

At the same time it should be noted that within the small percentage of the population, who are able to receive a higher education, gender equality is increasing. Even though, according to some students, some discrimination is still persisting in practice in different institutions, the overall trends in female access to universities are highly positive. There has been a rapid increase of female students although this increase is not yet reflected among the lecturers and professors or among other qualified professions. However, the large number of young women graduating from universities and obtaining qualifications equal to their male counter parts opens up a variety of opportunities for women to develop professionally as well as individuals, to promote gender equity within society and to contribute to the future development of the region.

Apart from general economic and social advantages within the region, the provisions for gender equality are also vital for the region's standing within the international community, as the government is aware. The international community, and especially the West, is currently placing great emphasis on appointing women into leading positions and also expects a similar emphasis from any region wishing to play a significant role in international dealings.

[1306] Interview AE, Erbil on 09/04/2012; AJ, Erbil on 20/04/2012; Interview AM, Erbil on 27/04/2012
[1307] Interview BW, Sulaimaniya on 08/08/2012; Interview BF, Erbil on 29/06/2012; Interview BB, Erbil on 24/06/2012
[1308] Kurdistan Regional Statistics Office, *Iraq Women Integrated Social and Health Survey*, 2.

The wider implications to the region of a lack of gender equality within the scholarly community will now be considered. Scholarly activities have traditionally been and often still are highly gendered. Women's opinions or findings were seldom published.[1309] This is especially the case Middle Eastern country, where scholarship, especially on women's issues, is still far from complete.[1310] In the Kurdistan Region also, scientific research on women and gender is still limited, although it exists.[1311] Until recently scholars writing about Middle Eastern women and being read in the West, were mainly from the West.[1312] These views shape the attitudes of the rest of the world towards the Middle East and may therefore have a negative effect on women's development. However with the increase of female scholars within the region, this development is likely to change. Experts and scholars can spread information, as well as new and critical ideas. Women participating to conflict transformation as feminist academics are crucial as a platform of communication as well as being the producers and distributors of ideas and new orders.[1313] As shown by the final research report on Female Iraqi Academics in Iraqi Kurdistan, the number of female post-graduate students, researchers, teachers and lecturers in the region has increased, but women are still marginalized when it comes to decision making posts, publishing and representing the region's institutions internationally.[1314] The female academics explained that while there is no legal discrimination between the sexes, a lack of a coherent and transparent system, as well as cultural and social attitudes and a lack of support structure when it comes to domestic responsibilities leads to practical discrimination.[1315] In addition, criticism remains that the government mainly supports one part of the population in becoming part of these numbers and that the other part of the population have hardly got a chance in getting into the system.

[1309] Jaquette Jane and Summerfield Gale (ed.), *Women and Gender Equity in Development Theory and Practice, Institutions, Resources, and Mobilization* (Duke University Press, Durham 2006) p.191

[1310] Sharoni, "Women and Gender in Middle East Studies," 28.

[1311] See e.g. Al-Tawil Namir, Hawler Medical University, "Research Article, Association of violence against women with religion and culture in Erbil Iraq: a cross-sectional study" (17 September 2012) http://www.biomedcentral.com/1471-2458/12/800/abstract (08.12.2012)

[1312] Yegenoglu Meyda, *Colonial fantasies, Towards a feminist reading of Orientalism* (Cambridge University Press, Cambridge 1998) p. 103

[1313] Julie Pateet and Barbara Harlow, "Gender and Political Change" *Middle East Report* 173 (1991): 7.

[1314] Nadje Al-Ali et.al, *Female Iraqi Academics in Iraqi Kurdistan: Roles, Challenges & Capacities* (Final Research Report, DelPHE Iraq) 2.

[1315] Ibid.pp.4-7

For a balanced and peaceful society, it is not possible to only support the one or the other element of society with advanced educational opportunities. A way still needs to be found in the Kurdistan region to provide opportunities to the whole population regardless of the social background.

It is this disparity in opportunity, which was criticized by the interviewees. While the majority of them agreed that within the education system the most support is still needed for the less advantaged in the general population including for women. The current problem within higher education is not numbers and gender equity, but rather social inequality.[1316] This loss of a high percentage of human resources for the government, as well as a loss of personal chances for individuals, is arguably reflected in the job market, as well as the social structure, and should thus be changed.

It can therefore be concluded that while equal access to higher education is in theory provided and gender equality in terms of merit is supported by the government, substantial developments are still necessary to ensure that also in practice all parts of the population have access to the higher education system. It is currently unthinkable that a girl from a remote village, who does not even have access to secondary education, would have the possibility travel to the UK for her PhD, whether she would be fit for a doctorate or not. This fact denies the country access to its full potential and leaves people behind, who might one day stand up and demand their rights.

Next to the inclusion of people from all elements of society and of women in particular, the quality of the higher education system, and the sensitivity to gender within the structure is vital when aiming for the enhancement of gender equality within society and positive development within the region at all levels. If and how this has been achieved in the Kurdistan Region and what consequences can be seen to follow, will be subject of the following section:

[1316] Interview BM, Erbil on 13/07/2012; Interview BU, Erbil on 24/07/2012; Interview BD, Erbil on 25/06/2012

2.   Quality of Higher Education – Searching for Critical Thinking and the Inclusion of Gender

"It is the duty of school teachers to raise awareness among children. It is also the duty of the universities and academic centers to conduct research on this area [of violence against women]."[1317]

In the Kurdistan Region, the quality of teaching is not only criticized when it comes to mandatory education, but also when it comes to higher education and scholarship. As with general schooling, access to institutes of higher education is of no value for the development of the region if they do not offer courses of high quality.

For instance several scholars at the international conference on Kurdish studies at the University of Exeter in September 2012, as well as teaching personnel from the University of Kurdistan Hawler, argued that many of the higher education institutions in the region today have an outdated system and a weak structure. Students and lecturers from different universities inside and outside of the Kurdistan Region were particularly critical of some institutes of higher educations which they believed are still too influenced by the political parties and too often accept not the highly qualified people with a good reputation, but rather family members or friends of party members.[1318]

In addition, many of the professors, especially at the more newly established universities, feel limited in their capacity to exercise professionalism and controlled by the system. Such a view was publicly stated by one former professor at the University of Kurdistan Hawler.[1319] Stories circulate about people, who were thrown out from university, because their input was against the political agenda and it was

---

[1317] Kurdistan Regional Government, "Prime Minister Barzani's speech".

[1318] Interview AF, Erbil on 09/04/2012; Interview BY, Sulaimaniya on 10/08/2012; Interview CH, Vienna on 05/11/2012; Interview CB, Vienna on 04/12/2012

[1319] See The Chronicle, "Apply to University of Kurdistan Hawler? Not Recommended" (27 May 2010) http://chronicle.com/forums/index.php?topic=69283.0 (Accessed on 08.12.2012)

said that there is in general no real freedom of speech, which results in a lack of critical thinking, a lack of knowledge circulation and control by politicians.[1320]

As experienced during field research in the region, control at the universities was high, and some of the students were afraid to discuss certain issues in public. At the same time, it needs to be noted that students nevertheless did discuss such issues and that the university system clearly produced a large number of active, reflective and critically thinking citizens.

The government recognises that the assurance of quality in the higher education sector remains a great challenge, which will need to be tackled, although at a different level than the challenges elaborated above. As recognized by the former Minister for Higher Education and Scientific Research, Professor Dlawer Abdul Aziz Ala'Aldeen, for a long time the government did not have a strategic long-term plan for its higher education system. As a consequence there are still problems of capacity and space in the different programmes; the quality of teaching and the style of learning are not as established as they might be, especially within Master's and PhD programmes; there are several problems with quality assurance in the graduation requirements, admission procedure and teaching structure; and finally most of the teachers from inside Kurdistan had not had the chance to increase their knowledge and experience internationally. To address the last mentioned issue the KRG is supporting more professors from outside.[1321] This need for transformation was met with a reform.

As part of its "Roadmap to Quality" the KRG sought to raise the quality of higher education and scientific research in the Kurdistan Region through a number of measures including the establishment of a system of quality assurance; reforming the curricula; heavily investing in the sector through the establishment of scholarship programmes and through the establishment of new universities; and finally initiating an administrative reform.[1322] These were all necessary and highly positive measures, which are already reflected in the general advances in the

---

[1320] See also: Salman Ahmed Rasul, "Higher Education in the Kurdistan Region of Iraqi" (6 January 2012) http://www.ekurd.net/mismas/articles/misc2012/1/state5770.htm (Accessed on 03.08.2013)

[1321] Ala'Aldeen, "Studying for Master's degree in Kurdistan Region"

[1322] Ministry of Higher Education and Scientific Research, *A Roadmap to Quality,* 16-20.

higher education sector and are promising to boost development in the region in the near term, if fully implemented. However, they arguably will not work to diminish social differences already created by the school system, and certain issues, which are vital for a positive academic exchange, such freedom of speech, are not discussed.

As part of the process, the KRG aims at reforming the undergraduate and postgraduate curriculum in a way to "*encourage students to think critically and become more creative self-learners*".[1323] If put into practice, this will encourage positive social development. In addition the reform promised to "*protect human rights, achieve social justice and to improve the learning and working environment*"[1324].

While all other aspects of the reform seem to be well thought through and carefully considered, the section on Protecting Human Rights and Establishing Social Justice is disappointing. While social justice issues, such as the granting of generous scholarships abroad are also included in the package of reforms,[1325] they are limited to "*reforming the recruitment and transfer system*" and "*to establish a Health and Safety Committee*".[1326] While both of these measures are important, they are limited in their potential. There are no provisions for the specific support of less advantaged students, whether financially or through quotas or other measures, such as raising awareness of higher education in schools.

Leaving aside class differences, movement can be seen in the inclusion of gender into the study and research curriculum. In the Kurdistan Region certain courses, such as medicine and engineering, are still regarded more highly than the social sciences. However it is the prevailing opinion that everybody shall receive a place to study according to his or her ability, as measured by the final marks in high school, without taking into account social issues and other pre-existing discrimination. As a result of various measures taken by the universities around the region it can be seen that gender and critical thinking are coming more to the fore.

[1323] Ibid.p.17
[1324] Ibid.p.12
[1325] Ibid.pp.57/58
[1326] Ibid.pp.88/89

Several universities including the Hawler Medical University include in their mission statements a commitment to the principle of equal opportunity without discrimination.[1327] The University of Duhok has as one of its objectives *"to promote secular, pluralistic and democratic principles with particular emphasis on gender equality, equal opportunity and human rights at large"*, as well as to *"encourage the spirit of debate, critical thinking and innovative approach in social, natural, applied, engineering and medical sciences"*.[1328] And the University of Kurdistan Hawler goes as far as saying that their philosophy is to teach the students how to think and not what to think.[1329]

At the University of Sulaimani, a Gender and Violence Studies Centre was established, funded by the British Council within its Development Projects in Higher Education (DelPHE-Iraq). The aim of the Centre is *"to provide robust evidence and recommendations to the government"*, according to its head, Dr Begikhani. As a consequence all sociology students have to complete one unit on gender and violence as part of their degree.[1330]

Salahaddin University-Hawler for example signed an agreement with the School of Oriental and African Studies at the University of London in joint research, supervision and student exchange in *"gender studies and women empowerment in the decision making processes for Kurdistan Region"*.[1331]

As a contribution to enhancing social and economic development in the region through gender equality, the University of Kurdistan Hawler (UKH) initiated a women empowerment program, which includes *"developing research capabilities and managerial skills"* among female academics through training sessions and

---

[1327] Hawler Medical University, "Vision and Mission" http://hmu.edu.iq/About/VisionandMission.aspx (Accessed on 08.12.2012)

[1328] University of Duhok, "Mission, Vision and Core Values" http://www.uod.ac/en/mission (Accessed on 08.12.2012)

[1329] University of Kurdistan, Hawler, "About UKH" http://www.ukh.ac/listArticls.php?ZID=1&CID=1 (Accessed on 08.12.2012)

[1330] Matthew Reisz, Times Higher Education "Iraqi Kurdish scholars put gender theory to the test" (13.10.2011) http://www.timeshighereducation.co.uk/story.asp?storycode=417730 (Accessed on 06.01.2013)

[1331] SUH, "London's SOAS Signs Agreement with SUH" (31.05.2012) http://www.suh-edu.com/index.php?option=com_content&view=article&id=484%3Alondons-soas-signs-agreement-with-suh&catid=1%3Alatest-news&Itemid=162&lang=en (Accessed on 08.12.2012)

workshops.[1332] Other initiatives included a women leadership seminar for the female students of UKH presented by Bayan Sami Abdul Rahman, the current KRG High Representative to the UK, who spoke to the students about her personal experiences.[1333] Furthermore, the university celebrated international women's day, during which Vice Chancellor Professor Serwan Baban emphasised that it is necessary to work for collective human rights and that *the development process in Kurdistan needs to harness 100% of its human resources and cannot proceed successfully without fully utilising the talents of women, i.e. some 50% of the population*"[1334], the university initiated Female Academic Network Workshops for female students at UKH, in which they are supported to strive for success,[1335] and the university has amongst its staff academics who are specialized in gender studies.[1336] In addition the university also participated in the workshop "sixteen days of activism to end violence against women", which took place from 29 November to third December 2012 under the slogan *from peace in the home to peace in the Society*", and which had at its purpose to raise awareness about gender based violence and to make the young generation fight against it.[1337]

Also the University of Zakho was very active in raising awareness *to combat domestic violence*"[1338], with speeches being held by personalities like MP Zakiya Sayed Saleh,[1339] Dr. Paru Karadaghi, the executive director of Kurdish Human Rights in the USA and Mr. Ahmed Musleh Saleh, the Director of the Office of

[1332] University of Kurdistan, Hawler, "UKH Leads Women Empowerment in Higher Education" http://www.ukh.ac/detailsArticls.php?ZID=1&CID=106&AID=602 (Accessed on 08.12.2012)
[1333] University of Kurdistan, Hawler, "Women Leadership Seminars to UKH Female Students" http://www.ukh.ac/detailsArticls.php?ZID=1&CID=106&AID=689 (Accessed on 08.12.2012)
[1334] University of Kurdistan, Hawler, "University of Kurdistan Hewler Celebrated International Women's Day" http://www.ukh.ac/detailsArticls.php?ZID=1&CID=106&AID=1006 (Accessed on 08.12.2012)
[1335] University of Kurdistan, Hawler, "Female Academic Network Workshop" http://www.ukh.ac/detailsArticls.php?ZID=1&CID=106&AID=1132 (Accessed on 08.12.2012)
[1336] University of Kurdistan, Hawler, "Katherine Carter" http://www.ukh.ac/detailsArticls.php?ZID=1&CID=106&AID=1141 (Accessed on 08.12.2012)
[1337] University of Kurdistan, Hawler, "UKH Students Fight Violence against Women" http://www.ukh.ac/detailsArticls.php?ZID=1&CID=106&AID=913 (Accessed on 08.12.2012)
[1338] University of Zakho, "First Day of (16 Days Campaign) To Combat Domestic Violence" (27 November 2012) http://www.uoz-krg.org/node/278 (Accessed on 12.12.2012)
[1339] University of Zakho, "(16 Days Campaign) To Combat Domestic Violence Activities from 29/11-3/12/2012 (10 December 1012) http://www.uoz-krg.org/node/281 (Accessed on 12.12.2012)

Domestic Violence in Zakho.[1340] They spoke on the role of women in society, as well as the role of the family and that of the parents in educating children in society.

However one has to remind oneself that the initiatives taken above only affect a small percentage of the people in higher education, who themselves comprise only a small percentage of the population as a whole. Nevertheless the potential of such measures should not be underestimated. Some female students at university argued that these programmes only reach *"those, who do not need it anyway"* and that they should rather increasingly reach women from less educated backgrounds as well as men.[1341] Nevertheless, the very existence of such measures points to the values of the region, and provides a foundation for the students, some of whom will most likely become the next leaders of Kurdistan and substantially influence the region's future development.

In addition, the various initiatives by the universities are partly reflected in the students' opinions. Most of the students questioned were very positive when it came to women's role in Kurdish society. They cherish their opportunities and are positive about future development in the region in general and also about issues of gender equality.[1342] Nevertheless many female students still have the feeling that despite their high level of education they will not be able to achieve high positions or that they will have to become housewives once they get married.[1343] At the same time, the open discussions among most students also showed that critical debate is flourishing amongst them and that women are generally supported in the higher education structure. However while gender inclusion within the university sector has not yet had any major influence on society as a whole, it has most certainly raised awareness amongst the small number of engaged students, which may eventually be reflected in the wider population.

All in all it can therefore be concluded that positive development in the university system, especially when it comes to gender inclusion, is under way. The

---

[1340] University of Zakho, "Second Day of (16 Days Campaign) To Combat Domestic Violence" (29 November 2012) http://www.uoz-krg.org/node/279 (Accessed on 12.12.2012)

[1341] See e.g. Interview BZ, Sulaimaniya on 10/08/2012

[1342] See e.g. Interview BL, Erbil on 12/07/2012; Interview AS, Sulaimaniya on 23/05/2012; Interview AT, Sulaimaniya on 24/05/2012

[1343] Interview AQ, Sulaimaniya on 19/05/2012; Interview AU, Sulaimaniya on 28/05/2012

government has worked hard and has invested a lot to ensure that the quality of the higher education system in the region is raised as quickly as possible. Within the structure of the higher education system, gender issues are slowly being put on centre stage, which will most certainly have a positive effect on the region's development, as it provides the female part of the population with the strength and the support, which they will need, if they pursue a career in the region. While there are still general problems of equity, including gender equity, the different institutions of higher education offer from their outset good and balanced opportunities for young men and women in the region. The sharp increase of numbers of universities and other institutes of higher education within the region provides ever more opportunities for citizens to access higher education, especially as university services are provided free. Considering that the number of female students is nearly as high as that of males, sexual equality can be said to have been achieved. The resulting increase in university graduates will push development within the region forward. It will also support the intended internationalization of the region, by building connections with professionals in other countries, as part of the sponsored PhD and Master programmes. From an individual point of view, the enhancement of the higher education sector provides the women involved with opportunities they would not otherwise have had and with the chance to pursue their career of choice. At the same time it has to be remembered that many of the current female students do not feel supported by society and cannot yet see themselves as having the same access to educational support or post university careers, as their male counterparts. Furthermore the current structure fails to support gender equality throughout the whole region, as there is a large part of the population, including an especially high proportion of women, who are in practice unable to access higher education, as they lack the essential prerequisites. This results in reduced opportunities for all, and consequential differentials between the different social groups, as well as a loss of resources for the region. As yet there is no emphasis on actively opening the higher education system to people from less advantaged backgrounds. Control by the ruling parties still persists, which, if not changed, could one day lead to unrest initiated by opponents of the current leaders or by elements of the population who feel left behind and discriminated against.

Hence in order to make the higher education sector work for long term positive development within the region, the sector needs to be opened up and the necessary prerequisites adjusted to allow access it have to all people, notwithstanding their background. This process should start with the older generation:

C.   Women's Education – Education by Women

"Since wars begin in the minds of the men, it is in the minds that the defences of peace must be constructed."[1344]

When considering education, especially education at a time of transformation, nobody can be excluded. It is not enough to merely consider the education of the six to twenty-one year olds; rather it is necessary to consider the education of the whole population. It is the older generation, who went through or actively took part in the wars, and it is they who must come to terms with their pasts. It is the older generation, which is currently influencing the dealings within the region, through the public as well as private actions they take every day. It is also the older generation, which educates the young generation, as mothers, fathers, and teachers. It follows that adult education, including the specific education of women, must also be seen as vital for the personal development of individuals, as well as society as a whole.

The aim of the following section is to discuss the influence of education on women, through the example of teaching literacy, as well as the role of women as educators for future development within the region.

1.   Literacy as a Way forward

"Illiteracy [...] is in fact a problem with serious and dangerous socio-economic implications. Any interventions to eradicate illiteracy should be viewed as developmental interventions."[1345]

[1344] UNESCO, *National Education Support Strategy, Republic of Iraq, 2010-2014*, 7.

In today's world illiteracy is seen as a serious problem for the individuals affected, and society as a whole. As a result of how the modern world is constructed, an inability to read and write constitutes a barrier in most day-to-day life, which results in dependency and a lack of choices in personal development. As demonstrated by UNESCO through the example of Iraq, high levels of illiteracy in a country hinder the developmental process in a country, as well as frustrate individuals in in their efforts to achieve their aspirations.[1346]

It is a common consequence of a prolonged armed conflict that levels of illiteracy, and in particular the percentage of illiterate women in the regions affected, is very high. This development can be observed around the world, and although exact numbers are often unclear, the effects of war on literacy are visible. In Rwanda the percentage of illiterate women, as measured after the genocide, was at 67,4 per cent, in Afghanistan it was 85 per cent and in Ethiopia 66,2 per cent.[1347]

For the Kurdistan Region in Iraq the long years of war and social exclusion have had similar effects. Education was scarce during the 1990s and consequently illiteracy rose. In 2000 the illiteracy rate amounted to 34 per cent, with over 60 per cent being women.[1348]

Despite great developments, the illiteracy rate in the three northern districts of Iraq is today still one of the highest in the country. An average of 26.3 per cent of the whole population is illiterate,[1349] according to the Kurdistan Region Statistics Office, and with an average of 36 to 40 per cent for women above fifteen.[1350] The very high illiteracy rate amongst women, compared to other parts of Iraq is ascribed to the lack of support for the region during the Baathist rule, as well as to the large differences between urban and rural life which still exist.

[1345] UNESCO Iraq Office, National Strategic Framework for Literacy in Iraq, 2011-2015 (UNESCO) 11.
[1346] Ibid.p.13
[1347] Petra Purkarthofer, *Gender und bewaffnete Konflikte, Vergleichsstudie,* (Vienna: Vienna Institute for International Dialogue and Cooperation, 2008) 10.
[1348] UNESCO Iraq Office, National Strategic Framework for Literacy in Iraq, 21.
[1349] Kurdistan Region Statistics Office, *Education,* 1.
[1350] IAU, *Women in Iraq Fact sheet.*

Once violence had decreased in the region, and the security situation became more stable, several sides lobbied for more educational opportunities for women, in order to improve their future prospects, and to support development in the region as a whole.

For example members of the Iraqi Council of Representatives and the Kurdistan Parliament-Iraq, as part of the international conference on *The Role of Women in Peace-Building, Reconciliation and Accountability in Iraq"* proposed to

> *"Make eliminating illiteracy a priority by supporting all government, private sector, and civil society literacy programmes, and make literacy a first step towards the socio-economic empowerment of women."*[1351]

Also the participants of the *"International Conference on Kurdish Women for Peace and Equality"* lobbied for the establishment of community culture centres, which provide professional training, as well as educational opportunities for women.[1352]

As a reaction to the need, the Ministry of Education initiated the "Illiteracy Free Kurdistan" campaign, which targeted everybody between the age of 15 and 45.[1353] In addition to the literacy and adult education initiative, the KRG introduced the "Accelerated Learning Program" in 2005, with the aim of attracting school drop outs back into education.[1354] According to a UNESCO report, for the academic year 2010/2011 there were 424 literacy centres present in the Kurdistan Region, which accommodated 19.330 learners, of which 57 per cent were women[1355] and 140 Accelerated Learning Schools with 20.212 learners, of which 46 per cent were women.[1356] In addition, the KRG declared as their goal to establish 3600 centres by 2015 with 150,000 learners to reduce illiteracy in the region to eight per cent[1357]

[1351] No Peace Without Justice, *The Role of Women in Peace-Building*, Recommendation 46.
[1352] The Kurdish National Congress of North America, *International Conference on Kurdish Women*, Suggestion 8.
[1353] UNESCO Iraq Office, National Strategic Framework for Literacy in Iraq, 21.
[1354] Ibid.p.21
[1355] Ibid.p.68
[1356] Ibid.p.71
[1357] Ibid.p.68

as well as to establish up to 800 Accelerated Learning Schools for 115.000 students.[1358]

The KRG was not alone with its initiative. As part of its strategy to support the improvement of Iraqi education UNESCO has established a priority to support the reduction of illiteracy especially amongst out-of-school children and women.[1359] An increase in the literacy rate is a concern for the region and also for the international community as a whole.

For this reason, UNESCO launched in 2010, in partnership with the Office of Her Highness Sheikha Mozah bint Nasser, First Lady of Qatar, the Literacy Initiative for Empowerment (LIFE) project in Iraq. This initiative aims at empowering civil society and the Iraqi Government to provide equal access to literacy and to reduce the illiteracy rate by 50 per cent by 2015.[1360] The Iraqi Ministry of Education, together with the Ministry of Education of the Kurdistan Region and UNESCO Iraq have developed a National Framework for the Literacy Strategy in Iraq for implementation until 2015.[1361]

Finally, the NGOs are also involved in promoting literacy in the region to maximise the outreach to the civil population. In the Kurdistan Region five Kurdish NGOs, namely the Civil Development Organisation, Al Messalla Organisation, Harikar, Alind Organisation for Youth Democratization and the Public Aid Organisation were chosen and sponsored to establish additional community learning centres.[1362]

The official statistics indicate that the campaigns have proven a big success. According to the Ministry of Education, the KRG has managed, through their "Illiteracy Free Kurdistan" campaign to decrease the illiteracy rate in 2010 to 16 per cent.[1363] While this number does not coincide with the percentage published by

---

[1358] Ibid.p.71

[1359] UNESCO, *National Education Support Strategy, Republic of Iraq, 2010-2014*, 13.

[1360] UNESCO Office for Iraq, "Involving local NGOs in Literacy programs in Iraq" (19 October 2011) http://www.unesco.org/new/en/iraq-office/about-this-office/single-view/news/involving_local_ngos_in_literacy_programs_in_iraq/ (Accessed on 09.01.2013)

[1361] UNESCO Iraq Office, National Strategic Framework for Literacy in Iraq, 2.

[1362] UNESCO Office for Iraq, "Involving local NGOs in Literacy programs in Iraq".

[1363] UNESCO Iraq Office, National Strategic Framework for Literacy in Iraq, 21.

the Kurdistan Region Statistics Office in 2012,[1364] it can nevertheless be assumed illiteracy throughout the region has decreased as a result of the campaign.

Even if some of the numbers are not totally accurate, it is arguable that by prioritising literacy, the leading parties are laying the foundations for boosting individual as well as national development, and for eliminating reasons for conflict from below. There are several grounds for supporting this theory:

According to IAU, households headed by an illiterate person are more likely to be deprived of basic needs. Such households are more likely to be disadvantaged when it comes to sufficient clean water, sanitation, food or electricity, than households headed by literate individuals.[1365] While it could be argued that it is not because of a lack of education that these individuals are suffering from a lack of basic necessities, but rather that they are unable to access education as a consequence of lacking the basic necessities of life. However, is clear that poverty and a lack of education often coincide, and it is thus vital to make education accessible, in order to provide the low- or no-income parts of the population with enhanced opportunities. Since women comprise the majority of the illiterate population, and since they most often manage the households, while the men are out working or seeking work, it is of great importance to consider literacy programmes through a gendered lens. It is important that women are provided with opportunities to access these programmes.

Furthermore, enhanced literacy not only provides the foundation to improve the living standards of the individual and her or his family, but also to boost the economic prosperity of the country. Literate and numerate people have an advantage in finding employment or in starting their own business, through which they can rails their families out of poverty. This in turn leads to further economic development throughout the country.

In addition educated mothers especially benefit their children through example. It has been argued that girls are more likely to attend schools if their mothers are

---

[1364] See above: 26.3%; Kurdistan Region Statistics Office, *Education*, 1.
[1365] IAU, *Literacy in Iraq Fact Sheet*.

educated, even if this happens in adulthood. The consequential education of the next generation will result in even further development of a nation.[1366]

Considering individual development, the vast changes in the Kurdistan Region over the past 10 years, the increased urbanization, and the level of international involvement the region is aiming for, it is inconceivable that part of the population could lead a prosperous life while remaining illiterate.

This also the opinion of most of the Kurdish population, who are, at least in theory, very much in favour of the idea of continuing education. According to the Kurdistan Regional Statistics Office, six out of ten women between 15 and 45, who did not complete their education, are interested in doing so.[1367] Also amongst the people interviewed several women were very supportive of the chances to continue education,[1368] although others were sceptical.[1369]

Finally, apart economic advantages, it is said that literacy programmes are able to support individual social development, including an enhancement of gender equality. As expressed by Leach and Dume, education is also a link between gender and violence.[1370] Literacy can have a positive effect on social participation and decision making, as it gives people the feeling that they have a voice.[1371] As explained by Colcough it can also provide people with more self-confidence resulting in less dependency on others. However, he continues that this will not be achieved by merely teach men and women to read and write. Literacy programmes will only truly empower women, when they are tied to income-generating activities, as well as to education in health and human rights.[1372]

Hence 'literacy' includes more than knowing the letters of the alphabet. Taking up the argument, several scholars, including Juliet McCaffery maintain that literacy is or should be more than merely learning how to read. Literacy can be significant in

---

[1366] Naomi Wolf, Al Jazeera, "Opinion, The price of oppressing your women" (5.10.2011) http://www.aljazeera.com/indepth/opinion/2011/10/2011102133713539233.html (Accessed on 5.12.2011)

[1367] Kurdistan Regional Statistics Office, *Iraq Women Integrated Social and Health Survey*, 1.

[1368] Interview AL, Erbil on 25/04/2012; Interview AW, Sulaimaniya on 01/06/2012

[1369] Interview AV, Sulaimaniya on 28/05/2012; Interview BG, Erbil on 02/07/2012

[1370] Leach and Dume (ed.), *Education, Conflict and Reconciliation*, 22.

[1371] IAU, *Literacy in Iraq Fact Sheet*.

[1372] Colclough, "Achieving Gender Equality in Education," 8.

changing individuals as well as society as a whole and in certain situations can challenge the social order. Whether and how literacy will influence people's lives is thereby dependent on the way it is taught. While it can be taught simply as a skill, without any specific background, the social model theory stresses that it is particularly important that *"literacy learned by adults should relate directly to their cultural and communal practices"*, which can then result in transformative literacy or literacy as a critical reflection. Literacy can consequently be used as a tool by the learner to take control over developments in their lives, and to engage with the world around them in a different way. This can be achieves by teaching critical analysis, problem solving, active methods of learning and context-related literacy, as part of literacy itself.[1373]

It follows that literacy's true transformative potential will only be achieved, if the aim for transformation is included into the programme.

Lessons form the failure to teach critical analysis and to read context as part of literacy programs could already be learned from Iraq in the 1980s, when, just as today, reading classes were conducted for all illiterate Iraqis between 15 and 45 years of age. As noted by Salvesberg, Hajo and Borck it was an important aim at the time to include rural women into modern society. However when the women were later asked about the usefulness of these classes, many were of the opinion that they had no use for reading and writing, since their lives remained the same in every other way. By not giving the graduates of these programmes the opportunities to put their skills to use, or by not providing them with the necessary expertise to achieve transformation by themselves, the literacy campaigns did not fulfil their potential.

Even today there persist problems surrounding the literacy initiatives. As analysed by UNESCO, while Iraq, including the Kurdistan Region, has the will and the possibility to decrease illiteracy within the population, there are still several challenges to be overcome. These include the effective deployment of human resources, an inadequate outreach to the population, the lack of enforcement of

---

[1373] Leach and Dume (ed.), *Education, Conflict and Reconciliation,* 136/7.

the compulsory education law, as well as a lack of including gender and cultural diversity within the curricula.[1374]

As with compulsory education, the great efforts by the authorities to support development in the region through enhanced literacy are limited by *inter alia* not reaching the whole population and by not including enough practical gender considerations in their programmes.

In order to provide opportunities for all parts of the population to enhance their education, to advance their personal development, as well as to support national development, it is vital to not only make literacy classes generally available, but to also provide the surrounding circumstances, which enable people to benefit from their new capabilities.

According to IAU, the most significant reasons for young illiterate women not attending school is their parents' refusal, followed by the distance to school and problems of financing.[1375] Hence the government should seek to achieve an environment where the parents support sending their girls to school. There are similar problems for older illiterate women. As described by Salih Waladbagi from the KurdishGlobe, women in the region respond very well to the literacy initiatives by the government and they are happy to study, but there are persisting problems of resources, as well as social and cultural impediments. These include the problem of being out in the evening, the lack of child care, the lack of transportation, and the lack of family support, which make it difficult for women to resume their studies.[1376] These problems could also be seen, when observing parts of the Kurdish population first hand. When older women with limited education were asked why they did not pursue further education after the war, the common replies were that they did not have the necessary finances, that they needed to pursue their responsibilities at home, that it was not seen as necessary anymore by the family, or that they felt too old. At the same time it has to be said

---

[1374] UNESCO Iraq Office, National Strategic Framework for Literacy in Iraq, 24-27.

[1375] IAU, *Literacy in Iraq Fact Sheet*.

[1376] Salih Waladbagi, "350.000 people being literate since 2000 in Kurdistan" (08 October 2011) http://www.kurdishglobe.net/display-article.html?id=6D96CE6D5F034867ABF590E232704E63 (Accessed on 09.01.2013)

that most of the families questioned strongly supported the education of their children and of the next generation.

It may be concluded that the support of literacy initiatives in the region in general is certainly needed and is positive for individual, as well as for national development. However is unclear to what extent the initiatives have yet influenced progress towards gender equality and development within the region. While the potential for development is certainly there, it is questionable whether the quality of the courses, as well as the level of their accessibility by all parts of the population is yet high enough to realise the potential. Even if the benefits are not clearly measurable, it is vital to continue these initiatives, as they provide people, and especially women, with the possibility to pursue education, which is arguably necessary in today's world and which will have an effect on the region's development in the long run.

While it is vital to give women, and men, the opportunities to become students once more, the most important roles in shaping the region's future arguably belong to the teachers, namely of teachers of their children, the next generation.

2.   Women as Educators for a New Generation

"It is necessary to remove the idea of war from the heads of the people and to work against the application of this idea."[1377]

Conflicts change the values and norms of a society. They make people much more tolerant towards violent behaviour, which is consequently difficult to reverse.[1378] It follows that after a time of conflict, especially after decades of internal conflict, there is a need to build up social relations from the bottom up. Hence not only the officials, but also groups within civil society are of great importance in the reconstruction of relationships born out of conflict. One way of doing so is through education, whether formal or informal, and it in this area that women are the most experienced, the most active,[1379] and also the most recognized. Interviewees both men and women, and from different social backgrounds, all agreed, whether they

---

[1377] Interview BO, Erbil on 18/07/2012

[1378] Christina Steenkamp, *Violence and Post-War Reconstruction, Managing Insecurity in the Aftermath of Peace Accords* (New York: I.B.Tauris, 2009) 29/30.

[1379] Golan, "Viewpoints," 94.

liked it or not, that an important, or even the most important role of a woman, is and always has been that of a mother.[1380] In their roles as educators, women have a profound influence on conflict transformation.

As explained by Al-Suwaiji, women have the ability to restore the Iraqi family, the personal one, as well as the national one. After decades of the government trying to turn different ethnic and religious groups against one another, and of having their informants and the secret police everywhere, it is a challenge to bring people together again and to restore positive values. Women are first and foremost in meeting this challenge through educating their children as well as everybody else around.[1381]

Further, women have a very important role as mothers and their teachings will influence their children and the next generation.

This fact was also recognized by some of the interviewees from the Kurdistan Region.[1382] It was the prevailing opinion among the interviewees that next to their role as workers, women have their most important role in their families, as nurturers, as well as as teachers. "Teaching" and conveying knowledge is seen by many as women's task or purpose, whether as teachers or as mothers in educating their children.[1383]

Nearly half of the interviewees (49%) believed that women especially should work in schools, as teachers. Teaching has good working hours and as with being a mother, is seen as a respectable calling for a woman in the Kurdistan Region.[1384] Teaching, especially at primary school level, has often been regarded as a "woman's job". In the Kurdistan Region the number of female teachers was often higher than that of male. In 2003 of 25,782 teachers there were 15,179 women in

---

[1380] See e.g. Interview AR, Sulaimaniya on 21/05/2012; Interview BB, Erbil on 24/06/2012; Interview AZ, Sulaimaniya on 06/06/2012; Interview BT, Erbil on 24/07/2012; Interview BU, Erbil on 24/07/2012
[1381] Woodrow Wilson International Center for Scholars, „Winning the Peace".
[1382] Interview BG, Erbil on 02/07/2012; Interview BK, Erbil on 12/07/2012; Interview AZ, Sulaimaniya on 06/06/2012
[1383] Interview BW, Sulaimaniya on 08/08/2012; Interview AX, Sulaimaniya on 03/06/2012; Interview CA, Sulaimaniya on 13/08/2012; Interview AI, Erbil on 16/04/2012
[1384] See e.g. Interview AZ, Sulaimaniya on 06/06/2012; Interview BQ, Erbil on 21/07/2012; Interview BJ, Erbil on 09/07/2012; Interview AF, Erbil on 09/04/2012

comparison to 10,603 men.[1385] As more fully elaborated above, schools, like family and social surroundings, can be considered as "human-making factories".[1386] Schools can change thinking and they will influence a person's mind for the rest of his or her life.[1387] Further, the teachers often provide role models for the children, and thereby play a decisive role in breaking down or in supporting stereotypes.[1388]

The results of the interviews conducted correlate with the results of the Kurdistan Regional Statistics Office, according to which the vast majority of men (71%) believe that it is women's main role to build up society and establish a household; while 24 per cent were of the opinion that the woman's most important role to give birth and raise their children.[1389]

The mother, especially in traditional societies, is the person who spends the most time with the child in the first years of its development. [1390] It is the parents who communicate values concerning war and peace to their children and mothers can have a great influence on the outlook of their children in these areas.[1391] The family is the first social institution which reinforces patriarchal relationships, which supports or works against gender discrimination and which influences social behaviour in general.[1392] The child will feel if something is important for the mother or not and will act accordingly. It follows that if the mother is a pacifist or puts a great emphasis on education, the child is likely though not inevitably to do so as well. Mothers are a driving force in forming their children, and through giving a young boy the feeling that he is superior to his female family members, and through giving a girl the feeling that it is her role to serve the men, the mother lays

---

[1385] Kurdistan Regional Government, "New School Year Starts".

[1386] Abu-Lughod (ed.), *Remaking Women*, 95.

[1387] Jolynn Shoemaker, "In War and Peace: Women and Conflict Prevention" *Civil Wars* 5(1) (2002): 49.

[1388] Colclough, "Achieving Gender Equality in Education," 7.

[1389] Kurdistan Regional Statistics Office, *Iraq Women Integrated Social and Health Survey, Men Influence* (I-WISH, October 2012) 1.

[1390] Kandiyoti (ed.), *Gendering the Middle East*, 206.

[1391] Judith Myers-Walls, Karen Myers-Bowman and Ann Pelo, „Parents as educators about war and peace" *Family Relations* 42(1) (1993): 66.

[1392] UNDP, *Arab Human Development Report 2005,* 16.

the foundation for the continuance of inequality between men and women in society.[1393]

As explained by a 20 year old house wife from Erbil, who had three children and had a very open and feminist outlook on the world,

> *"many of them (the women today) have an important position in the field of education and in educating. Some have educated their children in such a way that they can serve their home country. That is very great and a truly important role."*[1394]

Many people, especially from less educated backgrounds, see it as a "normal role" and not out of the ordinary that women have to educate the next generation and to pass on their national heritage to them. However, as explained by a young woman who herself had not finished school,[1395] women's roles as educators cannot be underestimated, and is in one way or another recognized by the whole of society.

About two thirds of the Kurds interviewed were of the opinion that women did not make a contribution to peace building, as they were not involved in high level politics.[1396] Amongst the one third who agreed that women have a role in conflict transformation, the majority saw this role in raising the next generation, as well as in supporting the men at home.[1397] As explained by different people in form of a metaphor, women in Kurdistan are the "interior ministry", caring for the family and society within, while men are the "exterior ministry" and depending on the position of the person the one or the other are slightly more important, but both are needed to stabilize the region.[1398]

Apart from supporting the decrease of violent behaviour, and supporting the increase of national development, it also falls upon the parents to convey gender ideologies to the next generation. With reference to gender equity within the households, several of the younger women interviewed complained that they were

---

[1393] Kandiyoti (ed.), *Gendering the Middle East,* 206.

[1394] Interview AI, Erbil on 16/04/2012

[1395] Interview AV, Sulaimaniya on 28/05/2012

[1396] See e.g. Interview BA, Erbil on 21/06/2012; Interview BN, Erbil on 17/07/2012; Interview BI, Erbil on 08/07/2012; Interview AX, Sulaimaniya on 03/06/2012; Interview AN, Erbil on 03/05/2012

[1397] See e.g. Interview BM, Erbil on 13/07/2012; Interview BX, Sulaimaniya on 09/08/2012; Interview AP, Sulaimaniya on 18/05/2012; Interview AJ, Erbil on 20/04/2012; Interview BB, Erbil on 24/06/2012

[1398] Interview CI, Vienna on 26/10/2012; Interview CK, Vienna on 20/10/2012

treated differently from their brothers, and that they had to fight harder to be allowed the same things as the male members of their families.[1399] These differences could also be witnessed, when observing family life, especially in more traditional households, where girls were rather taught the skills needed to become a good housewife and mother, while boys were encouraged to find a suitable career choice. When parents were then asked why they treated their children differently, the general reply was that they treated them equally, according to their roles in society[1400], or, when it came to individual freedom outside the house, that girls had to be treated differently for their protection.[1401]

The above statement seems to support one strand of criticism, which has been discussed time and time again in this thesis, namely that it is society, which is holding back the development of gender equality. While this might be true in certain individual circumstances, it cannot be accepted as a general conclusion. While parents might be the cause of restriction, they are also the cause of development and success for their children. This has been especially visible, when it came to the issue of education, as the majority of female students when asked how they achieved success in university despite possible social challenges, replied that it was due to their parents' support.[1402] Equally, when women with a visibly strong character were asked, where they thought they derived their personality from, one reason was often their mother. As explained by one woman:

> *"My mother was a really strong person. She just did everything she had to do and she wanted to do. She did not care if she sat with men or not, and she did not care how she dressed. My mother was a lot extremer than me. She always taught me that I could achieve everything I wanted in life and she made me to the person I am."[1403]*

It follows that mothers can have a great influence on the individual development of their children, and consequently also on the wider national development. However, for this to happen, support by society, as well as by the authorities, has to go hand

---

[1399] See e.g. Interview AJ, Erbil on 20/04/2012; Interview BY, Sulaimaniya on 10/08/2012

[1400] Interview BA, Erbil on 21/06/2012; Interview BR, Erbil on 22/07/2012; Interview BS, Erbil on 24/07/2012

[1401] Interview BE, Erbil on 26/06/2012; Interview BG, Erbil on 02/07/2012

[1402] Interview AJ, Erbil on 20/04/2012; Interview BB, Erbil on 24/06/2012; Interview BV, Sulaimaniya on 06/08/2012

[1403] Interview CH, Vienna on 05/11/2012

in hand. It is thus seen as detrimental and criticized by a considerable percentage of interviewees that the government and the public do not value the work of mothers sufficiently and that they are not well enough supported in their work of raising the next generation.[1404]

While the perceived lack of governmental support for mothers will most likely not directly change the way in which women raise their children, it is in general vital to recognize the role mothers are playing and to also make women aware of the importance of their position, especially as caretakers, in maintaining and reproducing a warlike society.[1405] It is necessary to make women aware of the importance of their roles in society, and especially of their roles as mothers. The norms and values with which they bring up their children can contribute on the one hand to discriminatory or violent behaviour, but on the other hand to open and positive contact with others, free of violence.[1406] This can lead to changes in thinking and to the prevention of future conflict.

The recognition of this role links to the previous consideration of the education of women, since, as mentioned by some, the role as a mother can only be properly fulfilled when the women themselves are educated. Currently the women are not sufficiently well educated, but are considered to be the educators of the next generation, which is simply not possible. This was also the opinion of more than half (60%) of the people interviewed. They agreed that women should participate in transformation as their role of mothers, but at the same time some were worried that women could convey the wrong ideas to their children. Several interviewees believed that women should only teach children, "*if they are educated enough*", which brings us back to the importance of educating women.[1407]

The section above argues that future development lies in the hands of every single person within society. Parents and especially mothers have the responsibility to

---

[1404] Interview BV, Sulaimaniya on 06/08/2012; Interview AP, Sulaimaniya on 18/05/2012

[1405] Development Studies Network, *Women, Gender and Development in the Pacific: Key Issues, Conflict and Peacemaking: Gender Perspectives*, (Australian National University 2000) 81.

[1406] Sorensen, *Women and Post-Conflict Reconstruction,* 11.

[1407] Interview AT, Sulaimaniya on 24/05/2012; Interview BC, Erbil on 25/06/2012; Interview BD, Erbil on 25/06/2012; Interview AY, Sulaimaniya on 04/06/2012; Interview BG, Erbil on 02/07/2012; Interview CJ, Vienna on 28/10/2012

influence the next generation in a way that enhances development at the individual as well as the regional level. Whether this is happening at the moment or not is very dependent on every individual. It is vital to make women aware of the important role they are playing. One way is to increase government support for housewives and women, or alternatively make such support more widely available as it cannot yet be felt by society as a whole.

As a general conclusion education has the ability to enhance positive development towards peace and social equality, but its potential until now has only partly been realised in the Kurdistan Region. While the government has clearly put a great effort into improving and enhancing education at all levels, from compulsory education, to higher education and adult education, these efforts have not yet been as successful as they might. The measures already undertaken, such as the building of new schools, the revision of the curriculum, the introduction of the "Roadmap to Quality" at university level, the initiation of a literacy campaign, and the support of international involvement at all levels, have certainly enhanced opportunities for the privileged classes in general, who have a feeling of positive development and peace within the region. However this is not the case for the lower classes. The reforms have not yet reached the general population and high quality education for children from less advantaged families is still scarce. This leads to families not sending their girls to school, especially at a later age, which results in their having the same social and economic problems as the previous generations. The same is true for the higher education system, where great developments have taken place, but large segments of the population are still excluded, and thus cannot feel the development of the region in the same way. Education in the Kurdistan Region might still, as argued by Seitz,[1408] be a tool to support social differences and inequalities rather than diminish them. Especially from a class perspective, gender equality is yet to be achieved. While the educational institutions for the upper classes can promote peace and gender equality within their system, the same cannot be said for the other educational institutions, and this leads to a general inequality within society.

[1408] Seitz, *Bildung und Konflikt*, 48/49.

From an individual point of view, this lack of equality and especially a lack of access to high quality education for all levels of society, impedes members of low income families, and especially girls, to fulfil their full potential. This results in possible social deprivation, economic hardship, or lack of self-fulfilment. The resulting loss of human potential for national development, the increasing disparity between social groups and the consequential lack of education for a substantial part of society are likely to increase the potential for conflict.

To redress these issues it would be advisable to further improve the quality of the schooling system by also viewing it from a gender perspective, to make higher education accessible to a higher percentage of the population, and to raise the status of mothers and teachers as educators for the next generation. The aim is to ensure that opportunities are given for all and that positive peace can be achieved at all levels. Finally, and maybe most importantly, there should be a special emphasis on diminishing the discrepancy between rich and poor, which might otherwise lead to the persistence of private violence and the flaring up of public violence once again.

VII. Conclusion

From the outset, it has been the aim of this thesis to research the effects of gender inclusive policies or the lack thereof on development in a region which is currently undergoing the process of conflict transformation; in this case: the Kurdistan Region.

It has been recognized today by the international community,[1409] as well as by academics[1410] that 'peace' is more than merely the laying down of arms and that the equality of men and women is hugely influential on development, arguably especially so after the cessation of violent conflicts.

[1409] United Nations. "Peace inextricably linked with equality between women and men says Security Council in International Women's Day statement".

[1410] See e.g.: Eifler and Seifert, *Gender Dynamics and Post-Conflict Reconstruction*; Enloe, *Nimo's War, Emma's War, Making Feminist Sense of the Iraq War*; or Pankhurst (ed.), *Gendered Peace, Women's Struggles for Post-War Justice and Reconciliation*.

Despite this knowledge, little has changed.[1411] Women are still often marginalized and gender inclusion is not seen as relevant at the time of peacemaking.[1412]

It was thus the aim to demonstrate on the example of a region currently in this situation, and which at the same time publicly set itself the task to stand up for the advancement of gender equality and for women in their society,[1413] what effect their gender policies have on the development of the region as a whole, as well as the development of their citizens on a more individual level.

A variety of different areas were considered, in order to give the reader a taste of the vast range of issues to be considered when it comes to developing a country or region, as well as to be able to derive to a realistic conclusion on the measures deployed by the KRG and the consequential effects on the region and society.

While this method proved far from fully inclusive, as the topics to be considered in a situation of conflict transformation seem never ending, it was possible to come to the general conclusion that while the KRG's actions to support women in the region are present to a certain extent, the policies in question have until now concentrated too much on quantity, i.e. sexual inclusion, rather than quality, i.e. gender inclusion. In addition, the fact that the policies deployed mainly target, or are accessible by, women from more advantaged family backgrounds, leads to inequality and an enhancement of the divide between rich and poor.

As could already be derived from an interpretation of previous research on similar subject matters, and as confirmed by the Kurdistan Region's citizens through their actions and points of views, it follows that the policies enacted by the government have not gone unnoticed and have had an effect on the development of the region, as well as its individuals, but with any positive effect remaining marginal.

The insufficient concentration on true gender equality, and especially the lack of attention to the inclusion of the different classes, has led to a loss of deeper transformative influence, which is visible in the current day-to-day life of the Kurds

---

[1411] Security Council, *Women and Peace and Security.*

[1412] Bonta, "Conflict Resolution among Peaceful Societies," 409.

[1413] RUDAW "Kurdistan Regional Government, PM Barzani kicks off campaign protecting women's rights, combating domestic violence".

in the region and which can be assumed to be detrimental to the region's development as a whole.

More specifically, when viewing in more detail the three different areas of involvement considered, the conclusions are:

A.   Politics

It has become consensus by academics and practitioners that inclusive involvement is needed in the political sphere in order to ensure development and the mitigation of conflict potential.[1414] Feminists in recent times have thereby particularly stressed that numbers are not enough and that it is vital to consider which type of women are getting involved.[1415] If done correctly, it is the presumption by the academics that equal representation on a political level will lead to enhanced appreciation of equality on the ground, and thus decrease conflict potential.[1416]

When it came to the issue of negotiations, it could be observed that the Kurdistan Region did not follow the recommendations by the international community[1417] and neither included women in numbers in their negotiations,[1418] nor gender considerations within the agreements reached as part of the negotiations,[1419] with the latter possibly, but not exclusively, being a consequence of the former.

[1414] Hunt, "Inclusive Security".
Suthanthiraraj and Ayo, *Promoting Women's Participation in Conflict and Post-Conflict Societies,* 11.
Caprioli and Boyer, "Gender, Violence and International Crisis," 505.
Zuckermann and Greenberg, "The Gender Dimensions of Post-Conflict Reconstruction," 79.
[1415] Al-Ali in Simon, "Kurdistan, Women in Iraq".
[1416] Melander, "Gender Equality and Intrastate Armed Conflict," 696.
[1417] Through Res 1325
[1418] Osman, "The Washington agreement, the negotiations".
Iraq Helsinki Project, "Invited Parties".
[1419] Osman, "The Washington agreement, the negotiations".
Sharifi, "Kurdish lawmaker".
Muhammed, "Problems with Baghdad are on the table".
Investors Iraq, "High-level Kurdish delegation to visit Baghdad to resolve the crisis file and Kirkuk oil".

Despite, or maybe because of, the lack of women and gender inclusion, the majority of the people interviewed were of the opinion that it would be advantageous to include women in this process.[1420]

As can be derived from previous findings by academics, and as also recognised by many among the interviewees, the lack of gender inclusion could be seen as taking away the chance for enhanced positive development on a national as well as individual level and has thus resulted in a loss of opportunities.

The situation was quite a different one when it came to the inclusion of women in parliament.

The KRG initiated the introduction of a quota and enshrined in its draft constitution that a minimum of 30 per cent of MPs have to be women.[1421] In addition, several committees specifically engaged with women's issues were created,[1422] women's inclusion was publicly promoted by the politicians in power,[1423] and conferences were held and sponsored to support women's standing in the political sphere as well as in society as a whole.[1424]

While all of this seemed to serve as a great starting point for a positive gender inclusion, the KRG arguably failed to take necessary further steps.

[1420] Interview BV, Sulaimaniya on 06/08/2012; Interview BN, Erbil on 17/07/2012; Interview BW, Sulaimaniya on 08/08/2012; Interview AJ, Erbil on 20/04/2012; Interview CI, Vienna on 26/10/2012; Interview CK, Vienna on 20/10/2012; Interview BQ, Erbil on 21/07/2012; Interview BR, Erbil on 22/07/2012; Interview CJ, Vienna on 28/10/2012; Interview CD, Vienna on 21/10/2012; Interview AN, Erbil on 03/05/2012; Interview BK, Erbil on 08/07/2012; Interview BS, Erbil on 24/07/2012

[1421] Draft of the Iraqi Kurdistan Region's Constitution 2009, Articles 41(2) and 106(2)

[1422] KRG, "The Kurdistan Parliament".
KRG-DFR, "Swedish rights training programme".
Rudaw, "New monitoring body established to protect women's rights".

[1423] PUKmedia, "President Barzani congratulates Kurdistan Women."
PUKmedia, "Dr. Masum: We wish woman to occupy sovereign position in Iraq".

[1424] Fallah, "Press Release Resolution and Suggestion".
No peace without justice, "International Conference on "The Role of Women in Peace-Building, Reconciliation and Accountability in Iraq"".
Chung, "Conference in Erbil Focuses on Women's Role in Politics".

It has been criticized that only so called 'token women' are present in Kurdistan's politics today,[1425] that only a certain class of women is in practice able to access the political sphere,[1426] and that they lack the necessary power.[1427]

The results of the actions taken by the KRG when it comes to women and gender inclusion into parliament are clearly visible in the region's development and within society.

While the efforts taken to increase the number of female MPs are certainly seen as positive by the international community and have also led to acceptance of female representatives by the population,[1428] the influence of the measures, just as the measures themselves, have until now only been on the surface.

On an individual level, the policies deployed cannot be seen to have resulted in increased gender equality, as the majority of the population in practice does not see themselves as being part of the development and many families would not allow their daughters to become politicians.[1429] In addition, as a consequence of their lack of power, und thus also a lack of accountability, many among the interviewees stated that they did not trust the capabilities of the female MPs.[1430]

The absence of actual power, as well as the non-existence of gender equal representation, also results in a loss for the development of region – as predicted by the academics[1431] – as many of their concerns are not heard, and their ideas not implemented.[1432]

It can thus be said that while the current measures certainly provide a starting point for the future, they are until now far from inclusive.

The issue of civil society organisations inside the region presents a similar picture.

[1425] Interview CB, Vienna on 04/12/2012

[1426] Al-Ali in Simon, "Kurdistan, Women in Iraq".

[1427] The Kurdish Globe, "Statistics suggest women's role is "weak" in government, politics and civil society".

[1428] See e.g. Interview AK, Erbil on 20/04/2012; Interview AR, Sulaimaniya on 21/05/2012; Interview AS, Sulaimaniya on 23/05/2012; Interview AT, Sulaimaniya on 24/05/2012

[1429] Interviews BY and BZ, Sulaimaniya on 10/08/2012

[1430] See e.g.: Interview BN, Erbil on 17/07/2012

[1431] Centre for Humanitarian Dialogue, "Women at the Peace Table - Nepal Roundtable".

[1432] Warvin, "Regional Parliament Denies Women Demand, Endorses Budget".
Hadi, "No one arrested for women provocation in Kurdistan Region, says MP"

While people in the region today have all the theoretical possibilities to found organisations and to let their voices being heard,[1433] and many are making great usage of these provisions,[1434] the government is said to merely support organisations of its liking.[1435]

Despite certain challenges it has been said that the continuous efforts of local women's groups and organisations have had an implication and positive influence for gender equality within the national development, as their tireless demands resulted in more gender focused legislation.[1436] Furthermore the NGOs are providing necessary services, which would otherwise be inaccessible in the region.[1437]

Considering the organisations' influence on women's personal lives, the situation looks different once more. Implementation of the gendered legislations is not consistent,[1438] and the different services provided by NGOs are not fully accessible to the population, as they are not widely known.[1439]

While the lack of support by the government for all organisations or initiatives equally, can thereby be seen as a detrimental factor for the influence of the grassroots level on development, the grassroots sector's scattered system and the lack of cooperation between the different organisations is equally detrimental.[1440]

Consequently it is positive that grassroots organisations in general have the possibility to blossom. Also many are also using these opportunities and are working hard to positively influence development in general, and gender equality in particular, in the region as well as to provide enhanced possibilities for local women, their lack of coherency and public presence leads to a lack of

---

[1433] Iraqi Constitution 2005 Article 20; Drat Constitution of the Kurdistan Region 2009 Articles 18, 21 and 26
[1434] Al-Ali and Pratt, "Between Nationalism and Women's Rights."
Al-Ali and Pratt, "Women's organizing and the conflict in Iraq since 2003".
[1435] Carpenter and Rubin, "Kurdistan's Troubled Democracy".
[1436] Al-Zubaidi, *Amendments to the Personal Status Law in Iraqi Kurdistan strengthen women's rights.*
[1437] Naggar, "Women's Rights in Iraqi Kurdistan".
Abdulrahman and Vormann, "Iraqi Kurdistan: Free yourself from FGM".
WADI, "Drei erfolgreich geführte Frauenzentren in Halabja, Kifri und Biara".
[1438] Al-Ali and Pratt, "Between Nationalism and Women's Rights," 342.
[1439] See e.g. Interview AZ, Sulaimaniya on 06/06/2012; Interview BB, Erbil on 24/06/2012; Interview BD, Erbil on 25/06/2012; Interview BF, Erbil on 29/06/2012
[1440] Al-Ali and Pratt, "Between Nationalism and Women's Rights," 344.

acknowledgment of their efforts by the local population, and hence to a lack of practical influence.[1441]

It can thus be seen that while positive measures are present in the political sphere, although more on certain levels than on others, their potential influence on society and consequently also on the region's development as a whole is minimalized by merely taking the initial steps and not implementing them to the fullest of their potential.

Following the assessment of academics and practitioners, who conducted research in other areas around the world, and following the evaluation of the interviews conducted, this leads to the conclusion that the policies deployed have until now only had a limited impact on the enhancement of gender equality and on the reduction of conflict potential on a nation, as well as individual level, within the region.

A comparable set of circumstances can be observed when it comes to the issue of economy:

B.   Economy

Since the fall of the Saddam regime and the cessation of armed conflict within the Kurdistan Region, economic prosperity had been one of the key aims of the KRG.

If deployed correctly, it has been agreed by experts that economic policies can constitute a key tool in managing peacebuilding.[1442] At the same time it has been agreed by the international community,[1443] and academics[1444] that gender inclusion in economic measures is vital for sustainable development.

While it is thus univocally agreed that women's inclusion is of great importance when considering national development, opinions are split on the advantages for women's individual development as well as the support of gender equality within society,[1445] the main argument being that without the necessary prerequisites, such

---

[1441] Interview AL, Erbil on 25/04/2012; Interview AM, Erbil on 27/04/2012
[1442] Raul Caruso, "On the Nature of Peace Economics," 1.
[1443] UNDP, *Powerful Synergies,* 3.
[1444] True, *The Political Economy of Violence against Women,* 85.
[1445] Heinrich Böll Stiftung, *Gender Politics Makes A Difference,* 52.

as a decrease in household chores, equal distribution of resources within the family, the recognition of non-marketed activities or the support by their social surroundings, the inclusion of women in the formal economic structure can be to their detriment.[1446] It follows that well thought-through and fully inclusive gender policies are necessary to ensure their positive effect on development.

In the Kurdistan Region, the foundation has been laid to include women into the formal economy,[1447] but it is arguable that the policies deployed are not sensitive enough to the practical circumstances.

When considering wider macroeconomic policies it could be observed that, as part of their official stance, Iraq and the Kurdistan Region, support gender inclusion into the economy,[1448] but this cannot be seen in practice.

Two of the main three foci of the KRG's path to economic success, namely internationalization of the region's economy and privatisation,[1449] are of minimal importance for the current practical day-to-day life of the majority of women in the region. Additionally it could not be seen that the KRG actively encourages a gender perspective within these areas.

The lack, or rather unclarity, of the KRG's consideration of gender as part of its national plan for economic success, could also be observed at the region's yearly budgeting.[1450] Despite the budget's great influential powers within the region, its usage is unclear, and gender consideration cannot be seen incorporated.[1451]

Considering the findings of feminist academics specialized in the area, the lack of gender inclusion as a whole in macroeconomic plans for the region can only result in a detriment for the region's development, as the policies will only target half of

---

[1446] UNDP, *Arab Human Development Report 2005*, 10.
Soderberg Jacobson, *Security on whose terms?*, 14.
Young and Scherrer (eds.), *Gender Knowledge*, 59/60.
[1447] See section V.A.2. on 'legal foundation'
[1448] IAU, *Iraq, The National Development Strategy*, 53/60.
Ministry of Planning – Republic of Iraq, *National Development Plan for the Years 2010-2014*, 18.
[1449] Law No.4 of 2006, Law of Investment in Kurdistan Region – Iraq
ILO, "Private Sector Development Programme".
[1450] Jamal, "Iraqi Kurdish State Budget Passes".
[1451] Warvin, "Regional Parliament Denies Women Demand, Endorses Budget".

the population, and will thus not be applicable to all. It follows that on an individual level, the lack of a clear gender inclusive strategy results in the people having the feeling that the majority of the female population in the region is not supported in their respective economic involvement,[1452] which leads to a lack of possibilities for the individuals, as well as a feeling of being treated in a discriminatory way, which in return fuels the possibility of conflict.

The situation is a slightly different one, when focusing solely on women's inclusion within the work force.

The KRG has been active in increasing the number of women in the labour market as part of its plan to increase economic productivity and to become more competitive internationally. Today, legislation provides equal access to work for men and women[1453] and the KRG is increasingly hiring female employees in the public sector.[1454]

While the slow increase of female workers[1455] provides the Kurdistan Region with a positive picture for the international community and makes available additional human resources for increasing economic prosperity within the region, it cannot be seen as supporting gender equality on a broader level. Lucrative employment possibilities are mainly seen as accessible to women from an upper class background, and women from low income families are seen as lacking equal opportunities.[1456]

As explained by the interviewees, as a consequence of society's preconceptions, it is not possible to women to accept any job,[1457] and it is said that the government is not active enough in improving this situation.[1458] The implementation of regulations for low-skilled employment is said to be scarce,[1459] part time jobs and

---

[1452] See e.g. Interview BO, Erbil on 18/07/1012; Interview AZ, Sulaimaniya on 06/06/2012; Interview BB, Erbil on 24/06/2012; Interview BC, Erbil on 25/06/2012; Interview BP, Erbil on 21/07/2012

[1453] Iraq Labor Code, Act No. 71 of 1987, Article 2

[1454] Mahmoud, "Steady Rise in Women Civil Servants".

[1455] Kurdistan Region Statistics Office, *Labour Force*, 2.

[1456] Interview CF, Vienna on 16/11/2012; Interview BS, Erbil on 24/07/2012; Interview BJ, Erbil on 09/07/2012

[1457] Interview AD, Erbil on 06/04/2012

[1458] Trades Union Congress, "Women in Iraqi Kurdistan".

[1459] Ibid.

flexible working hours are not widely on the agenda, and it is criticisable that the government is not providing women from less advantaged backgrounds with the skills necessary to succeed in the labour market.[1460]

Next to the criticism of one-sided support by the authorities, the majority of the people interviewed stated it is one of women's most important roles in Kurdish society to work,[1461] which resulted from the idea that all human resources are needed to build up the region.[1462] But just as it was the case with the theoretical support of women as politicians, support faded when it came to practically implementing the ideas within their own families.

This practical lack of backing by the government as well as society for women of all parts of society to participate in the labour force leads to a variety of consequences within the region.

On a national level, the lack of gender equality and the consequential very high percentage of 'economically inactive' women, leads to a lack in human resources and in a lack of development of gender equality, which in the long run is likely to minimize potential economic development, and thus supports conflict potential, which is increased if parts of the population lack in economic opportunities.

From an individual point of view, the lack of support results in a loss of opportunities, and thus in a loss of potential individual fulfilment, a loss of decrease in poverty, and in the subsistence of current patterns of male domination within the household and consequently results in no increase of gender quality. At the same time, it has been noted that this might equally be the case if job opportunities were offered, depending on which job opportunities these are.[1463]

[1460] IAU, *Iraq Labour Force Analysis 2003-2008*, 3.

[1461] Interview AF, Erbil on 09/04/2012; Interview AG, Erbil on 13/04/2012; Interview AK, Erbil on 20/04/2012; Interview AL, Erbil on 25/04/2012; Interview AP, Sulaimaniya on 18/05/2012

[1462] See e.g. Interview AM, Erbil on 27/04/2012; Interview AS, Sulaimaniya on 23/05/2012; Interview BB, Erbil on 24/06/2012; Interview BD, Erbil on 25/06/2012

[1463] UNDP, "Gender Inequality Index and related indicators".

Also when it comes to the setting up of businesses, women are in theory provided with the same possibilities as men, but specific gender sensitive measures, as well as wider support by society are lacking.[1464]

Just as with general employment, the reaction of the Kurdish population towards enhanced gender equality in business is in theory a positive one,[1465] while practical support is often lacking.[1466]

One measure adopted by the KRG to fight poverty and to empower women in this regard was the introduction of microfinance institutions within the region.[1467] While they arguably provide enhanced possibilities for starting up small businesses, especially for women in rural areas, or from less advantaged backgrounds, and to thus increase gender equality,[1468] their current influence is difficult to measure, as it is highly dependent on individual experience and no interviewee could be found, who was involved in the microfinance sector.

As a general conclusion it can thus be said that following current knowledge on the influence of gender equal provision in the economic sector or the lack thereof on development in a region at a time of conflict transformation, the mere concentration on numbers in the Kurdistan Region and the lack of support for creating a gender equal system at all levels of the economy is likely to be detrimental for national development, as a loss of human resources is the consequence, and it is disadvantageous to women's personal development, as many women are losing the chance to become economically active, and the ones who do, often suffer under a double burden.

These findings were supported by the reactions of the general public, who were in theory very much in favour of women's involvement, but who criticized the government's lack of support and who in practice often did not support gender equality within the system themselves.

[1464] Hacador, "The Big Success of women Entrepreneurs is a Kurdish Princess".

[1465] See e.g. Interview AP, Sulaimaniya on 18/05/2012; Interview AQ, Sulaimaniya on 19/05/2012; Interview AV, Sulaimaniya on 28/05/2012; Interview BC, Erbil on 25/06/212; Interview BD, Erbil on 25/06/2012

[1466] Interview AU, Sulaimaniya on 28/05/2012; Interview BM, Erbil on 13/07/2012

[1467] USAID Iraq, *State of Iraq's Microfinance Industry*, 5.

[1468] Johnson (ed.), *Small Change or Real Change?*, 54.

The consequential loss of resources for the region and individuals alike is likely to increase the potential in conflict over time, as the unequal support is likely to lead to an increase in the divide between rich and poor, rather than to equality, and will thus possibly fuel a feeling of hatred within the less advantaged parts of society.

One area, which has the capability to counter this development, but which once more shows similarities to the other areas discussed in the approach towards it by the government and its policies, is the area of education.

C.   Education

Whether for better or for worse, it seems agreed that education, whether inside or outside of educational institutions, is the most important and effective measure in influencing people's development.[1469]

According to the results of previous research conducted, the educational system is, either openly or through a 'hidden curriculum', the primary vehicle to either produce and legitimate inequalities and conflict within society,[1470] or to prevent future conflict from arising[1471] and to support the development of equality.[1472]

The positive effect of education has thereby be said to correlate with gender equality within the education system.[1473] Although it has been remarked that true gender equality will only be possible once a gender sensitive environment within the system is ensured[1474] and when high quality education for all is provided.[1475]

In the Kurdistan Region, all legal prerequisites have been laid down to make equality in education possible,[1476] and the KRG is aware that great improvement in the sector is needed and has worked hard to ensure that improvement is happening.

[1469] Seitz, *Bildung und Konflikt,* 48/49, 56.

[1470] Ibid., Shapiro, *Educating Youth for a World beyond violence,* 83.

[1471] Thyne, "ABC's, 123's, and the Golden Rule," 733.

[1472] Global Campaign for Peace Education, "Campaign Statement".

[1473] UNESCO Iraq Office, "Gender and Education for All".

[1474] Ibid.

[1475] Abu-Lughod, "Dialects of Women's Empowerment," 87.

[1476] Draft Constitution of the Kurdistan Region 2009, Article 27

In the case of children's schooling, the KRG has initiated the building of new schools,[1477] as well as the updating of the old curricula.[1478]

From a gender perspective, while the initiatives taken by the government have led to an improvement of numbers of young girls attending school,[1479] sexual equality has not yet been achieved within the school sector, arguably as a consequence of the lack of sufficient gender consideration when it came to the building of schools and its surrounding circumstances, such as geographical proximity adequate resources, teachers and change of ideologies of groups of the population.[1480] As confirmed by the interviewees, consequences are a great discrepancy in education between different social groups, as well as between the urban and the rural areas.[1481]

A similar situation persists when considering the quality of schooling, and specifically the inclusion of gender equality within the learning experience.

Great differences in the quality of education can be observed in the public and private sector education.[1482] In addition, a coherent framework for gender sensitive education is non-existent in the region. This was confirmed by the local population, who did not even consider gender considerations as being part of the school curriculum.[1483] While it was in general considered that further development of the sector is needed,[1484] education was by many not considered as being able to function as tool to bring transformation within society.[1485]

It follows that the government policies to improve the education system have until now not had a transformative effect, with gender equality neither existing in

---

[1477] Jamal, "Educational Reform in the Kurdistan Region of Iraq".

[1478] UNESCO, *World Data on Education, Iraq,* "The educational process".

[1479] Kurdistan Region Statistics Office, *Education,* 1.

[1480] UNICEF, *Girls Education in Iraq,* 20,21.

[1481] Interview BB, Erbil on 24/06/2012; Interview BY, Sulaimaniya on 10/08/2012; Interview BZ, Sulaimaniya on 10/08/2012

[1482] SABIS, "About SABIS".
Interview BY, Sulaimaniya on 10/08/2012

[1483] Interview AL, Erbil on 25/04/2012

[1484] Interview AS, Sulaimaniya on 23/05/2012; Interview BC, Erbil on 25/06/2012; Interview BT, Erbil on 24/07/2012

[1485] Interview CE, Vienna on 21/10/2012; Interview CK, Vienna on 20/10/2012

schools, as especially girls from low-income families often do not continue schooling after primary school, nor as part of the curriculum conveyed to the pupils.

As a consequence, gender equality is far from achieved and that once more potential human resources for the development of the region are lost, already at a very young age, which in return also results in possible unhappiness and the feeling of unfair treatment within less advantaged groups of society, which once more raises the conflict potential.

When considering women's individual situation, the loss of education for certain parts of the population leads to the subsistence of the patriarchal structure and to a loss of opportunities and feeling of equality for the young girls.

The problem of great discrepancy between the different parts of the population could also be observed in the case of higher education.

It is probably here that the government has made the biggest effort in ensuring the deployment and implementation of gender equal policies within the structure. New universities were opened to provide more young people with access to such,[1486] "A Roadmap to Quality" was introduced to increase quality at the institutions,[1487] and the different universities had been supported to incorporate gender study centres,[1488] and women empowerment programmes[1489] into their structure, and to raise awareness on combating domestic violence.[1490]

Even though there do not exist any provisions on positive discrimination or active encouragement of introducing female students into the higher education sector, the number of girls attending university is steadily rising. But just as in the case of MPs or government employees, it is mainly women from an advantaged family background who manage to go to university.

Despite the fact that university education is free in the region, boys and girls from less advantaged backgrounds are missing the possibility to access higher

---

[1486] Ala'Aldeen, "A determined push for higher education progress in Kurdistan".

[1487] Ministry of Higher Education and Scientific Research, *A Roadmap to Quality.*

[1488] Reisz, "Iraqi Kurdish scholars put gender theory to the test".

[1489] University of Kurdistan, Hawler, "UKH Leads Women Empowerment in Higher Education".

[1490] University of Zakho, "First Day of (16 Days Campaign) To Combat Domestic Violence".

education, as they often lack the necessary prerequisites, such as a good school education, or support by their social surroundings.

As explained by the interviewees, the government is thereby seen as mainly supporting already educated women,[1491] while not doing enough to support other women to get them to this point. In contrast, society is generally seen by the interviewees as supporting the mothers and housewives,[1492] possibly as a reaction to the considered lack of support by government. As a consequence, both groups of women feel treated unfairly.

The lack of consistent support once more leads to a loss of potential human resources for the region. Equally, it does not provide all women with the possibilities of enhancing their knowledge at university level, and thus cannot be said to fully support gender equality. Even the positive steps taken to ensure enhanced gender equality within the universities has to be considered with caution under this light, as it is merely accessible by a very small part of the population, although it has to be noted that it can be seen reflected positively on them.[1493]

It can thus be said that the 'inside' of the higher education system is mostly positive in the encouragement of positive development as well as gender equality within the region, but that access needs to be provided for all to make it fully successful.

One way of influencing the future generation's success in education is by educating their parents and by supporting them in educating their children.

The former has been aimed for by the KRG by introducing literacy programmes.[1494]

While the literacy initiatives as such could certainly be seen as positive, as a way of opening up employment possibilities, enhancing capabilities and creating role

[1491] Interview BX, Sulaimaniya on 09/08/2012; Interview BC, Erbil on 25/06/2012; Interview AW, Sulaimaniya on 01/06/2012; Interview AJ, Erbil on 20/04/2012; Interview AK, Erbil on 20/04/2012; Interview AL, Erbil on 25/04/2012; Interview AJ, Erbil on 25/04.2012

[1492] Interview AU, Sulaimaniya on 28/05/2012; Interview AG, Erbil on 13/04/2012; Interview BV, Sulaimaniya on 06/08/2012

[1493] See e.g. Interview BL, Erbil on 12/07/2012; Interview AS, Sulaimaniya on 23/05/2012; Interview AT, Sulaimaniya on 24/05/2012

[1494] UNESCO Iraq Office, National Strategic Framework for Literacy in Iraq, 21.

models for the younger generation, the arguable lack of sufficient gender consideration in its deployment,[1495] leads to a loss in its potential positive influence.

It can thus be seen that the government's actions, not only in training women for themselves, but supporting them in their roles as educators of the new generation has not been as extensive as would have been desirable.

For the interviewees the role of women as educators of their children, as well as children in general, is the most important.[1496] As the influence by mother on their children is substantial when it comes to the development of gender equality within society as well as to the general positive development for the region and to the decrease of conflict potential within the next generation, supporting them in their own development is vital, in order to ensure their positive influence on their children. But considering everything elaborated in this conclusion, this is only partly being done by the government at the moment.

Just as in the areas of politics and the economy, it can consequentially be concluded that the policies deployed by the KRG within the education sector are, while positive, not gender sensitive enough. Wider gender considerations are often not taken into account and the thereby created gap between the different groups of society, which results in a loss of potential in regional development, as well as in the advancement of gender equality.

When considering all the gender policies deployed, including the ones lacking, in the different areas, a general pattern can be observed. While the government has made an effort in introducing policies for the advancement of women's inclusion in every one of the three main areas discussed in this thesis, the deployment of gender inclusive policies within these main areas has been inconsistent. In addition, the policies deployed tend to merely focus on the increase of numbers, rather than the increase of gender inclusiveness, which has especially significant implications for the less wealthy part of the population, as the government policies

---

[1495] Ibid.pp.24-27.

[1496] Interview BW, Sulaimaniya on 08/08/2012; Interview AX, Sulaimaniya on 03/06/2012; Interview CA, Sulaimaniya on 13/08/2012; Interview AI, Erbil on 16/04/2012

in their practical implementation proved more successful for members of the upper classes, than for the rest of society.

Despite of a consequential loss of potential human resources for the region, the policies deployed can be seen as positive to a certain extent for the region's development, especially when it comes to positively influencing their standing within the international community.

For society on an individual level, the implications of the policies enacted are twofold. While the minority of the female population enjoys increased possibilities, a high standard of living, and a feeling of gender equality, for the majority of women, the policies do not seem to greatly influence their day to day life at the moment, and for many gender equality appears to be far from achieved. Considering thereby the definitions of peace by scholars, such as Galtung[1497] and Enloe,[1498] the lack of fully gender inclusive policies for all prevents women from experiencing peace, and thus prevents the region from creating sustainable peace. The great differences between the actions taken for the different social groups, and the consequential still existing divide between rich and poor is thereby one indicator for future conflict potential.

In order to work against this development and to ensure the achievement of gender equality within the region, as well as sustainable peace for the region and all its citizens, the KRG would have to use all their policies enacted until now as a starting point, and further develop them into more inclusive policies with a gender sensitive view, listen to the people influenced by these policies, and ensure the practical implementation for all levels of society.

As explained by representatives of the Kurdish population themselves:

Further development in the region, including the prevention of future conflict, requires a stop of corruption and an inclusive political system,[1499] the improvement

---

[1497] Galtung, *Peace,* 29/30.

[1498] Cynthia Enloe in Al-Ali, "Reconstructing Gender," 742.

[1499] Interview AY, Sulaimaniya on 04/06/2012; Interview AW, Sulaimainya on 01/06/2012; Interview AJ, Erbil on 20/04/2012

of the judiciary and the implementation of legislation,[1500] and respectful treatment without discrimination.[1501] Or as put by one young girl: All we need is

"Unity, Freedom and Love for All."[1502]

[1500] Interview BI, Erbil on 08/07/2012; Interview AG, Erbil on 13/4/2012

[1501] Interview AY, Sulaimaniya on 04/06/2012; Interview AR, Sulaimaniya on 21/05/2012; Interview AI, Erbil on 16/04/2012; Interview AE, Erbil on 09/04/2012

[1502] Interview AW, Sulaimaniya on 01/06/2012

VIII. Bibliography

Abdulla, Mufid, The Kurdistan Tribune "Asos Najib Abdullah: an exemplary KRG
minister" (20 October 2012) http://kurdistantribune.com/2012/asos-
najib-abdullah-exemplary-krg-minister/ (Accessed on 27.01.2013)

Abdulrahman, Sabah, UNAMI, "UNSC Resolution 1325: Fostering the role of
women in peace and security in Iraq"
http://unami.unmissions.org/Default.aspx?tabid=2792&ctl=Details&mid
=5079&ItemID=3512&language=en-US (Accessed on 16.10.2012)

Abdulrahman, Suaad and Vormann, Arvid, " Iraqi Kurdistan: Free yourself from
FGM – A new approach: Eye see Media"
http://www.mesop.de/2011/11/08/iraqi-kurdistan-free-yourself-from-
fgm-%e2%80%93-a-new-approach-eye-see-media/ (Accessed on
16.11.11)

AbuKhalil, As'ad, "Toward the Study of Women and Politics in the Arab World"
Spring Feminist Issues (1993): 3-19.

Abu-Lughod, Lila (ed.), *Remaking Women, Feminism and Modernity in the Middle
East,* Princeton: Princeton University Press, 1998.

Abu-Lughod, Lila, "Dialects of Women's Empowerment: The International Circuitry
of the *Arab Human Development Report 2005*" *Int. J. Middle East
Stud.* 41 (2009): 83-103.

Abu-Lughod, Lila, "Saving Muslim Women or Standing with Them?: On Images,
Ethics, and War in our Times" *Insayat* 1(1) (2003): 1-12.

Addison, Tony and Brück, Tilman, *Making Peace Work, The Challenges of Social
and Economic Reconstruction,* Basingstoke: Palgrave Macmillan,
2009.

Afshar, Haleh, "Women and Wars: Some Trajectories Towards a Feminist Peace"
Development in Practice 13(2/3) (2003): 178-188.

Ahmed, Rasheed Bakhtiar and Arif, Hussein Delshad, *Implementation of Iraqi
Labor Law 71 of 1987 in Dohuk Governorate,* Dohuk: Monitoring
Report, Hawar Printing Press – Dohuk 2012.

Akbar, Nooriahan, Al Jazeera, "Opinion, Afghan women fight back against
harassment" (13.07.2011)
http://www.aljazeera.com/indepth/opinion/2011/07/2011711133054075
80.html (Accessed on 5.12.2011)

Al Anfal Case no 1/C Second/2006

Ala'Aldeen, Dlawer Abdul Aziz, Minister for Higher Education and Scientific
Research, "Studying for Master's degree in Kurdistan Region,
Reforming the Master's Degree in the Kurdistan Region: Enhancing

Capacity and Quality" http://www.mhe-krg.org/node/117 (Accessed on 06.12.2012)

Ala'Aldeen, Dlawer, University World News, "A determined push for higher education progress in Kurdistan" (17 June 2012) http://www.universityworldnews.com/article.php?story=2012061506431 0850 (Accessed on 06.12.2012)

Al-Ali, Hashim, "Towards establishing a viable macroeconomic and medium-term fiscal framework integrated approach for the Iraqi economy" *International Journal of Contemporary Iraqi Studies* 6(2) (2012): 195-204.

Al-Ali, Nadje and Pratt, Nicola, "Conspiracy of Near Silence, Violence Against Iraqi Women" *Middle East Report* 258 (2011): 34-48.

Al-Ali, Nadje and Pratt, Nicola (ed.), *Women and War in the Middle East, Transnational Perspectives,* London: Zed Books, 2009.

Al-Ali, Nadje and Pratt, Nicola, "Between Nationalism and Women's Rights: The Kurdish Women's Movement in Iraq" *Middle East Journal of Culture and Communication* 4 (2011): 337-353.

Al-Ali, Nadje and Pratt, Nicola, "Women in Iraq: Beyond the Rhetoric" *Middle East Report* 239 (2006): 18-23.

Al-Ali, Nadje and Pratt, Nicola, "Women's organizing and the conflict in Iraq since 2003" *Feminist Review* 88 (2008): 74-85.

Al-Ali, Nadje, "Reconstructing Gender: Iraqi women between dictatorship, war, sanctions and occupation" *Third World Quarterly* 26(4-5) (2005): 739-758.

Al-Ali, Nadje, *Iraqi Women, Untold Stories from 1948 to the Present,* London Zed Books, 2007.

Al-Ali, Nadje, Muhammed, Muzhda, Kareem, Hataw, Salih, Dlaram, and Akreyi, Kawther, *Female Iraqi Academics in Iraqi Kurdistan: Roles, Challenges & Capacities*, Final Research Report, DelPHE Iraq.

Al-Hassan, Golley Nawar, "Is Feminism Relevant to Arab Women?" *Third World Quarterly* 25(3) (2004): 521-536.

Al-Jawaheri, Yasmin Husein, *Women in Iraq, The Gender Impact of International Sanctions,* London: I.B.Tauris, 2008.

Al-Karadaghi, Mustafa (Ed., Publ.) *Kurdistan times, A Biannual Political Journal, The Kurdish Nation has the Inalienable Right of Self Determination,* No.4, November 1995.

Al-Karadaghi, Mustafa (Publ.) *Kurdistan times, A Quarterly Political, Freedom and Democracy for Kurdish Nation,* No.1, Winter 1990.

Alsayid, Maamoon Mohammed, *Combating Physical Violence Against Women in Iraqi Kurdistan, The Contribution of Local Women's* Organisation, Thesis, Universitetet Tromso, Centre for Peace Studies 2009.

Alsumaria News, "Shoresh: Interview Kurdish delegation in Baghdad was a preliminary agreement to defer consideration of the contentious points" (18 June 2010) http://onedinar.forumotion.net/t17426-shoresh-interview-kurdish-delegation-in-baghdad-was-a-preliminary-agreement-to-defer-consideration-of-the-contentious-points (Accessed on 4.5.2012)

Al-Tawil, Namir, Hawler Medical University, "Research Article, Association of violence against women with religion and culture in Erbil Iraq: a cross-sectional study" (17 September 2012) http://www.biomedcentral.com/1471-2458/12/800/abstract (08.12.2012)

Al-Tikriti, Nabil, "War, State Collapse and the Predicament of Education in Iraq." In *Education and the Arab World: Political Projects, Struggles, and Geometries of Power, World Yearbook of Education 2010*, eds. André E. Mazawi and Ronald G. Sultana, 350-360. London: Routledge Press, 2009.

Al-Zubaidi, Layla, *Amdements to the Personal Status Law in Iraqi Kurdistan strengthen Women's Rights,* Heinrich Böll Stiftung, Interview, 2009.

Al-Zubaidi, Layla, *Amendments to the Personal Status Law in Iraqi Kurdistan strengthen women's rights,* Interview, Heinrich Böll Stiftung, 8 July 2009.

Al-Zubaidi, Layla, *Der Streit um Frauenrechte und das Personenstandsrecht: Testfall für die Demokratie im Irak,* Beirut: Heinrich Böll Stiftung, 2009.

American International School Kurdistan http://ais-k.org/ (Accessed on 04.01.2013)

Amin, Tareq, "KRG takes part in UN meeting on woman" (29 February 2012) http://www.iraqinews.com/variety/krg-takes-part-in-un-meeting-on-woman/ (Accessed on 03.08.2013)

Amnesty International, *Hope and Fear, Human Rights in The Kurdistan Region of Iraq,* London: Index: MDE 14/006/2009.

Amnesty International, *Reservations to the Convention on the Elimination of All Forms of Discrimination against Women, Weakening the protection of women from violence in the Middle East and North Africa region,* AI Index: IOR 51/009/2004, November 2004.

Anderlini, Sanam Naraghi and El-Bushra, Judy, *Post Conflict Reconstruction,* Inclusive security, Sustainable peace: A toolkit for advocacy and action.

Anderlini, Sanam Naraghi, *Women building Peace, What They Do, Why it Matters,* London: Lynne Rienner Publishers 2007.

Ashton, Charlotte, BBC-online "Iraq women: Winners or losers in a war-torn society?" (16.11.11) http://www.bbc.co.uk/news/world-middle-east-15743078 (Accessed on 27.11.11)

Askari, Ariz and Sagerma, Lawen, "Injustices have been committed" *soma, An Iraqi-Kurdish Digest* 49 (2008): 1.

Askari, Ariz, "A question of scruples" *soma, An Iraqi-Kurdish Digest* 49 (2008): 6.

Asuda, Combating Violence Against Women http://www.asuda.org/ (Accessed on 17.10.2012)

Badkhen, Anna, "Iraq: The Hidden Crime of Rape" (2009) http://www.pbs.org/frontlineworld/stories/pakistan802/video/video_index_baghdad.html (Accessed on 21.2.2012)

Bakker, Isabella and Silvey, Rachel, *Beyond States and Markets, the Challenge of Social Reproduction,* Milton Park: Routledge, 2008.

Bandarage, Asoka, "Women, Armed Conflict and Peacemaking in Sri Lanka: Toward a Political Economy Perspective" *Asian Politics & Policy* 2(4) (2010): 653-667.

Banister Soane, Ely, *To Mesopotamia and Kurdistan in Disguise: With historical notices of the Kurdish tribes and the Chaldeans of Kurdistan,* Boston: Adamant Media Corporation, 2005; original: 1928.

BBC online, "Iraq timeline" (21 May 2011) http://news.bbc.co.uk/2/hi/middle_east/737483.stm (Accessed on 10.10.2011)

BBC online, "Nobel Peace Prize recognises women rights activists" (7.10.2011) http://www.bbc.co.uk/news/world-europe-15211861 (Accessed on 7.10.2011)

BBC online, "Tripoli underground: Handbags, dinghies and secret emails" (3.12.2011) http://www.bbc.co.uk/news/magazine-16001247 (Accessed on 6.12.2011)

Beckwith, Karen (Review), "Bananas, Beaches & Bases: Making Feminist Sense of International Politics. By Cynthia Enloe" *The Journal of Politics* 53(1) (1991): 290-292.

Behera, Navniate Chadha (ed), *Gender, Conflict and Migration,* London: SAGE Publications, 2006.

Bell, Christine and O'Rourke, Catherine, "Peace agreements or pieces of paper? The impact of UNSC Resolution 1325 on peace processes and their agreements" *International & Comparative Law Quarterly* 59(4) (2010): 941-980.

Bell, Christine and O'Rourke, Catherine, *Opinion, UN Security Council 1325 and Peace Negotiations and Agreements,* Geneva: Center for Humanitarian Dialogue, March 2011.

Bell, Christine, *On the Law of Peace, Peace Agreements and the Lax Pacificatoria,* Oxford: Oxford University Press, 2008.

Berik, Günseli, Van der Meulen, Rodgers and Seguino, Stephanie, "Feminist Economics of Inequality, Development, and Growth" *Feminist Economics* 15(3) (2009): 1-33.

Bhatia, Michael, "Postconflict Profit: The Political Economy of Intervention" *Global Governance* 11(2) (2005): 205-224.

Bill of Rights for Kurdish Women

Bonta, Bruce, "Conflict Resolution among Peaceful Societies: The Culture of Peacefulness" *Journal of Peace Research* 33(4) (1996): 403-420.

Boudreaux, Andrea, "International Women's Day" (Arbil, Iraq, March 8, 2008) YouTube http://www.youtube.com/watch?v=4ooRd33Vu8A (Accessed on 7.12.2011)

Bouta, Tsjeard and Frerks, Georg, *Women's Roles in Conflict Prevention, Conflict Resolution and Post-Conflict Reconstruction, Literature Review and Institutional Analysis,* The Hague: Netherlands Institute of International Relations, Conflict Research Unit, 2002.

Boyce, James, "Aid for peace" *World Policy Journal* 15(2) (1998)

Boyer, Mark, et.al., "Gender and Negotiation: Some Experimental Findings from an International Negotiation Simulation" *International Studies Quarterly* 53 (2009): 23-47.

British International Schools, "Welcome to British International Schools in Kurdistan – Hawler" http://www.bis-kurdistan.co.uk/ (Accessed on 04.01.2013)

Brown, Lucy and Romano, David, "Women in Post-Saddam Iraq: One Step Forward or Two Steps Back?" *NWSA Journal* 18(3) (2006): 51-70.

Bryman, Alan, *Social Research Methods,* Third edition, Oxford: Oxford University Press, 2008.

Buchanan, Cate (ed.), *Women at the Indonesian peace table: Enhancing the contributions of women to conflict resolution,* Geneva: Center for Humanitarian Dialogue, November 2010.

Buck, Lori, Gallant, Nicole, and Nossal, Kim Richard, "Sanctions as a Gendered Instrument of Statecraft: The Case of Iraq" *Review of International Studies* 24(1) (1998): 69-84.

Buckley-Zistel, Susanne, *Conflict Transformation and Social Change in Uganda. Remembering after violence,* New York: Palgrave Macmillan, 2008.

Cahn, Naomi, "Women in Post-Conflict Reconstruction: Dilemmas and Directions" *William & Mary Journal of Women and the Law* 12(2) (2006): 335.

Cambridge International School-Kurdistan, "About CISK" http://www.cis-kurdistan.com/aboat-us/about-cisk.html (Accessed on 04.01.2013)

Caprioli, Mary and Boyer, Mark, "Gender, Violence and International Crisis" *Journal of Conflict Resolution* 45(4) (2001): 503-518.

Caprioli, Mary, "Primed for Violence: The Role of Gender Inequality in Predicting Internal Conflict" *International Studies Quarterly* 49(2) (2005): 161-178.

Carpenter, Scott and Rubin, Michael, Washington Post "Kurdistan's Troubled Democracy" (18 April 2009) http://www.meforum.org/2121/kurdistan-troubled-democracy (Accessed on 25.2.2012)

Carreiras, Helena and Kümmel, Gerhard (eds), *Women in the Military and in Armed Conflict*, Wiesbaden: VS Verlag für Sozialwissenschaften, 2008.

Cartier, Cyrille, "Iraqi Kurdish Women Voice Hopes for Constitution" (25 April 2006) http://womensenews.org/story/the-world/060425/iraqi-kurdish-women-voice-hopes-constitution (Accessed on 8.5.2012)

Caruso, Raul, "On the Nature of Peace Economics" *Peace Economics, Peace Science and Public Policy* 16(2) (2010): 1-13.

Center for Humanitarian Dialogue, *Meeting report, Oslo forum 2011, Annual Mediators' Retreat,* Oslo, Norway: 21-23 June 2011.

Center for Humanitarian Dialogue, *Peacemaking in Asia and the Pacific: Women's participation, perspectives and priorities* (Geneva: March 2011); Center for Humanitarian Dialogue, *Promoting gender issues in peace negotiations,* Annual Report 2010, Geneva: 2010.

Central Organisation for Statistics and Information Technology, Kurdistan Region Statistics Organisation, The World Bank, *Iraq Household Socio-Economic Survey, Volume II: Data Tables,* Tabulation Report, Volume II, IHSES-2007.

Centre for Humanitarian Dialogue, Vimeao, "Women at the Peace Table - Nepal Roundtable meeting Sept 2010" http://vimeo.com/16426911 (Accessed on 9.12.2011)

Centre for Humanitarian Dialogue, Vimeao, "Women in peacemaking – Africa" http://vimeo.com/8078047 (Accessed on 9.12.2011)

Chaliand, Gerard (ed.), *People without a country,* London: Zed Press, 1980.

Chandler, Robin, Wang, Lihua and Fuller, Linda (ed.), *Women, War and Violence, Personal Perspectives and Global Activism,* Basingstoke: Palgrave Macmillan, 2010.

Charter of the United Nations 1945

Chinkin and others, *Human Rights as General Norms and a State's Right to opt out, Reservations and Objections to Human Rights Conventions,* London: The British Institute of International and Comparative Law, 1997.

Chinkin, Christine and Charlesworth, Hilary, "Building Women into Peace: the international legal framework" *Third World Quarterly* 27(5) (2006): 937-957.

Christian Peacemaker Teams, *Kurdish Activists' Observations of Women's Rights in Iraqi Kurdistan between March 2012 and March 2013 and their hopes for the future,* Women's Rights, 2013.

Chung, Christian, Rudaw, "Conference in Erbil Focuses on Women's Role in Politics" (27.05.2012) http://www.rudaw.net/english/kurds/4780.html (Accessed on 16.10.2012)

Civil Pension Law No.33 of 1966

Clifford, James and Marcus, George (ed.), *Writing Culture, The Poetics and Politics of Ethnography,* Berkeley: University of California Press, 1986.

Cockburn, Cynthia, "'Democracy without Women Is No Democracy': Soviet Women Hold Their First Autonomous National Conference," *Feminist Review* 39 (1991): 141-148.

Cockburn, Cynthia, "Gender Relations as Causal in Militarization and War" *International Feminist Journal of Politics* 12(2) (2010): 139-157.

Cockburn, Cynthia, "On 'The Machinery of Dominance: Women, Men and Technical Know-How'" *Women's Studies Quarterly* 37(1/2) (2009): 269-273.

Cohn, Carol, "Feminist Peacemaking: In Resolution 1325, the United Nations Requires the Inclusion of Women in All Peace Planning and Negotiation" *The Women's Review of Books* 21(5) (2004): 8-9.

Cohn, Carol, Kinsella, Helen and Gibbings, Sheri, "Women, Peace and Security Resolution 1325" *International Feminist Journal of Politics* 6(1) (2010): 130-140.

Colclough, Christopher, "Achieving Gender Equality in Education: What Does It Take?" *Prospects* XXXIV/1 (2004): 3-10.

Constitution of Iraq 2005

Convention on the Elimination of All Forms of Discrimination Against Women 1979

Cooke, Miriam, *Women and the War Stories,* Berkeley: University of California Press, 1996.

Cuomo, Chris, "War is not just an event: Reflections on the significance of everyday violence" *Hypatia* 11(4) (1996): 30-45.

Danielle Mitterrand MLF International French School, Erbil http://erbilfrenchschool.com/about.php (Accessed on 04.01.2013)

Demir, Semra, "An Overview of Peace Education in Turkey: Definitions, Difficulties and Suggestions: A Qualitative Analysis" *Educational Sciences: Theory & Practice* 11(4) (2011): 1739-1745.

Deutsche Schule Erbil, "Willkommen" http://www.ds-e.org/ (Accessed on 04.01.2013)

Development Studies Network, *Women, Gender and Development in the Pacific: Key Issues, Conflict and Peacemaking: Gender Perspectives,* Australian National University 2000.

Diamond, Larry, "What went wrong in Iraq" *Foreign Affairs* 83(5) (2004): 34-56.

Djateng, Flaubert, Kayser, Christiane and Mavinga, Marie José, *Our contribution to peace: a patchwork of complementary actions,* Berlin: Civil Peace Services, 2009.

Doosky, Eli, Kurdish Globe, "Government works to reduce Kurdistan unemployment" (10 May 2011) http://www.krg.org/a/d.aspx?s=02010200&l=12&r=73&a=39943&s=010 000 (Accessed on 22.1.2013)

Draft Constitution of the Kurdistan Region 2009

Dworkin, Jonathan et.al, "The Long-Term Psychosocial Impact of a Surprise Chemical Weapons Attack on Civilians in Halabja, Iraqi Kurdistan" *The Journal of Nervous and Mental Disease* 196(10) (2008): 772-775.

Eifler, Christine and Seifert, Ruth (Hrsg), *Soziale Konstruktionen – Militär und Geschlächterverhältnis,* Münster: Westfälisches Dampfboot, 1999.

Eifler, Christine and Seifert, Ruth, *Gender Dynamics and Post-Conflict Reconstruction,* Frankfurt am Main: Peter Lang GmbH, 2009.

El-Kassem, Nadeen, "International Conference on Kurdish Women for Peace and Equality, March 8, 2007, Erbil, Southern Kurdistan" *Journal of Middle East Women's Studies* 3(3) (2007): 105-108.

El-Kassem, Nadeen, "The pitfalls of a 'democracy promotion' project for women of Iraq" *International Journal of Lifelong Education* 27(2) (2008): 129-151.

Engelhardt, Marc, *Starke Frauen für den Frieden, Die Nobelpreisträgerinnen Ellen Johnson Sirleaf, Leymah Gbowee und Tawakkul Karman,* Freiburg im Breisgau: Verlag Herder GmbH, 2011.

Enloe, Cynthia, "'Gender' Is Not Enough: The Need for a Feminist Consciousness" *International Affairs* 80(1) (2004): 95-97.

Enloe, Cynthia, "Police and Military in the Resolution of Ethnic Conflict" *Annals of the American Academy of Political and Social Science* 433 (1977): 137-149.

Enloe, Cynthia, "The Women behind the Warriors" *The Women's Review of Books* 10(5) (1993): 23-24.

Enloe, Cynthia, Connecticut College, Lectures, YouTube "Cynthia Enloe speaks on Women in Iraq" http://www.youtube.com/watch?v=BUVPm0vJINA (Accessed on 7.12.2011).

Enloe, Cynthia, *Globalization and Militarism, Feminists make the Link*, Plymouth: Rowman & Littlefield Publishers, 2007.

Enloe, Cynthia, *Nimo's War, Emma's War, Making Feminist Sense of the Iraq War,* Berkley: University of California Press, 2010.

Enloe, Cynthia, The Clarke Forum, YouTube "Women and Men in the Iraq War, What Can Feminist Curiosity Reveal" http://www.youtube.com/watch?v=XXUCLahznqs (Accessed on 7.12.2011)

Fallah, Soraya, World's Women for Life, "Press Release Resolution and Suggestion" (29.08.2009) http://www.wwfl.org/Persian/ (Accessed on 16.10.2012)

Fatma, Naib, Al Jazeera, "Women of the revolution" (19.2.2011) http://www.aljazeera.com/indepth/features/2011/02/2011217134411934738.html (Accessed on 5.12.2011)

Fischer-Tahir, Andrea , "Competition, cooperation and resistance: women in the political field in Iraq" *International Affairs* 86(6) (2010): 1381-1394.

Flach, Anja, *Frauen in der kurdischen Guerilla, Motivation, Identität und Geschlechterverhältnis in der Frauenarmee der PKK,* Köln: PapyRossa, 2007.

Ford, Nancy Gentile (Review), " Maneuvers: The International Politics of Militarizing Women's Lives by Cynthia Enloe" *The Journal of Military History* 65(4) (2001): 1175-1176.

Freedom House, "Iraq" (2004)
http://www.freedomhouse.org/template.cfm?page=173 (Accessed on 15.11.11)

Freedom House, "Women's Rights in the Middle East and North Africa 2010 – Iraq" (3 March 2010) http://www.unhcr.org/refworld/docid/4b990123c.html (Accessed on 22.2.2012)

Galtung, Johan, *Peace by Peaceful Means, Peace and Conflict, Development and Civilization,* Oslo: PRIO, International Peace Research Institute, 1996.

Galtung, Johan, *Peace: Research, Education, Action, Essays in Peace Research,* Volume 1, Copenhagen: Christian Ejlers, 1975.

Gardam, Judith and Charlesworth, Hilary, "Protection of Women in Armed Conflict" *Human Rights Quarterly* 22(1) (2000): 148-166.

Giles, Wenona and Hyndman, Jennifer (ed.), *Sites of Violence, Gender and Conflict Zones,* London: University of California Press, 2004.

Glaeser, Edward, Ponzetto, Giacomo and Shleifer, Andrei, "Why does democracy need education?" *Journal of Economic Growth* 12(2) (2007): 77-99.

Global Campaign for Peace Education, "Campaign Statement" http://www.peace-ed-campaign.org/statement.html (Accessed on 08.01.2013)

Global Fund for Women, "Top 10 Wins for Women's Movements", http://www.globalfundforwomen.org/impact/success-stories/top-10-wins-for-womens-movements (Accessed on 14.9.2011)

Goetz, Anne Marie and Hassim, Shireen (ed), *No Shortcuts to Power,* London: Zed Books, 2003.

Golan, Galia, "Viewpoints. The Role of Women in Conflict Resolution" *Palestine-Israel Journal* 11(2) (2004): 92-96.

Goodhand, Jonathan and Hulme, David, "From Wars to Complex Political Emergencies: Understanding Conflict and Peace-Building in the New World Disorder" *Third World Quarterly* 20(1) (1999): 13-26.

Goodhand, Jonathan, *Aiding Peace? The Roles of NGOs in Armed Conflict,* London: Lynne Rienner Publishers, 2006.

Grey, Sandra and Sawer, Marian, *Women's Movements, Flourishing or in abeyance?,* New York: Routledge, 2008.

Hacador, Solin, The Kurdistan Tribune "The Big Success of women Entrepreneurs is a Kurdish Princess" (24 December 2011) http://kurdistantribune.com/2011/big-success-of-women-entrepreneurs-kurdish-princess/ (Accessed on 27.01.2013)

Hadi, Dawan, Aknews, "No one arrested for women provocation in Kurdistan Region, says MP" (23.08.2012) http://www.aknews.com/en/aknews/3/322800/?AKmobile=true (Accessed on 16.10.2012)

Hague Appeal for Peace, "Global Campaign for Peace Education, Campaign Statement" (2003-2005) http://www.haguepeace.org/index.php?action=pe (Accessed on 15.07.2013)

Hamid, Zebari Abdel "Amendments Act of retirement and social security conference in Arbil" (30.10.2011) http://onedinar.forumotion.net/t37184-amendments-act-of-retirement-and-social-security-conference-in-arbil (Accessed on 27.01.2013)

Handrahan, Lori, "Conflict, Gender, Ethnicity and Post-Conflict Reconstruction" *Security Dialogue* 35(4) (2004): 431.

Hartwig, Elisabeth, *Rural African Women as Subjects of Social and Political Change, A Case Study of Women in Northwestern Cameroon,* Münster: LIT Verlag, 2005.

Hawler Medical University, "Vision and Mission" http://hmu.edu.iq/About/VisionandMission.aspx (Accessed on 08.12.2012)

Hawzhen, Rashadaddin, The Kurdish Globe, "Private schools provide better education in the region" (08 January 2011) http://www.kurdishglobe.net/display-article.html?id=1B11C0EEF9F7159B921BD87E606616E9 (Accessed on 05.01.2013)

Hedinger, Sandra, *Frauen über Kried und Frieden,* Frankfurt/Main: Campus, 2000.

Heinrich Böll Stiftung, *Gender Politics Makes A Difference, Experiences of the Heinrich Böll Foundation Across the World,* Berlin: Heinrich Böll Stiftung, 2009.

Hennerbichler, Ferdinand, *Die Kurden,* Mosonmagyaróvár: Edition fhe, 2004.

Human Rights Watch, "Iraqi Kurdistan: Law Banning FGM a Positive Step" (July 25, 2011) http://www.hrw.org/news/2011/07/25/iraqi-kurdistan-law-banning-fgm-positive-step (Accessed on 15.09.2011)

Human Rights Watch, *World Report 2012, Country Summary, Iraq,* January 2012.

Hunt, Swanee and Posa, Cristina, "Iraq's Excluded Women" *Foreign Policy* 143 (2004): 40-45.

Hunt, Swanee, "The Critical Role of Women Waging Peace" *Colum. J. Transnat'l L.* 41 (2002-2003): 557-572.

Hunt, Swanee, interviews with 15 Club of Madrid members on the importance of womens leadership in politics and peace processes, YouTube "Inclusive Security: The Importance of Women's Leadership in Conflict Resolution" (Club of Madrid's 2008 conference on Global Leadership for Shared Societies) http://www.youtube.com/watch?v=NgNgWBil950 (Accessed on 10.10.2011)

Hussein, Nabard, Rudaw, "Conflicting Unemployment Rates in Kurdistan" (07 March 2012) http://www.rudaw.net/english/kurds/4502.html (Accessed on 22.1.2013)

IAU, *Iraq – UN Women Project Activities by Governorate,* June 2011.

IAU, *Iraq Labour Force Analysis 2003-2008,* January 2009.

IAU, *Iraq, The National Development Strategy (2007-2010),* March 2007.

IAU, *Women in Iraq Fact sheet,* March 2012.

IFHS, *Republic of Iraq, Iraq Family Health Survey Report,* 2006/7.

ILO, "Private Sector Development Programme" (IRQ/08/01/UNQ, 2009-2011) (03 April 2012) http://www.ilo.org/public/english/region/arpro/beirut/what/projects/iraq/irq_08_01_unq.htm (Accessed on 22.1.2013)

Incesu, Fatma, *Die Stellung der Frauen in der kurdischen Gesellschaft,* Frankfurt am Main: Peter Lang, 2004.

Institute for International Law and Human Rights, *Women and the Law in Iraq,* Washington: December 2010.

Inter-Agency Information and Analysis Unit, UNESCO, "Literacy in Iraq Fact Sheet" (September 2010) http://www.iauiraq.org/documents/1050/Literacy%20Day%20Factsheet_Sep8.pdf (Accessed on 5.10.2011)

International Covenant on Economic, Social and Cultural Rights 1966

International Republican Institute, "Taskforce on Discrimination Against Women Launched in Iraq" (27.01.2012) http://www.iri.org/news-events-press-center/news/taskforce-discrimination-against-women-launched-iraq (Accessed on 17.10.2012)

International Trade Union Confederation, *2012 Annual Survey of Violations of Trade Union Rights – Iraq,* 6 June 2012.

Internationaler Verein für Menschenrechte in Kurdistan (Hrsg.), *Das Kurdische Volk – keine Zukunft ohne Menschenrechte,* Landesvertretung Niedersachsen: Dokumetation der internationalen Konferenz Bonn, 27. – 28. September 1991.

Inter-Parliamentary Union "IRAQ, Council of Representatives of Iraq" (31 July 2011) http://www.ipu.org/parline/reports/2151.htm (Accessed on 15.09.2011)

Inter-Parliamentary Union, "Women in National Parliaments" (31 August 2011) http://www.ipu.org/wmn-e/world.htm (Accessed on 10.10.2011)

Investors Iraq, "High-level Kurdish delegation to visit Baghdad to resolve the crisis file and Kirkuk oil" (6 August 2008) http://www.investorsiraq.com/archive/index.php/t-81206.html (Accessed on 3.5.2012)

IOM, *Sulaymaniyah, Governorate Profile, IDP and Returnee Assessment,* February 2010.

IOM-Iraq, *Female Headed Households,* Special Report 2011.

Iraq Helsinki Project, "Background" http://iraqhelsinkiproject.org/Default.aspx?pageId=500694 (Accessed on 11.5.2012)

Iraq Helsinki Project, "Helsinki Agreement" (28 April 2008) http://iraqhelsinkiproject.org/Default.aspx?pageId=500699 (Accessed on 1.3.2012)

Iraq Helsinki Project, "Invited Parties" http://iraqhelsinkiproject.org/Default.aspx?pageId=500702 (Accessed on 11.5.2012)

Iraq Labor Code, Act No. 71 of 1987

Iraq Legal Development Project, *The Status of Women in Iraq: Update to the Assessment of Iraq's De Jure and De Facto Compliance with International Legal Standards,* American Bar Association 2006.

Iraq: The Human Cost, "Widows in Iraq indicate scale of killing during U.S. war" http://mit.edu/humancostiraq/ (Accessed on 21.2.2012)

Iraqi Body Count, "Iraqi Deaths from Violence in 2010" (30 December 2010) http://www.iraqbodycount.org/analysis/numbers/2010/ (Accessed on 10.10.2011)

Iraqi Civil Code No. 40 of 1951

Iraqi Women's Democracy Initiative, "Fact Sheet, Women's issues" (30 April 2010) http://www.state.gov/s/gwi/rls/other/2010/141080.htm (Accessed on 27.2.2012)

Ismael, Shereen, "The lost generation of Iraq: children caught in the crossfire" *International Journal of Contemporary Iraqi Studies* 2(2) (2008): 151-163.

Jabar, Faleh and Dawod, Hosham (ed), *The Kurds, Nationalism and Politics,* London: SAQI, 2006.

Jabri, Vivienne, "Revisiting change and conflict: On Underlying Assumptions and the De-Politicisation of Conflict Resolution" *Berghof Research Center for Constructive Conflict Management* 5 (2006): 1-8.

Jad, Islah, "The NGO-isation of Arab Women's Movements" *IDS Bulletin* 35(4) (2004): 34-48.

Jamal, Randa, UN Assistance Mission for Iraq, "Educational Reform in the Kurdistan Region of Iraq" (19 August 2008) http://reliefweb.int/report/iraq/educational-reform-kurdistan-region-iraq (Accessed on 04.01.2013)

Jamal, Sangar, Niqash, "Iraqi Kurdish State Budget Passes – Eight Months Late, Against Strong Opposition" (12 July 2012) http://www.niqash.org/articles/?id=3085 (Accessed on 22.1.2013)

Jaquette, Jane and Summerfield, Gale (ed.), *Women and Gender Equity in Development Theory and Practice, Institutions, Resources, and Mobilization,* Durham: Duke University Press, 2006.

Jeong, Ho-Won, *Understanding Conflict and Conflict Analysis,* Thousand Oaks SAGE, 2008.

Johnson, Tina (ed.), *Small Change or Real Change? Commonwealth Perspectives on Financing Gender Equality,* London: Commonwealth Secretariat 2008.

Jordan, Ann, "Women and Conflict Transformation: Influences, Roles, and Experiences" *Development in Practice* 13(2/3) (2003): 239-251.

Kabeer, Naila, "Gender Equality and Women's Empowerment: A Critical Analysis of the Third Millennium Development Goal" *Gender and Development* 13(1) (2005): 13-24.

Kandiyoti, Deniz (ed.), *Gendering the Middle East, Emerging Perspectives,* London: L.B. Tauris Publishers, 1996.

Kandiyoti, Deniz (ed.), *Women, Islam and the State,* Basingstoke: Palgrave Macmillan, 1992.

Kandiyoti, Deniz, "Reconstruction & Women's Rights in Afghanistan," *ISIM Review* 20 (2007): 20.

Karam, Azza (ed.), *Women in Parliament: Beyond Numbers,* Stockholm: International IDEA Handbook Series 2, 1998.

Karam, Azza, "Women in War and Peace-building, The Roads traversed, the challenges ahead" *International Feminist Journal of Politics* 3(1) (2001): 2-25.

KDP, "Kurdistan Women Union" http://www.kdp.se/?do=women (Accessed on 15.10.2012)

Keddie, Nikki, *Women in the Middle East, Past and Present,* Princeton: Princeton University Press, 2007.

Kelly, Michael, "The Kurdish Regional Constitution within the Framework of the Iraqi Federal Constitution: A Struggle for Sovereignty, Oil, Ethnic Identity and the Prospects for a Reverse Supremacy Clause" *Pennsylvania State Law Review* 114(3) (2010): 707-808.

Kevane, Michael, *Women and Development in Africa, How Gender works,* London: Lynne Rienner Publishers, 2004.

Khidir, Jaafar Hussein, *The Kurds and Kurdistan and Recent Political Development of IKR,* Wien: Dissertation, Universität Wien, 2002.

Klages, Helmut, *Wertedynamik, Über die Wandelbarkeit des Selbstverständlichen,* Zürich: Edition Interfrom, 1988.

Korektel, "CEO – Ghada Gebara" http://www.korektel.com/top-links/about-us/ceo (Accessed on 27.01.2013)

Kreutzer, Schmidinger (Hg.), *Irak, Von der Republik der Angst zur bürgerlichen Demokratie?,* Freiburg: Ca Ira-Verlag, 2004.

KRG, "Council of Ministers finalises 2011 Kurdistan Region draft budget" (3 March 2011) http://www.krg.org/a/d.aspx?l=12&s=02010100&r=223&a=39080&s=010000 (Accessed on 22.1.2013)

KRG, "Kurdistan Investment Board Chairman visits Austria and Slovakia to discuss investment and trade opportunities" (January 2013) http://www.krg.org/a/print.aspx?l=12&smap=010000&a=46083 (Accessed on 22.1.2013)

KRG, "Kurdistan Regional Government ministers" (2009) http://www.krg.org/articles/detail.asp?smap=04060000&lngnr=12&rnr=159&anr=32148 (Accessed on 21.2.2012))

KRG, "Ministers Profiles, Ms Asos Najib Abdullah - Minister of Labour and Social Affairs" http://www.krg.org/articles/detail.asp?lngnr=12&smap=04090200&rnr=136&anr=32574 (Accessed on 15.10.2012)

KRG, "START Social Development Organisation concludes pilot women's skills programme" (11.10.2012) http://www.krg.org/articles/detail.asp?lngnr=12&smap=02010100&rnr=223&anr=45529 (Accessed on 15.10.2012)

KRG, "The Kurdistan Parliament"
http://www.krg.org/articles/detail.asp?rnr=160&lngnr=12&smap=04070 000&anr=15057 (Accessed on 15.10.2012)

KRG.org, "President Barzani receives senior Iraqi officials for talks" (30 April 2012) http://www.krg.org/articles/detail.asp?rnr=223&lngnr=12&smap=02010 100&anr=43764 (Accessed on 4.5.2012)

KRG-DFR, "Swedish rights training programme" (4 October 2011) http://dfr.krg.org/a/d.aspx?l=12&a=41303 (Accessed on 9.5.2012)

Krieger, Helmut, *Gender und bewaffnete Konflikte, Irak,* Vienna: Vienna Institute for International Dialogue and Cooperation, 2007.

Kurdish Human Rights Project, *The Role of Women in Civil society, Conflict Prevention, Resolution and Reconstruction,* Helsinki: OSCE Civil Society Forum, 2-3 December 2008.

Kurdish Human Rights Watch, "About us", http://www.khrw.org/?page_id=2 (Accessed on 16.11.11)

Kurdish Human Rights Watch, "Women's Programs" http://www.khrw.org/?page_id=90 (Accessed on 25.2.2012)

Kurdish Women's Rights Watch, front page, http://www.kwrw.org/ (Accessed on 16.11.11)

Kurdistan Board of Investment, "Education" http://www.kurdistaninvestment.org/education.html (Accessed on 06.12.2012)

Kurdistan board of investment, http://www.kurdistaninvestment.org/ (Accessed on 14.07.2013)

Kurdistan Region Draft Constitution 2009

Kurdistan Region Statistics Office, *Education,* Fact Sheet 2, October 2012.

Kurdistan Region Statistics Office, *Expenditures,* Fact Sheet 6, September 2012.

Kurdistan Region Statistics Office, *Labour Force,* Fact Sheet 3, September 2012.

Kurdistan Regional Government, "Fact sheet: Doing business in the Kurdistan Region" http://www.krg.org/p/p.aspx?l=12&s=050000&p=302 (Accessed on 14.07.2013)

Kurdistan Regional Government, "New School Year Starts" (22 September 2003) http://old.krg.org/news/index.asp (Accessed on 04.01.2013)

Kurdistan Regional Government, "Prime Minister Barzani's speech at launch of campaign to combat violence against women" (26 November 2012) http://www.krg.org/a/print.aspx?l=12&smap=010000&a=45955 (Accessed on 22.1.2013)

Kurdistan Regional Statistics Office, *Iraq Women Integrated Social and Health Survey, Knowledge and behavior of adolescent girls (10-14) age,* I-WISH, October 2012.

Kurth, Winfried, Janus, Ludwig und Galler, Florian (Hrsg), *Emotionale Strukturen, Nationen und Kriege,* Heidelberg: Mattes Verlag, 2007.

Kvinna till Kvinna Foundation, *Building Security – a contribution to the debate on security policy,* Stockholm 2011.

Lasky, Marjorie, *Iraqi Women under Siege,* CODEPINK/ Global Exchange 2006.

Lavin, Andrew, "Achieving Peace in Iraq through Negotiations: lessons learned from the Northern Ireland Peace Process" *Ohio State Journal on Dispute Resolution* 24(3) (2009): 571-612.

Law No.4 of 2006, Law of Investment in Kurdistan Region – Iraq

Leach, Fiona and Dume, Mairead (ed.), *Education, Conflict and Reconciliation, International Perspectives,* Bern: Peter Lang, 2007.

Lederach, John Paul and Moomaw, Jenner Janice (ed.), *A Handbook of International Peacebuilding, Into the Eye of the Storm,* San Francisco: Jossey-Bass A Wiley Imprint, 2002.

Lederach, John Paul, *Preparing for Peace, Conflict Transformation Across Cultures,* New York: Syracuse University Press, 1996.

Leezenberg, Michael, "Iraqi Kurdistan: contours of a post-civil war society", *Third World Quarterly* 26(4-5) (2005): 631-647.

Lidauer, Michael (ed.), *Women in Armed Conflict, Pilot Specialisation Course, International Civilian Peace-keeping and Peace-building Training Program, 12-24 October 2008,* Austrian Study Center for Peace and Conflict Resolution, December 2008.

Lovgren, Stefan, National Geographic News, "Nobel Peace Prize Goes to Micro-Loan Pioneers" (October 13, 2006) http://news.nationalgeographic.com/news/2006/10/061013-nobel-peace.html (Accessed on 15.09.2011)

Mac Ginty, Roger, *No war, no peace: the rejuvenation of stalled peace processes and peace accords,* Baskingstoke: Palgrave Macmillan, 2006.

Mahmoud, Nawzad, "Female Leaders Decline in Kurdistan" (Rudaw, in English – The Happening, 21.09.2011) http://www.rudaw.net/english/kurds/3993.html (Accessed on 1.10.2011)

Mahmoud, Nawzad, Rudaw, "Steady Rise in Women Civil Servants" (06 May 2012) http://www.rudaw.net/english/kurds/4707.html (Accessed on 27.01.2013)

Manning, Lory, "Military Women: Who They Are, What They Do, and Why It Matters" *The Women's Review of Books* 21(5) (2004): 7-8.

Marques, Jose and Bannon, Ian, *Central Amercia: Eduation Reform in a Post-Conflict Setting, Opportunities and Challenges,* CPR Working Papers, Paper No. 4, April 2003.

Mayer, Tamar (ed.), *Women and the Israeli Occupation: The Politics of Change,* London: Routledge, 1994.

Melander, Erik, "Gender Equality and Intrastate Armed Conflict" *International Studies Quarterly* 49(4) (2005): 695-714.

Meyda, Yegenoglu, *Colonial fantasies, Towards a feminist reading of Orientalism,* Cambridge University Press, Cambridge 1998.

Minister of Higher Education and Scientific Research, Kurdistan Region, Iraq, "A New PhD pathway in Kurdistan, Promoting Research and raising standards" http://www.mhe-krg.org/node/343 (Accessed on 06.12.2012)

Ministry of Higher Education and Scientific Research, "Equal Opportunities" http://www.mhe-krg.org/node/27 (Accessed on 06.12.2012)

Ministry of Higher Education and Scientific Research, "Higher Education in Kurdistan Region" http://www.mhe-krg.org/node/105 (Accessed on 06.12.2012)

Ministry of Higher Education and Scientific Research, "KRG-Scholarship program Human Capacity Development" http://www.mhe-krg.org/index.php?q=node/249 (Accessed on 06.12.2012)

Ministry of Higher Education and Scientific Research, "Universities in Kurdistan" http://www.mhe-krg.org/node/23 (Accessed on 06.12.2012)

Ministry of Higher Education and Scientific Research, *A Roadmap to Quality, Reforming the System of Higher Education and Scientific Research in the Kurdistan Region of Iraq, A Report on the Main Achievements, From 1ˢᵗ November 2009 to 1ˢᵗ September 2010,* Ministry of Higher Education and Scientific Research, Kurdistan Regional Government 2010.

Ministry of Planning – Republic of Iraq, *National Development Plan for the Years 2010-2014,* Baghdad 2010.

Ministry of Planning, "The Ministries of Planning, Education and Health announced the results of four RAND Projects to improve Region's health, Education and Economic Systems" (8 March 2011) http://www.mop-krg.org/index.jsp?sid=3&nid=52&y=2011&m=2&d=8&lng=en (Accessed on 04.01.2013)

Mlodoch, Karin, "'We Want to be Remembered as Strong Women, Not as Shepherds': Women Anfal Survivors in Kurdistan-Iraq Struggling for Agency and Acknowledgement" *Journal of Middle East Women's Studies* 8(1) (2012): 63-91

Moghadam, Valentine and Sadiqi, Fatima, "Women's Activism and the Public Sphere: An Introduction and Overview" *Journal of Middle East Women's Studies* 2(2) (2006): 1-7.

Moghadam, Valentine, "Patriarchy, The Taleban and politics of Public Space in Afghanistan" *Women's Studies International Forum* 25(1) (2002): 19-31.

Moghadam, Valentine, "Peacebuilding and Reconstruction with Women: Reflections on Afghanistan, Iraq and Palestine" *Development* 48(3) (2005): 63-72.

Moghadam, Valentine, *Modernizing women: gender and social change in the Middle East* (2nd Edition, Boulder: Lynne Rienner Publishers, 2003) 60.

Mohammed, Najiba, Rudaw "Kurdistan Govt To Introduce New System To Shelter Threatened Women" (16 November 2010) http://www.rudaw.net/english/culture_art/3298.html (Accessed on 27.01.2013)

Mohammed, Yanar, Organisation of Women's Freedom in Iraq "[Despite UN resolution 1325] Women of Iraq Left All Alone" (24 November 2010) http://www.global-sisterhood-network.org/content/view/2557/59/ (Accessed on 23.2.2012)

Mojab, Shahrzad and Gorman, Rachel, "Dispersed Nationalism: War, Diaspora and Kurdish Women's Organizing" *Journal of Middle East Women's Studies* 3(1) (2007): 58-85.

Mojab, Shahrzad, "Kurdish Women in the Zone of Genocide and Gendercide" *Al-Raida* XXI(103) (2003).

Mojab, Shahrzad, "Theorizing the Politics of 'Islamic Feminism'" *Feminist Review* 69 (2001): 124-146.

Mojab, Shahrzad, *Women of a Non-State Nation, The Kurds,* Costa Mesa: Mazda Publishers, 2001.

Muhammad, Najib, "Iraqi Kurdistan's private sector prefers female employees" (15 May 2010) http://www.ekurd.net/mismas/articles/misc2010/5/state3838.htm (Accessed on 27.01.2010)

Muhammed, Ako, "Problems with Baghdad are on the table" (29 October 2011) http://www.kurdishglobe.net/display-article.html?id=314A361429F26BAE682565C7423632C3 (Accessed on 3.5.2012)

Mustafa, Rabar Ruwayada, The Kurdish Globe, "'The opportunities are always there, but we need the right mindset for it' – Talar Faiq" (31 December 2012) http://www.kurdishglobe.net/display-article.html?id=DCA3483B1F76D860D6B9A36CDE2C203B (Accessed on 27.01.2013)

Myers-Walls, Judith, Myers-Bowman, Karen and Pelo, Ann, „Parents as educators about war and peace" *Family Relations* 42(1) (1993): 66-73.

Naggar, Mona, "Women's Rights in Iraqi Kurdistan: time for a Rethink" (21.3.2011) http://www.ekurd.net/mismas/articles/misc2011/3/state4880.htm (Accessed on 15.11.2011)

Nakaya, Sumie, "Women and gender equality in peace processes: from women at the negotiating table to postwar structural reforms in Guatemala and Somalia" *Global Governance* 9(4) (2003): 459-476.

Natali, Denise, "The Spoils of Peace in Iraqi Kurdistan" *Third World Quarterly* 28(6) (2007): 1111-1129.

Neissl, Eckstein, Arzt und Anker (Hrsg), *Männerkrieg und Frauenfrieden, Geschlechterdimensionen in kriegerischen Konflikten,* Wien: Promedia, 2003.

Neshat, Saeid, "A Look into the Women's Movement in Iraq" *Farzaneh* 6(11) (2004): 54-65.

Nester, William, *Globalization, War, and Peace in the Twenty-first Century* (New York: Palgrave MacMillan, 2010) 28.

No Peace Without Justice, "International Conference on "The Role of Women in Peace-Building, Reconciliation and Accountability in Iraq"" (Erbil, 27-28 January 2011) http://www.npwj.org/MENA/International-Conference-%E2%80%9CThe-Role-Women-Peace-Building-Reconciliation-and-Accountability-Iraq%E2%80%9D (Accessed on 1.10.2011)

No Peace Without Justice, *The Role of Women in Peace-Building, Reconciliation and Accountability in Iraq, Outcomes and Recommendations,* Erbil , Kurdistan-Iraq, 27-28 January 2011.

Nordstrom, Carolyn, "Women, economy, war" *International Review of the Red Cross* 92(877) (2010): 161-176.

Olson, Robert, *The Goat and The Butcher: Nationalism and State Formation in Kurdistan-Iraq since the Iraqi War,* Qosta Mesa: Mazda Publishers, 2005.

Opotow, Susan, Gerson, Janet and Woodside, Sarah, "From Moral Exclusion to Moral Inclusion: Theory for Teaching Peace" *Theory into Practice* 44(4) (2005): 303-318.

Osler, Audrey and Yahya, Chalank, "Challenges and complexity in human rights
        education, Teachers' understandings of democratic participation and
        gender equity in post-conflict Kurdistan-Iraq" *Education Inquiry* 4(1)
        (2013): 189-210.

Osman, Mahmoud, "The Washington agreement, the negotiations, the
        implementation and its prospects" (1 May 2001)
        http://kurdmedia.com/article.aspx?id=8013 (Accessed on 8.5.2012)

Pankhurst, Donna (ed.), *Gendered Peace, Women's Struggles for Post-War
        Justice and Reconciliation,* New York: Routledge, 2008.

Pankhurst, Donna, "The 'Sex War' and Other Wars: Towards a Feminist Approach
        to Peace Building" *Development in Practice* 13(2/3) (2003): 154-177.

Parliamentary Hearing at the United Nations, New York, 20-21 November 2008,
        Background document: Session II, "Sexual violence against women
        and children in armed conflict", http://www.ipu.org/splz-e/unga08/s2.pdf
        (Accessed on 13.9.2011)

Pateet, Julie and Harlow, Barbara, "Gender and Political Change" *Middle East
        Report* 173 (1991): 4-8.

Patriotic Union of Kurdistan, Leadership Council, "Program"
        http://www.pukpb.org/en/program (Accessed on 20.2.2013)

People's Development Association, front page,
        http://www.xelik.org/En/Default.aspx (Accessed on 16.11.11)

Posch, Walter und Brown, Nathan, *Kurdische Unabhängigkeitsbestrebungen und
        die irakische Verfassung,* Wien: Schriftreihe der
        Landesverteidigungsakademie, 03/2004.

Postgate, J.N. (ed.), *The Languages of Iraq, Ancient and Modern, The British
        School of Archaeology in Iraq,* Cambridge: Cambridge University
        Press, 2007.

Potter, Antonia, *Opinion, G is for Gendered: taking the mystery out of gendering
        peace agreements,* Geneva: Center for Humanitarian Dialogue, April
        2011.

Pratt, Nicola and Richter-Devroe, Sophie, "Critically Examining UNSCR 1325 on
        Women, Peace and Security" *International Feminist Journal of Peace*
        13(4) (2011): 489-503.

Pratt, Nicola, "Iraqi Women and UNSCR 1325: An Interview with Sundus Abbas,
        Director of the Iraqi Women's Leadership Institute, Baghdad, January
        2011" *International Feminist Journal of Peace* 13(4) (2011): 612-615.

Presse Agence France, "Kurdish women tell of rapes in Saddam's death camps"
        (10 October 2006) http://www.kurdishglobe.net/display-

article.html?id=B974F5B0DD6838F6A2EA19DB49F25E11 (Accessed on 23.2.2012)

Prime Minister Barzani, *Inaugral speech by KRG Prime Minister Nechirvan Barzani at the swearing in of the seventh KRG cabinet,* Erbil: inaugural speech, Kurdistan Parliament, 5 April 2012

Pugh, Michael, "Normative Values and Economic Deficits in Postconflict Transformation" *International Journal* 62(3) (2007): 478-493.

PUKmedia, "Dr. Masum: We wish woman to occupy sovereign position in Iraq" (8 March 2012) http://pukmedia.co/english/kurdish-women/178-dr-masum-we-wish-woman-to-occupy-sovereign-position-in-iraq (Accessed on 4.5.2012)

PUKmedia, "Kurdish delegation in Baghdad soon to discuss Separated Area" (3 October 2011) http://northerniraq.info/forums/viewtopic.php?f=1&t=7608#p57349 (Accessed on 3.5.2012)

PUKmedia, "President Barzani congratulates Kurdistan Women" (9 March 2012) http://pukmedia.co/english/kurdish-women/179-president-barzani-congratulates-kurdistan-women (Accessed on 4.5.2012)

Purkarthofer, Petra, *Gender und bewaffnete Konflikte, Vergleichsstudie*, Vienna: Vienna Institute for International Dialogue and Cooperation, 2008.

Rabar, Ruwayda Mustafah, "Kurdish women and their struggle for equality" (14 December 2010) http://www.ekurd.net/mismas/articles/misc2010/12/state4435.htm (Accessed on 23.2.2012)

Ramirez, Oriana, Operation 1325, Power to women in Peace Processes, "Women's Organisations Cooperating in Realising Resolution 1325, Expand collaboration between international missions and women's organisations" (25 November 2011) http://operation1325.se/en/nyheter/expand-collaboration-between-international-missions-and-women-s-organisations (Accessed on 23.2.2012)

Rashid, Amjad, Julian Havers (eds.), *Jobs for Iraq: An Employment and Decent Work Strategy*, International Labour Organisation 2007.

Rasul, Salman Ahmed, "Higher Education in the Kurdistan Region of Iraqi" (6 January 2012) http://www.ekurd.net/mismas/articles/misc2012/1/state5770.htm (Accessed on 03.08.2013)

Ratkovic, Viktorija and Wintersteiner, Werner (Eds.), *Yearbook Peace Culture 2010, Culture of Peace, A Concept and A Campaign Revisited*, Klagenfurt: Drava Verlag 2010.

Reardon, Betty, *Education for a culture of peace in a gender perspective,* Paris: The Teacher's Library, UNESCO Publishing, 2001.

Regan, Patrick and Paskeviciute, Aida, "Women's Access to Politics and Peaceful States" *Journal of Peace Research* 40(3) (2003): 287-302.

Reht, Elisabeth and Johnson-Sirleaf, Ellen, *Women, War, Peace: The Independent Experts' Assessment on the Impact of Armed Conflict on Women and Women's Role in Peace-building,* New York: UNIFEM, Progress of the World's Women 2002, Volume 1, 2002.

Reidar, Visser, "The Kurdish Issue in Iraq: A View from Baghdad at the Close of the Maliki Premiership" *The Fletcher Forum of World Affairs* 34(1) (2010): 77-93.

Reisz, Matthew, Times Higher Education "Iraqi Kurdish scholars put gender theory to the test" (13.10.2011) http://www.timeshighereducation.co.uk/story.asp?storycode=417730 (Accessed on 06.01.2013)

Resolution A/53/25 from November 10, 1998

Richmond, Oliver (Review), "Peace and Development: Strange Bedfellows? Postconflict Development: Meeting New Challenges by Gerd Junne; Willemijn Verkoren" *International Studies Review* 7(3) (2005): 437-440.

Richmond, Oliver, "A Genealogy of Peacemaking: The Creation and Re-Creation of Order" *Alternatives: Global, Local, Political* 26(3) (2001): 317-348.

Richmond, Oliver, "Emancipatory Forms of Human Security and Liberal Peacebuilding" *International Journal* 62(3) (2007): 458-477.

Rimmer, Stephen and Al-Ani, Mohammed, *Supporting Private Sector Development in Iraq,* World Bank, MENA Knowledge and Learning, Quick Notes Series, Number 48, November 2011.

Rolls, Sharon Bhagwan, "Women as Mediators in Pacific Conflict Zones", February 2007 http://www.isiswomen.org/index.php?option=com_content&task=view&id=436&Itemid=207_(Accessed on 14.09.2011)

Roni, Alasor, Ararat News and Publishing, "Minister Falah Mustafa: Kurdish Diaspora is an important asset for our future" (15.10.2012) http://www.krg.org/articles/detail.asp?smap=02010200&lngnr=12&rnr=73&anr=45562 (Accessed on 15.10.2012)

Rosenberg, Jennifer, 20th Century History Guide, "Top 5 Crimes of Saddam Hussein" http://history1900s.about.com/od/saddamhussein/a/husseincrimes.htm (Accessed on 25.2.2012)

Rudaw, "Kurdistan Regional Government, PM Barzani kicks off campaign protecting women's rights, combating domestic violence" (2 December 2012) http://www.krg.org/a/d.aspx?s=010000&l=12&a=46004 (Accessed on 22.1.2013)

Rudaw, "New monitoring body established to protect women's rights" (13 August 2012) http://www.krg.org/a/d.aspx?a=45015&l=12&r=73&s=02010200&s=010 000 (Accessed on 11.7.2013)

SABIS, "About SABIS" http://www.pppkurdistan-sabis.net/fakhir-mergasori/general/fakhir-about-sabis (04.01.2013) and SABIS, "Project Overview" http://www.pppkurdistan-sabis.net/fakhir-mergasori/general/fakhir-project-overview (Accessed on 04.01.2013)

SABIS, "Fees Structure" http://www.iscerbil-sabis.net/fees-structure/ (Accessed on 04.01.2013)

Sagerma, Jen, "Yes to gender equality" *soma, An Iraqi-Kurdish Digest* 49 (2008): 7.

Salim, Mehmet, und Kaufeldt, Ralf, *Daten und Fakten zu Kurden und Kurdistan, Eine Chronologie,* Köln: Pro Humanitate, 2002.

Salvesberg, Eva, Hajo, Siamend, und Borck, Carsten, *Kurdische Frauen und das Bild der kurdischen Frauen,* Münster: LIT Verlag, 2000.

Sarkisian, Lorin and Alasor, Roni, Ararat News-Publishing, "Minister Baban: Kurdish agricultural production should be self-sufficient and untimely provide food security for the region" (26 October 2012) http://www.araratnews.eu/nuce.php?aid=627 (Accessed on 27.01.2013)

Secretary-General, Report, *Improvement of the status of women in the United Nations system,* UN General Assembly, 65th session, Item 28(a), Advancement of women, 9.9.2010.

Security Council, *Women and Peace and Security,* Report of the Secretary-General 173, 2010.

Seewald, Magda Maria, *Bewaffnet mit Schwäche, kämpfen sie für den Frienden. Die Auswirkungen der Geschlechterverhältnisse im Israel-Palästina-Konflikt auf die Friendensarbeit von Frauen,* Wien: Dimplomarbeit, Universität Wien 2003.

Seitz, Klaus, *Bildung und Konflikt, Die Rolle von Bildung bei der Entstehung, Prävention und Bewältigung gesellschaftlicher Krisen – Konsequenzen für die Entwicklungszusammenarbeit,* Rossdorf: TZ-Verlagsgesellschaft, 2004.

Shapiro, Svi, *Educating Youth for a World beyond violence, A Pedagogy for Peace,* New York: Palgrave Macmillan, 2010.

Sharifi, Zia, "Kurdish lawmaker: Our delegation will visit Baghdad soon to discuss
the implementation of the Convention on the remaining Arbil" (23
November 2011) http://www.investorsiraq.com/archive/index.php/t-
164761.html (Accessed on 3.5.2012)

Sharoni, Simona, "Middle East Politics Through Feminist Lenses: Toward
Theorizing International Relations from Women's Struggles"
Alternatives: Global, Local, Political 18(1) (1993): 5-28.

Sharoni, Simona, "The Myth of Gender Equality and the Limits of Women's Political
Dissent in Israel" *Middle East Report* 207 (1998): 24-28.

Sharoni, Simona, "Women and Gender in Middle East Studies: Trends, Prospects
and Challenges" *Middle East Report* 205 (1997): 27-29.

Sharoni, Simona, "Women and the Gulf" *Off Our Backs* 21(2) (1991): 22.

Sharp, Heather, „Women challenge Jordan Nationality Law" (14.10.2011)
http://www.bbc.co.uk/news/world-middle-east-15306228 (Accessed on
16.10.2011)

Shepherd, Laura (ed), *Gender Matters in Global Politics, A feminist introduction to
international relations,* London: Routledge, 2010.

Shoemaker, Jolynn, "In War and Peace: Women and Conflict Prevention" *Civil
Wars* 5(1) (2002): 27-54.

Simon, James, "Kurdistan, Women in Iraq" (Video)
http://www.youtube.com/watch?v=x4POLH2O208 (Accessed on
15.11.11)

Sjoberg, Laura, *Gender and International Security, Feminist Perspectives,* London:
Routledge, 2010.

Sky, Emma, *Preventing Arab-Kurd Conflict in Iraq after the Withdrawal of US
Forces,* Washington: United Institution if Peace, Peacebrief 86, March
2011.

Social Welfare Law No. 126 of 1980

Soderberg Jacobson, Agneta, Kvinna till Kvinna Foundation, *Security on whose
terms? If men and women were equal,* Stockholm: 2009.

Sorensen, Brigitte, *Women and Post-Conflict Reconstruction, The War-torn
Societies Project,* Occasional Paper No. 3, 1998.

Stanek, Norbert, *Irak, Land zwischen Tradition und Fortschritt,* Wien: Druckkunst
Wien, 1980.

Stansfield, Gareth, *Iraqi Kurdistan. Political development and emergent
democracy,* London: RoutledgeCurzon, 2003.

Steenkamp, Christina, *Violence and Post-War Reconstruction, Managing Insecurity in the Aftermath of Peace Accords,* New York: I.B.Tauris, 2009.

Stilhoff Sörensen, Jens, *State Collapse and Reconstruction in the Periphery, Political Economy, Ethnicity and Development in Yugoslavia, Serbia and Kosovo,* New York: Berghahn Books, 2009.

SUH, "London's SOAS Signs Agreement with SUH" (31.05.2012) http://www.suh-edu.com/index.php?option=com_content&view=article&id=484%3Alondons-soas-signs-agreement-with-suh&catid=1%3Alatest-news&Itemid=162&lang=en (Accessed on 08.12.2012)

Suthanthiraraj, Kavitha and Ayo, Cristina, *Promoting Women's Participation in Conflict and Post-Conflict Societies, How Women Worldwide are Making and Building Peace,* Global Action to Prevent War, NGO Working Group on Women, Peace and Security, Women's International League for Peace and Freedom, August 2010.

Tamang, Stella, "Peace Teachers: The History of Tamang Women as Conflict Mediators And Why the Human Rights Movement Must Listen to Them" (2004) http://www.culturalsurvival.org/publications/cultural-survival-quarterly/nepal/peace-teachers-history-tamang-women-conflict-mediator (Accessed on 14.09.2011)

Taylor, Sarah and Mader, Kristina, *Mapping Women, Peace and Security in the UN Security Council, Report of the NGOWG Monthly Action Points, 2009-2010,* NGO Working Group on Women, Peace and Security, October 2010.

Taylor-Lind, Anastasia, "Warrior Women" (2003) http://www.bbc.co.uk/wales/southeast/sites/newport/pages/article_peshmerga.shtml (Accessed on 23.2.2012)

Tehranian, Majid (ed.), *Bridging a Gulf, Peacebuilding in West Asia,* London: I.B. Tauris, 2003.

The Chronicle, "Apply to University of Kurdistan Hawler? Not Recommended" (27 May 2010) http://chronicle.com/forums/index.php?topic=69283.0 (Accessed on 08.12.2012)

The Guardian, "Time for revenge" (28 February 2003) http://www.guardian.co.uk/world/2003/feb/28/gender.uk1 (Accessed on 23.2.2012)

The Illuminate Consulting Group, UK Higher Education International Unit, *UK Higher Education engagement with Iraq,* Research Series/4, June 2009.

The International Committee of the Red Cross in Iraq, *Women in War,* March 2009.

The Kurdish Globe, "KURDISTAN: Kurdish Women Seek More Participation in Government" (4 February 2012)

http://www.peacewomen.org/news_article.php?id=4629&type=news
(Accessed on 21.2.2012)

The Kurdish Globe, "Statistics suggest women's role is "weak" in government,
politics and civil society" (1 October 2011)
http://www.kurdishglobe.net/display-
article.html?id=9EDBB488AE5FA5A57B17A5F41D521667 (Accessed
on 21.2.2012)

The Kurdish National Congress of North America, *International Conference on
Kurdish Women for Peace and Equality, Resolution and Suggestions,*
Press Release – March 20, 2007.

The World Bank, *Gender Equality and Development,* Washington: World
Development Report, 2012.

Thyne, Clayton, "ABC's, 123's, and the Golden Rule: The Pacifying Effect of
Education on Civil War, 19080-1999" *International Studies Quarterly*
50(4) (2006): 733-754.

Tickner, Ann, *Gender in International Relations, Feminist Perspectives on
Achieving Global Security,* New York: Columbia University Press,
1992.

Tonias, Nuria and Villellas, Ana, *The Kurdistan Autonomous Region: Risks and
Challenges for Peace*, Quaderns de Construccio de Pau, Escola de
Cultura de Pau, July 2009.

Touma, Juliette, UNDP Iraq, *Women's Economic Empowerment Conference held
in Baghdad,* UNAMI Newsletter, Issue 27, October 2012.

Trades Union Congress, "Women in Iraqi Kurdistan – demanding their rights at
work and at home" (19 May 2010)
http://www.tuc.org.uk/international/tuc-17949-f0.cfm (Accessed on
29.01.2013)

True, Jacqui, *The Political Economy of Violence against Women,* Oxford: Oxford
University Press, 2012.

Turnbull, Colin, *The Mountain People,* London: Picador, Pan Books, 1974.

Tuyizere, Alice, *Peace, Gender and Development, The Role of Religion and
Culture,* Kampala: Makerere University, Fountain Publishers Ltd, 2007.

UCDP, "Conflict Encyclopedia" Uppsala Universitet
http://www.ucdp.uu.se/gpdatabase/search.php (Accessed on
12.09.2011)

UN Economic and Social Council 2010 Resolution 45/4 Women Economic
Empowerment

UN Iraq, *Women in Iraq Factsheet*, March 2013.

UN Security Council Resolution 1325 (2000), adopted by the SC at its 4213th
meeting on 31 October 2000

UNAMI, "Facts and Figures"
http://unami.unmissions.org/Default.aspx?tabid=2835&language=en-
US (Accessed on 8.5.2012)

UNAMI, "UN in Iraq, Frequently Asked Questions"
http://unami.unmissions.org/Default.aspx?tabid=3431&language=en-
US (Accessed on 8.5.2012)

UNdata, "Iraq", http://data.un.org/CountryProfile.aspx?crName=Iraq (Accessed on
16.09.2011)

Undata, "United Kingdom",
http://data.un.org/CountryProfile.aspx?crName=United%20Kingdom
(Accessed on 16.09.2011)

UNDEF, "News from the Field: Human rights education and promotion in Northern
Iraq" (11 February 2008)
http://www.un.org/democracyfund/XNewsIraq_ConcordiaProject.htm
(Accessed on 9.5.2012)

UNDP – Iraq, *Women's Economic Empowerment, Integrating Women into the Iraqi
Economy,* March 2012.

UNDP Iraq, *Budget Execution Support in the Kurdistan Regional Government,*
Project Document, April 2009.

UNDP, *Arab Human Development Report 2005, Executive Summary,* (2005)
http://www.arab-hdr.org/publications/contents/2005/execsum-05e.pdf
(Accessed on 28.11.11)

UNDP, Human Development Reports, "Gender Inequality Index and related
indicators" (2011)
http://hdr.undp.org/en/media/HDR_2011_EN_Table4.pdf (Accessed on
09.12.2011)

UNDP, *Powerful Synergies, Gender Equality, Economic Development and
Environmental Sustainability,* Report, September 2012.

UNESCO Iraq Office, *Literacy Initiative for Empowerment in Iraq 2010-2015,*
Literacy Needs Assessment Report, UNESCO.

UNESCO Iraq Office, Literacy Network for Iraq, "Gender and Education for All"
http://www.lifeforiraq.org/en/content/gender-and-education-all
(Accessed on 09.01.2013)

UNESCO Iraq Office, National Strategic Framework for Literacy in Iraq, 2011-2015,
UNESCO.

UNESCO Iraq Office, *The Power of Literacy, Stories from Iraq,* IQ/2011/PI/H/1 2011.

UNESCO Office for Iraq, "Involving local NGOs in Literacy programs in Iraq" (19 October 2011) http://www.unesco.org/new/en/iraq-office/about-this-office/single-view/news/involving_local_ngos_in_literacy_programs_in_iraq/ (Accessed on 09.01.2013)

UNESCO, International Bureau of Education, *World Data on Education, Iraq,* IBE/2011/CP/WDE/IQ, 7th Edition 2010/2011.

UNESCO, *World Atlas of Gender Equality in Education,* Paris: UNESCO, 2012.

UNESCO, World Education Forum, *The Dakar Framework for Action, Education for All: Meeting our Collective Commitments,* ED-2000/WS/27, Dakar, Senegal, 26-28 April 2000.

UNICEF, *Girls Education in Iraq,* 2010.

UNIFEM, "Establishing Women's Caucus within the main Political Blocks of the Iraqi Parliament" (November 2006) http://www.unifem.org.jo/pages/articledetails.aspx?aid=1082 (Accessed on 8.5.2012)

UNIFEM, "Iraq" (2007) http://www.utoronto.ca/wwdl/bibliography_war/UNIFEM%20-%20Iraq%20-%20women%20war%20and%20peace.htm (Accessed on 17.09.2011)

UNIFEM, "Towards Iraqi Gender Sensitive Constitution" (November 2006) http://www.unifem.org.jo/pages/articledetails.aspx?aid=1083 (Accessed on 8.5.2012)

UNIFEM, Facts & Figures on VAW, "Crimes against Women in Situations of Armed Conflict" http://www.unifem.org/gender_issues/violence_against_women/facts_figures.php?page=7 (Accessed on 12.09.2011)

United Nations and World Bank, *Joint Iraq Needs Assessment,* October 2003.

United Nations Economic and Social Commission for Asia and the Pacific, *Women and Armed Conflict, A Regional Analysis on Asian and the Pacific,* Bangkok: December 2009.

United Nations Security Council Resolution 1546 (2004), adopted by the Security Council at its 4987th meeting, on 8 June 2004.

United Nations Security Council Resolution 661, adopted on 6 August 1990.

United Nations Security Council Resolution 666, adopted on 13 September 1990.

United Nations Security Council Resolution 687, adopted on 3 April 1991.

United Nations Security Council Resolution 986, adopted on 14 April 1995.

United Nations, *Beijing Platform for Action* 1995

United Nations. Press Release SC/6816. "Peace inextricably linked with equality between women and men says Security Council in International Women's Day statement" (8. March 2000) http://www.un.org/News/Press/docs/2000/20000308.sc6816.doc.html. (Accessed on 10.10.2011)

United States - Kurdistan Business Council, http://uskbc.org/ (Accessed on 14.07.2013)

United States Forces - Iraq PAO, "Female Iraqi Soldiers explore roles, ethics at seminar" (22 February 2010) http://www.usf-iraq.com/news/press-releases/female-iraqi-soldiers-explore-roles-ethics-at-seminar (Accessed on 23.2.2012)

University Act, Ministry of Higher Education and Scientific Research, Kurdistan Region Iraq, http://www.mhe-krg.org/node/28 (Accessed on 06.12.2012)

University of Duhok, "Financial Aid" http://www.uod.ac/en/financialaid (Accessed on 08.12.2012)

University of Duhok, "Mission, Vision and Core Values" http://www.uod.ac/en/mission (Accessed on 08.12.2012)

University of Duhok, "The University" http://www.uod.ac/en/university (Accessed on 08.12.2012)

University of Duhok, "Undergraduate Admission" http://www.uod.ac/en/undergraduateadmission (Accessed on 08.12.2012)

University of Duhok, http://www.uod.ac/en/ (Accessed on 08.12.2012)

University of Kurdistan, Hawler, "About UKH" http://www.ukh.ac/listArticls.php?ZID=1&CID=1 (Accessed on 08.12.2012)

University of Kurdistan, Hawler, "Female Academic Network Workshop" http://www.ukh.ac/detailsArticls.php?ZID=1&CID=106&AID=1132 (Accessed on 08.12.2012)

University of Kurdistan, Hawler, "Katherine Carter" http://www.ukh.ac/detailsArticls.php?ZID=1&CID=106&AID=1141 (Accessed on 08.12.2012)

University of Kurdistan, Hawler, "UKH Leads Women Empowerment in Higher
Education"
http://www.ukh.ac/detailsArticls.php?ZID=1&CID=106&AID=602
(Accessed on 08.12.2012)

University of Kurdistan, Hawler, "UKH Students Fight Violence against Women"
http://www.ukh.ac/detailsArticls.php?ZID=1&CID=106&AID=913
(Accessed on 08.12.2012)

University of Kurdistan, Hawler, "University of Kurdistan Hewler Celebrated
International Women's Day"
http://www.ukh.ac/detailsArticls.php?ZID=1&CID=106&AID=1006
(Accessed on 08.12.2012)

University of Kurdistan, Hawler, "Women Leadership Seminars to UKH Female
Students"
http://www.ukh.ac/detailsArticls.php?ZID=1&CID=106&AID=689
(Accessed on 08.12.2012)

University of Sulaimani, "Study" http://www.univsul.org/E_U_Xwendin.aspx
(Accessed on 08.12.2012)

University of Zakho, "(16 Days Campaign) To Combat Domestic Violence Activities
from 29/11-3/12/2012 (10 December 1012) http://www.uoz-
krg.org/node/281 (Accessed on 12.12.2012)

University of Zakho, "First Day of (16 Days Campaign) To Combat Domestic
Violence" (27 November 2012) http://www.uoz-krg.org/node/278
(Accessed on 12.12.2012)

University of Zakho, "Second Day of (16 Days Campaign) To Combat Domestic
Violence" (29 November 2012) http://www.uoz-krg.org/node/279
(Accessed on 12.12.2012)

UNPO, *Presidential and Parliamentary Elections, Kurdistan Region of Iraq, 25 July
2009,* Election Observation Report, 2009.

Unrepresented Nations and Peoples Organisation, "Iraqi Kurdistan: Condemning
Femicide" (14 September 2012) http://www.unpo.org/article/14855
(Accessed on 03.08.2013)

USAID Iraq, *Provincial Economic Growth Program, State of Iraq's Microfinance
Industry,* Tijara, June 2011.

USAID Iraq, *State of Iraq's Microfinance Industry,* Tijara, June 2010.

USAID, *Kurdistan Region, Economic Development Assessment,* RTI International,
Local Governance Project, Final Report, December 2008.

Van Bruinessen, Martin, *Kurdish Ethno-Nationalism Versus Nation-Building States,
Collected Articles,* Istanbul: The Isis Press, 2000.

WADI and Zhyan group, "No bargaining about Women's Rights Issues in Iraqi
        Kurdistan" (8 March 2013)
        http://www.ekurd.net/mismas/articles/misc2013/3/state6907.htm
        (Accessed on 03.08.2013)

WADI, "Drei erfolgreich geführte Frauenzentren in Halabja, Kifri und Biara"
        http://www.wadi-
        online.de/index.php?option=com_content&view=article&id=79&Itemid=
        16 (Accessed on 16.11.11)

WADI, front page, http://www.wadi-online.de/ (Accessed on 16.11.11)

Waite, Louise, "How Is Household Vulnerability Gendered? Female-headed
        Households in the Collectives of Suleimaniyah, Iraqi Kurdistan"
        Disasters 24(2) (2000): 153-172.

Waladbagi, Salih, "350.000 people being literate since 2000 in Kurdistan" (08
        October 2011) http://www.kurdishglobe.net/display-
        article.html?id=6D96CE6D5F034867ABF590E232704E63 (Accessed
        on 09.01.2013)

Waladbagi, Salih, Kurdish Globe "Foreign Workers treated poorly in Kurdistan" (25
        June 2011) http://www.kurdishglobe.net/display-
        article.html?id=905044227805C6DD07851D94CE14711E (Accessed
        on 27.01.2013)

Waladbagi, Salih, The Kurdish Globe, "Anti-domestic violence law in Kurdistan" (3
        April 2012) http://www.kurdishglobe.net/display-
        article.html?id=2465D8372C87030A2C08D36A5B17ABD2 (Accessed
        on 8.5.2012)

Warvin, "Regional Parliament Denies Women Demand, Endorses Budget"
        (24.06.2012)
        http://www.warvin.org/drejaE.aspx?=hewal&jmara=335&Jor=4
        (Accessed on 15.10.2012)

Webel, Charles and Galtung, Johan, *Handbook of Peace and Conflict Studies,*
        New York: Routledge, 2007.

WFD, "UK MPs share experience with women counterparts in Kurdistan
        Parliament" (28.02.2012) http://www.wfd.org/wfd-
        news/latest/news.aspx?p=109549 (Accessed on 16.10.2012)

Williams, Nick, Los Angeles Times, "Kurdish leaders, Baghdad hold political talks
        WAR IN THE GULF" (21 April 1991)
        http://articles.baltimoresun.com/1991-04-
        21/news/1991111053_1_baghdad-kurdish-saddam-hussein (Accessed
        on 4.5.2012)

Wolf, Naomi, Al Jazeera, "Opinion, The price of oppressing your women"
        (5.10.2011)

http://www.aljazeera.com/indepth/opinion/2011/10/2011102133713539
233.html (Accessed on 5.12.2011)

Wölte, Sonja, *Human Rights Violations against Women during War and Conflict,*
Geneva: Women's International League for Peace and Freedom,
Report of a Roundtable Discussion parallel to the UN Commission on
Human Rights, 1997.

Women Empowerment Organisation, "WEO Profile", http://www.weoiraq.org/
(Accessed on 17.10.2012)

Woodrow Wilson International Center for Scholars, „Winning the Peace: Forum
Explores Role of Women in Post-Conflict Iraq"
http://www.wilsoncenter.org/index.cfm?fuseaction=news.print&news
(Accessed on 10.1.2011)

Workers' Pension and Social Security Scheme under Law No. 19 of 1971

World Bank, "Gender Dimensions of Private Sector Development, Capacity
Building for Women in Business, The Example of Iraq" *PSD Gender
Notes* 1(1) (2004): 1-4.

World Declaration on Education for All 1990

Yildiz, Kerim, *The Kurds in Iraq, The past, present and future,* London: Pluto Press
in association with Kurdish Human Rights Project, 2004.

Young, Brigitte and Scherrer, Christoph (eds.), *Gender Knowledge and Knowledge
Networks in International Political Economy,* Baden-Baden: Nomos,
2010.

Yuval-Davis, Nira, *Gender & Nation,* London: SAGE Publications, 1997.

Zarindast, Karen, „Afghan MP forced to stop hunger strike after 13 days"
(14.10.2011) http://www.bbc.co.uk/news/world-south-asia-15318141
(Accessed on 16.10.2011)

Zuckermann, Elaine and Greenberg, Marcia, "The Gender Dimensions of Post-
Conflict Reconstruction: An Analytical Framework for Policymakers"
Gender and Development 12(3) (2004): 70-82.

Zülch, Tilman, *Völkermord an den Kurden, Eine Dokumentation der Gesellschaft
für bedrohte Völker,* München: Luchterhand Literaturverlag 1991.

IX.   Appendix

A.   Field Research - Information on Interviews & Interviewees

Note: This section was deleted from the publicly available version of this thesis, for reasons of anonymity.

B.   Map of Iraq and the Kurdistan Region

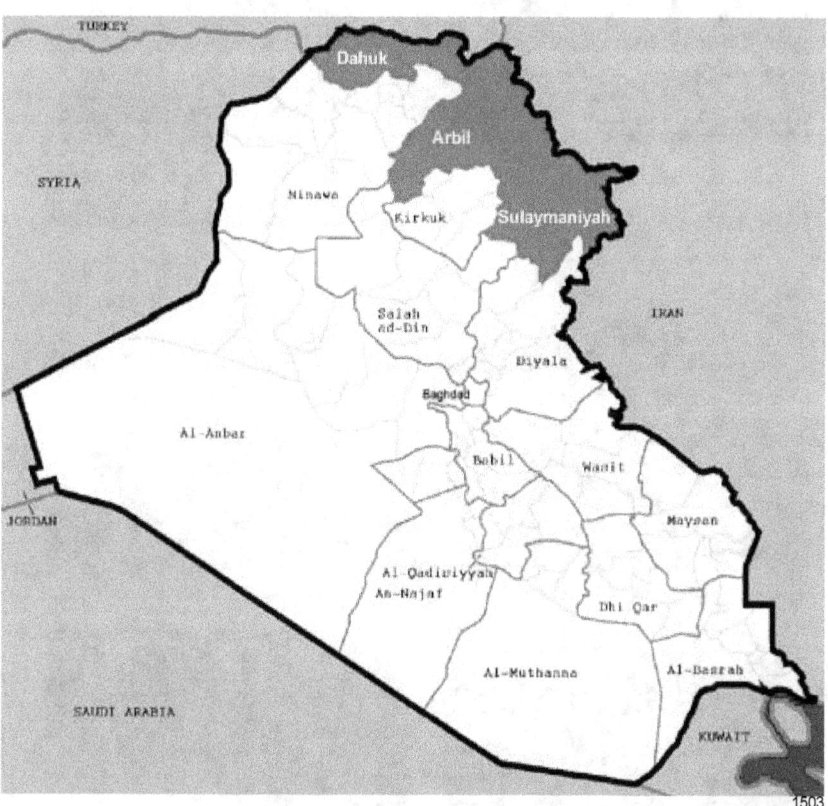

ERBIL

Erbil Centre

Erbil Centre

Erbil Citadel

Erbil Citadel

Erbil Citadel Museum

Erbil Centre

Erbil Market

Erbil Food Market

View of Erbil with Minara

Erbil Fabric Market

Erbil - Ankawa

Erbil development

Erbil Gated Community

Erbil German Village

Erbil Majidi Mall

Erbil Family Mall

CELEBRATIONS

Erbil Majidi Mall, New Years Eve 2011

Erbil Citadel, New Years Eve 2011

Erbil Nawroz Celebrations 2012

Erbil Shanidar Park

Erbil Minara Park

Erbil Primary School

Erbil University of Kurdistan Hawler

Erbil Statue of Dove

Erbil near UKH

Erbil Parliament

Erbil Parliament

On the Way to Shaqlawa

Castle near Salahaddin

Shaqlawa

Gai Beg

Bekhal

On the Way to Rwandz

Rwandz

Dohuk Dam

Dukan

On the Way to Sulaimaniya

Sulaimaniya Centre

Park near University of Sulaimani

Sulaimaniya Azadi Park

Sulaimaniya Kurdistan Women's Union

Sulaimaniya Amna Suraka Museum

Halabja Memorial

Ahmadawa

Village next to the Iranian Border

POLITICS

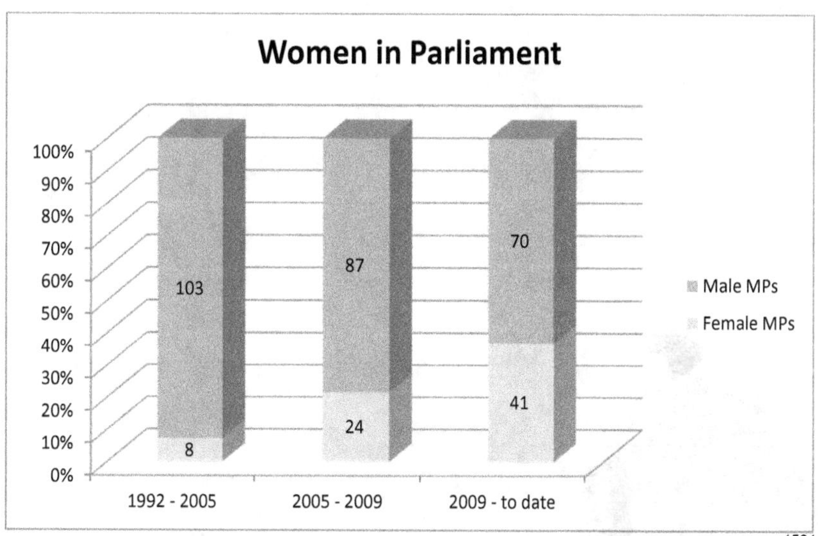

1504

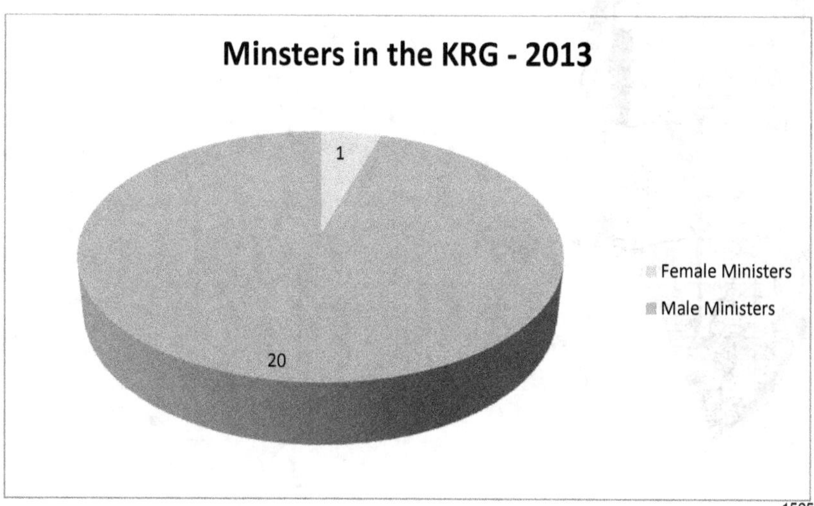

1505

[1504] The Kurdish Globe, "Statistics suggest women's role is "weak" in government, politics and civil society".

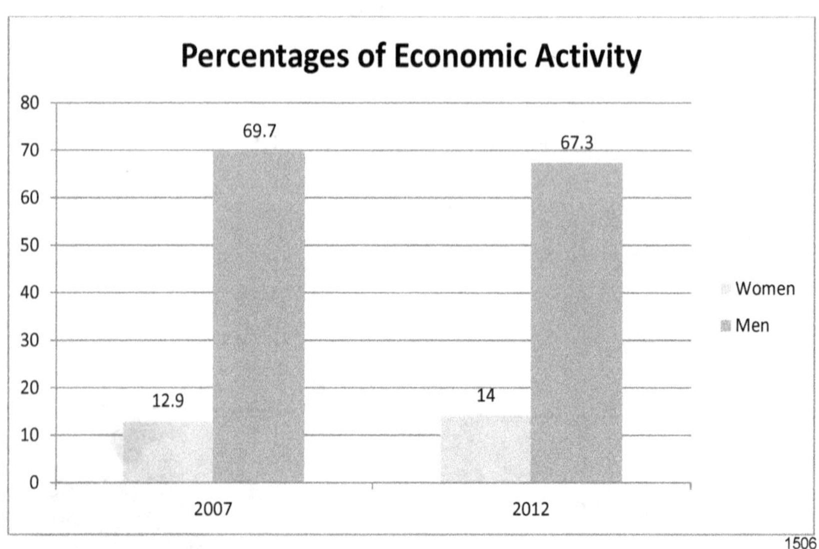

1506

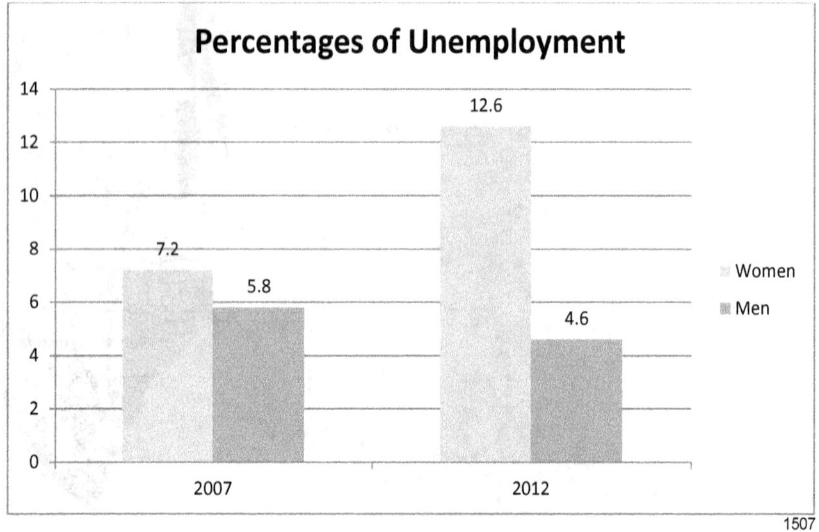

1507

[1505] KRG, "Kurdistan Regional Government ministers".

[1506] Central Organisation for Statistics and Information Technology, *Iraq Household Socio-Economic Survey,* 290.; Kurdistan Region Statistics Office, *Labor Force.*

[1507] Ibid.

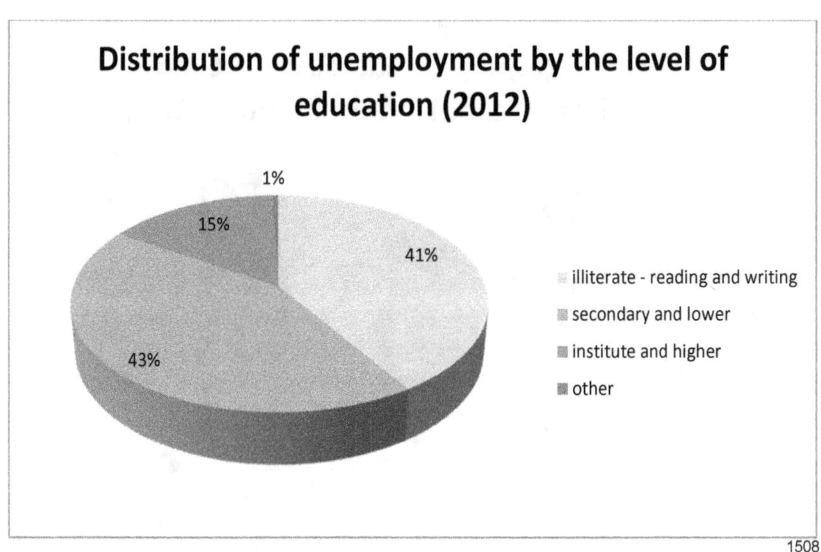

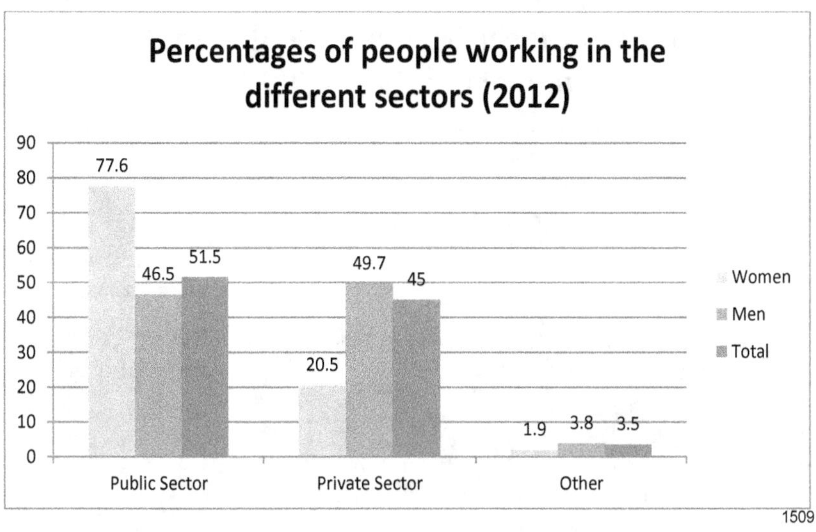

[1508] Kurdistan Region Statistics Office, *Labor Force*
[1509] Ibid.

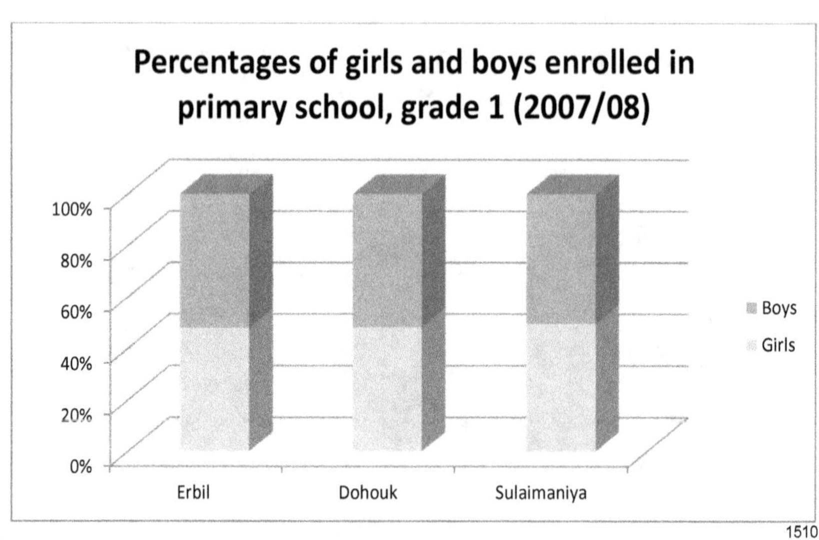

1510

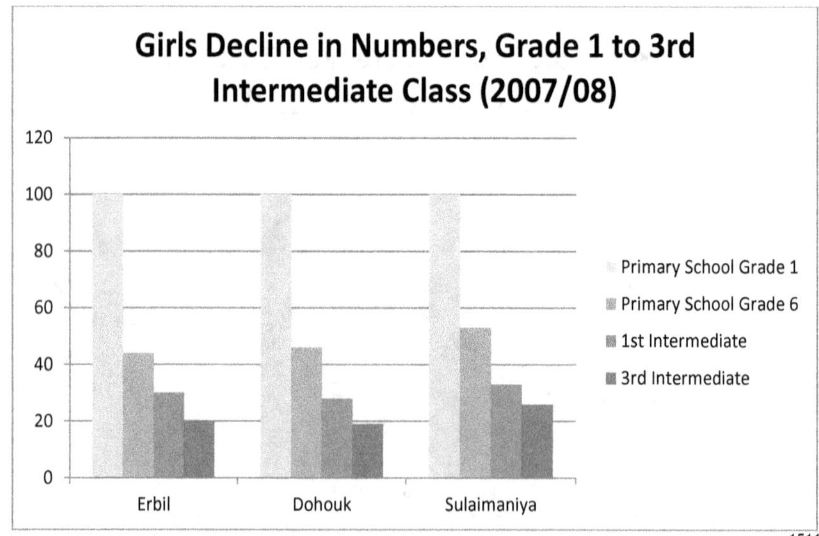

1511

[1510] UNICEF, *Girls Education in Iraq*.
[1511] Ibid.

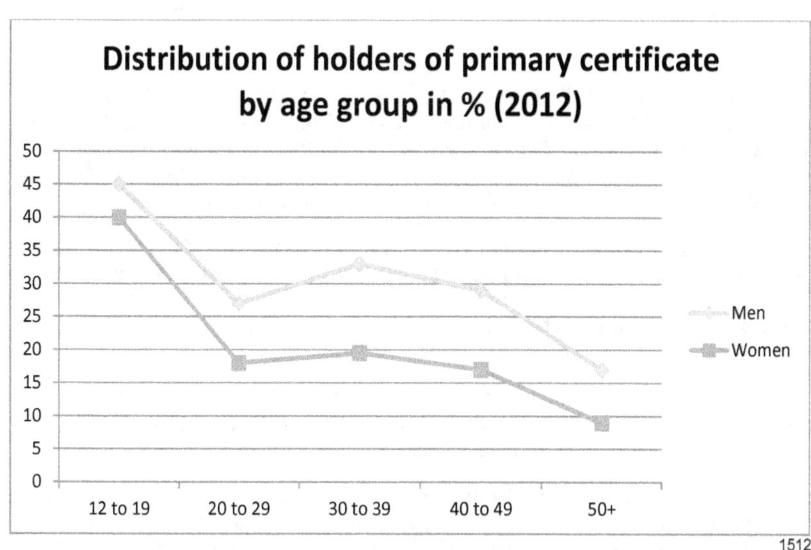

1512

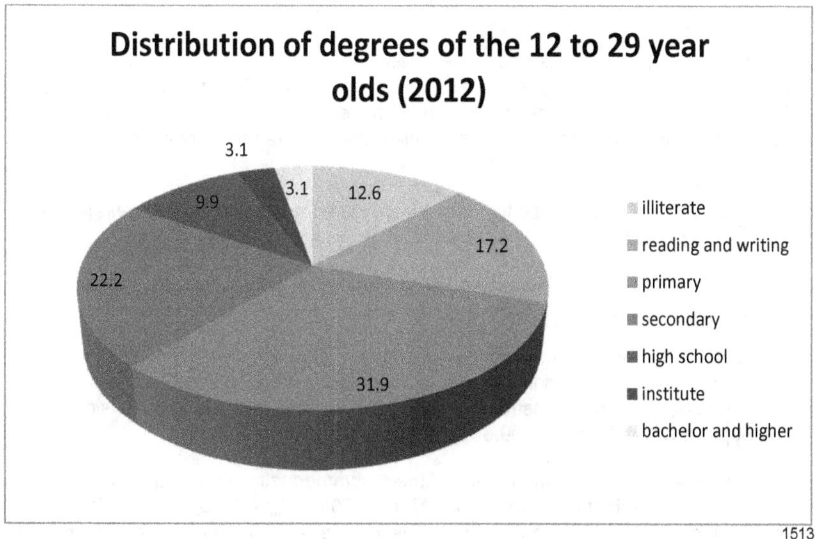

1513

[1512] Kurdistan Region Statistics Office, *Education.*
[1513] Ibid.

Adopted by the Security Council at its 4213th meeting, on 31 October 2000

The Security Council,

Recalling its resolutions 1261 (1999) of 25 August 1999, 1265 (1999) of 17 September 1999, 1296 (2000) of 19 April 2000 and 1314 (2000) of 11 August 2000, as well as relevant statements of its President, and *recalling also* the statement of its President to the press on the occasion of the United Nations Day for Women's Rights and International Peace (International Women's Day) of 8 March 2000 (SC/6816),

Recalling also the commitments of the Beijing Declaration and Platform for Action (A/52/231) as well as those contained in the outcome document of the twenty-third Special Session of the United Nations General Assembly entitled "Women 2000: Gender Equality, Development and Peace for the Twenty-First Century" (A/S-23/10/Rev.1), in particular those concerning women and armed conflict,

Bearing in mind the purposes and principles of the Charter of the United Nations and the primary responsibility of the Security Council under the Charter for the maintenance of international peace and security,

Expressing concern that civilians, particularly women and children, account for the vast majority of those adversely affected by armed conflict, including as refugees and internally displaced persons, and increasingly are targeted by combatants and armed elements, and *recognizing* the consequent impact this has on durable peace and reconciliation,

Reaffirming the important role of women in the prevention and resolution of conflicts and in peace-building, and *stressing* the importance of their equal participation and full involvement in all efforts for the maintenance and promotion of peace and security, and the need to increase their role in decision-making with regard to conflict prevention and resolution,

Reaffirming also the need to implement fully international humanitarian and human rights law that protects the rights of women and girls during and after conflicts,

Emphasizing the need for all parties to ensure that mine clearance and mine awareness programmes take into account the special needs of women and girls,

Recognizing the urgent need to mainstream a gender perspective into peacekeeping operations, and in this regard *noting* the Windhoek Declaration and the Namibia Plan of Action on Mainstreaming a Gender Perspective in Multidimensional Peace Support Operations (S/2000/693),

Recognizing also the importance of the recommendation contained in the statement of its President to the press of 8 March 2000 for specialized training for all peacekeeping personnel on the protection, special needs and human rights of women and children in conflict situations,

Recognizing that an understanding of the impact of armed conflict on women and girls, effective institutional arrangements to guarantee their protection and full participation in the peace process can significantly contribute to the maintenance and promotion of international peace and security,

Noting the need to consolidate data on the impact of armed conflict on women and girls,

1. *Urges* Member States to ensure increased representation of women at all decision-making levels in national, regional and international institutions and mechanisms for the prevention, management, and resolution of conflict;

2. *Encourages* the Secretary-General to implement his strategic plan of action (A/49/587) calling for an increase in the participation of women at decisionmaking levels in conflict resolution and peace processes;

3. *Urges* the Secretary-General to appoint more women as special representatives and envoys to pursue good offices on his behalf, and in this regard *calls on* Member States to provide candidates to the Secretary-General, for inclusion in a regularly updated centralized roster;

4. *Further urges* the Secretary-General to seek to expand the role and contribution of women in United Nations field-based operations, and especially among military observers, civilian police, human rights and humanitarian personnel;

5. *Expresses* its willingness to incorporate a gender perspective into peacekeeping operations, and *urges* the Secretary-General to ensure that, where appropriate, field operations include a gender component;

6. *Requests* the Secretary-General to provide to Member States training guidelines and materials on the protection, rights and the particular needs of women, as well as on the importance of involving women in all peacekeeping and peacebuilding measures, *invites* Member States to incorporate these elements as well as HIV/AIDS awareness training into their national training programmes for military and civilian police personnel in preparation for deployment, and *further requests* the Secretary-General to ensure that civilian personnel of peacekeeping operations receive similar training;

7. *Urges* Member States to increase their voluntary financial, technical and logistical support for gender-sensitive training efforts, including those undertaken by relevant funds and programmes, inter alia, the United Nations Fund for Women and United Nations Children's Fund, and by the Office of the United Nations High Commissioner for Refugees and other relevant bodies;

8. *Calls on* all actors involved, when negotiating and implementing peace agreements, to adopt a gender perspective, including, inter alia:

(a) The special needs of women and girls during repatriation and resettlement and for rehabilitation, reintegration and post-conflict reconstruction;

(b) Measures that support local women's peace initiatives and indigenous processes for conflict resolution, and that involve women in all of the implementation mechanisms of the peace agreements;

(c) Measures that ensure the protection of and respect for human rights of women and girls, particularly as they relate to the constitution, the electoral system, the police and the judiciary;

9. *Calls upon* all parties to armed conflict to respect fully international law applicable to the rights and protection of women and girls, especially as civilians, in particular the obligations applicable to them under the Geneva Conventions of 1949 and

the Additional Protocols thereto of 1977, the Refugee Convention of 1951 and the Protocol thereto of 1967, the Convention on the Elimination of All Forms of Discrimination against Women of 1979 and the Optional Protocol thereto of 1999 and the United Nations Convention on the Rights of the Child of 1989 and the two Optional Protocols thereto of 25 May 2000, and to bear in mind the relevant provisions of the Rome Statute of the International Criminal Court;

10. *Calls on* all parties to armed conflict to take special measures to protect women and girls from gender-based violence, particularly rape and other forms of sexual abuse, and all other forms of violence in situations of armed conflict;

11. *Emphasizes* the responsibility of all States to put an end to impunity and to prosecute those responsible for genocide, crimes against humanity, and war crimes including those relating to sexual and other violence against women and girls, and in this regard *stresses* the need to exclude these crimes, where feasible from amnesty provisions;

12. *Calls upon* all parties to armed conflict to respect the civilian and humanitarian character of refugee camps and settlements, and to take into account the particular needs of women and girls, including in their design, and recalls its resolutions 1208 (1998) of 19 November 1998 and 1296 (2000) of 19 April 2000;

13. *Encourages* all those involved in the planning for disarmament, demobilization and reintegration to consider the different needs of female and male ex-combatants and to take into account the needs of their dependants;

14. *Reaffirms* its readiness, whenever measures are adopted under Article 41 of the Charter of the United Nations, to give consideration to their potential impact on the civilian population, bearing in mind the special needs of women and girls, in order to consider appropriate humanitarian exemptions;

15. *Expresses* its willingness to ensure that Security Council missions take into account gender considerations and the rights of women, including through consultation with local and international women's groups;

16. *Invites* the Secretary-General to carry out a study on the impact of armed conflict on women and girls, the role of women in peace-building and the gender dimensions of peace processes and conflict resolution, and *further invites* him to submit a report to the Security Council on the results of this study and to make this available to all Member States of the United Nations;

17. *Requests* the Secretary-General, where appropriate, to include in his reporting to the Security Council progress on gender mainstreaming throughout peacekeeping missions and all other aspects relating to women and girls;

18. *Decides* to remain actively seized of the matter.

The States Parties to the present Convention,

Noting that the Charter of the United Nations reaffirms faith in fundamental human rights, in the dignity and worth of the human person and in the equal rights of men and women,

Noting that the Universal Declaration of Human Rights affirms the principle of the inadmissibility of discrimination and proclaims that all human beings are born free and equal in dignity and rights and that everyone is entitled to all the rights and freedoms set forth therein, without distinction of any kind, including distinction based on sex,

Noting that the States Parties to the International Covenants on Human Rights have the obligation to ensure the equal rights of men and women to enjoy all economic, social, cultural, civil and political rights,

Considering the international conventions concluded under the auspices of the United Nations and the specialized agencies promoting equality of rights of men and women,

Noting also the resolutions, declarations and recommendations adopted by the United Nations and the specialized agencies promoting equality of rights of men and women,

Concerned, however, that despite these various instruments extensive discrimination against women continues to exist,

Recalling that discrimination against women violates the principles of equality of rights and respect for human dignity, is an obstacle to the participation of women, on equal terms with men, in the political, social, economic and cultural life of their countries, hampers the growth of the prosperity of society and the family and makes more difficult the full development of the potentialities of women in the service of their countries and of humanity,

Concerned that in situations of poverty women have the least access to food, health, education, training and opportunities for employment and other needs,

Convinced that the establishment of the new international economic order based on equity and justice will contribute significantly towards the promotion of equality between men and women,

Emphasizing that the eradication of apartheid, all forms of racism, racial discrimination, colonialism, neo-colonialism, aggression, foreign occupation and domination and interference in the internal affairs of States is essential to the full enjoyment of the rights of men and women,

Affirming that the strengthening of international peace and security, the relaxation of international tension, mutual co-operation among all States irrespective of their social and economic systems, general and complete disarmament, in particular nuclear disarmament under strict and effective international control, the affirmation of the principles of justice, equality and mutual benefit in relations among countries and the realization of the right of peoples under alien and colonial domination and foreign occupation to self-determination and independence, as well as respect for national sovereignty and territorial integrity, will promote social progress and development and as a consequence will contribute to the attainment of full equality between men and women,

Convinced that the full and complete development of a country, the welfare of the world and the cause of peace require the maximum participation of women on equal terms with men in all fields,

Bearing in mind the great contribution of women to the welfare of the family and to the development of society, so far not fully recognized, the social significance of maternity and the role of both parents in the family and in the upbringing of children, and aware that the role of women in procreation should not be a basis for discrimination but that the upbringing of children requires a sharing of responsibility between men and women and society as a whole,

Aware that a change in the traditional role of men as well as the role of women in society and in the family is needed to achieve full equality between men and women,

Determined to implement the principles set forth in the Declaration on the Elimination of Discrimination against Women and, for that purpose, to adopt the measures required for the elimination of such discrimination in all its forms and manifestations,

Have agreed on the following:

PART I

Article I

For the purposes of the present Convention, the term "discrimination against women" shall mean any distinction, exclusion or restriction made on the basis of sex which has the effect or purpose of impairing or nullifying the recognition, enjoyment or exercise by women, irrespective of their marital status, on a basis of equality of men and women, of human rights and fundamental freedoms in the political, economic, social, cultural, civil or any other field.

Article 2

States Parties condemn discrimination against women in all its forms, agree to pursue by all appropriate means and without delay a policy of eliminating discrimination against women and, to this end, undertake: (a) To embody the principle of the equality of men and women in their national constitutions or other appropriate legislation if not yet incorporated therein and to ensure, through law and other appropriate means, the practical realization of this principle;

(b) To adopt appropriate legislative and other measures, including sanctions where appropriate, prohibiting all discrimination against women;

(c) To establish legal protection of the rights of women on an equal basis with men and to ensure through competent national tribunals and other public institutions the effective protection of women against any act of discrimination;

(d) To refrain from engaging in any act or practice of discrimination against women and to ensure that public authorities and institutions shall act in conformity with this obligation;

(e) To take all appropriate measures to eliminate discrimination against women by any person, organisation or enterprise;

(f) To take all appropriate measures, including legislation, to modify or abolish existing laws, regulations, customs and practices which constitute discrimination against women;

(g) To repeal all national penal provisions which constitute discrimination against women.

Article 3

States Parties shall take in all fields, in particular in the political, social, economic and cultural fields, all appropriate measures, including legislation, to en sure the full development and advancement of women , for the purpose of guaranteeing them the exercise and enjoyment of human rights and fundamental freedoms on a basis of equality with men.

Article 4

1. Adoption by States Parties of temporary special measures aimed at accelerating de facto equality between men and women shall not be considered discrimination as defined in the present Convention, but shall in no way entail as a consequence the maintenance of unequal or separate standards; these measures shall be discontinued when the objectives of equality of opportunity and treatment have been achieved.

2. Adoption by States Parties of special measures, including those measures contained in the present Convention, aimed at protecting maternity shall not be considered discriminatory.

Article 5

States Parties shall take all appropriate measures: (a) To modify the social and cultural patterns of conduct of men and women, with a view to achieving the elimination of prejudices and customary and all other practices which are based on the idea of the inferiority or the superiority of either of the sexes or on stereotyped roles for men and women;

(b) To ensure that family education includes a proper understanding of maternity as a social function and the recognition of the common responsibility of men and women in the upbringing and development of their children, it being understood that the interest of the children is the primordial consideration in all cases.

Article 6

States Parties shall take all appropriate measures, including legislation, to suppress all forms of traffic in women and exploitation of prostitution of women.

PART II

Article 7

States Parties shall take all appropriate measures to eliminate discrimination against women in the political and public life of the country and, in particular, shall ensure to women, on equal terms with men, the right: (a) To vote in all elections and public referenda and to be eligible for election to all publicly elected bodies;

(b) To participate in the formulation of government policy and the implementation thereof and to hold public office and perform all public functions at all levels of government;

(c) To participate in non-governmental organisations and associations concerned with the public and political life of the country.

Article 8

States Parties shall take all appropriate measures to ensure to women, on equal terms with men and without any discrimination, the opportunity to represent their Governments at the international level and to participate in the work of international organisations.

Article 9

1. States Parties shall grant women equal rights with men to acquire, change or retain their nationality. They shall ensure in particular that neither marriage to an alien nor change of nationality by the husband during marriage shall automatically change the nationality of the wife, render her stateless or force upon her the nationality of the husband.

2. States Parties shall grant women equal rights with men with respect to the nationality of their children.

PART III

Article 10

States Parties shall take all appropriate measures to eliminate discrimination against women in order to ensure to them equal rights with men in the field of education and in particular to ensure, on a basis of equality of men and women: (a) The same conditions for career and vocational guidance, for access to studies and for the achievement of diplomas in educational establishments of all categories in rural as well as in urban areas; this equality shall be ensured in pre-school, general, technical, professional and higher technical education, as well as in all types of vocational training;

(b) Access to the same curricula, the same examinations, teaching staff with qualifications of the same standard and school premises and equipment of the same quality;

(c) The elimination of any stereotyped concept of the roles of men and women at all levels and in all forms of education by encouraging coeducation and other types of education which will help to achieve this aim and, in particular, by the revision of textbooks and school programmes and the adaptation of teaching methods;

(d) The same opportunities to benefit from scholarships and other study grants;

(e) The same opportunities for access to programmes of continuing education, including adult and functional literacy programmes, particulary those aimed at reducing, at the earliest possible time, any gap in education existing between men and women;

(f) The reduction of female student drop-out rates and the organisation of programmes for girls and women who have left school prematurely;

(g) The same Opportunities to participate actively in sports and physical education;

(h) Access to specific educational information to help to ensure the health and well-being of families, including information and advice on family planning.

Article 11

1. States Parties shall take all appropriate measures to eliminate discrimination against women in the field of employment in order to ensure, on a basis of equality of men and women, the same rights, in particular: (a) The right to work as an inalienable right of all human beings;

(b) The right to the same employment opportunities, including the application of the same criteria for selection in matters of employment;

(c) The right to free choice of profession and employment, the right to promotion, job security and all benefits and conditions of service and the right to receive vocational training and retraining, including apprenticeships, advanced vocational training and recurrent training;

(d) The right to equal remuneration, including benefits, and to equal treatment in respect of work of equal value, as well as equality of treatment in the evaluation of the quality of work;

(e) The right to social security, particularly in cases of retirement, unemployment, sickness, invalidity and old age and other incapacity to work, as well as the right to paid leave;

(f) The right to protection of health and to safety in working conditions, including the safeguarding of the function of reproduction.

2. In order to prevent discrimination against women on the grounds of marriage or maternity and to ensure their effective right to work, States Parties shall take appropriate measures: (a) To prohibit, subject to the imposition of sanctions, dismissal on the grounds of pregnancy or of maternity leave and discrimination in dismissals on the basis of marital status;

(b) To introduce maternity leave with pay or with comparable social benefits without loss of former employment, seniority or social allowances;

(c) To encourage the provision of the necessary supporting social services to enable parents to combine family obligations with work responsibilities and participation in public life, in particular through promoting the establishment and development of a network of child-care facilities;

(d) To provide special protection to women during pregnancy in types of work proved to be harmful to them.

3. Protective legislation relating to matters covered in this article shall be reviewed periodically in the light of scientific and technological knowledge and shall be revised, repealed or extended as necessary.

Article 12

1. States Parties shall take all appropriate measures to eliminate discrimination against women in the field of health care in order to ensure, on a basis of equality of men and women, access to health care services, including those related to family planning.

2. Notwithstanding the provisions of paragraph I of this article, States Parties shall ensure to women appropriate services in connection with pregnancy, confinement and the post-natal period, granting free services where necessary, as well as adequate nutrition during pregnancy and lactation.

Article 13

States Parties shall take all appropriate measures to eliminate discrimination against women in other areas of economic and social life in order to ensure, on a basis of equality of men and women, the same rights, in particular: (a) The right to family benefits;

(b) The right to bank loans, mortgages and other forms of financial credit;

(c) The right to participate in recreational activities, sports and all aspects of cultural life.

Article 14

1. States Parties shall take into account the particular problems faced by rural women and the significant roles which rural women play in the economic survival of their families, including their work in the non-monetized sectors of the economy, and shall take all appropriate measures to ensure the application of the provisions of the present Convention to women in rural areas.

2. States Parties shall take all appropriate measures to eliminate discrimination against women in rural areas in order to ensure, on a basis of equality of men and women, that they participate in and benefit from rural development and, in particular, shall ensure to such women the right:

(a) To participate in the elaboration and implementation of development planning at all levels;

(b) To have access to adequate health care facilities, including information, counselling and services in family planning;

(c) To benefit directly from social security programmes;

(d) To obtain all types of training and education, formal and non-formal, including that relating to functional literacy, as well as, inter alia, the benefit of all community and extension services, in order to increase their technical proficiency;

(e) To organize self-help groups and co-operatives in order to obtain equal access to economic opportunities through employment or self employment;

(f) To participate in all community activities;

(g) To have access to agricultural credit and loans, marketing facilities, appropriate technology and equal treatment in land and agrarian reform as well as in land resettlement schemes;

(h) To enjoy adequate living conditions, particularly in relation to housing, sanitation, electricity and water supply, transport and communications.

PART IV

Article 15

1. States Parties shall accord to women equality with men before the law.

2. States Parties shall accord to women, in civil matters, a legal capacity identical to that of men and the same opportunities to exercise that capacity. In particular, they shall give women equal rights to conclude contracts and to administer property and shall treat them equally in all stages of procedure in courts and tribunals.

3. States Parties agree that all contracts and all other private instruments of any kind with a legal effect which is directed at restricting the legal capacity of women shall be deemed null and void.

4. States Parties shall accord to men and women the same rights with regard to the law relating to the movement of persons and the freedom to choose their residence and domicile.

Article 16

1. States Parties shall take all appropriate measures to eliminate discrimination against women in all matters relating to marriage and family relations and in particular shall ensure, on a basis of equality of men and women: (a) The same right to enter into marriage;

(b) The same right freely to choose a spouse and to enter into marriage only with their free and full consent;

(c) The same rights and responsibilities during marriage and at its dissolution;

(d) The same rights and responsibilities as parents, irrespective of their marital status, in matters relating to their children; in all cases the interests of the children shall be paramount;

(e) The same rights to decide freely and responsibly on the number and spacing of their children and to have access to the information, education and means to enable them to exercise these rights;

(f) The same rights and responsibilities with regard to guardianship, wardship, trusteeship and adoption of children, or similar institutions where these concepts exist in national legislation; in all cases the interests of the children shall be paramount;

(g) The same personal rights as husband and wife, including the right to choose a family name, a profession and an occupation;

(h) The same rights for both spouses in respect of the ownership, acquisition, management, administration, enjoyment and disposition of property, whether free of charge or for a valuable consideration.

2. The betrothal and the marriage of a child shall have no legal effect, and all necessary action, including legislation, shall be taken to specify a minimum age for marriage and to make the registration of marriages in an official registry compulsory.

PART V

Article 17

1. For the purpose of considering the progress made in the implementation of the present Convention, there shall be established a Committee on the Elimination of Discrimination against Women (hereinafter referred to as the Committee) consisting, at the time of entry into force of the Convention, of eighteen and, after ratification of or accession to the Convention by the thirty-fifth State Party, of twenty-three experts of high moral standing and competence in the field covered by the Convention. The experts shall be elected by States Parties from among their nationals and shall serve in their personal capacity, consideration being given to equitable geographical distribution and to the representation of the different forms of civilization as well as the principal legal systems.

2. The members of the Committee shall be elected by secret ballot from a list of persons nominated by States Parties. Each State Party may nominate one person from among its own nationals.

3. The initial election shall be held six months after the date of the entry into force of the present Convention. At least three months before the date of each election the Secretary-General of the United Nations shall address a letter to the States Parties inviting them to submit their nominations within two months. The Secretary-General shall prepare a list in alphabetical order of all persons thus nominated, indicating the States Parties which have nominated them, and shall submit it to the States Parties.

4. Elections of the members of the Committee shall be held at a meeting of States Parties convened by the Secretary-General at United Nations Headquarters. At that meeting, for which two thirds of the States Parties shall constitute a quorum, the persons elected to the Committee shall be those nominees who obtain the largest number of votes and an absolute majority of the votes of the representatives of States Parties present and voting.

5. The members of the Committee shall be elected for a term of four years. However, the terms of nine of the members elected at the first election shall expire at the end of two years; immediately after the first election the names of these nine members shall be chosen by lot by the Chairman of the Committee.

6. The election of the five additional members of the Committee shall be held in accordance with the provisions of paragraphs 2, 3 and 4 of this article, following the thirty-fifth ratification or accession. The terms of two of the additional members elected on this occasion shall expire at the end of two years, the names of these two members having been chosen by lot by the Chairman of the Committee.

7. For the filling of casual vacancies, the State Party whose expert has ceased to function as a member of the Committee shall appoint another expert from among its nationals, subject to the approval of the Committee.

8. The members of the Committee shall, with the approval of the General Assembly, receive emoluments from United Nations resources on such terms and conditions as the Assembly may decide, having regard to the importance of the Committee's responsibilities.

9. The Secretary-General of the United Nations shall provide the necessary staff and facilities for the effective performance of the functions of the Committee under the present Convention.

Article 18

1. States Parties undertake to submit to the Secretary-General of the United Nations, for consideration by the Committee, a report on the legislative, judicial, administrative or other measures which they have adopted to give effect to the provisions of the present Convention and on the progress made in this respect: (a) Within one year after the entry into force for the State concerned;

(b) Thereafter at least every four years and further whenever the Committee so requests.

2. Reports may indicate factors and difficulties affecting the degree of fulfilment of obligations under the present Convention.

Article 19

1. The Committee shall adopt its own rules of procedure.

2. The Committee shall elect its officers for a term of two years.

Article 20

1. The Committee shall normally meet for a period of not more than two weeks annually in order to consider the reports submitted in accordance with article 18 of the present Convention.

2. The meetings of the Committee shall normally be held at United Nations Headquarters or at any other convenient place as determined by the Committee. (amendment, status of ratification)

Article 21

1. The Committee shall, through the Economic and Social Council, report annually to the General Assembly of the United Nations on its activities and may make suggestions and general recommendations based on the examination of reports and information received from the States Parties. Such suggestions and general recommendations shall be included in the report of the Committee together with comments, if any, from States Parties.

2. The Secretary-General of the United Nations shall transmit the reports of the Committee to the Commission on the Status of Women for its information.

Article 22

The specialized agencies shall be entitled to be represented at the consideration of the implementation of such provisions of the present Convention as fall within the scope of their activities. The Committee may invite the specialized agencies to submit reports on the implementation of the Convention in areas falling within the scope of their activities.

PART VI

Article 23

Nothing in the present Convention shall affect any provisions that are more conducive to the achievement of equality between men and women which may be contained: (a) In the legislation of a State Party; or

(b) In any other international convention, treaty or agreement in force for that State.

Article 24

States Parties undertake to adopt all necessary measures at the national level aimed at achieving the full realization of the rights recognized in the present Convention.

Article 25

1. The present Convention shall be open for signature by all States.

2. The Secretary-General of the United Nations is designated as the depositary of the present Convention.

3. The present Convention is subject to ratification. Instruments of ratification shall be deposited with the Secretary-General of the United Nations.

4. The present Convention shall be open to accession by all States. Accession shall be effected by the deposit of an instrument of accession with the Secretary-General of the United Nations.

Article 26

1. A request for the revision of the present Convention may be made at any time by any State Party by means of a notification in writing addressed to the Secretary-General of the United Nations.

2. The General Assembly of the United Nations shall decide upon the steps, if any, to be taken in respect of such a request.

Article 27

1. The present Convention shall enter into force on the thirtieth day after the date of deposit with the Secretary-General of the United Nations of the twentieth instrument of ratification or accession.

2. For each State ratifying the present Convention or acceding to it after the deposit of the twentieth instrument of ratification or accession, the Convention shall enter into force on the thirtieth day after the date of the deposit of its own instrument of ratification or accession.

Article 28

1. The Secretary-General of the United Nations shall receive and circulate to all States the text of reservations made by States at the time of ratification or accession.

2. A reservation incompatible with the object and purpose of the present Convention shall not be permitted.

3. Reservations may be withdrawn at any time by notification to this effect addressed to the Secretary-General of the United Nations, who shall then inform all States thereof. Such notification shall take effect on the date on which it is received.

Article 29

1. Any dispute between two or more States Parties concerning the interpretation or application of the present Convention which is not settled by negotiation shall, at the request of one of them, be submitted to arbitration. If within six months from the date of the request for arbitration the parties are unable to agree on the organisation of the arbitration, any one of those parties may refer the dispute to the International Court of Justice by request in conformity with the Statute of the Court.

2. Each State Party may at the time of signature or ratification of the present Convention or accession thereto declare that it does not consider itself bound by paragraph I of this article. The other States Parties shall not be bound by that paragraph with respect to any State Party which has made such a reservation.

3. Any State Party which has made a reservation in accordance with paragraph 2 of this article may at any time withdraw that reservation by notification to the Secretary-General of the United Nations.

Article 30

The present Convention, the Arabic, Chinese, English, French, Russian and Spanish texts of which are equally authentic, shall be deposited with the Secretary-General of the United Nations.

IN WITNESS WHEREOF the undersigned, duly authorized, have signed the present Convention.

G.   Constitution of Iraq 2005

Constitution of Iraq

The Iraqi constitution was approved by a national referendum held on 15 October 2005. The text was drafted by the Iraq Constitutional Committee. The following is an unofficial English translation by the Associated Press of the final approved text of the constitution.

The Preamble

In the name of God, the Most merciful, the Most compassionate

{We have honored the sons of Adam}

We, the people of Mesopotamia, the homeland of the apostles and prophets, resting place of the virtuous imams, cradle of civilization, crafters of writing, and home of numeration. Upon our land the first law made by man was passed, and the oldest pact of just governance was inscribed, and upon our soil the saints and companions of the Prophet prayed, philosophers and scientists theorized, and writers and poets excelled;

Acknowledging God's right over us, and in fulfillment of the call of our homeland and citizens, and in a response to the call of our religious and national leaderships and the determination of our great authorities and of our leaders and politicians, and in the midst of international support from our friends and those who love us, marched for the first time in our history towards the ballot boxes by the millions, men and women, young and old, on the thirtieth of January 2005, invoking the pains of sectarian oppression inflicted by the autocratic clique and inspired by the tragedies of Iraq's martyrs, Shiite and Sunni, Arabs and Kurds and Turkmen and from all other components of the people, and recollecting the darkness of the ravage of the holy cities and the South in the Sha'abaniyya uprising and burnt by the flames of grief of the mass graves, the marshes, Al-Dujail and others and articulating the sufferings of racial oppression in the massacres of Halabcha, Barzan, Anfal and the Fayli Kurds and inspired by the ordeals of the Turkmen in Bashir and the sufferings of the people of the western region, as is the case in the remaining areas of Iraq where the people suffered from the liquidation of their leaders, symbols, and Sheiks and from the displacement of their skilled individuals and from drying out of its cultural and intellectual wells, so we sought hand in hand and shoulder to shoulder to create our new Iraq, the Iraq of the future, free from sectarianism, racism, complex of regional attachment, discrimination, and exclusion.

Accusations of being infidels, and terrorism did not stop us from marching forward to build a nation of law. Sectarianism and racism have not stopped us from marching together to strengthen our national unity, following the path of peaceful transfer of power, adopting the course of just distribution of resources, and providing equal opportunity for all.

We, the people of Iraq, who have just risen from our stumble, and who are looking with confidence to the future through a republican, federal, democratic, pluralistic system, have resolved with the determination of our men, women, elderly, and youth to respect the rule of law, to establish justice and equality, to cast aside the politics of aggression, to pay attention to women and their rights, the elderly and their concerns, and children and their affairs, to spread the culture of diversity, and to defuse terrorism.

We, the people of Iraq, of all components and across the spectrum, have taken upon ourselves to decide freely and by choice to unite our future, to take lessons from yesterday for tomorrow, and to enact this permanent Constitution, through the values and ideals of the heavenly messages and the findings of science and man's civilization. The adherence to this Constitution preserves for Iraq its free union of people, of land, and of sovereignty.

Section One
Fundamental Principles

Article 1:
The Republic of Iraq is a single federal, independent and fully sovereign state in which the system of government is republican, representative, parliamentary, and democratic, and this Constitution is a guarantor of the unity of Iraq.

Article 2:
First: Islam is the official religion of the State and is a foundation source of legislation:
A. No law may be enacted that contradicts the established provisions of Islam
B. No law may be enacted that contradicts the principles of democracy.
C. No law may be enacted that contradicts the rights and basic freedoms stipulated in this Constitution.

Second: This Constitution guarantees the Islamic identity of the majority of the Iraqi people and guarantees the full religious rights to freedom of religious belief and practice of all individuals such as Christians, Yazidis, and Mandean Sabeans.

Article 3:
Iraq is a country of multiple nationalities, religions, and sects. It is a founding and active member in the Arab League and is committed to its charter, and it is part of the Islamic world.

Article 4:
First: The Arabic language and the Kurdish language are the two official languages of Iraq. The right of Iraqis to educate their children in their mother tongue, such as Turkmen, Syriac, and Armenian shall be guaranteed in government educational institutions in accordance with educational guidelines, or in any other language in private educational institutions.

Second: The scope of the term "official language" and the means of applying the provisions of this article shall be defined by a law and shall include:

A. Publication of the Official Gazette, in the two languages;

B. Speech, conversation, and expression in official domains, such as the Council of Representatives, the Council of Ministers, courts, and official conferences, in either of the two languages;

C. Recognition and publication of official documents and correspondence in the two languages;

D. Opening schools that teach the two languages, in accordance with the educational guidelines;

E. Use of both languages in any matter enjoined by the principle of equality such as bank notes, passports, and stamps.

Third: The federal and official institutions and agencies in the Kurdistan region shall use both languages.

Fourth: The Turkomen language and the Syriac language are two other official languages in the administrative units in which they constitute density of population.

Fifth: Each region or governorate may adopt any other local language as an additional official language if the majority of its population so decides in a general referendum.

Article 5:
The law is sovereign. The people are the source of authority and legitimacy, which they shall exercise in a direct, general, secret ballot and through their constitutional institutions.

Article 6:
Transfer of authority shall be made peacefully through democratic means as stipulated in this Constitution.

Article 7:
First: Any entity or program that adopts, incites, facilitates, glorifies, promotes, or justifies racism or terrorism or accusations of being an infidel (takfir) or ethnic cleansing, especially the Saddamist Ba'ath in Iraq and its symbols, under any name whatsoever, shall be prohibited. Such entities may not be political pluralism in Iraq. This shall be regulated by law.

Second: The State shall undertake to combat terrorism in all its forms, and shall work to protect its territories from being a base, pathway, or field for terrorist activities.

Article 8:
Iraq shall observe the principles of good neighborliness, adhere to the principle of non-interference in the internal affairs of other states, seek to settle disputes by peaceful means, establish relations on the basis of mutual interests and reciprocity, and respect its international obligations.

Article 9:
First:
A - The Iraqi armed forces and security services will be composed of the components of the Iraqi people with due consideration given to their balance and representation without discrimination or exclusion. They shall be subject to the control of the civilian authority, shall defend Iraq, shall not be used as an instrument to oppress the Iraqi people, shall not interfere in the political affairs, and shall have no role in the transfer of authority.

B - The formation of military militias outside the framework of the armed forces is prohibited.

C - The Iraqi armed forces and their personnel, including military personnel working in the Ministry of Defense or any subordinate departments or organisations, may not stand for election to political office, campaign for candidates, or participate in other activities prohibited by Ministry of Defense regulations. This ban includes the activities of the personnel mentioned above acting in their personal or professional capacities, but shall not infringe upon the right of these personnel to cast their vote in the elections.

D - The Iraqi National Intelligence Service shall collect information, assess threats to national security, and advise the Iraqi government. This Service shall be under civilian control, shall be subject to legislative oversight, and shall operate in accordance with the law and pursuant to the recognized principles of human rights.

E- The Iraqi Government shall respect and implement Iraq's international obligations regarding the non-proliferation, non-development, non-production, and non-use of nuclear, chemical, and biological weapons, and shall prohibit associated equipment, materiel, technologies, and delivery systems for use in the development, manufacture, production, and use of such weapons.

Second: Military service shall be regulated by law.

Article 10:
The holy shrines and religious sites in Iraq are religious and civilizational entities. The State is committed to assuring and maintaining their sanctity, and to guaranteeing the free practice of rituals in them.

Article 11:
Baghdad is the capital of the Republic of Iraq.

Article 12:
First: The flag, national anthem, and emblem of Iraq shall be regulated by law in a way that symbolizes the components of the Iraqi people.

Second: A law shall regulate honours, official holidays, religious and national occasions and the Hijri and Gregorian calendar.

Article 13:
First: This Constitution is the preeminent and supreme law in Iraq and shall be binding in all parts of Iraq without exception.

Second: No law that contradicts this Constitution shall be enacted. Any text in any regional constitutions or any other legal text that contradicts this Constitution shall be considered void.

Section Two

Rights and Liberties

Chapter One
[Rights]

First: Civil and Political Rights

Article 14:
Iraqis are equal before the law without discrimination based on gender, race, ethnicity, nationality, origin, color, religion, sect, belief or opinion, or economic or social status.

Article 15:
Every individual has the right to enjoy life, security and liberty. Deprivation or restriction of these rights is prohibited except in accordance with the law and based on a decision issued by a competent judicial authority.

Article 16:
Equal opportunities shall be guaranteed to all Iraqis, and the state shall ensure that the necessary measures to achieve this are taken.

Article 17:
First: Every individual shall have the right to personal privacy so long as it does not contradict the rights of others and public morals.

Second: The sanctity of the homes shall be protected. Homes may not be entered, searched, or violated, except by a judicial decision in accordance with the law.

Article 18:
First: Iraqi citizenship is a right for every Iraqi and is the basis of his nationality.

Second: Anyone who is born to an Iraqi father or to an Iraqi mother shall be considered an Iraqi. This shall be regulated by law.

Third:
A. An Iraqi citizen by birth may not have his citizenship withdrawn for any reason. Any person who had his citizenship withdrawn shall have the right to demand its reinstatement. This shall be regulated by a law.
B. Iraqi citizenship shall be withdrawn from naturalized citizens in cases regulated by law.

Fourth: An Iraqi may have multiple citizenships. Everyone who assumes a senior, security or sovereign position must abandon any other acquired citizenship. This shall be regulated by law.

Fifth: Iraqi citizenship shall not be granted for the purposes of the policy of population settlement that disrupts the demographic composition of Iraq.

Sixth: Citizenship provisions shall be regulated by law. The competent courts shall consider the suits arising from those provisions.

Article 19:
First: The judiciary is independent and no power is above the judiciary except the law.

Second: There is no crime or punishment except by law. The punishment shall only be for an act that the law considers a crime when perpetrated. A harsher punishment than the applicable punishment at the time of the offense may not be imposed.

Third: Litigation shall be a protected and guaranteed right for all.

Fourth: The right to a defense shall be sacred and guaranteed in all phases of investigation and the trial.

Fifth: The accused is innocent until proven guilty in a fair legal trial. The accused may not be tried for the same crime for a second time after acquittal unless new evidence is produced.

Sixth: Every person shall have the right to be treated with justice in judicial and administrative proceedings.

Seventh: The proceedings of a trial are public unless the court decides to make it secret.

Eighth: Punishment shall be personal.

Ninth: Laws shall not have retroactive effect unless stipulated otherwise. This exclusion shall not include laws on taxes and fees.

Tenth: Criminal laws shall not have retroactive effect, unless it is to the benefit of the accused.

Eleventh: The court shall appoint a lawyer at the expense of the state for an accused of a felony or misdemeanor who does not have a defense lawyer.

Twelfth:
A. Unlawful detention shall be prohibited.
B. Imprisonment or detention shall be prohibited in places not designed for these purposes, pursuant to prison laws covering health and social care, and subject to the authorities of the State.

Thirteenth: The preliminary investigative documents shall be submitted to the competent judge in a period not to exceed twenty-four hours from the time of the arrest of the accused, which may be extended only once and for the same period.

Article 20:
Iraqi citizens, men and women, shall have the right to participate in public affairs and to enjoy political rights including the right to vote, elect, and run for office.

Article 21:
First: No Iraqi shall be surrendered to foreign entities and authorities.

Second: A law shall regulate the right of political asylum in Iraq. No political refugee shall be surrendered to a foreign entity or returned forcibly to the country from which he fled.

Third: Political asylum shall not be granted to a person accused of committing international or terrorist crimes or to any person who inflicted damage on Iraq.

Second: Economic, Social and Cultural Liberties

Article 22:
First: Work is a right for all Iraqis in a way that guarantees a dignified life for them.

Second: The law shall regulate the relationship between employees and employers on economic bases and while observing the rules of social justice.

Third: The State shall guarantee the right to form and join unions and professional associations, and this shall be regulated by law.

Article 23:
First: Private property is protected. The owner shall have the right to benefit, exploit and dispose of private property within the limits of the law.

Second: Expropriation is not permissible except for the purposes of public benefit in return for just compensation, and this shall be regulated by law.

Third:

A. Every Iraqi shall have the right to own property anywhere in Iraq. No others may possess immovable assets, except as exempted by law.

B. Ownership of property for the purposes of demographic change is prohibited.

Article 24:

The State shall guarantee freedom of movement of Iraqi manpower, goods, and capital between regions and governorates, and this shall be regulated by law.

Article 25:

The State shall guarantee the reform of the Iraqi economy in accordance with modern economic principles to insure the full investment of its resources, diversification of its sources, and the encouragement and development of the private sector.

Article 26:

The State shall guarantee the encouragement of investment in the various sectors, and this shall be regulated by law.

Article 27:

First: Public assets are sacrosanct, and their protection is the duty of each citizen.

Second: The provisions related to the preservation of State properties, their management, the conditions for their disposal, and the limits for these assets not to be relinquished shall all be regulated by law.

Article 28:

First: No taxes or fees shall be levied, amended, collected, or exempted, except by law.

Second: Low income earners shall be exempted from taxes in a way that guarantees the preservation of the minimum income required for living. This shall be regulated by law.

Article 29:

First:

A. The family is the foundation of society; the State shall preserve it and its religious, moral, and national values.

B. The State shall guarantee the protection of motherhood, childhood and old age, shall care for children and youth, and shall provide them with the appropriate conditions to develop their talents and abilities.

Second: Children have the right to upbringing, care and education from their parents. Parents have the right to respect and care from their children, especially in times of need, disability, and old age.

Third: Economic exploitation of children in all of its forms shall be prohibited, and the State shall take the necessary measures for their protection.

Fourth: All forms of violence and abuse in the family, school, and society shall be prohibited.

Article 30:

First: The State shall guarantee to the individual and the family - especially children and women – social and health security, the basic requirements for living a free and decent life, and shall secure for them suitable income and appropriate housing.

Second: The State shall guarantee social and health security to Iraqis in cases of old age, sickness, employment disability, homelessness, orphanhood, or unemployment, shall work to protect them from ignorance, fear and poverty, and shall provide them housing and special programs of care and rehabilitation, and this shall be regulated by law.

Article 31:
First: Every citizen has the right to health care. The State shall maintain public health and provide the means of prevention and treatment by building different types of hospitals and health institutions.

Second: Individuals and entities have the right to build hospitals, clinics, or private health care centers under the supervision of the State, and this shall be regulated by law.

Article 32:
The State shall care for the handicapped and those with special needs, and shall ensure their rehabilitation in order to reintegrate them into society, and this shall be regulated by law.

Article 33:
First: Every individual has the right to live in safe environmental conditions.

Second: The State shall undertake the protection and preservation of the environment and its biological diversity.

Article 34:
First: Education is a fundamental factor for the progress of society and is a right guaranteed by the state. Primary education is mandatory and the state guarantees that it shall combat illiteracy.

Second: Free education in all its stages is a right for all Iraqis.

Third: The State shall encourage scientific research for peaceful purposes that serve humanity and shall support excellence, creativity, invention, and different aspects of ingenuity.

Fourth: Private and public education shall be guaranteed, and this shall be regulated by law.

Article 35:
The state shall promote cultural activities and institutions in a manner that befits the civilizational and cultural history of Iraq, and it shall seek to support indigenous Iraqi cultural orientations.

Article 36:
Practicing sports is a right of every Iraqi and the state shall encourage and care for such activities and shall provide for their requirements.

Chapter Two
[Liberties]

Article 37:

First:
A. The liberty and dignity of man shall be protected.

B. No person may be kept in custody or investigated except according to a judicial decision.

C. All forms of psychological and physical torture and inhumane treatment are prohibited. Any confession made under force, threat, or torture shall not be relied on, and the victim shall have the right to seek compensation for material and moral damages incurred in accordance with the law.

Second: The State shall guarantee protection of the individual from intellectual, political and religious coercion.

Third: Forced labor, slavery, slave trade, trafficking in women or children, and sex trade shall be prohibited.

Article 38:
The State shall guarantee in a way that does not violate public order and morality:
A. Freedom of expression using all means.
B. Freedom of press, printing, advertisement, media and publication.
C. Freedom of assembly and peaceful demonstration, and this shall be regulated by law.

Article 39:
First: The freedom to form and join associations and political parties shall be guaranteed, and this shall be regulated by law.

Second: It is not permissible to force any person to join any party, society, or political entity, or force him to continue his membership in it.

Article 40:
The freedom of communication and correspondence, postal, telegraphic, electronic, and telephonic, shall be guaranteed and may not be monitored, wiretapped, or disclosed except for legal and security necessity and by a judicial decision.

Article 41:
Iraqis are free in their commitment to their personal status according to their religions, sects, beliefs, or choices, and this shall be regulated by law.

Article 42:
Each individual shall have the freedom of thought, conscience, and belief.

Article 43:
First: The followers of all religions and sects are free in the:
A- Practice of religious rites, including the Husseini rituals.
B- Management of religious endowments (waqf), their affairs, and their religious institutions, and this shall be regulated by law.

Second: The State shall guarantee freedom of worship and the protection of places of worship.

Article 44:
First: Each Iraqi has freedom of movement, travel, and residence inside and outside Iraq.

Second: No Iraqi may be exiled, displaced, or deprived from returning to the homeland.

Article 45:
First: The State shall seek to strengthen the role of civil society institutions, and to support, develop and preserve their independence in a way that is consistent with peaceful means to achieve their legitimate goals, and this shall be regulated by law.

Second: The State shall seek the advancement of the Iraqi clans and tribes, shall attend to their affairs in a manner that is consistent with religion and the law, and shall uphold their noble human values in a way that contributes to the development of society. The State shall prohibit the tribal traditions that are in contradiction with human rights.

Article 46:
Restricting or limiting the practice of any of the rights or liberties stipulated in this Constitution is prohibited, except by a law or on the basis of a law, and insofar as that limitation or restriction does not violate the essence of the right or freedom.

<u>**Section Three**</u>

<u>**Federal Powers**</u>

Article 47:
The federal powers shall consist of the legislative, executive, and judicial powers, and they shall exercise their competencies and tasks on the basis of the principle of separation of powers.

<u>**Chapter one**</u>
<u>**[The Legislative Power]**</u>

Article 48:
The federal legislative power shall consist of the Council of Representatives and the Federation Council.

<u>**First: The Council of Representatives**</u>

Article 49:
First: The Council of Representatives shall consist of a number of members, at a ratio of one seat per 100,000 Iraqi persons representing the entire Iraqi people. They shall be elected through a direct secret general ballot. The representation of all components of the people shall be upheld in it.

Second: A candidate to the Council of Representatives must be a fully qualified Iraqi.

Third: A law shall regulate the requirements for the candidate, the voter, and all that is related to the elections.

Fourth: The elections law shall aim to achieve a percentage of representation for women of not less than one-quarter of the members of the Council of Representatives.

Fifth: The Council of Representatives shall promulgate a law dealing with the replacement of its members on resignation, dismissal, or death.

Sixth: It is not permissible to combine membership in the Council of Representatives with any work or other official position.

Article 50:
Each member of the Council of Representatives shall take the following constitutional oath before the Council prior to assuming his duties:

"I swear by God Almighty to carry out my legal duties and responsibilities with devotion and integrity and preserve the independence and sovereignty of Iraq, and safeguard the interests of its people, and ensure the safety of its land, sky, water, wealth, and federal democratic system, and I shall endeavor to protect public and private liberties, the independence of the judiciary, and pledge to implement legislation faithfully and neutrally. God is my witness."

Article 51:
The Council of Representatives shall establish its bylaws to regulate its work.

Article 52:
First: The Council of Representatives shall decide, by a two-thirds majority, the authenticity of membership of its member within thirty days from the date of filing an objection.

Second: The decision of the Council of Representatives may be appealed before the Federal Supreme Court within thirty days from the date of its issuance.

Article 53:
First: Sessions of the Council of Representatives shall be public unless, for reasons of necessity, the Council decides otherwise.

Second: Minutes of the sessions shall be published by means considered appropriate by the Council.

Article 54:
The President of the Republic shall call upon the Council of Representatives to convene by a presidential decree within fifteen days from the date of the ratification of the general election results. Its eldest member shall chair the first session to elect the speaker of the Council and his two deputies. This period may not be extended by more than the aforementioned period.

Article 55:
The Council of Representatives shall elect in its first session its speaker, then his first deputy and second deputy, by an absolute majority of the total number of the Council members by direct secret ballot.

Article 56:
First: The electoral term of the Council of Representatives shall be four calendar years, starting with its first session and ending with the conclusion of the fourth year.

Second: The new Council of Representatives shall be elected forty-five days before the conclusion of the preceding electoral term.

Article 57:
The Council of Representatives shall have one annual term, with two legislative sessions, lasting eight months. The bylaws shall define the method to convene the sessions. The

session in which the general budget is being presented shall not end until approval of the budget.

Article 58:
First: The President of the Republic, the Prime Minister, the Speaker of the Council of Representatives, or fifty members of the Council of Representatives may call the Council to an extraordinary session. The session shall be restricted to the topics that necessitated the call for the session.

Second: The legislative session of the Council of Representatives may be extended for no more than 30 days to complete the tasks that require the extension, based on a request from the President of the Republic, the Prime Minister, the Speaker of the Council, or fifty members of the Council of Representatives.

Article 59:
First:
The Council of Representatives quorum shall be achieved by an absolute majority of its members.

Second:
Decisions in the sessions of the Council of Representatives shall be made by a simple majority after quorum is achieved, unless otherwise stipulated.

Article 60:
First:
Draft laws shall be presented by the President of the Republic and the Council of Ministers.

Second:
Proposed laws shall be presented by ten members of the Council of Representatives or by one of its specialized committees.

Article 61:
The Council of Representatives shall be competent in the following:
First: Enacting federal laws.

Second: Monitoring the performance of the executive authority.

Third: Electing the President of the Republic.

Fourth: Regulating the ratification process of international treaties and agreements by a law, to be enacted by a two-thirds majority of the members of the Council of Representatives.

Fifth: Approving the appointment of the following:
A. The President and members of the Federal Court of Cassation, the Chief Public Prosecutor, and the President of Judicial Oversight Commission by an absolute majority, based on a proposal from the Higher Juridical Council.
B. Ambassadors and those with special grades, based on a proposal from the Council of Ministers.
C. The Iraqi Army Chief of Staff, his assistants, those of the rank of division commander and above, and the director of the intelligence service, based on a proposal from the Council of Ministers.

Sixth:
A. Questioning the President of the Republic, based on a petition with cause, by an absolute majority of the members of the Council of Representatives.

B. Relieving the President of the Republic by an absolute majority of the Council of Representatives after being convicted by the Federal Supreme Court in one of the following cases:
1 - Perjury of the constitutional oath.
2 - Violating the Constitution.
3 - High treason.

Seventh:
A. A member of the Council of Representatives may direct questions to the Prime Minister and the Ministers on any subject within their specialty and each of them shall answer the members' questions. Only the member who has asked the question shall have the right to comment on the answer.

B. At least twenty-five members of the Council of Representatives may raise a general issue for discussion in order to inquire about a policy and the performance of the Council of Ministers or one of the Ministries and it shall be submitted to the Speaker of the Council of Representatives, and the Prime Minister or the Ministers shall specify a date to come before the Council of Representatives to discuss it.

C. A member of the Council of Representatives, with the agreement of twenty-five members, may direct an inquiry to the Prime Minister or the Ministers to call them to account on the issues within their authority. The debate shall not be held on the inquiry except after at least seven days from the date of submission of the inquiry.

Eighth:
A. The Council of Representatives may withdraw confidence from one of the Ministers by an absolute majority and he shall be considered resigned from the date of the decision of withdrawal of confidence. A vote of no confidence in a Minister may not be held except upon his request or on the basis of a request signed by fifty members after the Minister has appeared for questioning before the Council. The Council shall not issue its decision regarding the request except after at least seven days from the date of its submission.

B.
1 - The President of the Republic may submit a request to the Council of Representatives to withdraw confidence from the Prime Minister.
2 - The Council of Representatives may withdraw confidence from the Prime Minister based on the request of one-fifth of its members. This request shall not be submitted except after an inquiry directed at the Prime Minister and after at least seven days from the date of submitting the request.
3 - The Council of Representatives may decide to withdraw confidence from the Prime Minister by an absolute majority of the number of its members.

C. The Government is deemed resigned in case of withdrawal of confidence from the Prime Minister.

D. In case of a vote of withdrawal of confidence in the Council of Ministers as a whole, the Prime Minister and the Ministers continue in their positions to run everyday business for a period not to exceed thirty days until a new Council of Ministers is formed in accordance with the provisions of Article 76 of this Constitution.

E. The Council of Representatives may question independent commission heads in accordance with the same procedures related to the Ministers. The Council shall have the right to relieve them by absolute majority.

Ninth:
A. To consent to the declaration of war and the state of emergency by a two-thirds majority based on a joint request from the President of the Republic and the Prime Minister.

B. The state of emergency shall be declared for a period of thirty days, which can be extended after approval each time.

C. The Prime Minister shall be delegated the necessary powers which enable him to manage the affairs of the country during the period of the declaration of war and the state of emergency. These powers shall be regulated by a law in a way that does not contradict the Constitution.

D. The Prime Minister shall present to the Council of Representatives the measures taken and the results during the period of the declaration of war and the state of emergency within 15 days from the date of its end.

Article 62:
First: The Council of Ministers shall submit the draft general budget bill and the closing account to the Council of Representatives for approval.

Second: The Council of Representatives may conduct transfers between the sections and chapters of the general budget and reduce the total of its sums, and it may suggest to the Council of Ministers that they increase the total expenses, when necessary.

Article 63:
First: A law shall regulate the rights and privileges of the speaker of the Council of Representatives, his two deputies, and the members of the Council of Representatives.

Second:
A. A member of the Council of Representatives shall enjoy immunity for statements made while the Council is in session, and the member may not be prosecuted before the courts for such.

B. A Council of Representatives member may not be placed under arrest during the legislative term of the Council of Representatives, unless the member is accused of a felony and the Council of Representatives members consent by an absolute majority to lift his immunity or if he is caught in flagrante delicto in the commission of a felony.

C. A Council of Representatives member may not be arrested after the legislative term of the Council of Representatives, unless the member is accused of a felony and with the consent of the speaker of the Council of Representatives to lift his immunity or if he is caught in flagrante delicto in the commission of a felony.

Article 64:
First: The Council of Representatives may be dissolved by an absolute majority of the number of its members, or upon the request of one-third of its members by the Prime Minister with the consent of the President of the Republic. The Council shall not be

dissolved during the period in which the Prime Minister is being questioned.

Second: Upon the dissolution of the Council of Representatives, the President of the Republic shall call for general elections in the country within a period not to exceed sixty days from the date of its dissolution. The Council of Ministers in this case is deemed resigned and continues to run everyday business.

Second: The Federation Council

Article 65:
A legislative council shall be established named the "Federation Council," to include representatives from the regions and the governorates that are not organized in a region. A law, enacted by a two-thirds majority of the members of the Council of Representatives, shall regulate the formation of the Federation Council, its membership conditions, its competencies, and all that is connected with it.

Chapter Two
[The Executive Power]

Article 66:
The federal executive power shall consist of the President of the Republic and the Council of Ministers and shall exercise its powers in accordance with the Constitution and the law.

First: The President of the Republic

Article 67:
The President of the Republic is the Head of the State and a symbol of the unity of the country and represents the sovereignty of the country. He shall guarantee the commitment to the Constitution and the preservation of Iraq's independence, sovereignty, unity, and the safety of its territories, in accordance with the provisions of the Constitution.

Article 68:
A nominee to the Presidency of the Republic must be:
First: An Iraqi by birth, born to Iraqi parents.

Second: Fully qualified and must be over forty years of age.

Third: Of good reputation and political experience, known for his integrity, uprightness, fairness, and loyalty to the homeland.

Fourth: Free of any conviction of a crime involving moral turpitude.

Article 69:
First: The provisions for nomination to the office of the President of the Republic shall be regulated by law.

Second: The provisions for nomination to the office of one or more Vice Presidents of the Republic shall be regulated by law.

Article 70:
First: The Council of Representatives shall elect a President of the Republic from among the candidates by a two-thirds majority of the number of its members.

Second: If none of the candidates receive the required majority vote then the two candidates who received the highest number of votes shall compete and the one who receives the majority of votes in the second election shall be declared President.

Article 71:
The President shall take the constitutional oath before the Council of Representatives according to the language stipulated in Article 50 of the Constitution.

Article 72:
First: The President of the Republic's term in office shall be limited to four years. He may be re-elected for a second time only.

Second:
A - The President of the Republic's term in office shall end with the end of the term of the Council of Representatives.

B - The President of the Republic shall continue to exercise his duties until after the end of the election and the meeting of the new Council of Representatives, provided that a new President of the Republic is elected within thirty days from the date of its first convening.
C - In case the position of the President of the Republic becomes vacant for any reason, a new President shall be elected to complete the remaining period of the President's term.

Article 73:
The President of the Republic shall assume the following powers:
First: To issue a special pardon on the recommendation of the Prime Minister, except for anything concerning a private claim and for those who have been convicted of committing international crimes, terrorism, or financial and administrative corruption.

Second: To ratify international treaties and agreements after the approval by the Council of Representatives. Such international treaties and agreements are considered ratified after fifteen days from the date of receipt by the President.

Third: To ratify and issue the laws enacted by the Council of Representatives. Such laws are considered ratified after fifteen days from the date of receipt by the President.

Fourth: To call the elected Council of Representatives to convene during a period not to exceed fifteen days from the date of approval of the election results and in the other cases stipulated in the Constitution.

Fifth: To award medals and decorations on the recommendation of the Prime Minister in accordance with the law.

Sixth: To accredit ambassadors.

Seventh: To issue Presidential decrees.

Eighth: To ratify death sentences issued by the competent courts.

Ninth: To perform the duty of the High Command of the armed forces for ceremonial and honorary purposes.

Tenth: To exercise any other presidential powers stipulated in this Constitution.

Article 74:
A law shall fix the salary and the allowances of the President of the Republic.

Article 75:
First: The President of the Republic shall have the right to submit his resignation in writing to the Speaker of the Council of Representatives, and it shall be considered effective after seven days from the date of its submission to the Council of Representatives.

Second: The Vice President shall replace the President in case of his absence.

Third: The Vice President shall replace the President of the Republic in the event that the post of the President becomes vacant for any reason whatsoever. The Council of Representatives must elect a new President within a period not to exceed thirty days from the date of the vacancy.

Fourth: In case the post of the President of the Republic becomes vacant, the Speaker of the Council of Representatives shall replace the President of the Republic in case he does not have a Vice President, on the condition that a new President is elected during a period not to exceed thirty days from the date of the vacancy and in accordance with the provisions of this Constitution.

Second: Council of Ministers

Article 76:
First: The President of the Republic shall charge the nominee of the largest Council of Representatives bloc with the formation of the Council of Ministers within fifteen days from the date of the election of the President of the Republic.

Second: The Prime Minister-designate shall undertake the naming of the members of his Council of Ministers within a period not to exceed thirty days from the date of his designation.

Third: If the Prime Minister-designate fails to form the Council of Ministers during the period specified in clause "Second," the President of the Republic shall charge a new nominee for the post of Prime Minister within fifteen days.

Fourth: The Prime Minister-designate shall present the names of his members of the Council of Ministers and the ministerial program to the Council of Representatives. He is deemed to have gained its confidence upon the approval, by an absolute majority of the Council of Representatives, of the individual Ministers and the ministerial program.

Fifth: The President of the Republic shall charge another nominee to form the Council of Ministers within fifteen days in case the Council of Ministers did not win the vote of confidence.

Article 77:
First: The conditions for assuming the post of the Prime Minister shall be the same as those for the President of the Republic, provided that he has a college degree or its equivalent and is over thirty-five years of age.

Second: The conditions for assuming the post of Minister shall be the same as those for members of the Council of Representatives, provided that he holds a college degree or its equivalent.

Article 78:
The Prime Minister is the direct executive authority responsible for the general policy of the State and the commander-in-chief of the armed forces. He directs the Council of Ministers, presides over its meetings, and has the right to dismiss the Ministers, with the consent of the Council of Representatives.

Article 79:
The Prime Minister and members of the Council of Ministers shall take the constitutional oath before the Council of Representatives according to the language stipulated in Article 50 of the Constitution.

Article 80:
The Council of Ministers shall exercise the following powers:
First: To plan and execute the general policy and general plans of the State and oversee the work of the ministries and departments not associated with a ministry.

Second: To propose bills.

Third: To issue rules, instructions, and decisions for the purpose of implementing the law.

Fourth: To prepare the draft of the general budget, the closing account, and the development plans.

Fifth: To recommend to the Council of Representatives that it approve the appointment of undersecretaries, ambassadors, state senior officials, the Chief of Staff of the Armed Forces and his deputies, division commanders or higher, the Director of the National Intelligence Service, and heads of security institutions.

Sixth: To negotiate and sign international agreements and treaties, or designate any person to do so.

Article 81:
First: The President of the Republic shall take up the office of the Prime Minister in the event the post becomes vacant for any reason whatsoever.

Second: If the event mentioned in "First" of this Article occurs, the President shall charge another nominee to form the Council of Ministers within a period not to exceed fifteen days in accordance with the provisions of Article 76 of this Constitution.

Article 82:
A law shall regulate the salaries and allowances of the Prime Minister and Ministers, and anyone of their grade.

Article 83:
The responsibility of the Prime Minister and the Ministers before the Council of Representatives is of a joint and personal nature.

Article 84:
First: A law shall regulate the work and define the duties and authorities of the security institutions and the National Intelligence Service, which shall operate in accordance with the principles of human rights and shall be subject to the oversight of the Council of Representatives.

Second: The National Intelligence Service shall be attached to the Council of Ministers.

Article 85:
The Council of Ministers shall establish internal bylaws to organize the work therein.

Article 86:
A law shall regulate the formation of ministries, their functions, and their specializations, and the authorities of the minister.

Chapter Three
[The Judicial Power]

Article 87:
The judicial power is independent. The courts, in their various types and levels, shall assume this power and issue decisions in accordance with the law.

Article 88:
Judges are independent, and there is no authority over them except that of the law. No power shall have the right to interfere in the judiciary and the affairs of justice.

Article 89:
The federal judicial power is comprised of the Higher Juridical Council, the Federal Supreme Court, the Federal Court of Cassation, the Public Prosecution Department, the Judiciary Oversight Commission, and other federal courts that are regulated in accordance with the law.

First: Higher Juridical Council

Article 90:
The Higher Juridical Council shall oversee the affairs of the judicial committees. The law shall specify the method of its establishment, its authorities, and the rules of its operation.

Article 91:
The Higher Juridical Council shall exercise the following authorities:
First: To manage the affairs of the judiciary and supervise the federal judiciary.

Second: To nominate the Chief Justice and members of the Federal Court of Cassation, the Chief Public Prosecutor, and the Chief Justice of the Judiciary Oversight Commission, and to present those nominations to the Council of Representatives to approve their appointment.

Third: To propose the draft of the annual budget of the federal judicial authority, and to present it to the Council of Representatives for approval.

Second: Federal Supreme Court

Article 92:
First: The Federal Supreme Court is an independent judicial body, financially and administratively.

Second: The Federal Supreme Court shall be made up of a number of judges, experts in Islamic jurisprudence, and legal scholars, whose number, the method of their selection, and the work of the Court shall be determined by a law enacted by a two-thirds majority of the members of the Council of Representatives.

Article 93:
The Federal Supreme Court shall have jurisdiction over the following:

First: Overseeing the constitutionality of laws and regulations in effect.

Second: Interpreting the provisions of the Constitution.

Third: Settling matters that arise from the application of the federal laws, decisions, regulations, instructions, and procedures issued by the federal authority. The law shall guarantee the right of direct appeal to the Court to the Council of Ministers, those concerned individuals, and others.

Fourth: Settling disputes that arise between the federal government and the governments of the regions and governorates, municipalities, and local administrations.

Fifth: Settling disputes that arise between the governments of the regions and governments of the governorates.

Sixth: Settling accusations directed against the President, the Prime Minister and the Ministers, and this shall be regulated by law.

Seventh: Ratifying the final results of the general elections for membership in the Council of Representatives.

Eight:
A. Settling competency disputes between the federal judiciary and the judicial institutions of the regions and governorates that are not organized in a region.
B. Settling competency disputes between judicial institutions of the regions or governorates that are not organized in a region.

Article 94:
Decisions of the Federal Supreme Court are final and binding for all authorities.

Third: General Provisions

Article 95:
The establishment of special or extraordinary courts is prohibited.

Article 96:
The law shall regulate the establishment of courts, their types, levels, and jurisdiction, and the method of appointing and the terms of service of judges and public prosecutors, their discipline, and their retirement.

Article 97:
Judges may not be removed except in cases specified by law. Such law will determine the particular provisions related to them and shall regulate their disciplinary measures.

Article 98:
A judge or public prosecutor is prohibited from the following:
First: Combining a judicial position with legislative and executive positions and any other

employment.

Second: Joining any party or political organisation or performing any political activity.

Article 99:
A law shall regulate the military judiciary and shall specify the jurisdiction of military courts, which are limited to crimes of a military nature committed by members of the armed forces and security forces, and within the limits established by law.

Article 100:
It is prohibited to stipulate in the law the immunity from appeal for any administrative action or decision.

Article 101:
A State Council may be established, specialized in functions of the administrative judiciary, issuing opinions, drafting, and representing the State and various public commissions before the courts except those exempted by law.

Chapter Four
[Independent Commissions]

Article 102:
The High Commission for Human Rights, the Independent Electoral Commission, and the Commission on Public Integrity are considered independent commissions subject to monitoring by the Council of Representatives, and their functions shall be regulated by law.

Article 103:
First: The Central Bank of Iraq, the Board of Supreme Audit, the Communication and Media Commission, and the Endowment Commissions are financially and administratively independent institutions, and the work of each of these institutions shall be regulated by law.

Second: The Central Bank of Iraq is responsible before the Council of Representatives. The Board of Supreme Audit and the Communication and Media Commission shall be attached to the Council of Representatives.

Third: The Endowment Commissions shall be attached to the Council of Ministers.

Article 104:
A commission named The Martyrs' Foundation shall be established and attached to the Council of Ministers, and its functions and competencies shall be regulated by law.

Article 105:
A public commission shall be established to guarantee the rights of the regions and governorates that are not organized in a region to ensure their fair participation in managing the various state federal institutions, missions, fellowships, delegations, and regional and international conferences. The commission shall be comprised of representatives of the federal government and representatives of the regions and governorates that are not organized in a region, and shall be regulated by a law.

Article 106:
A public commission shall be established by a law to audit and appropriate federal

revenues. The commission shall be comprised of experts from the federal government, the regions, the governorates, and its representatives, and shall assume the following responsibilities:

First: To verify the fair distribution of grants, aid, and international loans pursuant to the entitlement of the regions and governorates that are not organized in a region.

Second: To verify the ideal use and division of the federal financial resources.

Third: To guarantee transparency and justice in appropriating funds to the governments of the regions and governorates that are not organized in a region in accordance with the established percentages.

Article 107:
A council named the Federal Public Service Council shall be established and shall regulate the affairs of the federal public service, including appointments and promotions, and its formation and competencies shall be regulated by law.

Article 108:
Other independent commissions may be established by law, according to need and necessity.

Section Four

Powers of the Federal Government

Article 109:
The federal authorities shall preserve the unity, integrity, independence, and sovereignty of Iraq and its federal democratic system.

Article 110:
The federal government shall have exclusive authorities in the following matters:
First: Formulating foreign policy and diplomatic representation; negotiating, signing, and ratifying international treaties and agreements; negotiating, signing, and ratifying debt policies and formulating foreign sovereign economic and trade policy.

Second: Formulating and executing national security policy, including establishing and managing armed forces to secure the protection and guarantee the security of Iraq's borders and to defend Iraq.

Third: Formulating fiscal and customs policy; issuing currency; regulating commercial policy across regional and governorate boundaries in Iraq; drawing up the national budget of the State; formulating monetary policy; and establishing and administering a central bank.

Fourth: Regulating standards, weights, and measures.
Fifth: Regulating issues of citizenship, naturalization, residency, and the right to apply for political asylum.
Sixth: Regulating the policies of broadcast frequencies and mail.
Seventh: Drawing up the general and investment budget bill.

Eighth: Planning policies relating to water sources from outside Iraq and guaranteeing the rate of water flow to Iraq and its just distribution inside Iraq in accordance with international laws and conventions.

Ninth: General population statistics and census.

Article 111:
Oil and gas are owned by all the people of Iraq in all the regions and governorates.

Article 112:
First: The federal government, with the producing governorates and regional governments, shall undertake the management of oil and gas extracted from present fields, provided that it distributes its revenues in a fair manner in proportion to the population distribution in all parts of the country, specifying an allotment for a specified period for the damaged regions which were unjustly deprived of them by the former regime, and the regions that were damaged afterwards in a way that ensures balanced development in different areas of the country, and this shall be regulated by a law.

Second: The federal government, with the producing regional and governorate governments, shall together formulate the necessary strategic policies to develop the oil and gas wealth in a way that achieves the highest benefit to the Iraqi people using the most advanced techniques of the market principles and encouraging investment.

Article 113:
Antiquities, archeological sites, cultural buildings, manuscripts, and coins shall be considered national treasures under the jurisdiction of the federal authorities, and shall be managed in cooperation with the regions and governorates, and this shall be regulated by law.

Article 114:
The following competencies shall be shared between the federal authorities and regional authorities:
First: To manage customs, in coordination with the governments of the regions and governorates that are not organized in a region, and this shall be regulated by a law.

Second: To regulate the main sources of electric energy and its distribution.

Third: To formulate environmental policy to ensure the protection of the environment from pollution and to preserve its cleanliness, in cooperation with the regions and governorates that are not organized in a region.

Fourth: To formulate development and general planning policies.

Fifth: To formulate public health policy, in cooperation with the regions and governorates that are not organized in a region.

Sixth: To formulate the public educational and instructional policy, in consultation with the regions and governorates that are not organized in a region.

Seventh: To formulate and regulate the internal water resources policy in a way that guarantees their just distribution, and this shall be regulated by a law.

Article 115:
All powers not stipulated in the exclusive powers of the federal government belong to the authorities of the regions and governorates that are not organized in a region. With regard

to other powers shared between the federal government and the regional government, priority shall be given to the law of the regions and governorates not organized in a region in case of dispute.

<u>**Section Five**</u>

<u>**Powers of the Regions**</u>

<u>**Chapter One**</u>
<u>**[Regions]**</u>

Article 116:
The federal system in the Republic of Iraq is made up of a decentralized capital, regions, and governorates, as well as local administrations.

Article 117:
First: This Constitution, upon coming into force, shall recognize the region of Kurdistan, along with its existing authorities, as a federal region.

Second: This Constitution shall affirm new regions established in accordance with its provisions.

Article 118:
The Council of Representatives shall enact, in a period not to exceed six months from the date of its first session, a law that defines the executive procedures to form regions, by a simple majority of the members present.

Article 119:
One or more governorates shall have the right to organize into a region based on a request to be voted on in a referendum submitted in one of the following two methods:
First: A request by one-third of the council members of each governorate intending to form a region.

Second: A request by one-tenth of the voters in each of the governorates intending to form a region.

Article 120:
Each region shall adopt a constitution of its own that defines the structure of powers of the region, its authorities, and the mechanisms for exercising such authorities, provided that it does not contradict this Constitution.

Article 121:
First: The regional powers shall have the right to exercise executive, legislative, and judicial powers in accordance with this Constitution, except for those authorities stipulated in the exclusive authorities of the federal government.

Second: In case of a contradiction between regional and national legislation in respect to a matter outside the exclusive authorities of the federal government, the regional power shall have the right to amend the application of the national legislation within that region.

Third: Regions and governorates shall be allocated an equitable share of the national revenues sufficient to discharge their responsibilities and duties, but having regard to their resources, needs, and the percentage of their population.

Fourth: Offices for the regions and governorates shall be established in embassies and diplomatic missions, in order to follow cultural, social, and developmental affairs.

Fifth: The regional government shall be responsible for all the administrative requirements of the region, particularly the establishment and organisation of the internal security forces for the region such as police, security forces, and guards of the region.

Chapter Two
[Governorates that are not incorporated in a region]

Article 122:
First: The governorates shall be made up of a number of districts, sub-districts, and villages.

Second: Governorates that are not incorporated in a region shall be granted broad administrative and financial authorities to enable them to manage their affairs in accordance with the principle of decentralized administration, and this shall be regulated by law.

Third: The governor, who is elected by the Governorate Council, is deemed the highest executive official in the governorate to practice his powers authorized by the Council.

Fourth: A law shall regulate the election of the Governorate Council, the governor, and their powers.

Fifth: The Governorate Council shall not be subject to the control or supervision of any ministry or any institution not linked to a ministry. The Governorate Council shall have independent finances.

Article 123:
Powers exercised by the federal government can be delegated to the governorates or vice versa, with the consent of both governments, and this shall be regulated by law.

Chapter Three
[The Capital]

Article 124:
First: Baghdad in its municipal borders is the capital of the Republic of Iraq and shall constitute, in its administrative borders, the governorate of Baghdad.

Second: This shall be regulated by a law.

Third: The capital may not merge with a region.

Chapter Four
[The Local Administrations]

Article 125:
This Constitution shall guarantee the administrative, political, cultural, and educational rights of the various nationalities, such as Turkomen, Chaldeans, Assyrians, and all other constituents, and this shall be regulated by law.

<u>**Section Six**</u>

<u>**Final and Transitional Provisions**</u>

<u>**Chapter One**</u>
<u>**[Final Provisions]**</u>

Article 126:
First: The President of the Republic and the Council of the Ministers collectively, or one-fifth of the Council of Representatives members, may propose to amend the Constitution.

Second: The fundamental principles mentioned in Section One and the rights and liberties mentioned in Section Two of the Constitution may not be amended except after two successive electoral terms, with the approval of two-thirds of the members of the Council of Representatives, the approval of the people in a general referendum, and the ratification by the President of the Republic within seven days.

Third: Other articles not stipulated in clause "Second" of this Article may not be amended, except with the approval of two-thirds of the members of the Council of Representatives, the approval of the people in a general referendum, and the ratification by the President of the Republic within seven days.

Fourth: Articles of the Constitution may not be amended if such amendment takes away from the powers of the regions that are not within the exclusive powers of the federal authorities, except by the approval of the legislative authority of the concerned region and the approval of the majority of its citizens in a general referendum.

Fifth:
A - An amendment is considered ratified by the President of the Republic after the expiration of the period stipulated in clauses "Second" and "Third" of this Article, in case he does not ratify it.

B - An amendment shall enter into force on the date of its publication in the Official Gazette.

Article 127:
The President of the Republic, the Prime Minister, members of the Council of Ministers, the Speaker of the Council of Representatives, his two Deputies, members of the Council of Representatives, members of the Judicial Authority, and people of special grades may not use their influence to buy or rent any state properties, to rent or sell any of their assets to the state, to sue the state for these assets, or to conclude a contract with the state under the pretense of being building contractors, suppliers, or concessionaires.

Article 128:
The laws and judicial judgments shall be issued in the name of the people.

Article 129:
Laws shall be published in the Official Gazette and shall take effect on the date of their publication, unless stipulated otherwise.

Article 130:
Existing laws shall remain in force, unless annulled or amended in accordance with the

provisions of this Constitution.

Article 131:
Every referendum mentioned in this Constitution is deemed successful with the approval of the majority of the voters unless otherwise stipulated.

Chapter Two
[Transitional Provisions]

Article 132:
First: The State shall guarantee care for the families of the martyrs, political prisoners, and victims of the oppressive practices of the defunct dictatorial regime.

Second: The State shall guarantee compensation to the families of the martyrs and the injured as a result of terrorist acts.

Third: A law shall regulate matters mentioned in clauses "First" and "Second" of this Article.

Article 133:
The Council of Representatives shall adopt in its first session the bylaws of the Transitional National Assembly until it adopts its own bylaws.

Article 134:
The Iraqi High Tribunal shall continue its duties as an independent judicial body, in examining the crimes of the defunct dictatorial regime and its symbols. The Council of Representatives shall have the right to dissolve it by law after the completion of its work.

Article 135:
First: The High Commission for De-Ba'athification shall continue its functions as an independent commission, in coordination with the judicial authority and the executive institutions within the framework of the laws regulating its functions. The Commission shall be attached to the Council of Representatives.

Second: The Council of Representatives shall have the right to dissolve this Commission by an absolute majority after the completion of its function.

Third: A nominee to the positions of the President of the Republic, the Prime Minister, the members of the Council of Ministers, the Speaker, the members of the Council of Representatives, the President, members of the Federation Council, their counterparts in the regions, or members of the judicial commissions and other positions covered by de-Ba'athification statutes pursuant to the law may not be subject to the provisions of de-Ba'athification.

Fourth: The conditions stated in clause "Third" of this Article shall remain in force unless the Commission stated in item "First" of this Article is dissolved.

Fifth: Mere membership in the dissolved Ba'ath party shall not be considered a sufficient basis for referral to court, and a member shall enjoy equality before the law and protection unless covered by the provisions of De-Ba'athification and the directives issued according to it.

Sixth: The Council of Representatives shall form a parliamentary committee from among its members to monitor and review the executive procedures of the Higher Commission for De-Ba'athification and state institutions to guarantee justice, objectivity, and transparency and to examine their consistency with the laws. The committee's decisions shall be subject to the approval of the Council of Representatives.

Article 136:
First: The Property Claims Commission shall continue its functions as an independent commission in coordination with the judicial authority and the executive institutions in accordance with the law. The Property Claims Commission shall be attached to the Council of Representatives.

Second: The Council of Representatives shall have the right to dissolve the Commission by a two-thirds majority vote of its members.

Article 137:
Application of the provisions of the articles related to the Federation Council, wherever it may be cited in this Constitution, shall be postponed until the Council of Representatives issues a decision by a two-thirds majority vote in its second electoral term that is held after this Constitution comes into force.

Article 138:
First: The expression "the Presidency Council" shall replace the expression "the President of the Republic" wherever the latter is mentioned in this Constitution. The provisions related to the President of the Republic shall be reactivated one successive term after this Constitution comes into force.

Second:
A. The Council of Representatives shall elect the President of the State and two Vice Presidents who shall form a Council called the "Presidency Council," which shall be elected by one list and with a two-thirds majority.

B. The provisions to remove the President of the Republic present in this Constitution shall apply to the President and members of the Presidency Council.

C. The Council of Representatives may remove a member of the Presidency Council with a three-fourths majority of the number of its members for reasons of incompetence and dishonesty.

D. In the event of a vacant seat in the Presidency Council, the Council of Representatives shall elect a replacement by a two-thirds majority vote of its members.

Third: Members of the Presidency Council shall be subject to the same conditions as a member of the Council of Representatives and must:
A. Be over forty years of age.
B. Enjoy good reputation, integrity and uprightness.
C. Have quit the dissolved (Ba'ath) Party ten years prior to its fall, in case he was a member of it.
D. Have not participated in suppressing the 1991 and Al-Anfal uprisings. He must not have committed a crime against the Iraqi people.

Fourth: The Presidency Council shall issue its decisions unanimously and any member may delegate to one of the two other members to take his place.

Fifth:
A - Legislation and decisions enacted by the Council of Representatives shall be forwarded to the Presidency Council for their unanimous approval and for its issuance within ten days from the date of delivery to the Presidency Council, except the stipulations of Articles 118 and 119 that pertain to the formation of regions.

B - In the event the Presidency Council does not approve, legislation and decisions shall be sent back to the Council of Representatives to reexamine the disputed issues and to vote on them by the majority of its members and then shall be sent for the second time to the Presidency Council for approval.

C - In the event the Presidency Council does not approve the legislation and decisions for the second time within ten days of receipt, the legislation and decisions are sent back to the Council of Representatives, which has the right to adopt it by three-fifths majority of its members, which may not be challenged, and the legislation or decision shall be considered ratified.

Sixth: The Presidency Council shall exercise the powers of the President of the Republic stipulated in this Constitution.

Article 139:
The Prime Minister shall have two deputies in the first electoral term.

Article 140:
First: The executive authority shall undertake the necessary steps to complete the implementation of the requirements of all subparagraphs of Article 58 of the Transitional Administrative Law.

Second: The responsibility placed upon the executive branch of the Iraqi Transitional Government stipulated in Article 58 of the Transitional Administrative Law shall extend and continue to the executive authority elected in accordance with this Constitution, provided that it accomplishes completely (normalization and census and concludes with a referendum in Kirkuk and other disputed territories to determine the will of their citizens), by a date not to exceed the 31st of December 2007.

Article 141:
Legislation enacted in the region of Kurdistan since 1992 shall remain in force, and decisions issued by the government of the region of Kurdistan, including court decisions and contracts, shall be considered valid unless they are amended or annulled pursuant to the laws of the region of Kurdistan by the competent entity in the region, provided that they do not contradict with the Constitution.

Article 142:
First: The Council of Representatives shall form at the beginning of its work a committee from its members representing the principal components of the Iraqi society with the mission of presenting to the Council of Representatives, within a period not to exceed four months, a report that contains recommendations of the necessary amendments that could be made to the Constitution, and the committee shall be dissolved after a decision is made regarding its proposals.

Second: The proposed amendments shall be presented to the Council of Representatives all at once for a vote upon them, and shall be deemed approved with the agreement of the absolute majority of the members of the Council.

Third: The articles amended by the Council of Representatives pursuant to item "Second" of this Article shall be presented to the people for voting on them in a referendum within a period not exceeding two months from the date of their approval by the Council of Representatives.

Fourth: The referendum on the amended Articles shall be successful if approved by the majority of the voters, and if not rejected by two-thirds of the voters in three or more governorates.

Fifth: Article 126 of the Constitution (concerning amending the Constitution) shall be suspended, and shall return into force after the amendments stipulated in this Article have been decided upon.

Article 143:
The Transitional Administrative Law and its Annex shall be annulled on the seating of the new government, except for the stipulations of Article 53(A) and Article 58 of the Transitional Administrative Law.

Article 144:
This Constitution shall come into force after the approval of the people thereon in a general referendum, its publication in the Official Gazette, and the seating of the government that is formed pursuant to this Constitution.

Iraq - Kurdistan Parliament

June 23, 2009

Draft Constitution of the Iraqi Kurdistan Region

Prepared by: The Committee for Revising the Draft Constitution of the Iraqi Kurdistan Region

June 23, 2009

The Preamble

We, the People of Iraqi Kurdistan,

Acknowledging that successive generations of our people have suffered from oppression, persecution, tyranny and campaigns of genocide, that they have been deprived and dispossessed of their rights to freedom, equality and justice, which were granted by God to all of mankind; carrying out crimes against humanity and ethnic cleansing the history has rarely witnessed the unprecedented; presented by the removal of about four thousands five hundred villages and change demographic features in large parts of Iraq-Kurdistan by forced displacement of its population, forcing them to change their nationality, using chemical weapons and other internationally forbidden weapons against civilian in Halabcha city, Balisan, Karmyan, Bahdinan and other wide areas, and gave thousands of Fayli Kurds to their death in the fields of chemical testing and genocide campaigns after that of the remaining abandoned out of Iraq and their Iraq nationality was shot down, followed by genocide campaigns including more than eight thousands of Baraznis, and the Anfal genocide operation that claimed more than 182 thousand people. [TC: The paragraph in Red above has been added to 2009 version]

Cherishing the leaders and symbols of the Kurdish Liberation Movement, its Peshmerga fighters, and its devoted martyrs; appreciating the sacrifices they offered for our freedom, for the defense of our dignity, the protection of our nation, and in order to safeguard our right to determine our destiny in our own complete free will ;

Honoring the mission, the goals and the values for which they sacrificed so much;

Aiming to establish a developed and cultivated Kurdish society which prides itself on its ethnic and religious groups, is open to all, unleashes the energies of its citizens, and where a spirit of fraternity and tolerance prevails;

Seeking to build Kurdistan as a nation united for all, founded upon democratic values, enlightened by the principles of human rights, where law and justice prevail ;

Striving to anchor good governance that emanates from our free will, embodies our hopes, and honors our sacrifices;

Our choices have become unified, and our desire converges with that of the other components of the people of Iraq and its national forces for Iraqi Kurdistan to be a federal region within the federal state of Iraq;

As an embodiment of this desire, and a fulfillment of these aims, we have adopted this constitution.

Section One
Fundamental Principles

Article 1:
The Iraqi Kurdistan Region is a region within the Federal State of Iraq. It is a democratic republic with a parliamentary political system that is based on political pluralism, the principle of separation of powers, and the peaceful transfer of power through direct, general, and periodic elections that use a secret ballot.

Article 2:
<u>First:</u> The Iraqi Kurdistan Region is a geographical historical entity consisting of Dohuk governorate with its existing administrative borders, Kirkuk, Sulaymaniyah, Arbil, and districts of 'Aqrah, Shaikhan, Sinjar, Talkaif, Qaraqush, and townshipsh of Zamar, Ba'asheeqa, and Aski Kalak from Nineveh province, districts of Khanaqeen and Mandali from Diyala province with its administrative boarder before 1968.
[TC: Item first above reflects the new text in 2009, however, the text in Red below reflects 2008 version]
<u>First:</u> The Iraqi Kurdistan Region is a geographical, historical and political entity that includes all of the areas indicated in Article 143 of the Federal Constitution, and the other areas that shall be recovered according to Article 140 of the aforementioned Constitution.

<u>Second:</u> The political borders of the Region shall be determined through the implementation of Article 140 of the Federal Constitution.
<u>Third:</u> A new region may not be established within the borders of the Iraqi Kurdistan Region.

Article 3:
<u>First:</u> The people are the source of authority and the basis of its legitimacy; said authority shall be exercised by the people through their constitutional institutions. The Constitution and the laws of the Kurdistan Region are sovereign and supersede all laws issued by the Iraqi government outside of the exclusive jurisdiction of the Federal Authorities, as stipulated in Article 110 of the Constitution of the Federal Republic of Iraq.
<u>Second:</u> In accordance with Article 115 and Paragraph 2 of Article 121 of the Federal Constitution, in the event that the federal law deals with matters within the exclusive jurisdiction of the federal authorities, as listed in Article 110 of the Federal Constitution, or with other matters outside this jurisdiction, this shall not detract from the sovereignty and supremacy of the Constitution and laws of the Kurdistan Region, nor shall it limit the powers of the Region's authorities.

Article 4:

The Parliament of Kurdistan may put into effect in the Region any federal law that is outside the exclusive jurisdiction of the federal authorities, as stipulated in Article 110 of the Federal Constitution of the Republic of Iraq.

Article 5:

The people of the Kurdistan Region are composed of Kurds, Turkmens, Arabs, Chaldo-Assyrian-Syriacs, Armenians and others who are citizens of Kurdistan.

<u>Second:</u> The right to citizenship in the Region shall be regulated by law.
[TC: The item (Second) in Red above is not included in the new constitution].

Article 6:

This Constitution confirms and respects the Islamic identity of the majority of the people of Iraqi Kurdistan. It considers the principles of Islamic *Sharia* as one of the main sources of legislation. Likewise, this Constitution upholds and respects all the religious rights of Christians, Yazidis, and others, and it guarantees to every individual in the Region freedom of belief and the freedom to practice their religious rites and rituals. It is not allowed:
First: Enact a law inconsistent with the provisions of the fundamentals of Islam.
Second: Enact a law inconsistent with Democracy principals.

Third: Enact a law inconsistent with the rights and fundamental freedoms contained in this constitution.
[TC: The items in Red above have been added to 2009 edition]

Article 7:

The people of Iraqi Kurdistan shall have the right to determine their own destiny, and they have chosen, out of their own free will, to be a federal region within Iraq, as long as Iraq abides by the federal, democratic, parliamentary and pluralistic system, and remains committed to the human rights of individuals and groups, as stipulated in the Federal Constitution.

Article 8:

<u>First:</u> International treaties and agreements which the Federal Government enters into with any foreign state or party, and which affect the status or rights of the Kurdistan Region shall be effective in the Region if said treaties and agreements meet with the approval of an absolute majority of the Members of the Parliament of Kurdistan.
<u>Second:</u> Treaties and agreements which the Federal Government enters into with foreign states shall not be effective in the Kurdistan Region if they deal with matters outside the Federal Government's exclusive jurisdiction, in accordance with Article 110 of the Federal Constitution, unless an absolute majority of the Members of the Parliament of Kurdistan approve the implementation of said treaties and agreements in the Region.
<u>Third:</u> The Kurdistan Region shall have the right to enter into agreements with foreign states or with regions within foreign states regarding issues that do not lie within the exclusive jurisdiction of the federal authorities, as stipulated in Article 110 of the Federal Constitution.
<u>Fourth:</u> An agreement concluded between the Kurdistan Region and the governments of foreign states shall be submitted to the Federal Government to secure its approval. Said agreement shall not be effective if the Federal Government refuses to approve it for legal reasons.

Article 9:

With regard to the Federal Government, the Region shall have a fundamental and constitutional right to:

First:, An equitable share of federal income, including international grants, aid, and loans, pursuant to Articles 106 and 112 of the Federal Constitution. This share shall be determined according to the principle of demographic proportionality and equality, while taking into consideration the policy of genocide, scorching and destruction that afflicted Iraqi Kurdistan during previous regimes and deprived its people of their entitlements.
Second: Equitable participation, in a balanced and proportionate manner, in the administration of the different institutions of the federal state, in academic deputations and scholarships, in delegations and in regional and international conferences. Pursuant to Article 105 of the Federal Constitution, positions in Federal Government offices that are located in the Kurdistan Region shall be entrusted to the citizens of the Region.

Article 10:

The city of Erbil (Hewlêr[1514]) shall be the capital of the Kurdistan Region. The parliament may select another city in Kurdistan as the capital.

Article 11:

First: The Iraqi Kurdistan Region shall have its own flag, which shall be flown side-by-side with the federal flag. The Kurdistan Region shall have its own national emblem, national anthem, and National Day (Noruz[1515]). This shall be regulated by law.
Second: The flag shall be composed of a red [stripe], a white [stripe], and a green [stripe]. A yellow sun with twenty-one rays emanating from it shall be located in the middle. The dimensions of the flag and the meaning of its components shall be determined by law.
Third: A law shall be enacted to regulate official holidays, badges and medals.

Article 12:

The defensive Peshmerga Forces shall guard the Kurdistan Region in accordance with item Five of Article (121) of the constitution. The organisation and duties of these forces shall be regulated by law. Armed militias may not be formed outside of the scope of the law.

Article 13:

No fee or tax may be imposed, modified or waived in the Kurdistan Region without the approval of the parliament of Kurdistan, who must pass a law to that effect.

Article 14:

First: Kurdish and Arabic shall be the two official languages of the Kurdistan Region. This Constitution guarantees the right of the citizens of the Kurdistan Region to educate their children in their mother tongue, including Turkmen, Assyrian, and Armenian, in the government's educational institutions and in accordance with pedagogical guidelines.

Second: Along with Kurdish and Arabic, Turkmen and Assyrian shall be official languages in administrative districts that are densely populated by speakers of Turkmen and Assyrian. This shall be regulated by law.
Third: Concerning the official language, Article 4 of the Federal Constitution shall be adopted wherever there exists a legal possibility to apply its provisions in the Kurdistan Region.

Article 15:

The Kurdistan Region shall adopt a competitive legal market economy, which encourages and embraces economic development on modern foundations, as well as public and private investment. Monopolies shall not be allowed, except as regulated by law.

[1514] Translator's Note: This is the transliteration of the Kurdish name for Erbil.
[1515] Translator's Note: Noruz is the day celebrating the Kurdish New Year.

Article 16:
In light of their responsibility to current and future generations, all Regional Authorities must protect the environment, the essential means of subsistence, and the natural and human environment in the Kurdistan Region. The law shall regulate the establishment of protected areas, wild areas, natural parks and public gardens, in order to protect nature, wildlife, wilderness and natural plants and animals, and to preserve them in their natural state. The law shall not permit the erection of buildings or any motorized activity in these zones.

Article 17:
First: The general sources and components of natural resources, surface and ground water, unextracted minerals, quarries, and mines are a public resource. A law which protects these resources for current and future generations shall regulate the extraction, exploitation or management of said resources, and the conditions for their allocation.
Second: Lands and public property in the Region are the property of the people of Kurdistan. A law shall regulate their allocation and exploitation.

Section Two
Fundamental Rights
Chapter One
Civil and Political Rights

Article 18 – Commitment and Application:
First: The legislative, executive and judicial authorities of the Kurdistan Region shall be committed to upholding the fundamental rights listed in this Constitution, considering them a basic element of legislation that must be applied and implemented, as these are the fundamental rights of the Region's citizens.
Second: Whenever application of stipulations and provisions related to the fundamental rights listed in this Constitution is possible, such stipulation and provisions shall be mandatory for natural and juridical persons, while taking into consideration the nature of the right and the nature of the duty imposed by this right.
Third: Within the Kurdistan Region, the fundamental rights granted in this Constitution to natural persons shall also be granted to juridical persons, where applicable.
Ninth: There is no coercion in matters of religion. Every person has the right to freedom of religion, belief, thought and conscience. The Government of the Region shall guarantee the freedom of Muslims, Christians, Yazidis and others to worship and to practice their rites and the rituals of their religions without being exposed [to danger]. The government of the Region shall guarantee the sanctity of mosques, churches, and places of worship. In order to safeguard their sanctity and the holiness of their message, therefore, it is forbidden for parties, groups or persons to use mosques, churches or places of worship as a place for party activity or political activity.
   1.   It is forbidden for parties, groups or persons to use mosques, churches or places of worship as a place for party activity or political activity.
   2.   It is forbidden for men of religion to use mosques, churches or places of worship as a pulpit to promote their factional or political ideas.
[TC: Item (1.) and (2.) above deleted from 2009 version, however, item (1.) above was merged with item (Ninth) above, while Item (2.) is not included]

Tenth: Every person shall have the right to freedom of expression. The freedom and diversity of the press and other media must be guaranteed. This right shall not apply to libel, infringement of others' rights, sacrilege, provocation to violence, or the incitement of hatred between the groups of the people of Kurdistan.

<u>Eleventh:</u> The right to access information technology shall be guaranteed by law.
<u>Twelfth:</u> The Government of the Region shall guarantee the freedom of communication and correspondence by post, telegram, telephone, and electronic means. Such communication and correspondence may not be subject to surveillance, wiretapping, or disclosure unless for legal or security requirements, and when authorized by a judicial decision.
<u>Thirteenth:</u> The Government of the Kurdistan Region shall be responsible for youth welfare, for developing the faculties and abilities of the young generation, and encouraging their initiative. The Government shall establish the institutions required to train young people and to empower them to keep up with worldwide scientific and technological developments, so that they can play an effective role in society and invest their talents in economic, social and scientific development. The Government shall lay out programs and plans to achieve this purpose.
<u>Fourteenth:</u> Every citizen shall have the right to practice sports. The Government of the Kurdistan Region shall encourage sporting activities, establish dedicated sporting institutions, and provide the necessary requirements for them.
<u>Fifteenth:</u> Artistic and literary expression and scientific research shall be free from any restrictions. Academic freedom to perform scientific research must be guaranteed and encouraged. Universities and scientific centers must be supported and sponsored; their sanctity upheld, and the elements of their moral character guaranteed. Their administrative apparatus must be developed on a decentralized basis.
<u>Sixteenth:</u> The Government of the Region shall be responsible for protecting intellectual property, copyright, publication rights, patents, and registered trademarks.
<u>Eighteenth:</u>

1. The freedom to found [political] parties shall be guaranteed and regulated by law, provided that the internal order, organisations, and activities of the party, as well as the rights of its members, abide by the fundamental principles of democracy and human rights, and by the provisions of this Constitution. The party must also respect the flag of Kurdistan and its national anthem.
2. The party may not be the branch of a foreign party, or beholden to foreign interests or entities.
3. A party shall be considered in violation of the Constitution if it seeks through its goals, its activities, or the behavior of its followers to violate the fundamental democratic system of the Kurdistan Region or to remove this system; or if it seeks in the aforementioned manner to threaten the unity of the Region, or the peaceful coexistence of its ethnic and religious groups. The Constitutional Court shall be the agency charged with deciding [whether or not the party is considered in violation of the Constitution] , and it shall take this decision in light of the imputed Constitutional violation, and the extent of its danger.
4. Any entity or approach that adopts, instigates, facilitates, glorifies, promotes, or justifies ethnic or sectarian cleansing or a chauvinist, fascist, racist, terrorist, or *takfiri*[1516] ideology shall be prohibited. The authorities of Iraqi Kurdistan shall be committed to combating terrorism in all its forms, and shall work to protect the territories of the Region from becoming a center or a gateway or a platform for terrorist activity.
5. A party must disclose to the relevant authorities specified in the law its revenues and sources of funding, and how it disposes of them.

[1516] Translator's Note: *Takfiri* means 'declaring others infidels' (*kufar*). It is a process often used by extremist Sunni groups against other Muslims and non-Muslims alike, thereby justifying the use of violence against them. The translator has chosen to keep the Arabic term, as no single English expression accurately renders the meaning of the Arabic.

3. Parties shall be forbidden from using religion, quotations from holy books, or religious rites and rituals to discredit others for the purpose of achieving partisan or electoral goals.

[TC: Item (3.) in Red above was included in 2008 version; however, this item is eliminated from the 2009 constitution].

<u>Nineteenth:</u> Collective expulsions shall be forbidden.

<u>Twentieth:</u> Within the limits of the law, every person shall have the right to own, inherit, or bequeath his possessions and his property that he has obtained by legal means. Private property shall be protected. It may not be seized or confiscated except in the public interest, and in accordance with a law which provides for fair and immediate compensation being paid at the latest on the date the property is seized, unless the owner agrees [otherwise] by written approval.[1517]

<u>Nineteenth:</u> The right of political asylum shall be guaranteed. A refugee shall not be expelled or returned to a state where he was persecuted. The Geneva Convention [Relating to the Status of Refugees] , adopted on 28 July 1951, and the Protocol [Relating to the Status of Refugees] of 31 January 1967 shall be taken into consideration and respected.

[TC: The item in Red above was eliminated from 2009 constitution. There were (21) items in 2008 version, while only (20) items are included in Article 18 above of 2009 version]

Article 20:

<u>First:</u> All are equal before the law.

<u>Second:</u> All forms of discrimination on the basis of race, color, sex, language, social background, nationality, origin, religion, belief, thought, age, social, political or economic status, or handicap are prohibited. The principle of equality shall not prevent redressing the effects and consequences of past injustice perpetrated by former regimes against the citizens of Kurdistan and its ethnic, religious and linguistic groups.

<u>Third:</u> Men and women shall be equal before the law. The Government of the Region must seek to remove all obstacles hindering equality in all spheres of life, and in civil, political, social, cultural and economic rights. The Government of the Region guarantees that all shall enjoy their rights, as stipulated in this Constitution and the international charters signed by the State of Iraq.

Article 21 –Citizenship Rights:

<u>First:</u> Any citizen who has reached 18 years of age shall have the right to vote in any election or referendum organized in the area of his residence within the Region of Kurdistan.

<u>Second:</u> Any citizen who has reached 18 years of age shall have the right to hold public office.

<u>Third:</u> Freedom of residence, movement and travel shall be guaranteed, within the limits of the law.

<u>Fourth:</u> Every citizen shall have the right to submit a complaint or petition with the authorities of the Region, who may not refuse to accept it. Whoever has submitted a complaint or petition has to right to receive a prompt response. A refusal to deliver said response, or a delay in arriving at the response with no legal justification shall entail legal responsibility.

Article 22 – The Right to a Fair Trial

[1517] Translator's Note: The Arabic text is unclear as to what the "owner's written approval" refers to. The translator's best guess is reflected in his rendering of the Arabic text.

First: The investigating authority shall submit preliminary investigative documents to a competent judge within a period not exceeding twenty-four hours from the time at which the accused was apprehended. This period may only be extended once, for another period of twenty-four hours.

Second: [Arbitrary] detention of individuals shall be prohibited. No one shall be arrested or imprisoned except in accordance with the law, and based on an order issued to that effect by a competent judicial authority. Any arrested individual must be informed, immediately and in his own language, of the charge brought against him. The apprehended individual has the right of recourse to an attorney. During the investigation and the trial, the court shall appoint an attorney, who shall serve at the Government's expense, to defend the accused charged with committing a felony or a misdemeanor and who does not have an attorney to defend him.

Third: The accused shall be innocent until proven guilty in a fair and legal trial. After being released, the accused shall not be tried again on the same charge, unless new evidence appears.

Fourth: Every one shall have the right to a fair and speedy trial before a competent court.

Fifth: No act shall be considered a crime and no punishment shall be imposed except as stipulated by law. No one may be convicted on account of an act or an omission which did not constitute a criminal offence at the time it was committed.

Sixth:
1. No law shall have a retroactive effect, unless the text of the law stipulates otherwise. This shall not apply to taxes and fees.
2. Penal law shall not have a retroactive effect, unless this is more favorable for the accused.

Seventh: Punishment shall be individual.

Eighth: No heavier punishment shall be imposed than the one that was applicable at the time the criminal offence was committed.

Ninth: No one shall be tried or punished twice by criminal or penal procedures for an offense of which they were already acquitted or convicted in accordance with the law.

Tenth: Civilians may not be tried before a military court.

Eleventh: No one may be detained or imprisoned except in locations designated for this purpose and in conformity with the law. Such locations must include health and social services, and be subject to the authority of the Government.

Twelfth: The religious beliefs and moral principles of prisoners must be respected.

Chapter Two
Social and Economic Rights

Article 23:
First: The Government of the Kurdistan Region shall be responsible for the welfare of the families of the martyrs of the Kurdish People's Liberation Movement and the welfare of the families of the Peshmerga martyrs. The Government shall also be responsible for the welfare of the families of victims of *Al-Anfal* campaign, and victims of the chemical attacks and those affected by permanent disabilities as a result thereof. Qualified individuals from these groups, and their children, shall be given priority in accessing work opportunities, in accordance with the law.

Second: The authorities of the Kurdistan Region shall seek for the Federal Government of Iraq to assume its constitutional, legal and moral responsibilities toward the victims mentioned in the preceding paragraph, including political prisoners, who have suffered from the policies of repression practiced by successive central governments, by compensating said victims, and guaranteeing their right to secure healthcare and a dignified means of livelihood.

Article 24:
First: Everyone shall have the right to a standard of living adequate for a dignified life, including food, clothing and housing.
Second: Everyone shall have the right to obtain healthcare and medical treatment, regardless of their ability to assume the expenses thereof.
Third: Everyone shall have the right to social security, especially in cases of motherhood, sickness, unemployment, injury, disability, old age, displacement, and loss of one's means of livelihood in circumstances beyond one's control
Fourth: Everyone shall have the right to work in a profession or an occupation to which he or she freely consents.
Fifth: Every worker shall have the right to equal pay for equal work. The relations between workers and employers shall be regulated by law and founded on economic bases, while taking into account the rules of social justice.

Article 25:
The authorities of the Region must ensure the welfare of the handicapped and persons with special needs, and train them in order to integrate them into society. This shall be regulated by law.

Article 26:
The Government of the Region shall guarantee the right to form and to freely join professional associations, unions, organisations and federations. This shall be regulated by law.

Article 27 – Education and Family:
First: The Government of the Region shall guarantee free education at the primary, secondary and university levels. The Government shall also guarantee vocational training and technical education. Education shall be compulsory until the completion of the primary level.
Second: The Government of the Region shall be in charge of the campaign against illiteracy.
Third: The family is the fundamental core of society. Therefore, mothers and children must be protected, and the economic exploitation of children must be prohibited.
Fourth: The government of the Region shall guarantee the establishment of special homes to protect and care for women who have, for social reasons, lost their family security.
Fifth: All forms of discrimination, violence and abuse in society, school, and in the family shall be forbidden.

Article 28 – Consumers' Rights
The Government of the Kurdistan Region must protect consumers' rights. It must create legal means to empower consumers to defend their rights and establish consumer associations and federations

Chapter Three
Ethnic and Religious Rights of the Different Groups of the Kurdistan Region

Article 29:
People belonging to one of the ethnic or religious groups shall have the right to legal recognition of their names, and the right to use the traditional, local names of places in their language, while abiding by the provisions of the language law in the Kurdistan Region.

Article 30:

First: The provisions of the personal status law for the followers of one religion may not be imposed on the followers of another religion.

Second: The followers of non-Muslim religions and sects, such as Christians, Yazidis and others may establish their own religious councils and may follow the provisions specific to the personal status law of their [faiths]. Such personal status provisions shall be determined by law, and personal status cases shall be heard before a personal status court. The provisions of personal status laws specific to non-Muslim religions and sects shall remain in effect in the Kurdistan Region as long as they are not amended or annulled by law.

[TC: Article 30 was consists of three items in 2008 version. However, items (Second) & (Third) in the 2008 version were merged and reflected in item (Second) above of 2009 version]

Article 31 – The Authorities' Commitment to Guaranteeing Equality

The authorities in the Kurdistan Region must guarantee the principle of effective equality among people belonging to ethnic and religious groups and must seek to achieve this equality. The authorities must create the conditions which will ensure that the identity of these ethnic and religious groups is preserved, and must take the necessary measures to reinforce this identity.

Article 32 – The Authorities' Commitment to Avoiding Forced Expulsions

First: The authorities in the Region must protect people belonging to ethnic and religious groups from any measure aiming at forced expulsion. Likewise, the authorities must support and encourage these people to establish their own specific leagues and associations, and ensure the continuity of such leagues and associations.

Second: The Government of the Kurdistan Region shall be committed to preventing any intentional change in population percentages in the areas inhabited by ethnic or religious groups. This shall not affect the process of equitable restitution for the policies of Arabization and forced displacement practiced by the Baathist regime in Iraqi Kurdistan, particularly in the city of Kirkuk.

Article 33

The authorities in the Kurdistan Region shall strengthen the principle of mutual respect between all of the Region's inhabitants, particularly in the fields of education, media and general culture. The authorities shall create the necessary conditions for persons belonging to ethnic or religious groups to participate effectively in all fields of life.

Article 34

Every religious group in the Region shall have the right to establish a council to develop, organize, and advance its cultural and social affairs, and its heritage. This shall be regulated by law.

Article 35

This Constitution guarantees autonomy to the Turkmen, Arabs and Chaldo-Assyrian-Syriacs wherever they represent a majority of the population. This shall be regulated by law.

Article 36

The provisions contained in this Chapter shall be considered additional rights to the rights of ethnic and religious groups mentioned in this Constitution.

Chapter Four

Article 37 – International Agreements, Charters and Laws

Everyone shall have the right to enjoy the rights mentioned in the international agreements, charters, covenants and declarations on human rights that have been ratified and acceded to by Iraq. In addition, everyone shall have the right to enjoy the rights guaranteed by this Constitution and by international law.

Article 38 – Scope of Restrictions on Rights

<u>First</u>: No restriction may be placed on the exercise of civil, political, social, economic and cultural rights, or on the rights of ethnic and religious groups recognized in this Constitution, unless such a restriction is imposed by law. Such a restriction may only infringe upon the essence of these rights to the extent that is necessary and acceptable in a democratic and peaceful society built upon diversity, dignity, equality and freedom. Any restriction that is imposed and that conflict with [this principle] shall be null and void.

<u>Second</u>: Anyone who is directly concerned [by a restriction imposed on his rights] may appeal to the Region's Constitutional Court against the measure or the law restricting these rights.

Section Three
The Authorities of the Kurdistan Region
Chapter One
The Parliament of Kurdistan

Article 39:

The Authorities of the Iraqi Kurdistan Region shall be comprised of:
<u>First</u>: the Legislative Authority (the Parliament of Kurdistan).
<u>Second</u>: the Executive Authority.
<u>Third</u>: the Judicial Authority.

Article 40:

The Parliament of Kurdistan shall be the legislative authority, and it shall be the authority for settling decisive issues affecting the people of the Kurdistan Region. Members of the Parliament shall be elected directly by secret ballot in a free and general election.

Article 41:

<u>First</u>: The law shall determine the manner used to elect the members of the Parliament of Iraqi Kurdistan, the timing of the election, how the election is conducted, and the proportion of representation.

<u>Second</u>: Fair representation of all geographic localities, ethnic and religious groups shall be taken into consideration when organizing a system for electing members, as well as guaranteeing that no less than 30% of the seats in the parliament of Iraqi Kurdistan be reserved for women representatives.

<u>Third</u>: A Member of Parliament shall represent all the groups that make up the people of Iraqi Kurdistan, regardless of his or her political, ethnic and religious affiliation, or his or her electoral district.

Article 42:

<u>First</u>: The Parliament shall be elected for a term of four years, starting from the day of its first assembly.

<u>Second</u>: The Parliament shall convene at the invitation of the President of the Kurdistan Region, within fifteen days of the announcement of the final election results. If an invitation to convene is not issued, then the Parliament shall convene automatically at 12 p.m. on the day following this fifteen day period.

Article 43:
The Parliament shall hold its first session under the chairmanship of its oldest Member,
and shall elect by secret ballot a Speaker, a Deputy Speaker, and a Secretary General
chosen from its Members.

Article 44:
Before assuming their duties, Members of Parliament shall take the following
Constitutional oath:
"I swear by God Almighty to protect the interests of the people of the Kurdistan Region, to
safeguard the Region's unity and dignity, to protect the rights and freedoms of its citizens,
and to protect public funds. I swear by God Almighty to abide by the provisions of the
Constitution, and to perform the duties of a member [of this Parliament] faithfully and
loyally."

Article 45:
Upon taking the Constitutional oath, a Member of Parliament shall be considered to have
resigned from his [previous] position. He shall have the right to return to that position, or to
a similar one, at the end of his term in Parliament. The length of the term served as a
Member of Parliament shall be taken into account for purposes of promotion,
advancement, seniority and retirement.

Article 46:
A Member of the Parliament of Kurdistan may not serve simultaneously as a member in
the Federal Parliament, in local and municipal councils, or in the civil service. A Member
of Parliament shall be dedicated exclusively to parliamentary work; and shall be forbidden
from practicing any other profession while serving in Parliament.

Article 47:
First: Parliament shall hold two sessions a year, each lasting four months. Parliamentary
procedure shall define how these sessions are held.
Second: The parliamentary session in which the general budget is proposed shall not be
concluded until the budget is approved. Based on the request of the President of the
Kurdistan Region, or the Speaker of the Parliament of Kurdistan, or the President of the
Council of Ministers, or twenty-five Members of Parliament, a parliamentary session may
also be extended for a period not exceeding thirty days to complete other tasks whose
importance requires such an extension.

Article 48:
An absolute majority of the Members of Parliament shall constitute a quorum. Resolutions
shall be issued by a majority vote of those in attendance, unless parliamentary law or
procedure specify otherwise. If equal votes are cast, the Speaker of the Parliament shall
cast the deciding vote.

Article 49:
Ten Members of Parliament, or a competent parliamentary committee, may introduce bills
or draft resolutions to Parliament.

Article 50:
First: A Member of Parliament may question the Prime Minister, his Deputy, and the
Ministers regarding matters that concern the Council of Ministers or one of the Ministries.
Parliamentary law and procedure shall organize the questioning of these officials.

<u>Second</u>: Ten Members of Parliament may request to interpellate the Prime Minister or the Members of the Council of Ministers. The interpellation shall not take place until eight days after the date on which the request for the interpellation arrived at the Prime Minister's office. If the interpellation results in a request for a motion of no-confidence in the Prime Minister, or one of the Ministers, the motion shall be passed by the agreement of two-thirds of the Members of Parliament in the case of the Prime Minister, and by the agreement of an absolute majority of the Members of Parliament in the case of a Minister.

Article 51:
The Speaker of the Parliament, the Deputy Speaker, the Secretary General, and the Members of Parliament shall be entitled to rights and privileges which ensure their independence and their livelihood. Such rights and privileges shall be fixed and regulated by law.

Article 52:
Parliamentary law and procedure shall determine and regulate the details of Parliament's work processes, and the manner in which its ordinary and extraordinary sessions are held, organized and conducted. Parliamentary law and procedure shall also address the situations in which membership is terminated, and how vacant seats should be filled.

Article 53:
The Parliament shall exercise the following powers, in addition to any other powers which the laws in force in the Region have delegated to it:
<u>First</u>: Settle decisive issues affecting the people of Kurdistan, by a vote of a majority of two-thirds of its members.
<u>Second</u>: Approve proposed constitutional amendments, according to (Article 120/ Fourth) of this Constitution.
[TC: Article 120 in Red above was 118 in 2009 version]
<u>Third</u>:
1. Legislate, amend and repeal laws in all matters in Kurdistan, except for issues that lie wholly within the exclusive legislative jurisdiction of the Federal Authorities, according to Article 110 of the Federal Constitution.
2. Approve the entry into force of federal laws in the Kurdistan Region, and amend their application, in accordance with the law. However, laws that lie wholly within the exclusive legislative jurisdiction of the Federal Authorities, according to Article 110 of the Federal Constitution, shall be exempt from this process, and shall be applied in the Region upon their entry into force according to the provisions of the Federal Constitution.

<u>Fourth</u>: Take measures to impeach the President or Vice President of the Kurdistan Region, by the agreement of a majority of two-thirds of Parliament's members, on account of perjury of the constitutional oath, serious violation of the Constitution, or high treason.
<u>Fifth</u>: Pass motions of confidence and no-confidence in the Government and its members, by an absolute majority of the Members of Parliament.
<u>Sixth</u>: Monitor the activities of the executive branch, and hold the Prime Minister, the Deputy Prime Minister, and the Ministers accountable, in accordance with parliamentary law and procedure.
<u>Seventh</u>: Approve the general budget for Kurdistan and its final accounts; transfer between [appropriation] sections; and approve expenditures not referred to in the budget.
<u>Eighth</u>: Approve general development plans.
<u>Ninth</u>: Levy, amend, annul, or grant exemptions to taxes and duties.
<u>Tenth</u>: Settle, by an absolute majority vote of those present, the validity of a Member of Parliament's membership. This decision shall be subject to appeal before the Region's Constitutional Court within thirty days of the date on which it is issued.

Eleventh: Put in place parliamentary procedure, appoint parliamentary staff and employees and fix their salaries, and estimate the parliament's budget.
Twelfth: Form permanent, temporary, and investigative committees.
Thirteenth: Confirm, by an absolute majority of its members, the nomination of members to the Constitutional Court for the Kurdistan Region.
Fourteenth: Confirm, by an absolute majority of its members, the nomination of the heads of the independent Authorities and Commissions listed in Article 107 of this Constitution.

Article 54:
The Parliament may not relinquish its legislative authority, except as stipulated in the seventh paragraph of Article 65 of this Constitution.

Article 55:
First: Members of Parliament shall enjoy parliamentary immunity, and may speak freely within the boundaries outlined in parliamentary procedure.
Second: The freedom of Members of Parliament may not be restricted, nor may they be put under surveillance without the approval of Parliament.
Third: Except in cases of *flagrante delicto*, Members of Parliament may not be prosecuted, interrogated or searched; their residences and offices may not be searched; nor may they be apprehended by any authority while Parliament is in session without prior authorization from Parliament.
Fourth: Except in cases of *flagrante delicto*, Members of Parliament may not be prosecuted, interrogated or searched; their residences and offices may not be searched; nor may they be apprehended by any authority while Parliament is not in session without prior authorization from the Speaker of the Parliament.

Article 56:
First: Parliament may dissolve itself by the approval of a majority of two-thirds of its members.
Second: The President of the Region shall issue a decree to dissolve Parliament in the following situations:
   1. Resignation of more than half of the Parliament's Members.
   2. Failure to achieve quorum for a parliamentary meeting within sixty days of the date on which Parliament was invited to convene after being elected.
   3. Parliament's failure to pass a motion of confidence in three different and successive proposed cabinets.
Third: A decree shall be issued ordering that elections be held for the Parliament of Kurdistan and fixing the election date within fifteen days of the date on which Parliament was dissolved, or within the two-month period preceding the end of its electoral term.
[TC: Item Third in Red above has been eliminated from the 2009 version].

Article 57:
If Parliament is dissolved, or its electoral term comes to an end, a decree should be issued to hold the elections and determine the date of the elections within 15 days from the date of dissolution or ninety days period preceding the end of its electoral term, provided that to be hold no later than ninety days following the dissolution or be within ninety days prior to the end of its electoral term date.

Article 57:
If Parliament is dissolved, or its electoral term comes to an end, new elections shall be held to elect a new Parliament within a period not exceeding 60 days from the date on which Parliament was dissolved, or within the sixty day period preceding the end of its electoral term.

[TC: Article 57 in Red above represents the 2008 version]

Article 58:
If Parliament is dissolved based on the provisions of Article 56 of this Constitution, or if Parliament's electoral term comes to an end, and new elections are delayed or unfeasible due to extraordinary circumstances, Parliament shall remain in session and continue to perform its duties and exercise its constitutional authorities until a new parliament is elected and its first session held. In this case, the decree dissolving Parliament shall be considered suspended until elections for the new parliament are held.

Chapter Two
The Executive Authority

Article 59:
The executive authority shall be composed of The President of Kurdistan Region and the Council of Ministers. The executive authority shall exercise its powers in accordance with the Constitution and the law.

First: The President of Iraq Kurdistan

Article 60:
First: The President of the Kurdistan Region holds the highest office of the executive authority. He is the Commander-in-Chief of the Regional Guard (the Peshmerga). He shall represent the people of the Region and act on their behalf in all national events. He shall be in charge of coordination between Federal and Regional Authorities.
Second: The President of the Region shall choose a Vice President who shall assist him in performing his duties. The Vice President shall take the place of the President in case of the President's absence. The Vice President shall also be the Deputy Commander-in-Chief of the Regional Guard (the Peshmerga), provided that to have the consent of parliament by absolute majority of its members.
[TC: The text in Red above has been added to 2009 constitution]

Article 61:
The President of the Kurdistan Region shall be elected directly by secret ballot in a general election by the citizens of the Kurdistan Region. The law shall determine the manner of this election.

Article 62:
If the President of the Region, or the Vice President, is impeached by a vote of a majority of two-thirds of the members the Members of Parliament on account of perjury of the constitutional oath, serious violation of the Constitution, or high treason, and is then found guilty by the Region's Constitutional Court, he shall be removed from his position.

Article 63:
Before assuming their duties, the President of the Kurdistan Region and the Vice President shall take the following constitutional oath before the Parliament of Kurdistan:

"I swear by God Almighty to protect the rights, achievements, unity, and interests of the people of Iraq Kurdistan. I swear by God Almighty to perform my duties faithfully and loyally, and to adhere to the Constitution of the Kurdistan Region."

Article 64:

The President of the Kurdistan Region shall be elected for a term of four years, beginning on the date on which he takes the constitutional oath. He may only be reelected once for a second term.

Article 65:
In addition to any other powers granted to him by the law, the President of the Region shall exercise the following powers:
First: Propose draft laws and resolutions to the Parliament of the Kurdistan Region.
Second: Promulgate laws and resolutions legislated by the Parliament of Kurdistan within fifteen days of receiving them. During this period, the President shall have the right to oppose the law or resolution in entirety or in part, and to send the law or resolution back to Parliament for reconsideration. Parliament's decision regarding such a law or resolution shall then be final. If the President fails to promulgate such laws and resolutions within the aforementioned period and does not oppose them, they shall be considered promulgated and shall be published in the Official Gazette.
Third: Issue a decree for the holding of general elections for the Parliament of Iraqi Kurdistan when Parliament is dissolved or at the end of its electoral term. This shall be done in accordance with Article 56 of this Constitution, while respecting the period set forth in Article 57 herein.
Fourth:, Issue a decree inviting the Parliament of Kurdistan to hold the first session of its electoral term, within ten days of the date on which final election results are announced. Should the President fail to call Parliament [into session], the Parliament shall convene automatically on the day following the end of the aforementioned period.
Fifth: Issue a decree dissolving the Parliament of Kurdistan in the situations that are set forth in this Constitution.
Sixth: Issue a decree dismissing a Minister, based on a proposal brought forward by the Prime Minister.
Eighth: In cases of war, occupation, insurrection, chaos, natural disasters, epidemics, or other unexpected emergencies, the President shall have the power to declare a state of emergency, after consulting with the Speaker of the Parliament and the Prime Minister of Kurdistan, and obtaining their consent. The initial period [of the state of emergency] must be no longer than one month. Subsequent extensions shall be approved by an absolute majority of the Members of Parliament; each extension shall be no longer than three months. Provisions related to a state of emergency shall be regulated by law.
Ninth: Grant special pardons to convicted persons, by issuing a decree in accordance with the law.
Tenth: Approve death sentences, or commute them to life imprisonment.
Twelfth: Allow federal armed forces to enter Iraq Kurdistan territory when necessary, after obtaining the approval of the Parliament of Iraq Kurdistan and defining the mission of these forces, as well as the location and duration of their stay in the Region.
Thirteenth: Send the Regional Guard (the Peshmerga) or the Domestic Security Forces [on a mission] outside of the Region, with the approval of the Parliament of Kurdistan.
Fourteenth:
  A. Charge the candidate of the majority parliamentary bloc with forming a government within forty five days of the date on which so charged.
  B. If the first candidate fails to form a government within forty-five days of being so charged, the President of the Kurdistan Region shall charge another candidate from the same bloc with forming a government.
  C. If the second candidate fails to form a government, the President of the Kurdistan Region may choose whoever he considers fitting, and charge him with forming a government.
  D. The person charged with forming a government may be a Member of Parliament, or not.

Fifteenth: Issue a decree ordering the government to form, after it has obtained a vote of confidence from the Parliament.

Sixteenth: Issue a decree ordering the resignation of the government or of a Minister after [Parliament] has passed a motion of a no-confidence in either of them.

Seventeenth: Issue a decree accepting the resignation of the government or of a Minister, and charging them with continuing to act as a caretaker government until a new government is formed.

Eighteenth: Issue a decree appointing the members of the Constitutional Court, after the Parliament [of Kurdistan is not mentioned] has confirmed the nominees.

Nineteenth: Issue a decree appointing judges, the Head of the Judiciary Inspection Department, as well as the Head and the members of the Public Prosecution, after these individuals have been nominated by the Judiciary Council in Kurdistan.

Twentieth: Issue a decree appointing the heads of the independent authorities and commissions listed in Article 107 of this Constitution, after their nomination has been approved by the Parliament of Kurdistan.

Twenty-First: Issue a resolution establishing special offices for the Kurdistan Region in foreign countries, based on a proposal from the Prime Minister, and in coordination with the competent agency of the Federal Government.

Twenty-Second: Appoint individuals to special grades, based on the nomination of the competent Minister and the approval of the Council of Ministers.

Twenty-Third: Confer military ranks on the officers of the Regional Guard (the Peshmerga) and the Domestic Security Force; and issue decrees, according to the laws in force, discharging them or retiring them.

Twenty-Fourth: Issue a decree awarding medals and badges, as pursuant to the law.

Article 66:
The salaries and allowances of the President and Vice President of the Kurdistan Region shall be specified by law.

Article 67:
The President of the Kurdistan Region shall have an office whose organisation, privileges and responsibilities shall be specified by law.

Article 68:
First: If the President of the Kurdistan Region resigns, dies, or becomes afflicted with a handicap that prevents him from carrying out his presidential duties, his successor shall be elected within sixty days for a period of four years, in accordance with Article 64 of this Constitution.

Second: When the office of President of the Kurdistan Region becomes vacant, the Speaker of the Parliament [of Kurdistan is not mentioned], in accordance with the first paragraph of this Article, shall assume the duties of the presidential office until a new President is elected within sixty days of the day on which the office becomes vacant.

Third: The Vice President of the Kurdistan Region shall assume the duties of the President of the Kurdistan Region when the latter is absent from the Kurdistan Region, is on leave, or is temporarily incapable of performing his duties.

Fourth: If the President's term comes to an end, but the holding of new presidential elections is impossible because of war or natural disasters, the President of the Region shall continue to perform his duties until the aforementioned obstacles have been removed, and a new President of the Region has been elected.

Second: The Council of Ministers of the Iraq Kurdistan Region

Article 69:

The Council of Ministers of the Iraq Kurdistan Region is the executive and administrative authority in the Kurdistan Region.

Article 70:
First: The Council of Ministers shall be composed of a Prime Minister, a Deputy Prime Minister or Deputy Prime Ministers, and [other] Ministers. The formation of the Council of Ministers shall be determined by law.
Second: A nominee shall be charged with forming a government according to the provisions of the fourteenth paragraph of Article 65 of this Constitution.
[TC: In "Second" above, Article 104 replaced by Article 65]
Third: The Prime Minister-designate shall select his Deputy or Deputies and the Ministers from among the Members of the Parliament of Kurdistan; or he may select other individuals who meet the requirements necessary to become Members of the Parliament of Kurdistan.
Fourth: The Prime Minister-designate shall present a list of the members of his government to the President of the Kurdistan Region for his approval.
Fifth: Following the approval of the President of the Kurdistan Region, the Prime Minister-designate shall present the members of his government to the Parliament of Kurdistan, requesting a vote of confidence in the government.
Sixth: The Prime Minister shall preside over cabinet sessions, except for those sessions that are attended by the President of the [Kurdistan is not mentioned] Region.

Article 71:
Before beginning their official duties and after obtaining Parliament's vote of confidence, the Prime Minister and members of the Council of Ministers shall take the following constitutional oath: "I swear by God Almighty to protect loyally the unity of the people and the territory of Iraq Kurdistan, to respect the Constitution and the laws that are in effect, to protect public funds, and to safeguard fully the interests of the people."

Article 72:

Fair representation of the groups making up the people of Iraq Kurdistan shall be taken into account in the formation of the Council of Ministers of the Kurdistan Region.

Article 73:
The Prime Minister and the Ministers shall be jointly accountable to the Parliament of Kurdistan for matters related to the Council of Ministers. Each Minister shall be individually, primarily, and directly responsible for the activities of his Ministry.

Article 74:
The Council of Ministers shall exercise the following powers and authorities:
First: Implement laws, resolutions, decrees, and regulations; protect the security of Iraq Kurdistan and its public funds.
Second: Outline the general policy of the Kurdistan Region, in coordination with the President of the Kurdistan Region; and implement this policy after it is approved by the Parliament.
Third: Prepare the draft general budget for Kurdistan.
Fourth: Draft bills and resolutions and submit them to the Parliament of Kurdistan.
Fifth: Issue regulations and executive and administrative resolutions, in accordance with the Constitution and law.
Sixth: Prepare projects for development plans, and implement such projects after they are approved by the Parliament.
Seventh: Form a joint administration with the Federal Government to manage the oil and gas extracted from [fields in] Iraq Kurdistan and put into commercial production before

August 15, 2005. Revenues received from these fields must be distributed fairly in accordance with the principles specified in Article 112 of the Federal Constitution, and with the oil and gas laws of the Kurdistan Region. For the purposes of enforcing the provision of this paragraph, the scale of commercial production shall be defined as the production of no less than five thousand (5,000) barrels per day for a period of twelve (12) months.
Eighth: Work jointly with the Federal Government to formulate the strategic policies necessary to develop oil and gas resources. All matters related to the Region's resources must meet with the approval of the Parliament of Kurdistan.
Ninth: Manage, in accordance with the laws of the Kurdistan Region, all exploration, production, management, development, sales, marketing, and export activities, as well as all other operations, required for crude oil and gas fields, [including] oil and gas that has not been extracted or that has been extracted but not put into commercial production before August 15, 2005. For the purposes of enforcing the provision of this paragraph, commercial production shall be defined as the production of no less than five thousand (5000) barrels per day for a period of twelve (12) months.
Tenth: Exercise executive powers pertaining to all matters in the Kurdistan Region that do not lie within the exclusive jurisdiction of the federal authorities, in accordance with Article 110 of the Federal Constitution.
Eleventh: Exercise those powers the Federal Authorities and the Kurdistan Authorities jointly authorize it to exercise, in accordance with the provisions of the Federal Constitution.
Twelfth: Oversee, direct, follow up, monitor, and coordinate the activities of the ministries, institutions and public utilities in Kurdistan.
Thirteenth: Appoint, promote, dismiss, discharge or retire employees in accordance with the law and in a manner that does not conflict with the provisions of this Constitution, or the laws that are issued based on these provisions.
Fourteenth: Propose the establishment of special offices for the Region's cultural, social and developmental affairs in the embassies and diplomatic missions, and manage such offices.
Fifteenth: Organize and administer the Regional Guard (the Peshmerga), in order to protect the region, as well as the police, the security agencies, and other internal security forces.
Fifteenth: Organize and administer the Regional Guard (the Peshmerga), in order to protect the region, as well as the police, the security agencies, and other internal security forces.

Fourteenth: Nominate representatives of the Region, with the approval of the Parliament of Kurdistan, to Independent Federal Authorities and to federal positions at or above the rank of general director.
[TC: Fourteenth in Red above was eliminated from the 2009 constitution and replaced with the contents of Item Sixteenth in Red below, yet Article 74 was consists of 16 items in 2008 constitution, while only 15 items are included in 2009 constitution]
Sixteenth: Propose the establishment of special offices for the Region's cultural, social and developmental affairs in the embassies and diplomatic missions, and manage such offices.

Article 75:

First: In the following situations, the Council of Ministers shall be considered to have resigned, and the cabinet shall be charged with acting as a caretaker government until a new government is formed:

1. Acceptance of the Prime Minister's resignation.
2. A vote of no confidence in the Prime Minister by the Parliament of Iraq Kurdistan.

3. Beginning of a new term for the Parliament of Kurdistan.
4. Beginning of a new term for the President of the Kurdistan Region.
5. Death of the Prime Minister.

<u>Second:</u> A Minister shall be considered to have resigned if the Parliament of Iraq Kurdistan passes a motion of no confidence in him.

Article 76:
<u>First:</u> The law shall regulate the impeachment and trial of the Prime Minister, the Deputy Prime Minister, and [other] Ministers.
<u>Second:</u> The law shall determine the salaries, benefits, and privileges of the Prime Minister, the Deputy Prime Minister, and the Ministers.

Chapter Three
The Judicial Authority
First: General Principles

Article 77:
The judicial authority in the Region is independent. It shall be composed of the Judicial Council, the Constitutional Court, the Court of Cassation, the Judiciary Inspection Department, the Public Prosecution Office, and of the various levels and types of courts, and their cadres. The law shall regulate the manner in which these bodies are formed, the conditions and procedures for appointing their members, and for holding these members accountable.

Article 78:
The judiciary shall be independent and subject to no authority except that of the law.

Article 79:
The judiciary shall have general jurisdiction over all natural and legal persons in Kurdistan.

Article 80:
Judicial rulings and decisions shall be issued and implemented in the name of the people.

Article 81:
All judges shall be appointed for an unlimited term, with compulsory retirement at an age specified by law. Judges may not be removed, except in the cases specified by law. Judges must be provided with suitable working conditions, and granted remuneration that is consistent with the dignity of their office and the scale of their duties, and that guarantees their independence. While judges in office, their remuneration may not be diminished, nor may their working conditions be changed.

Article 82:
Judges and members of the Public Prosecution shall be prohibited from:
<u>First:</u> Simultaneously holding a judicial position and a legislative or executive position, or any other job.
<u>Second:</u> Being affiliated with a political party or organisation.

Article 83:
Court sessions shall be public, unless the court decides in favor of a closed session, for the sake of public morals, or sanctity of the family. In the case of a closed session, the ruling must be pronounced in an open session.

Article 84:

It shall be forbidden to establish special or extraordinary courts in Kurdistan.

Article 85:
The law shall regulate which courts have jurisdiction to investigate crimes of a military nature committed by members of the Regional Guard (the Peshmerga), or by members of the internal security forces, as well as crimes committed by members of these forces against each other.

Article 86:
It shall be prohibited for laws to stipulate that the courts are forbidden from hearing cases arising from such laws.

Article 87:
It shall be prohibited for laws to stipulate that any executive or administrative resolution or procedure is immune from appeal.

Article 88:
The law shall guarantee the impartiality of the administration, and that any individual who abuses his power shall be punished.

Article 89:
Anyone injured as a result of the misconduct or negligence of staff members from the Kurdistan Government's Departments or Authorities, while said staff members are performing their jobs, shall be entitled to claim compensation from the aforementioned agencies.

Article 90:
Judicial decisions must be implemented. Refusal to implement them, or obstructing their implementation, shall be considered a criminal offense punishable by law. If the accused is a civil servant or an individual charged with performing a public service, then in addition to receiving a punitive sanction, he shall be dismissed from his position. The judgment beneficiary shall have the right to bring an action directly before the competent court, and if he has suffered any harm, the government shall guarantee him full compensation. This compensation shall not detract from the subordinate's responsibility.

Second: The Constitutional Court

Article 91:
The Constitutional Court of Iraq Kurdistan shall be established by law.

Article 92:
First: The Constitutional Court of Kurdistan shall be composed of seven members, including the Chief Justice. Members shall be selected from among judges, law professors, and lawyers who have a total of at least twenty years of practice in the judicial or legislative field, in teaching or in legal practice.
Second: The President of the Kurdistan Region, in consultation with the Judicial Council, shall nominate the members of the Constitutional Court.
Third: After the Parliament of Kurdistan has confirmed, by a majority of two-thirds of its members, the nominees to the Constitutional Court, the President of the Kurdistan Region shall issue a decree appointing these nominees as members of the Court.

Article 93:
The Court shall elect its Chief Justice from among its members.

Article 94:
Before beginning their duties, the Chief Justice and members of the Constitutional Court shall take the legal oath of office before the President of the Kurdistan Region.

Article 95:
The Constitutional Court shall have jurisdiction over the following matters:
First: Explain the stipulations of the articles of the Kurdistan Region's Constitution.
Second:
1. Monitor the constitutionality of the laws, based on a request from the President of the Kurdistan Region, the Council of Ministers, ten Members of Parliament, or any concerned party.
2. Decide the legality of decrees, regulations, resolutions and instructions, based on the request of any concerned party.

Third: Settle appeals brought before [the Constitutional Court] that arise from an ongoing case before a [lower] court and are related to the unconstitutionality of a law or the illegality of a resolution, regulation, or instruction. The aforementioned [lower] court must adjourn the case until the result of the appeal is decided.
Fourth: Certify the results of referendums and of general elections for the President of the Region, the Parliament of Iraq Kurdistan, and local and municipal councils.
Fifth: Decide on the constitutionality of proposed amendments to the Constitution of the Kurdistan Region, and decide whether said amendments conform to the requirements listed in Article 120 of this Constitution.
[TC: In Fifth above (Article 120) was (Article 118) in 2008 version]
Sixth: Try the President or Vice President of the Kurdistan Region after they have been impeached by the Parliament in accordance with Article 62 of this Constitution. The conviction of the President or the Vice President requires the agreement of at least five of the Court's members.
No punishment may be inflicted on them except removing them from their positions.
[TC: The text in Red above was eliminated from 2009 version]
Seventh: Settle cases brought before the Court in accordance with Article 19, Paragraph 18 / 3 of this Constitution.
[TC: In Seventh above (3) was (4) in the 2008 version]
Eighth: Settle appeals related to the validity of membership, and lift the immunity of parliamentary members.

Article 96:
The law shall determine the conditions for membership in the Court, the Court's work processes, and how the Court accepts cases, motions and appeals.

Article 97:
The rulings of the Constitutional Court shall be final and binding for all. If the Court, in deciding the constitutionality of laws, or the legality of decrees, regulations, resolutions and instructions, resolves that any law, decree, regulation, resolution or instruction violates the Constitution or the law, the Court should notify the concerned authority in Kurdistan, so that this authority may take the necessary measures to remove or correct the constitutional violations.

Third: The Judicial Council

Article 98:
First: The Judiciary Council shall be composed of the President of the Court of Cassation and his deputies, the Head of the Judiciary Inspection Department, the Head of the Public Prosecution; and the presiding judges of the appellate district courts in Kurdistan.

Second: The Judiciary Council shall manage the affairs of the judiciary, guarantee its independence, and oversee judicial agencies, in accordance with the law.

Article 99:
First: The judicial authority shall have its own special budget that shall be appended to the budget of the Region. This budget shall be financed through judicial fees and fines collected in accordance with the law, and by the funds which the Government of Kurdistan provides for this purpose.
Second: The Judicial Council shall be responsible for preparing an annual draft budget for the judicial authority, and shall consult the Constitutional Court regarding the allocations set aside for it. The Judicial Council shall present the draft budget to the Parliament of Iraq Kurdistan for its approval. The final figure for this budget must be incorporated into the annual budget of the Kurdistan Region.

Section Four
First: The Public Prosecution

Article 100:
The Public Prosecution shall represent society in defending justice, protecting legality, public order, the security of the region and of its public funds, and in protecting families and individuals and their freedoms. This shall be regulated by law.

Second: The Shura [Advisory] Council

Article 101:
A Shura Council of the Iraq Kurdistan Region shall be established. The missions and authorities of the Shura Concil shall be regulated by a law.

[TC: Contents of Article 101 in Red below was eliminated and replaced by the text shown in Article 101 above]

Second: The Shura [Advisory] Council
Article 101:

First: A Shura Council of the Kurdistan Region shall be established by law. It shall have jurisdiction in the following matters:

1. Settle appeals regarding punitive and disciplinary measures, and employment issues related to employees of government departments.

2. Settle issues involving a conflict of jurisdiction between Ministries and government institutions and departments, at the request of the Prime Minister's office.

3. Study, prepare or draft bills for Kurdistan, at the request of the President of the Kurdistan Region, the Council of Ministers, the competent Ministries, or non-ministerial agencies.

4. Express its opinion and offer advice on legal matters brought before it by Ministries and non-ministerial agencies; settle issues over which these entities differ when the parties in the case appeal to the Council. In such cases, the opinion of the council shall be binding on these parties.

5. Any other jurisdiction entrusted to the Council by law.

Second: Administrative courts shall be established in the region; their makeup and their duties shall be determined by law.

Section Five
Local Administrations and Municipal Councils

Article 102:

Administrative divisions in the Kurdistan Region shall be as follows: governorates, districts, counties and villages. The establishment of these administrative divisions, the designation or change of their capitals, the settling or modification of their boundaries, and the separation of one administrative unit to attach it to other such units shall take place in accordance with the law.

Article 103:
<u>First</u>: In order to achieve democracy, administrative decentralization shall be applied, continuously developed and activated in running the administrative units of Kurdistan (governorates, districts, counties and villages), because it is one of the indispensable tools for the participation of the Region's citizens in running the administrative unit's general affairs. Each administrative unit shall have a local council, chosen by secret ballot in direct and general elections. The method in which these councils are elected, as well as their powers and duties, shall be clarified by law.
<u>Second</u>: Each administrative unit shall have an executive council chaired by the chief officer of that administrative unit. The law shall clarify how this council is formed, determine its powers and duties, and define its relationship to the local council of the same administrative unit and to the central Ministries and institutions of Kurdistan.

Article 104:
The capital of each governorate, district, county, or village with a population of at least 3,000 people shall have a municipality managed by an elected municipal council which shall provide public services to its citizens in accordance with the law.

Article 105:
<u>First</u>: Local and municipal councils shall enjoy the status of a legal person.
<u>Second</u>: Each administrative or municipal unit shall have its own independent budget.

Article 106:
<u>First</u>: Equitable representation of the ethnic groups living within an administrative unit or municipality shall be taken into account in the composition of local and municipal councils. This process shall be regulated by law.
<u>Second</u>: The electoral law for local and municipal councils must aim to ensure that at least (30%) of the councils' members are women.

Section Six
Independent Authorities and Commissions

Article 107:
<u>First</u>: The following entities shall be established by law:
    1. The Independent High Authority for Elections and Referenda in Iraq Kurdistan.
    2. The Financial Auditing and Integrity Board.
    3. The Public Authority for the Safety and Quality of Local and Imported Products.
<u>Second</u>: The following entities shall be established by law:
    1. The Advisory Council for Economic and Social Affairs.
    2. The task of this Council shall be to provide advice to the office of the President of the Region, the Parliament, and the Council of Ministers on economic and social affairs.

[TC: contents of Article 107 below was changed and replaced by the above contents of 2009 version]

Article 107:
First: The following entities shall be established by law:
1. The Independent High Authority for Elections and Referenda in Kurdistan.
2. The Civil Service Board.
3. The Financial Auditing and Integrity Board.
4. The Commission for the Protection of the People's Rights (Ombudsman)
5. The Special Commission for the Rights of the Faylee Kurds.
6. The Public Authority for the Safety and Quality of Local and Imported Products.
7. The Independent Authority of Kurdistan for Media and Communications.

Second: The following entities shall be established by law:
A. The Advisory Council for Economic and Social Affairs.
B. The task of this Council shall be to provide advice to the office of the President of the Region, the Parliament, and the Council of Ministers on economic and social affairs.

Article 108:
First: The authorities and commissions included in the first paragraph of Article 107 of this Constitution shall be subject to oversight by the Parliament of Kurdistan. The law shall regulate the relationship of each aforementioned authority or commission to the Parliament.
Second: Other authorities and commissions may be formed by law, in addition to those mentioned in the first paragraph of Article 107 of this Constitution.

Article 109:
A Council called (The Council of the Regions Security) shall be formed. This Council shall be linked to the President of the Region. The powers and duties of this Council shall be regulated by the law.
[TC: Article 109 above was added to 2009 version; however, Article 109 in 2008 version is included in **Section Seven / Financial Provision** with a different text]

Section Seven
Financial Provisions

[TC: **Section Seven** in 2008 version starts with Article 109, yet starts with Article 110 in 2009 version, so, Article 109 is now part of Section Six

Article 110:
Low income individuals shall be exempt from taxes in a manner that ensures a fair minimum standard of living. This process shall be regulated by law.

Article 111:
The revenues of the Kurdistan Region shall be composed of the following:
First: Kurdistan's share of the federal government's general budget, originating from proceeds from oil and gas resources, customs duties, and other federal revenues, including loans, grants, gifts and aid.
Second: Proceeds from taxes, fees, and charges for public utilities; and from the revenues of public institutions and companies.
Third: Charges collected from the administration and levying of federal taxes and customs fees, and other federal revenues in the Region.

<u>Fourth</u>: Proceeds from the regional government's investments and resources.
<u>Fifth:</u> Grants and gifts.
<u>Sixth</u>: Domestic and foreign loans specific to the Region.
<u>Seventh:</u> Financial support provided by the federal government to the Government of the Region.

Article 112:
The fiscal year shall be specified by law.

Article 113:
<u>First:</u> A budget law for the Kurdistan Region, including estimated revenues and expenditures, shall be legislated every fiscal year.
<u>Second:</u> The draft budget for the [next] fiscal year shall be presented to the Parliament of Iraq Kurdistan three months prior to the end of the fiscal year.
<u>Third:</u> In the event that the preparation or presentation of the budget is delayed for any reason beyond the beginning of the fiscal year, the Government of Kurdistan shall, each month the budget is delayed, disburse one twelfth of the approved appropriations in the budget of the elapsed fiscal year.

Article 114:
The President and Vice President of the Kurdistan Region, the Speaker of the Parliament of Kurdistan, Members of Parliament, the Prime Minister and the Deputy Prime Minister, Ministers, judges, public prosecutors and deputy public prosecutors, individuals with special grades, general directors, and individuals of these ranks shall be prohibited from buying or renting any public property in Iraq Kurdistan. The aforementioned individuals shall also be prohibited from leasing or selling any part of their property to the regional authorities, and from entering into contracts (either directly or by proxy) as concessionaires, suppliers, or contractors.

Section Eight
Implementation, Explanation and Amendment of the Constitution

Article 115:
Pursuant to Article 126 / Fourth of the federal Constitution, no amendment to the federal Constitution shall be enacted if it diminishes those powers exercised by the authorities of the Kurdistan Region that do not lie within the exclusive jurisdiction of the federal authorities, unless the agreement of the Region's Parliament to said amendment has been secured, and a majority of voters in a referendum indicate the agreement of the people of Kurdistan to this amendment.

Article 116:
In addition to its normal areas of jurisdiction, the Kurdistan Court of Cassation shall have the authority to explain the stipulations of this Constitution, and to settle appeals that arise from ongoing cases before the courts and that are related to the unconstitutionality of laws, or the illegality of resolutions, decrees, regulations and instructions. The Court of Cassation shall exercise these authorities until the Constitutional Court of Kurdistan is formed.

Article 117:
Laws shall be published in the official Kurdistan gazette (*Waqai'i Kurdistan* [Kurdistan Events]), and shall come into force on the date of their publication, unless the given law stipulates otherwise.

Article 118:

This Constitution shall be considered ratified after it has been approved in a public referendum by a majority of the voters of the people of the Kurdistan Region.

Article 119:
In case of amend the sequence of the materials of the Federal Constitution, which was considered in the present Constitution the parliament of Iraq Kurdistan, by a majority vote of those present, shall correct the sequence based on it.
[TC: Article 119 was added to 2009 version]

Article 120:
First: The Constitution may be amended according to the procedures mentioned in this article, provided that the amendment not infringe upon the integrity of Iraqi Kurdistan's republican and democratic system, or upon its territorial unity, and provided that the amendment not undermine the basic right and freedoms set forth in the Constitution.
Second: Together, the President of the Kurdistan Region and the Council of Ministers, or half of the Members of Parliament, may propose a constitutional amendment.
Third: After reviewing the proposed amendment within forty-five days, the Constitutional Court shall determine whether the proposed amendment conflicts the conditions set forth in the first paragraph of this article.
Fourth: The Parliament of Iraq Kurdistan may approve the proposed [amendment] by a majority of two-thirds of its members.
Fifth: The majority of the voters of the people of Iraq Kurdistan shall agree to the amendment in a general referendum.

Article 121:
The citizens of the Region shall have the right to a referendum. Twenty-five percent of eligible voters in the Region shall have the right to request a referendum on a particular issue, provided that such a referendum is conducted and regulated by law.

Article 122:
First: This Constitution shall go into effect sixty days after the date on which it is approved in a general referendum. The President of the Kurdistan Region shall be responsible for publishing this Constitution in the official gazette (*Waqai'i Kurdistan*) within ten days of the date on which it is approved in a general referendum.
Second: All of the laws in force on the date on which this Constitution comes into effect shall remain in force as long as they are not amended or annulled in accordance with the provisions of this Constitution.